Eben Tourjée

Tribute of Praise

a collection of hymns and tunes for public and social worship, and for use in the

family circle

Eben Tourjée

Tribute of Praise
a collection of hymns and tunes for public and social worship, and for use in the family circle

ISBN/EAN: 9783337286323

Printed in Europe, USA, Canada, Australia, Japan

Cover: Foto ©Lupo / pixelio.de

More available books at **www.hansebooks.com**

THE

of Praise.

A COLLECTION OF

AND T

FOR

SOCIAL

THE FA

BOSTON:
FOR SALE BY JAMES P. MAGEE,
33 BROMFIELD STREET.

PUBLISHERS' NOTICE.

WE have been desirous to furnish a book which should be generally acceptable and useful to all Christian congregations. To this end, the compilers, Rev. W. McDonald and L. F. Snow, Esq., have called to their aid the services and suggestions of eminent clergymen of the various denominations; among them Rev. J. O. Means, D.D. (Congregationalist), Rev. Alvah Hovey, D.D. (Baptist),* and Rev. David Patten, D. D. (Methodist), and they cherish the confident belief that the results will be found entirely satisfactory. The whole has been under the able direction and supervision of Dr. EBEN TOURJÉE, to whose ardent and enthusiastic labors in the cause of church music, the great popular uprising in favor of congregational singing, during the last three years, is largely due. They desire particularly to state that Dr. TOURJÉE's connection with the work has been with him *a labor of love*, undertaken solely in the interests of congregational psalmody, at the sacrifice of other important interests, and without expectation of reward.

Special obligations are acknowledged to Messrs O. Ditson & Co., for the use of tunes of Dr. Lowell Mason and others; to Messrs. Biglow & Main, for tunes of Wm. B. Bradbury and others; to Dr. H. L. Hastings, George Kingsley, F. J. Huntington, Wm. G. Fischer, Asa Hull, O. Snow, Philip Phillips, G. F. Root, Rev. Robt. Lowry, Rev. L. Hartsough, the publishers of "Songs of Gladness," and others who have kindly allowed the use of their compositions. Most of the tunes used being copyright property, parties desiring to use them in other collections will please make application to the authors, or proprietors, and not to the publishers.

M. H. SARGENT,
Treasurer Congregational Publishing Society.

* See Baptist Edition.

THOMAS H. LENFEST, MUSIC PRINTER, BOSTON.

Entered, according to Act of Congress, in the year 1871, by M. H. SARGENT, Treasurer, in the office of the Librarian of Congress, at Washington, D. C.

INTRODUCTION.

The publication of the present work will, it is hoped and believed, greatly facilitate the adoption of a service song in our churches and social meetings *in which all shall participate.* In its preparation very extensive researches have been made in both European and American Psalmody. Dignified, striking melodies, easily learned and remembered, have been selected, and the contents enriched by fifty of the most popular and useful of the German and English Chorals. Thousands of Christians, in every age since LUTHER, have been edified and blessed by singing and listening to these grand old tunes. May the day soon come when they shall be sung in every church throughout America.

The tunes in the second part have been selected especially for use in social meetings. Many of them are already extensively known; and others have become very popular wherever introduced, and will, it is believed, be found generally useful.

Especial care has been taken to adopt such hymns as are appropriate for singing, and it is believed that they are sufficiently varied and numerous to satisfy the wants of every phase of Christian experience.

CHANTING.

This form of sacred music, the most devotional as well as the most ancient method of worshipping by song, has of late years been entirely abandoned in most churches. The Psalms of David were thus sung nearly three thousand years ago, and it was the only kind of music known to the church during the first six centuries of the Christian Era. A revival of this primitive, simple style of worship is highly desirable.

The single chant consists of two divisions or strains, the first containing three and the second four bars. The double chant consists of four divisions of three and four bars arranged alternately.

The first note of each division is called the reciting or chanting note, to which most of the syllables in each line are chanted; the remaining notes constitute what is called the cadence, to which the last few syllables in each line are sung.

"It is important to understand that the first or reciting note, which on paper occupies so small a space, but in practice often absorbs nearly all the words of the line, is the characteristic and principal note of the chant,—that which distinguishes it from all other forms of music, and is the source at once of all its beauty and all its difficulty. We may indeed call it THE CHANT, as the terminal notes which often attract much more notice, are, according to their names, only a cadence-inflection, or alteration of tone, and are sometimes wanting altogether.

"The distinguishing principle of the chant is, that in its origin, and in its truest forms, it is simply *musical* recitation — *reading or reciting in musical tones.* It is a method by which 'a congregation may, in a pleasing and devotional manner, read together the words of God.' In the tune we seek, as it were, to adorn the words, to increase their emotion by the addition of musical passages of corresponding emotional character. All that the chant adds to the words is musical *tone,* with terminal inflections, intended to resemble those of ordinary speech."—*Anglican Chant Book.*

The Gregorian chants are universally considered models of this plain, dignified species of church song, and may be used *antiphonally* with fine effect by the choirs.

The modern double chant resembles the ornamental style of psalmody more than the simplicity of the ancient chant; and though highly useful to the choir, is much less practicable for the congregation. In correct chanting, the words must be delivered as rapidly and plainly as in deliberate reading; special care being taken to avoid drawling the notes of the cadence. The final syllable of participles and adjectives should have a precise articulation, as in the words bless-ed, sav-ed, redeem-ed. Observing these directions, with practice under a skilful leader, any congregation may as readily learn to chant as to read aloud.

CHOIR AND CONGREGATIONAL SINGING.

The following suggestions result from long experience, and it is believed that wherever adopted, they will be followed by most gratifying results.

1. An organ and a choir are essential to the proper maintenance of singing as an element of worship in church service.

2. The organ should be of sufficient power to sustain and lead the congregation in the general song; and should contain such a variety of registers as will furnish a suitable accompaniment to the choir, and at the same time give the organist proper scope for the voluntaries. Its appropriate position is in the rear of the pulpit.

3. The organist and chorister should be well fitted for their respective positions, both by their musical knowledge, and by their religious character.

4. The first organ voluntary should be dignified, devout, bringing the first offerings of adoration and prayer which arise from the assembled multitude: all mere displays of execution by the player are out of place, and inconsistent with the impressive services of the house of God. In the concluding voluntary the solemn truths uttered, and the emotions awakened in the hearts of the people by the sermon, should be deepened by the sympathetic tones of the organ. Otherwise it is better dispensed with altogether.

5. The choir, wherever practicable, may be arranged in three divisions, located each side of the pulpit, one composed principally of children, another of adults, and the third of solo voices, and should consist of at least twenty-four trained voices (sixty would be much better), whose duty will be, —

First: To sing music bequeathed to us by the great masters, ancient and modern, the correct rendering of which will serve to impress the minds of the people with the sacredness and beauty of divine worship, and prepare their hearts for the prayers and songs which are to follow. All secular music should be rigorously excluded; long solos and *virtuoso* display should seldom be permitted, as their tendency is rather to produce a critical than devotional frame of mind; in fact, each hymn, chant, or anthem should be given as an individual act of worship by every participant.

Second: To assist and lead the congregation in the general song.

Here all must remember that choir and congregation are now to become an assembly of devout worshippers, raising heart and voice in one united song of praise to a common Father and Redeemer.

6. Congregational singing should be introduced at least twice in each service. In order to prepare the people for joining generally in this exercise, "Praise Meetings" should be frequently held under the joint direction of the pastor and chorister, in which the congregation may join in singing familiar tunes.

The choir should always be present, and lend their assistance by singing with the congregation; by introducing from time to time new tunes which may be sung by the congregation at subsequent meetings; and also by occasionally

INTRODUCTION.

singing appropriate select pieces. The pastor should frequently intersperse the singing exercises with short addresses, containing incidents concerning the hymns or tunes, and other remarks appropriate to the occasion. As far as practicable, it should be relieved from the formality of a regular service, and rendered social and attractive, by which means it will inevitably become one of the most desirable and popular meetings of the church.

When properly conducted, such meetings cannot fail to awaken the people to a new interest in church music, infuse them with the spirit of song, quicken their religious life, and give a new impetus to every department of church labor. Indeed, so great has been their influence that, in several instances, powerful revivals have resulted from their introduction. The regular weekly prayer meeting may be most appropriately and profitably prefaced by a half hour's service of this character.

7. The tunes which the congregation are expected to sing should be selected by the chorister with reference to their adaptation to the hymn and to their familiarity to the people.* If the tune set to the hymn in the tune book is not generally known, another which is familiar should be chosen, and its name and the page where it may be found, announced by the minister.

8. The organist should give out the tune by playing the melody upon the great organ with loud stops, and the harmony upon the swell or choir organ. The *tempo* must never be taken so fast but that the congregation can easily join.

9. *The minister and congregation should rise while the organist is playing the last line of the prelude*, the congregation always facing the pulpit.

10. At the conclusion of the prelude the congregation and choir should join together upon the *first* word of the hymn. The choir may sing either the harmony or the melody, but *the congregation should invariably sing the melody*. In order to facilitate this, the key of the tunes has been arranged, wherever practicable, so that the melody shall not ascend above E. The organist should accompany the choir and congregation generally with the full organ, and confine himself solely to the notes of the tune.

11. The congregation should be invited, encouraged, and exhorted, if necessary, to join with heart and voice in this delightful service. *All* should sing, and sing "lustily"; and all endeavors to produce artistic effects should be avoided.

12. The last note of each line should be sustained whenever the musical structure of the tunes will admit.

13. If any interlude is played, it should not exceed in length four bars of the tune. When the interlude is omitted, the pedal note should be continued between the verses.

14. At the conclusion of the hymn the organist may play a few chords, giving a *decrescendo* effect while the congregation are being seated.

15. Wherever practicable, it is desirable that the singing should be accompanied by one or more brass instruments. The congregation are thereby sustained and borne along, and the devotional effect is very greatly improved.

16. If it is desired that *all* should join in the singing, there must be no lack of tune books in the pews.

The importance of congregational singing is being felt more and more in all our churches; and if this work shall help to hasten on the day, when from every congregation in the land, shall ascend one general song of praise from the united voices of all the worshippers, we shall feel that our labor has not been in vain.

EBEN TOURJÉE.

---

* Fugue tunes are quite unsuited for congregational use. A few have, however, been introduced into the present volume in deference to the earnest wishes of friends, to whom they are exceedingly precious. In general, the tune upon the opposite page may be substituted.

Order of Worship.

Morning Service.

1. ORGAN VOLUNTARY.

2. THE LORD'S PRAYER offered by Minister and People, or the PRAYER OF INVOCATION by the Minister, followed by the LORD'S PRAYER, by Minister and People.   [Congregation bowed down.]

> OUR FATHER WHICH ART IN HEAVEN,
> HALLOWED BE THY NAME.
> THY KINGDOM COME.
> THY WILL BE DONE IN EARTH,
> AS IT IS IN HEAVEN.
> GIVE US THIS DAY OUR DAILY BREAD;
> AND FORGIVE US OUR TRESPASSES,
> AS WE FORGIVE THOSE WHO TRESPASS AGAINST US.
> AND LEAD US NOT INTO TEMPTATION;
> BUT DELIVER US FROM EVIL:
> FOR THINE IS THE KINGDOM,
> AND THE POWER, AND THE GLORY,
> FOREVER, AMEN.

3. The Minister, Choir and Congregation unite in singing (without prelude) the DOXOLOGY.   [All standing.]

> Praise God from whom all blessings flow,
> Praise him all creatures here below;
> Praise him above, ye heavenly host,
> Praise Father, Son, and Holy Ghost.

4. The Congregation remain standing and repeat after the Minister the APOSTLES' CREED.

I believe in God the Father, Almighty,
Maker of Heaven and Earth;
And in Jesus Christ his only begotten Son our Lord;
Who was conceived by the Holy Ghost,
Born of the Virgin Mary,
Suffered under Pontius Pilate,
Was crucified, dead, and buried;
The third day he rose from the dead;
He ascended into Heaven,
And sitteth at the right hand of God the Father Almighty;
From thence he shall come to judge the quick and the dead.
I believe in the Holy Ghost;
The Holy Catholic Church,
The communion of saints;
The forgiveness of sins;
The resurrection of the body;
And the life everlasting, Amen.

5. The Choir sing the Gloria Patri.*

> Glory be to the Father, and to the Son, and to the Holy Ghost; as it was in the beginning, is now, and ever shall be, world without end. Amen.

6. A Lesson from the Psalter† is read by the Minister and Congregation responsively. [The Congregation standing.]

7. Selection by the Choir; viz., a Chant, Te Deum, Motett, or Anthem. [Congregation seated.]

---

* This plan may be occasionally varied by singing a familiar chant before the Gloria Patri. See pp. 265—279.

† The practice of reading the Psalms and other selections of scripture, by the congregation and minister, alternately, might with great profit be introduced in all our churches.
Arrangements of the Psalms for this purpose have been published by several denominations.

8. READING OF THE SCRIPTURE LESSON. [Congregation seated.]

9. PRAYER OF GENERAL CONFESSION AND SUPPLICATION: [The Congregation bowing their heads or kneeling.]

10. The NOTICES are given by the Minister.

11. A HYMN is read or announced by the Minister, and sung by the Minister, Choir and Congregation to a familiar tune. [All standing.]

12. SERMON.

13. THE CLOSING HYMN sung by Choir and Congregation. [The congregation standing.]

14. The Congregation being seated, the PRAYER FOR A BLESSING ON THE WORD is offered by the Minister, and then, while the people are still bowed down, he pronounces the

15. BENEDICTION.

Evening Service.

1. ORGAN VOLUNTARY.

2. Singing of a HYMN by Choir and Congregation. [All standing.]

3. Reading of a LESSON from the PSALTER by the Minister and Congregation responsively. [The Congregation still standing.]

4. PRAYER. [The Congregation bowed down.]

5. The Choir sing the GLORIA IN EXCELSIS DEO (see page 268), or a Chant followed by the GLORIA PATRI; or a PSALM may be read and chanted responsively by the Minister and Choir. [The Congregation seated.]

6. SINGING OF AN ANTHEM by the Choir, or of a hymn by Choir and Congregation.

7. SERMON.

8. The Closing Hymn, sung by Choir and Congregation. [All standing.]

9. The Prayer for a Blessing on the Word is offered by the Minister, following which, while the people are bowed down, he pronounces the

10. Benediction.

Communion Service.

I. Organ Prelude.

II. Singing of a Hymn by the Choir and Congregation. [Congregation standing.]

III. Reading of the Scripture Lesson.

IV. Prayer of General Confession and Supplication.

V. The ten Commandments are read by the Minister, after each of which (excepting the last), the following response may be said or sung :*

Lord, have mercy upon us, and incline our hearts to keep this law.

After the last commandment the following response should be used:

Lord, have mercy upon us, and write all these, thy laws, in our hearts, we beseech thee.

VI. Any persons who are to be admitted to the church on confession of faith, are invited to present themselves before the Congregation, and are then received according to the forms prescribed in the Church manual.

VII. Any persons to be received by letter from other churches are invited to rise from their places and are then received according to forms prescribed in the Church manual.

---

* The responses may be omitted to all but the last commandment, if thought expedient.

VIII. The SACRAMENTAL COLLECTION for the poor is taken, the Minister reading select portions of Scripture.

IX. THE NOTICES are read by the Minister.

X. A HYMN is read by the Minister and sung by the Choir and Congregation.

XI. THE PRAYER OF CONFESSION is offered.

XII. ADMINISTRATION OF THE SACRAMENT.

XIII. ADDRESS by the Pastor.

XIV. PRAYER.

XV. Singing of a HYMN by Choir and Congregation.

XVI. BENEDICTION.

Commandments.

God spake all these words, saying,

I am the LORD thy GOD, which have brought thee out of the land of Egypt, out of the house of bondage.

I.

Thou shalt have no other gods before me.

II.

Thou shalt not make unto thee any graven image, or any likeness of anything that is in heaven above, or that is in the earth beneath, or that is in the water under the earth. Thou shalt not bow down thyself to them, nor serve them; for I the Lord thy God am a jealous God, visiting the iniquity of the fathers upon the children unto the third and fourth generation of them that hate me; and shewing mercy unto thousands of them that love me, and keep my commandments.

III.

Thou shalt not take the name of the Lord thy God in vain; for the Lord will not hold him guiltless that taketh his name in vain.

IV.

Remember the sabbath day, to keep it holy. Six days shalt thou labor, and do all thy work; but the seventh day is the sabbath of the Lord thy God; in it thou shalt not do any work, thou, nor thy son, nor thy daughter, thy manservant, nor thy maidservant, nor thy cattle, nor thy stranger that is within thy gates; for in six days the Lord made heaven and earth, the sea, and all that in them is, and rested the seventh day; wherefore the Lord blessed the sabbath day and hallowed it.

V.

Honor thy father and thy mother; that thy days may be long upon the land which the Lord thy God giveth thee.

VI.

Thou shalt not kill.

VII.

Thou shalt not commit adultery..

VIII.

Thou shalt not steal.

IX.

Thou shalt not bear false witness against thy neighbor.

X.

Thou shalt not covet thy neighbor's house, thou shalt not covet thy neighbor's wife, nor his manservant, nor his maidservant, nor his ox, nor his ass, nor anything that is thy neighbor's.

RESPONSES TO THE COMMANDMENTS. *

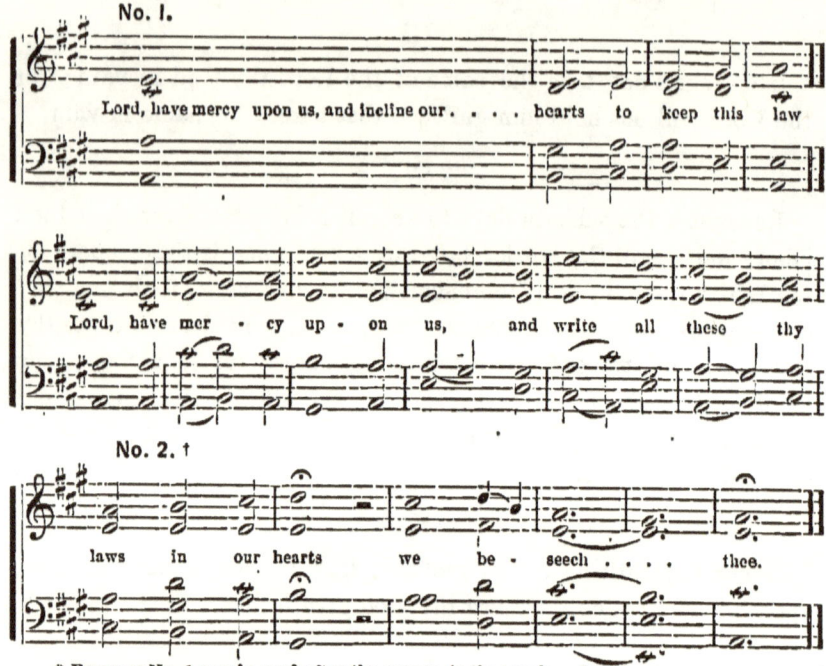

* Response No. 1 may be used after the prayer, to the words,—*Lord have mercy upon us, and incline thine ear to hear our prayer.*

† No. 2 should be used after the last commandment only.

GLORIA PATRI.

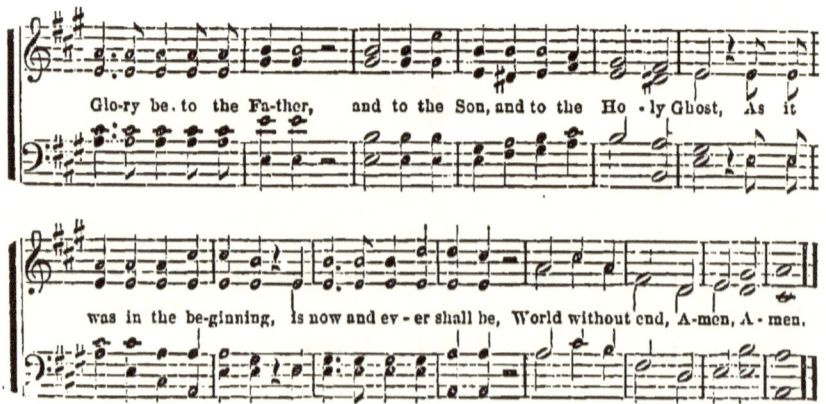

THE

TRIBUTE OF PRAISE,

OR

HYMNS AND TUNES

FOR

PUBLIC AND SOCIAL WORSHIP.

EISENACH. L. M.

1. With all my pow'rs of heart and tongue, I'll praise my Maker in my song; Angels shall hear the notes I raise, Approve the song, and join the praise.

2 To God I cried, when troubles rose;
He heard me, and subdued my foes;
He did my rising fears control,
And strength diffused thro' all my soul.

3 Amid a thousand snares I stand,
Upheld and guarded by thy hand;
Thy words my fainting soul revive,
And keep my dying faith alive;

4 I'll sing thy truth and mercy, Lord;
I'll sing the wonders of thy word;
Not all thy works and names below
So much thy power and glory show.

2   *Jesus reigns.*

1 Come, let us tune our loftiest song,
  And raise to Christ our joyful strain:
Worship and thanks to him belong,
  Who reigns, and shall forever reign.

2 His sov'reign power our bodies made;
  Our souls are his immortal breath;
And when his creatures sinn'd, he bled,
  To save us from eternal death.

3 Burn every breast with Jesus' love;
  Bound every heart with rapt'rous joy;
And saints on earth, with saints above,
  Your voices in his praise employ.

4 Extol the Lamb with loftiest song,
  Ascend for him our cheerful strain;
Worship and thanks to him belong,
  Who reigns and shall forever reign.

3   *Living bread.*

1 Thy presence, gracious God, afford;
  Prepare us to receive thy word:
Now let thy voice engage our ear,
  And faith be mix'd with what we hear.

2 Distracting thoughts and cares remove,
  And fix our hearts and hopes above;
With food divine may we be fed,
  And satisfied with living bread.

3 To us the sacred word apply,
  With sov'reign power and energy;
And may we, in thy faith and fear,
  Reduce to practice what we hear.

4 Father, in us thy Son reveal;
  Teach us to know and do thy will:
Thy saving power and love display,
  And guide us to the realms of day.

4   *The sacramental seal.*

1 Come, Father, Son, and Holy Ghost,
  Honor the means ordain'd by thee;
Make good our apostolic boast,
  And own thy glorious ministry.

2 We now thy promised presence claim;
  Sent to disciple all mankind,—
Sent to baptize into thy name,—
  We now thy promised presence find.

3 Father, in these reveal thy Son;
  In these, for whom we seek thy face,
The hidden mystery make known,
  The inward, pure, baptizing grace.

4 Jesus, with us thou always art,
  Effectual make the sacred sign;
The gift unspeakable impart,
  And bless the ordinance divine.

5 Eternal Spirit, from on high,
  Baptizer of our spirits thou,
The sacramental seal apply,
  And witness with the water now.

BAVA. * L. M.

5 *The heavenly Guest invited.*
1 Savior of all, to thee we bow,
  And own thee faithful to thy word;
  We hear thy voice, and open now
  Our hearts to entertain our Lord.

2 Come in, come in, thou heavenly Guest;
  Delight in what thyself hast given;
  On thy own gifts and graces feast,
  And make the contrite heart thy heaven.

3 Smell the sweet odor of our prayers;
  Our sacrifice of praise approve;
  And treasure up our gracious tears,
  Who rest in thy redeeming love.

4 Beneath thy shadow let us sit;
  Call us thy friends, and love, and bride;
  And bid us freely drink and eat
  Thy dainties, and be satisfied.

6 *The vow sealed at the cross.*
1 Lord, I am thine, entirely thine,
  Purchased and saved by blood divine;
  With full consent thine I would be,
  And own thy sov'reign right in me.

2 Grant one poor sinner more a place
  Among the children of thy grace;
  A wretched sinner, lost to God,
  But ransomed by Immanuel's blood.

3 Thine would I live—thine would I die;
  Be thine through all eternity;
  The vow is past beyond repeal,
  And now I set the solemn seal.

4 Here, at that cross where flows the blood
  That bought my guilty soul for God,—
  Thee, my new Master, now I call,
  And consecrate to thee my all.

7 *The spirit of the ancient worthies.*
1 O for that flame of living fire,
  Which shone so bright in saints of old:
  Which bade their souls to heaven aspire,—
  Calm in distress, in danger bold.

2 Where is that spirit, Lord, which dwelt
  In Abrah'm's breast, and seal'd him thine?
  Which made Paul's heart with sorrow melt,
  And glow with energy divine?—

3 That Spirit, which from age to age
  Proclaim'd thy love, and taught thy ways?
  Brighten'd Isaiah's vivid page,
  And breath'd in David's hallow'd lays?

4 Is not thy grace as mighty now
  As when Elijah felt its power;
  When glory beam'd from Moses' brow,
  Or Job endur'd the trying hour?

5 Remember, Lord, the ancient days;
  Renew thy work; thy grace restore;
  And while to thee our hearts we raise,
  On us thy Holy Spirit pour.

* This tune is found in the best collections of Psalmody. From its constant publication in all the olden collections, it may be supposed to have been a special favorite. It is fully equal in every thing but recollections and associations to the "Tune of Tunes," even "The Old Hundredth."

BRIDGEWATER. * L. M. EDSON.

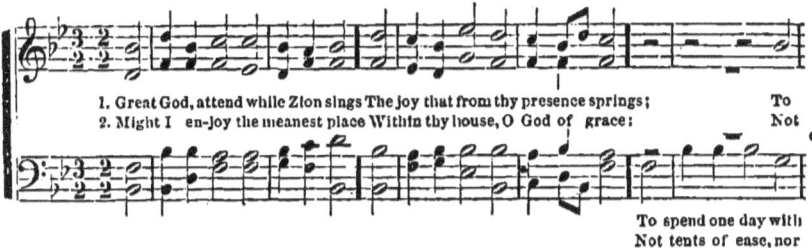

1. Great God, attend while Zion sings The joy that from thy presence springs; To spend one day with
2. Might I en-joy the meanest place Within thy house, O God of grace: Not tents of ease, nor

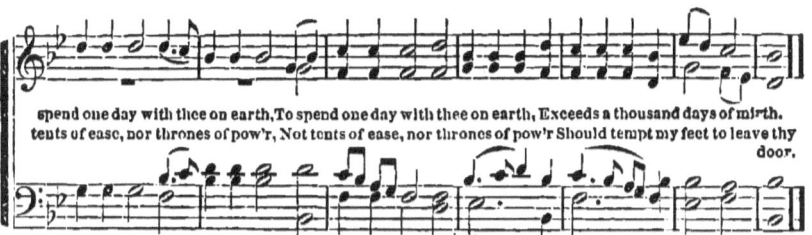

spend one day with thee on earth, To spend one day with thee on earth, Exceeds a thousand days of mirth.
tents of ease, nor thrones of pow'r, Not tents of ease, nor thrones of pow'r Should tempt my feet to leave thy door.

thee on earth, To spend one day with thee on earth, Ex-ceeds a thou - sand days of mirth.
thrones of pow'r, Not tents of ease, nor thrones of pow'r Should tempt my feet . . to leave thy door.

3 God is our Sun, he makes our day ;
   God is our shield, he guards our way,
   From all the' assaults of hell and sin,
   From foes without and foes within.

4 All needful grace will God bestow,
   And crown that grace with glory too ;
   He gives us all things, and withholds
   No real good from upright souls.

9   *The joys of the Sabbath.*
1 Sweet is the work, my God, my King,
   To praise thy name, give thanks, and sing;
   To show thy love by morning light,
   And talk of all thy truth by night.

2 Sweet is the day of sacred rest ;
   No mortal cares shall seize my breast ;
   O may my heart in tune be found,
   Like David's harp of solemn sound.

3 When grace has purified my heart,
   Then I shall share a glorious part :
   And fresh supplies of joy be shed,
   Like holy oil to cheer my head.

4 Then shall I see, and hear, and know
   All I desired or wished below ;
   And every power find sweet employ
   In that eternal world of joy.

10   *The gospel feast.*
1 Come, sinners, to the gospel feast ;
   Let every soul be Jesus' guest :
   Ye need not one be left behind,
   For God hath bidden all mankind.

2 Sent by my Lord, on you I call ;
   The invitation is to all :—
   Come all the world ! come, sinner, thou !
   All things in Christ are ready now.

3 Come, all ye souls by sin oppressed,
   Ye restless wand'rers after rest ;
   Ye poor, and maimed, and halt, and blind
   In Christ a hearty welcome find.

4 My message as from God receive ;
   Ye all may come to Christ and live :
   O let his love your hearts constrain,
   Nor suffer him to die in vain.

5 See him set forth before your eyes,
   That precious, bleeding sacrifice :
   His offered benefits embrace,
   And freely now be saved by grace.

Doxology.
Praise God, from whom all blessings flow ;
Praise him, all creatures here below ;
Praise him above, ye heavenly host,
Praise Father, Son and Holy Ghost

* See foot note on p. 3d. of Introduction.

HAMBURG. L. M.

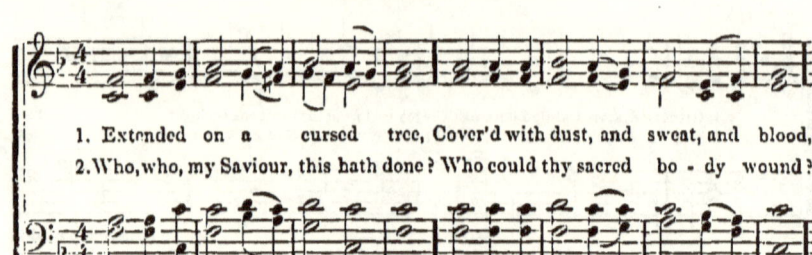

1. Extended on a cursed tree, Cover'd with dust, and sweat, and blood,
2. Who, who, my Saviour, this hath done? Who could thy sacred bo-dy wound?

See there, the King of glo-ry see! Sinks and expires the Son of God.
No guilt thy spot-less heart hath known, No guile hath in thy lips been found.

3 I, I alone have done the deed;
'Tis I thy sacred flesh have torn;
My sins have caused thee, Lord, to bleed,—
Pointed the nail, and fix'd the thorn.

4 For me the burden to sustain
Too great, on thee, my Lord, was laid:
To heal me, thou hast borne the pain;
To bless me, thou a curse wast made.

5 My Savior, how shall I proclaim,
How pay, the mighty debt I owe?
Let all I have, and all I am,
Ceaseless, to all, thy glory show.

6 Still let thy tears, thy groans, thy sighs,
O'erflow my eyes, and heave my breast,
Till, loosed from flesh and earth I rise,
And ever in thy bosom rest.

12 *Original and actual sin.*
1 Lord, we are vile, conceived in sin,
And born unholy and unclean;
Sprung from the man whose guilty fall
Corrupts his race, and taints us all.

2 Soon as we draw our infant breath
The seeds of sin grow up for death;
Thy law demands a perfect heart,
But we're defiled in every part.

3 Behold, we fall before thy face;
Our only refuge is thy grace:
No outward forms can make us clean;
The leprosy lies deep within.

4 Nor bleeding bird, nor bleeding beast,
Nor hyssop branch, nor sprinkling priest,
Nor running brook, nor flood, nor sea,
Can wash the dismal stain away.

5 Jesus, thy blood, thy blood alone,
Hath power sufficient to atone;
Thy blood can make us white as snow
No Jewish types could cleanse us so.

6 While guilt disturbs and breaks our peace,
Nor flesh nor soul hath rest or ease;
Lord, let us hear thy pard'ning voice,
And make these broken hearts rejoice.

13 *Sustaining grace prayed for.*
1 Taught by our Lord, we will not pray
Out of the world to be removed;
But keep us, in our evil day,
Till patient faith is fully proved.

2 From sin, the world, and Satan's snare,
The members of thy Son defend,
Till all thy character we bear,
And grace matured in glory end.

HURSLEY. L. M.

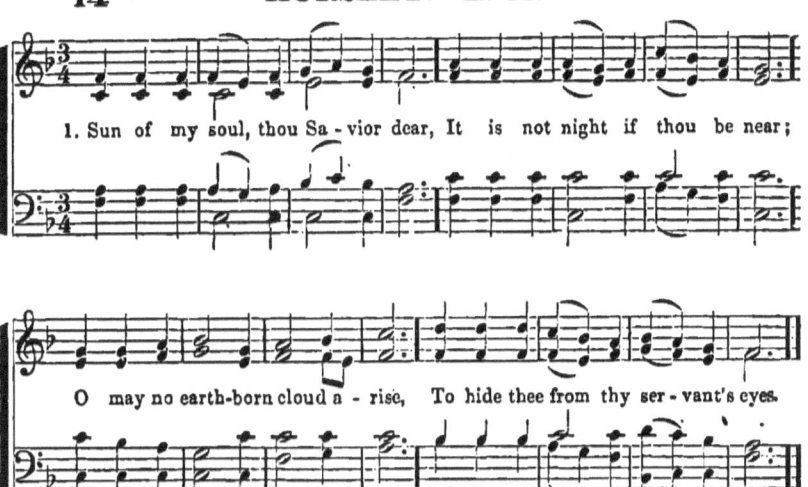

1. Sun of my soul, thou Sa-vior dear, It is not night if thou be near; O may no earth-born cloud a-rise, To hide thee from thy ser-vant's eyes.

2 Abide with me from morn till eve,
For without thee I cannot live;
Abide with me when night is nigh,
For without thee I dare not die.

3 If some poor wandering child of thine
Have spurned to-day the voice divine,
Now, Lord, the gracious work begin;
Let him no more lie down in sin.

4 Watch by the sick; enrich the poor
With blessings from thy boundless store;
Be every mourner's sleep to-night,
Like infants' slumbers, pure and light.

5 Come near and bless us when we wake,
Ere through the world our way we take;
Till in the ocean of thy love
We lose ourselves in heaven above.

15 *The only plea.*

1 Jesus, the sinner's friend, to thee,
Lost and undone, for aid I flee;
Weary of earth, myself, and sin:
Open thine arms, and take me in.

2 Pity and heal my sin-sick soul;
'Tis thou alone canst make me whole;
Dark, till in me thine image shine,
And lost, I am, till thou art mine.

3 At last I own it cannot be
That I should fit myself for thee:
Here, then, to thee I all resign;
Thine is the work, and only thine.

4 What shall I say thy grace to move?
Lord, I am sin,—but thou art love:
I give up every plea beside,—
Lord, I am lost—but thou hast died.

16 *Seeking deliverance and rest.*

1 Awaked from sin's delusive sleep,
My heavy guilt I feel, and weep;
Beneath a weight of woes oppress'd,
I come to thee, my Lord, for rest.

2 Now, from thy throne of grace above,
Look down upon my soul in love;—
That smile shall sweeten all my pain,
And make my soul rejoice again.

3 By thy divine, transforming power,
My ruin'd nature now restore;
And let my life and temper shine,
In blest resemblance, Lord, to thine.

17 *Helpless, in sin and misery.*

1 Whom man forsakes, thou wilt not leave,
Ready the outcast to receive:
Though all my simpleness I own,
And all my faults to thee are known.

2 Ah! wherefore did I ever doubt?
Thou wilt in nowise cast me out,—
A helpless soul, that comes to thee
With only sin and misery.

3 Lord, I am sick,—my sickness cure:
I want,—do thou enrich the poor:
Under thy mighty hand I stoop,
O lift the abject sinner up.

4 Lord, I am blind,—be thou my sight;
Lord, I am weak,—be thou my might;
A helper of the helpless be,
And let me find my all in thee.

WOODWORTH. L. M.
WM. B. BRADBURY

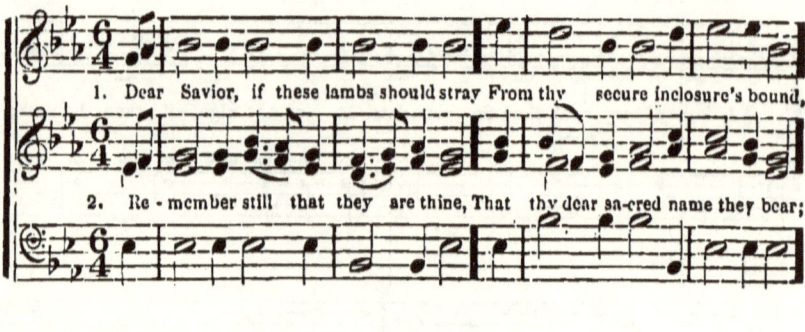

1. Dear Savior, if these lambs should stray From thy secure inclosure's bound,
2. Re-member still that they are thine, That thy dear sa-cred name they bear;

And, lured by world-ly joys a-way, Among the thoughtless crowd be found.
Think that the seal of love di-vine, The sign of covenant grace they wear.

3 In all their erring, sinful years,
  Oh, let them ne'er forgotten be!
Remember all the prayers and tears
  Which made them consecrate to thee.

4 And when these lips no more can pray,
  These eyes can weep for them no more,
Turn thou their feet from folly's way;
  The wanderers to thy fold restore.

19 *Trust in Christ at the hour of death.*
1 Jesus, in whom but thee above
  Can I repose my trust, my love?
  And shall an earthly object be
  Loved in comparison with thee?

2 How soon, O Lord, will life decay!
  How soon this world will pass away!
  Ah! what can mortal friends avail,
  When heart, and strength, and life shall fail?

3 O, then, be thou, my Savior, nigh,
  And I will triumph while I die;
  My strength, my portion is divine,
  And Jesus is forever mine!

20 *With Christ in heaven.*
1 As when the weary traveler gains
  The hight of some o'erlooking hill,
His heart revives, if o'er the plains
He sees his home, though distant still—

2 So when the Christian pilgrim views,
  By faith, his mansion in the skies,
  The sight his fainting strength renews,
  And wings his speed to reach the prize.

3 " 'T is there," he says, " I am to dwell
  With Jesus in the realms of day;
  Then shall I bid my cares farewell,
  And he shall wipe my tears away."

21 *" There am I in the midst of them."*
1 Where two or three, with sweet accord,
  Obedient to their sov'reign Lord,
  Meet to recount his acts of grace,
  And offer solemn prayer and praise;

2 "There," says the Savior, " will I be,
  Amid this little company;
  To them unveil my smiling face,
  And shed my glories round the place.'

3 We meet at thy command, dear Lord,
  Relying on thy faithful word;
  Now send thy Spirit from above,
  Now fill our hearts with heavenly love.

22   MELCOMBE. L. M.   J. WEBBE.

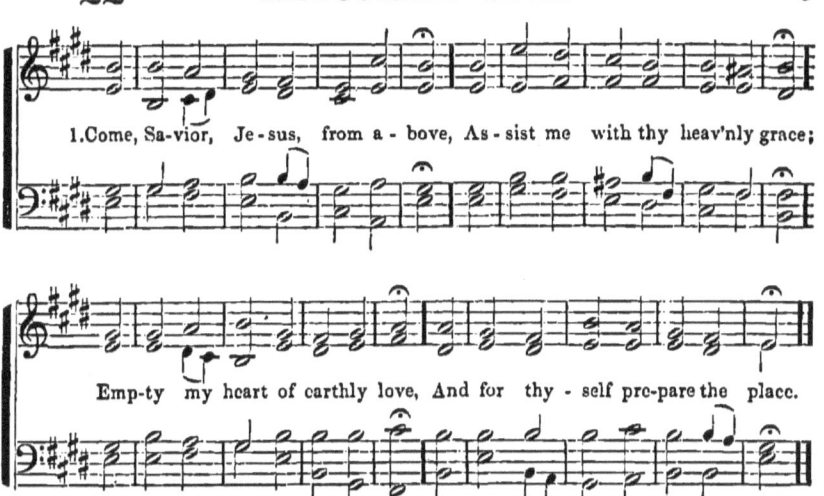

1. Come, Savior, Jesus, from above,
As-sist me with thy heav'nly grace;
Empty my heart of earthly love,
And for thyself prepare the place.

2 O let thy sacred presence fill,
And set my longing spirit free;
Which pants to have no other will,
But night and day to feast on thee.

3 While in this region here below,
No other good will I pursue:
I'll bid this world of noise and show,
With all its glittering snares, adieu.

4 That path with humble speed I'll seek,
In which my Savior's footsteps shine,
Nor will I hear, nor will I speak,
Of any other love but thine.

5 Henceforth may no profane delight
Divide this consecrated soul;
Possess it thou, who hast the right,
As Lord and Master of the whole.

6 Nothing on earth do I desire,
But thy pure love within my breast;
This, only this, will I require,
And freely give up all the rest.

23   *Just as I am.*

1 Just as I am, without one plea,
But that thy blood was shed for me,
And that thou bid'st me come to thee,
O Lamb of God, I come! I come!

2 Just as I am, and waiting not
To rid my soul of one dark blot;
To thee whose blood can cleanse each spot,
O Lamb of God, I come! I come!

3 Just as I am, though tossed about
With many a conflict, many a doubt;
Fightings within, and fears without,
O Lamb of God, I come! I come!

4 Just as I am,— poor, wretched, blind;
Sight, riches, healing of the mind,
Yea, all I need, in thee to find,
O Lamb of God, I come! I come!

5 Just as I am — thou wilt receive,
Wilt welcome, pardon, cleanse, relieve;
Because thy promise I believe,
O Lamb of God, I come! I come!

6 Just as I am — thy love unknown,
Hath broken every barrier down;
Now, to be thine alone, yea, thine alone,
O Lamb of God, I come! I come!

24   *Long suffering.*

1 God of my life, to thee belong
The grateful heart, the joyful song:
Touch'd by thy love, each tuneful chord
Resounds the goodness of the Lord.

2 Yet why, dear Lord, this tender care?
Why doth thy hand so kindly rear
A useless cumberer of the ground,
On which so little fruit is found?

3 Still let the barren fig-tree stand,
Upheld and fostered by thy hand;
And let its fruit and verdure be
A grateful tribute, Lord, to thee.

25 MILLER. L. M.
Dr. Miller.

1. Great God, indulge my humble claim;
Be thou my hope, my joy, my rest;
The glories that compose thy name,
Stand all engaged to make me blest.

2 Thou great and good, thou just and wise,
Thou art my Father and my God;
And I am thine, by sacred ties,—
Thy son, thy servant bought with blood.

3 With heart, and eyes, and lifted hands,
For thee I long, to thee I look;
As travelers in thirsty lands
Pant for the cooling water brook.

4 I'll lift my hands, I'll raise my voice,
While I have breath to pray or praise;
This work shall make my heart rejoice,
And fill the remnant of my days.

26 *Light for those who sit in darkness.*

1 Though now the nations sit beneath
The darkness of o'erspreading death,
God will arise with light divine,
On Zion's holy towers to shine.

2 That light shall shine on distant lands,
And wand'ring tribes, in joyful bands,
Shall come, thy glory, Lord, to see,
And in thy courts to worship thee.

3 O light of Zion, now arise!
Let the glad morning bless our eyes;
Ye nations, catch the kindling ray,
And hail the splendors of the day.

27 *Anticipating the Heavenly Sabbath.*

1 Lord of the Sabbath, hear us pray,
In this thy house, on this thy day;
And own, as grateful sacrifice,
The songs which from thy servants rise.

2 Thine earthly Sabbaths, Lord, we love,
But there's a nobler rest above;
To that our lab'ring souls aspire,
With ardent hope, and strong desire.

3 No more fatigue, no more distress,
Nor sin, nor hell shall reach the place;
No sighs shall mingle with the songs
Which warble from immortal tongues.

4 No rude alarms of raging foes;
No cares to break the long repose;
No midnight shade, no clouded sun;
But sacred, high, eternal noon.

5 O long-expected day, begin;
Dawn on these realms of woe and sin:
Fain would we leave this weary road,
And sleep in death, to rest with God.

28 *Self-dedication to the Lord.*

1 O Lord, thy heavenly grace impart,
And fix my frail, inconstant heart;
Henceforth my chief desire shall be
To dedicate myself to thee.

2 Thy glorious eye pervadeth space;
Thy presence, Lord, fills every place;
And wheresoe'er my lot may be,
Still shall my spirit rest with thee.

3 Renouncing every worldly thing,
And safe beneath thy spreading wing,
My sweetest thought henceforth shall be,
That all I want I find in thee.

DUANE ST. L. M.

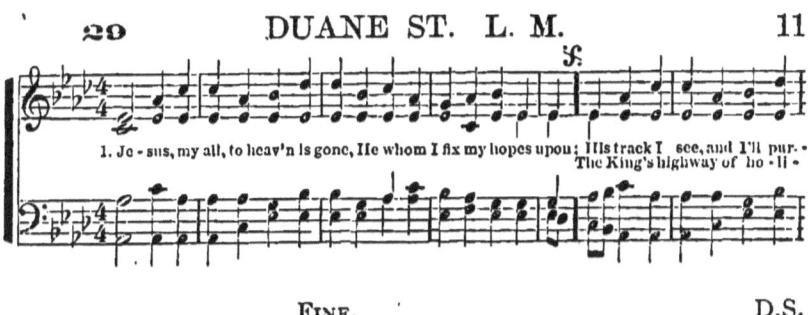

1. Je-sus, my all, to heav'n is gone, He whom I fix my hopes upon; His track I see, and I'll pursue the narrow way, till him I view. The way the holy prophets went, The road that leads from banish-
The King's highway of ho-li-
ness, I'll go, for all his paths are peace. *ment,*

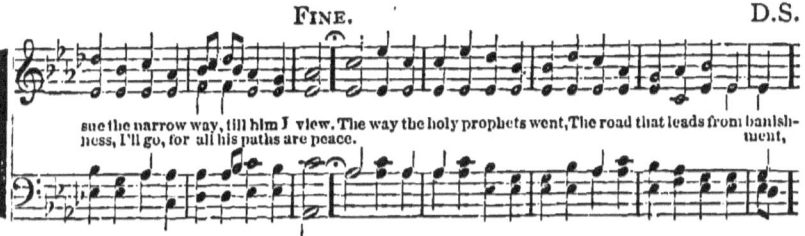

3 This is the way I long have sought,
And mourn'd because I found it not;
My grief a burden long has been,
Because I was not saved from sin.

4 The more I strove against its power,
I felt its weight and guilt the more;
Till late I heard my Savior say,—
Come hither, soul, I am the way.

5 Lo! glad I come; and thou, blest Lamb,
Shalt take me to thee, as I am:
Nothing but sin have I to give,—
Nothing but love shall I receive.

6 Then will I tell to sinners round,
What a dear Savior I have found;
I'll point to thy redeeming blood,
And say,—Behold the way to God.

30 *The Unspeakable Gift.*
1 Happy the man who finds the grace,
The blessing of God's chosen race;
The wisdom coming from above,
The faith that sweetly works by love.

2 Happy, beyond description, he
Who knows the Savior died for me!
The gift unspeakable obtains,
And heavenly understanding gains.

3 Wisdom divine! who tells the price
Of wisdom's costly merchandise?
Wisdom to silver we prefer,
And gold is dross compared to her.

4 Her hands are fill'd with length of days,
True riches, and immortal praise,—
Riches of Christ on all bestow'd,
And honor that descends from God.

5 To purest joys she all invites,—
Chaste, holy, spiritual delights;
Her ways are ways of pleasantness,
And all her flowery paths are peace.

6 Happy the man who wisdom gains;
Thrice happy, who his guest retains:
He owns, and shall forever own,
Wisdom, and Christ, and heaven are one.

31 *The New Covenant.*
1 O God, most merciful and true,
Thy nature to my soul impart;
'Stablish with me the covenant new,
And stamp thine image on my heart.

2 To real holiness restored,
O let me gain my Savior's mind,
And in the knowledge of my Lord,
Fullness of life eternal find.

3 Remember, Lord, my sins no more,
That I may them forget;
But, sunk in guiltless shame, adore,
With speechless wonder at thy feet.

4 O'erwhelm'd with thy stupendous grace,
I shall not in thy presence move;
But breathe unutterable praise,
And rapt'rous awe, and silent love.

5 Then every murm'ring thought and vain,
Expires, in sweet confusion lost;
I cannot of my cross complain,—
I cannot of my goodness boast.

6 Pardon'd for all that I have done,
My mouth as in the dust I hide;
And glory give to God alone,—
My God in Jesus pacified.

32 SESSIONS. L. M.
By permission of L. O. Emerson.

1. Shepherd of souls, with pitying eye, The thousands of our Israel see;
To thee in their be-half we cry, Ourselves but new-ly found in thee.

2. See where o'er desert wastes they err,.... And neither food nor feeder have;
Nor fold, nor place of refuge near, For no man cares.... their soul to save.

3 Thy people, Lord, are sold for naught,
   Nor know they their Redeemer nigh;
They perish, whom thyself hast bought;
   Their souls for lack of knowledge die.

4 Why should the foe thy purchase seize?
   Remember, Lord, thy dying groans:
The meed of all thy suff'rings these;
   O claim them for thy ransom'd ones!

33   *The light yoke and easy burden.*

1 O that my load of sin were gone;
   O that I could at last submit
At Jesus' feet to lay it down—
   To lay my soul at Jesus' feet.

2 Rest for my soul I long to find:
   Savior of all, if mine thou art,
Give me thy meek and lowly mind,
   And stamp thine image on my heart.

3 Break off the yoke of inbred sin,
   And fully set my spirit free;
I cannot rest till pure within,—
   Till I am wholly lost in thee.

4 Fain would I learn of thee, my God;
   Thy light and easy burden prove;
The cross all stain'd with hallow'd blood,
   The labor of thy dying love.

5 I would, but thou must give the power,
   My heart from every sin release;
Bring near, bring near the joyful hour,
   And fill me with thy perfect peace.

34   *The vow sealed at the cross.*

1 Lord, I am thine, entirely thine,
   Purchased and saved by blood divine:
With full consent thine I would be,
   And own thy sov'reign right in me.

2 Grant one poor sinner more a place
   Among the children of thy grace;
A wretched sinner, lost to God,—
   But ransom'd by Immanuel's blood.

3 Thine would I live—thine would I die;
   Be thine through all eternity;
The vow is past beyond repeal,
   And now I set the solemn seal.

4 Here, at that cross where flows the blood,
   That bought my guilty soul for God,—
Thee, my new Master, now I call,
   And consecrate to thee my all.

5 Do thou assist a feeble worm,
   The great engagement to perform;
Thy grace can full assistance lend,
   And on that grace I dare depend.

35   RETREAT. L. M.   T. HASTINGS.
By Permission.

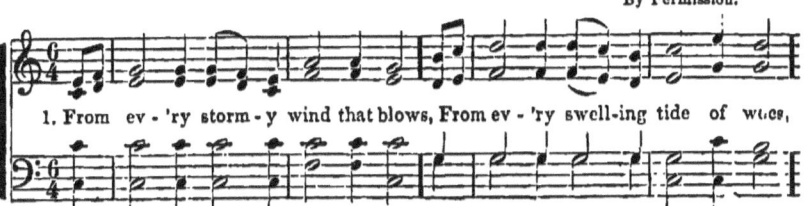

1. From ev-'ry storm-y wind that blows, From ev-'ry swell-ing tide of woes,

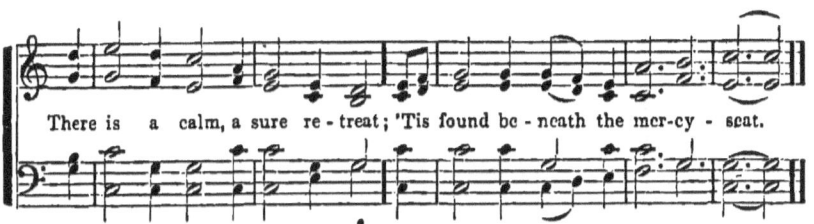

There is a calm, a sure re-treat; 'Tis found be-neath the mer-cy-seat.

2 There is a place where Jesus sheds
The oil of gladness on our heads;
A place than all besides more sweet,—
It is the blood-bought mercy-seat.

3 There is a scene where spirits blend,
Where friend holds fellowship with friend;
Though sunder'd far, by faith they meet,
Around one common mercy-seat.

4 Ah! whither could we flee for aid,
When tempted, desolate, dismay'd?
Or how the hosts of hell defeat,
Had suff'ring saints no mercy-seat?

5 There, there on eagles' wings we soar,
And sin and sense molest no more;
And heaven comes down our souls to greet,
While glory crowns the mercy-seat.

36   *Blessings of Prayer.*

1 What various hindrances we meet,
In coming to a mercy-seat;
Yet who that knows the worth of prayer,
But often wishes to be there?

2 Prayer makes the darken'd cloud withdraw,
Prayer climbs the ladder Jacob saw;
Gives exercise to faith and love;
Brings every blessing from above.

3 Restraining prayer, we cease to fight;
Prayer keeps the Christian's armor bright;
And Satan trembles when he sees
The weakest saint upon his knees.

37   *For the Savior's protection.*

1 Jesus, I fain would walk in thee,—
From nature's every path retreat;
Thou art my Way,—my Leader be,
And set upon the rock my feet.

2 Uphold me, Savior, or I fall;
O reach me out thy gracious hand:
Only on thee for help I call,—
Only by faith in thee I stand.

38   *His loving kindness is better than life.*

1 O God, thou art my God alone;
Early to thee my soul shall cry;
A pilgrim in a land unknown,—
A thirsty land, whose springs are dry.

2 Thee, in the watches of the night,
When I remember, on my bed,
Thy presence makes the darkness light;
Thy guardian wings are round my head.

3 Better than life itself, thy love;
Dearer than all beside to me;
For whom have I in heaven above,
Or what on earth, compared to thee.

4 Praise with my heart, my mind, my voice,
For all thy mercy I will give;
My soul shall still in God rejoice,—
My tongue shall bless thee while I live.

BRENTFORD. L. M.

1. Now be my heart inspired to sing The glo-ries of my Sa-vior King; Je-sus, the Lord, how heav'n-ly fair His form! how bright his beauties are!

2 O'er all the sons of human race,
He shines with a superior grace;
Love from his lips divinely flows,
And blessings all his state compose.

3 Thy throne, O God, forever stands,
Grace is the sceptre in thy hands;
Thy laws and works are just and right,
Justice and grace are thy delight.

4 God, thine own God, has richly shed
His oil of gladness on thy head;
And with his sacred Spirit blest
His first-born Son above the rest.

40 *The divine teacher.*

1 How sweetly flow'd the gospel's sound
From lips of gentleness and grace;
While list'ning thousands gather'd round,
And joy and rev'rence fill'd the place.

2 From heaven he came, of heaven he spoke,
To heaven he led his foll'wers' way;
Dark clouds of gloomy night he broke,
Unveiling an immortal day.

3 Come, wand'rers, to my Father's home;
Come, all ye weary ones, and rest.
Yes, sacred Teacher! we will come,
Obey, and be forever blest.

4 Decay, then, tenements of dust!
Pillars of earthly pride, decay!
A nobler mansion waits the just,
And Jesus has prepared the way.

41 *All-sufficiency of his grace.*

1 Ho! every one that thirsts, draw nigh:
'Tis God invites the fallen race:
Mercy and free salvation buy,—
Buy wine, and milk, and gospel grace.

2 Come to the living waters, come!
Sinners, obey your Maker's call;
Return, ye weary wand'rers, home,
And find his grace is free for all.

3 See from the Rock a fountain rise;
For you in healing streams it rolls;
Money ye need not bring, nor price,
Ye lab'ring, burden'd, sin-sick souls.

4 Nothing ye in exchange shall give;
Leave all you have, and are, behind;
Frankly the gift of God receive;
Pardon and peace in Jesus find.

42 *No success without God's blessing.*

1 Except the Lord our labor bless,
In vain shall we desire success;
Except his guardian power restrain,
The watchman waketh but in vain.

2 'Tis useless toil our stores to keep,—
Early to rise, and late to sleep,—
Unless the Lord, who reigns on high,
His providential care supply.

3 Grant, Lord, that we may ever flee
For guidance and for help to thee;
Thy blessing ask, whate'er we do,
And in thy strength our work pursue.

SEASONS. L. M. — PLEYEL.

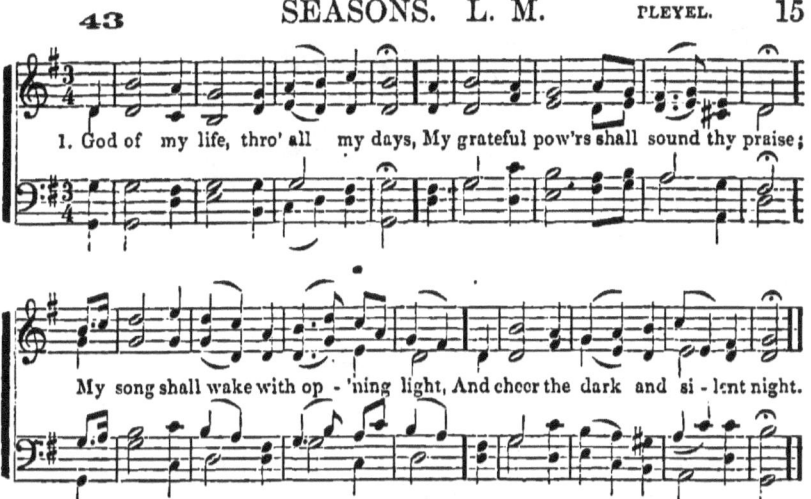

1. God of my life, thro' all my days,
My grateful pow'rs shall sound thy praise;
My song shall wake with op'ning light,
And cheer the dark and silent night.

2 When anxious cares would break my rest,
And griefs would tear my throbbing breast,
Thy tuneful praises, raised on high,
Shall check the murmur and the sigh.

3 When death o'er nature shall prevail,
And all the powers of language fail,
Joy through my swimming eyes shall break,
And mean the thanks I cannot speak.

4 But O, when that last conflict's o'er,
And I am chain'd to earth no more,
With what glad accents shall I rise
To join the music of the skies!

5 Soon shall I learn th' exalted strains,
Which echo thro' the heavenly plains;
And emulate, with joy unknown,
The glowing seraphs round the throne.

6 The cheerful tribute will I give,
Long as a deathless soul shall live:
A work so sweet, a theme so high,
Demands and crowns eternity.

44 *Christ and his Church.*

1 The King of saints, how fair his face,
Adorned with majesty and grace!
He comes with blessings from above,
And wins the nations to his love.

2 At his right hand, our eyes behold
The queen, arrayed in purest gold;
The world admires her heavenly dress,
Her robe of joy and righteousness.

3 O happy hour, when thou shalt rise
To his fair palace in the skies!
And all thy sons, a numerous train,
Each like a prince in glory reign.

4 Let endless honors crown his head;
Let every age his praises spread;
While we with cheerful songs approve
The condescensions of his love.

45 *Seeking the pastures of Christ.*

1 Thou, whom my soul admires above
All earthly joy, and earthly love,—
Tell me, dear Shepherd, let me know,
Where do thy sweetest pastures grow?

2 Where is the shadow of that rock,
That from the sun defends thy flock?
Fain would I feed among thy sheep,
Among them rest, among them sleep.

3 Why should thy bride appear like one
That turns aside to paths unknown?
My constant feet would never rove,—
Would never seek another love.

4 The footsteps of thy flock I see;
Thy sweetest pastures here they be;
A wondrous feast thy love prepares, [tears,
Bought with thy wounds, and groans, and]

5 His dearest flesh he makes my food,
And bids me drink his richest blood;
Here, to these hills, my soul would come
Till my Beloved lead me home.

FEDERAL STREET. L. M.

H. K. OLIVER.

1. If Lord, I have ac-ceptance found With thee, or fa-vor in thy sight,

2. O may I hear thy warn-ing voice, And timely fly from dan-ger near;

Still with thy grace and truth sur - round, And arm me with thy Spir-it's might.

With rev'rence un-to thee re - joice, And love thee with a fil-ial fear:

3 Still hold my soul in second life,
   And suffer not my feet to slide:
Support me in the glorious strife,
   And comfort me on every side.

4 O give me faith, and faith's increase;
   Finish the work begun in me;
Preserve my soul in perfect peace,
   And let me always rest on thee.

17 *The hidings of the Father's face.*

1 From Calvary a cry was heard,—
   A bitter and heart-rending cry;
My Savior! every mournful word
   Bespeaks thy soul's deep agony.

2 A horror of great darkness fell
   On thee, thou spotless, holy One!
And all the swarming hosts of hell
   Conspired to tempt God's only Son.

3 The scourge, the thorns, the deep disgrace,—
   These thou couldst bear, nor once repine;
But when Jehovah veiled his face,
   Unutterable pangs were thine.

4 Let the dumb world its silence break;
   Let pealing anthems rend the sky,

Awake, my sluggish soul, awake!
   He died, that we might never die.

5 Lord! on thy cross I fix mine eye;
   If e'er I lose its strong control,
O, let that dying, piercing cry,
   Melt and reclaim my wandering soul.

48 *Morning and evening mercies.*

1 My God, how endless is thy love;
   Thy gifts are every evening new;
And morning mercies from above,
   Gently descend like early dew.

2 Thou spread'st the curtains of the night,
   Great Guardian of my sleeping hours;
Thy sov'reign word restores the light,
   And quickens all my drowsy powers.

3 I yield myself to thy command;
   To thee devote my nights and days;
Perpetual blessings from thy hand
   Demand perpetual songs of praise

Doxology.

Praise God, from whom all blessings flow,
Praise him, all creatures here below;
Praise him above, ye heavenly host;
Praise Father, Son, and Holy Ghost.

EASTON. L. M.   MOZART.

1. O deem not they are blest a-lone, Whose lives a peace-ful ten-or keep;
For God, who pi-ties them, has shown A blessing for the eyes that weep.

2 The light of smiles shall fill again
The lids that overflow with tears:
And weary hours of woe and pain,
Are promises of happier years.

3 There is a day of sunny rest,
For every dark and troubled night;
Though grief may bide an evening guest,
Yet joy shall come with early light.

4 Nor let the good man's trust depart,
Though life its common gifts deny,—
Though with a pierced and broken heart,
And spurn'd of men, he goes to die.

5 For God has mark'd each sorrowing day,
And number'd every secret tear;
And heaven's eternal bliss shall pay
For all his children suffer here.

---

50   *Vows remembered and renewed.*

1 O happy day, that fix'd my choice
On thee, my Savior and my God!
Well may this glowing heart rejoice,
And tell its raptures all abroad.

2 O happy bond, that seals my vows,
To him who merits all my love;
Let cheerful anthems fill his house,
While to that sacred shrine I move.

3 'Tis done, the great transaction's done;
I am my Lord's, and he is mine;

He drew me, and I follow'd on,
Charm'd to confess the voice divine.

4 Now rest, my long-divided heart;
Fix'd on this blissful centre, rest;
Nor ever from thy Lord depart:
With him of every good possess'd.

5 High heaven, that heard the solemn vow,
That vow renew'd shall daily hear;
Till in life's latest hour I bow,
And bless in death a bond so dear.

---

51   *Rejoicing at the table, with godly sorrow.*

1 To Jesus, our exalted Lord,
The name by heaven and earth adored,
Fain would our hearts and voices raise
A cheerful song of sacred praise.

2 But all the notes which mortals know,
Are weak, and languishing, and low;
Far, far above our humble songs,
The theme demands immortal tongues

3 Yet while around his board we meet,
And humbly worship at his feet,
O let our warm affections move
In glad returns of grateful love!

4 Let humble, penitential woe,
In tears of godly sorrow flow;
And thy forgiving smiles impart
Life, hope, and joy to every heart

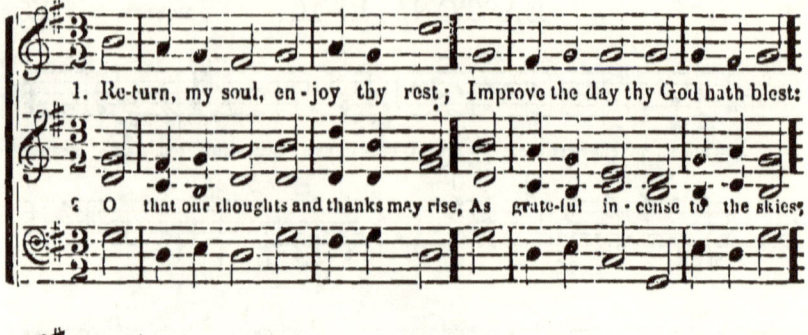

1. Return, my soul, en-joy thy rest; Improve the day thy God hath blest:
2. O that our thoughts and thanks may rise, As grateful incense to the skies;

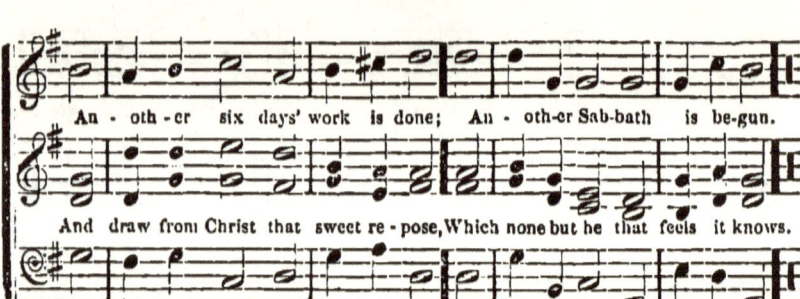

Another six days' work is done; Another Sabbath is begun.
And draw from Christ that sweet repose, Which none but he that feels it knows.

3 This heavenly calm within the breast,
Is the dear pledge of glorious rest,
Which for the Church of God remains,
The end of cares, the end of pains.

4 In holy duties, let the day,
In holy comforts, pass away;
How sweet, a Sabbath thus to spend,
In hope of one that ne'er shall end.

---

53 *Love which passeth knowledge.*

1 Of Him who did salvation bring,
I could forever think and sing;
Arise, ye needy,—he'll relieve;
Arise, ye guilty,—he'll forgive.

2 Ask but his grace, and lo, 'tis given;
Ask, and he turns your hell to heaven:
Though sin and sorrow wound my soul,
Jesus, thy balm will make it whole.

3 To shame our sins he blush'd in blood;
He closed his eyes to show us God:
Let all the world fall down and know,
That none but God such love can show.

4 Insatiate to this spring I fly;
I drink, and yet am ever dry:

Ah! who against thy charms is proof?
Ah! who that loves, can love enough?

---

54 *The bliss of assurance.*

1 Lord, how secure and blest are they
Who feel the joys of pardon'd sin; [sea,
Should storms of wrath shake earth and
Their minds have heaven and peace within.

2 The day glides sweetly o'er their heads,
Made up of innocence and love;
And soft, and silent as the shades,
Their nightly minutes gently move.

3 Quick as their thoughts, their joys come on
But fly not half so swift away:
Their souls are ever bright as noon,
And calm as summer evenings be.

4 How oft they look to the' heavenly hills,
Where groves of living pleasure grow;
And longing hopes, and cheerful smiles,
Sit undisturb'd upon their brow.

5 They scorn to seek earth's golden toys,
But spend the day, and share the night,
In numb'ring o'er the richer joys
That heaven prepares for their delight

AMES. L. M.
Dr. L. MASON.

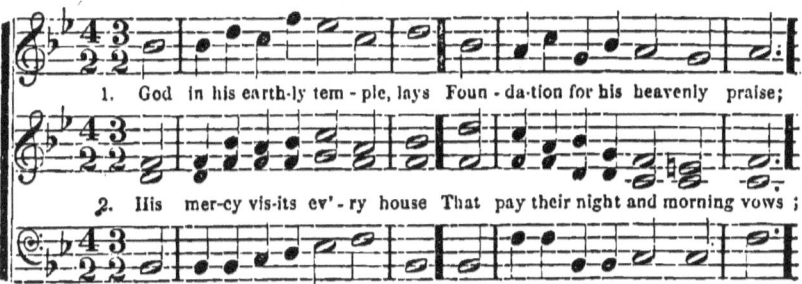

1. God in his earth-ly tem-ple, lays Foun-da-tion for his heavenly praise;
2. His mer-cy vis-its ev'-ry house That pay their night and morning vows;
3. What glories were described of old! What wonders are of Zi-on told!

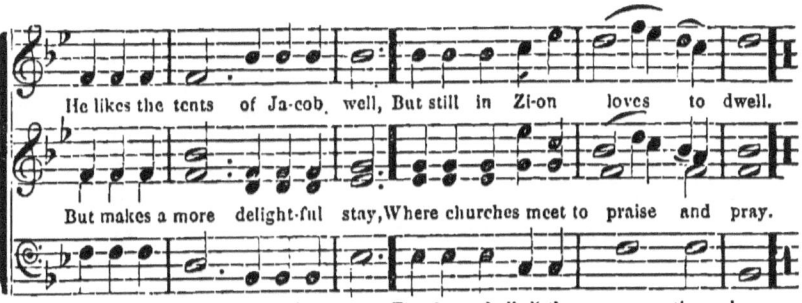

He likes the tents of Ja-cob well, But still in Zi-on loves to dwell.
But makes a more delight-ful stay, Where churches meet to praise and pray.
Thou ci-ty of our God be-low, Thy fame shall all the na-tions know.

---

56 *Heavenly zeal.*

1 O King of glory, thy rich grace
  Our feeble thought surpasses far;
Yea, e'en our crimes, though numberless,
  Less num'rous than thy mercies are.

2 Still, Lord, thy saving health display,
  And arm our souls with heavenly zeal;
So, fearless, shall we urge our way
  Through all the powers of earth and hell.

57 *All things are now ready.*

1 Sinners, obey the gospel word;
  Haste to the supper of my Lord;
  Be wise to know your gracious day;
  All things are ready,—come away.

2 Ready the Father is to own,
  And kiss his late-returning son;
  Ready your loving Savior stands,
  And spreads for you his bleeding hands.

3 Ready the Spirit of his love,
  Just now the stony to remove;
  To apply and witness with the blood,
  And wash and seal the sons of God.

4 The Father, Son, and Holy Ghost,
  Are ready with their shining host:
  All heaven is ready to resound,—
  The dead's alive! the lost is found!

58 *There remaineth a rest for the people of God*

1 Come, O thou greater than our heart,
  And make thy faithful mercies known:
  The mind which was in thee impart:
  Thy constant mind in us be shown.

2 O let us by thy cross abide,
  Thee, only thee, resolved to know,
  The Lamb for sinners crucified,
  A world to save from endless wo.

3 Take us into thy people's rest,
  And we from our own works shall cease
  With thy meek Spirit arm our breast,
  And keep our minds in perfect peace.

4 Jesus, for this we calmly wait;
  O let our eyes behold thee near!
  Hasten to make our heaven complete
  Appear, our glorious God, appear!

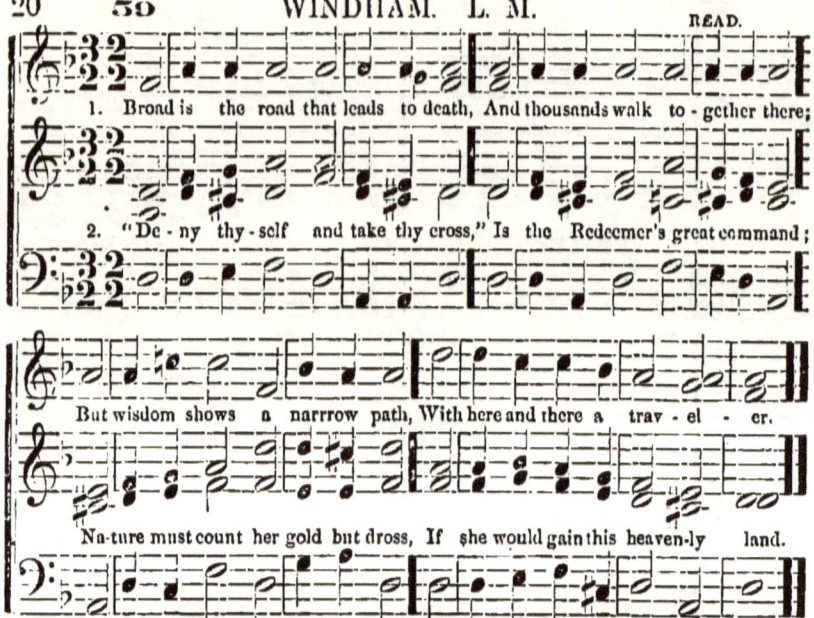

60. *The sinner's only hope.*

1 Wherewith, O Lord, shall I draw near,
  And bow myself before thy face?
How in thy purer eyes appear?
  What shall I bring to gain thy grace?

2 Will gifts delight the Lord Most High?
  Will multiplied oblations please?
Thousands of rams his favor buy,
  Or slaughter'd hecatombs appease?

3 Can these avert the wrath of God?
  Can these wash out my guilty stain?
Rivers of oil, and seas of blood,
  Alas! they all must flow in vain.

4 Who would himself to thee approve,
  Must take the path thyself hast trod;
Justice pursue, and mercy love,
  And humbly walk by faith with God.

5 But though my life henceforth be thine,
  Present for past can ne'er atone:
Though I to thee the whole resign,
  I only give thee back thine own.

6 Guilty I stand before thy face;
  On me I feel thy wrath abide;
'T is just the sentence should take place;
  'T is just,—but O, thy Son hath died!

61. *Deprecating eternal death.*

1 Father, if I may call thee so,
  Regard my fearful heart's desire:
Remove this load of guilty wo,
  Nor let me in my sins expire.

2 I tremble, lest the wrath divine,
  Which bruises now my wretched soul,
Should bruise this wretched soul of mine
  Long as eternal ages roll.

3 I deprecate that death alone,—
  That endless banishment from thee;
O save, and give me to thy Son,
  Who suffer'd, wept, and bled for me.

62. *The sacrifice of a broken heart.*

1 Though I have grieved thy Spirit, Lord,
  Thy help and comfort still afford;
And let a wretch come near thy throne
  To plead the merits of thy Son.

2 A broken heart, my God, my King,
  Is all the sacrifice I bring;
Thou God of grace, wilt thou despise
  A broken heart for sacrifice?

3 My soul lies humbled in the dust,
  And owns the dreadful sentence just:
Look down, O Lord, with pitying eye,
  And save a soul condemn'd to die.

TRIBUTE OF PRAISE. 21

63 *Deprecating the withdrawal of the Spirit.*
1 Stay, thou insulted Spirit, stay,
  Though I have done thee such despite;
Nor cast the sinner quite away,
  Nor take thine everlasting flight.
2 Though I have steel'd my stubborn heart,
  And shaken off my guilty fears;
And vex'd and urg'd thee to depart,
  For many long rebellious years.
3 Though I have most unfaithful been,
  Of all who e'er thy grace received;
Ten thousand times thy goodness seen;
  Ten thousand times thy goodness grieved:
4 Yet, O! the chief of sinners spare,
  In honor of my great High Priest;
Nor in thy righteous anger swear
  T' exclude me from thy people's rest.

64 *The fountain gushing from his side.*
1 Ye that pass by, behold the Man—
  The Man of griefs condemn'd for you:
The Lamb of God, for sinners slain,
  Weeping to Calvary pursue.
2 His sacred limbs they stretch, they tear;
  With nails they fasten to the wood;
His sacred limbs, exposed and bare,
  Or only cover'd with his blood.
3 Behold his temples, crown'd with thorn;
  His bleeding hands, extended wide;
His streaming feet, transfix'd and torn;
  The fountain gushing from his side!
4 O thou dear suff'ring Son of God,
  How doth thy heart to sinners move;
Sprinkle on us thy precious blood,
  And melt us with thy dying love.

65 *Condemned, but pleading the promises.*
1 Show pity, Lord, O Lord, forgive;
  Let a repenting rebel live.
Art not thy mercies large and free?
  May not a sinner trust in thee?
2 My crimes are great, but don't surpass
  The power and glory of thy grace;
Great God, thy nature hath no bound,—
  So let thy pard'ning love be found.
3 O wash my soul from every sin,
  And make my guilty conscience clean;
Here on my heart the burden lies,
  And past offences pain my eyes.
4 My lips with shame my sins confess,
  Against thy law, against thy grace;
Lord, should thy judgments grow severe,
  I am condemn'd, but thou art clear.
5 Should sudden vengeance seize my breath,
  I must pronounce thee just, in death;
And if my soul were sent to hell,
  Thy righteous law approves it well.
6 Yet save a trembling sinner, Lord,
  Whose hope, still hov'ring round thy word,
Would light on some sweet promise there,—
  Some sure support against despair.

66 *The dreadful day.*
1 The day of wrath, that dreadful day,
  When heaven and earth shall pass away,
What power shall be the sinner's stay?
  How shall he meet that dreadful day—
2 When, shriv'ling like a parched scroll,
  The flaming heavens together roll;
And, louder yet, and yet more dread,
  Swells the high trump that wakes the dead?
3 O, on that day, that wrathful day,
  When man to judgment wakes from clay,
Be thou, O Christ, the sinner's stay,
  Though heaven and earth shall pass away.

67 *The grave shall restore its trust.*
1 Unveil thy bosom, faithful tomb;
  Take this new treasure to thy trust:
And give these sacred relics room
  To slumber in the silent dust.
2 Nor pain, nor grief, nor anxious fear
  Invade thy bounds: no mortal woes
Can reach the peaceful sleeper here,
  While angels watch the soft repose.
3 So Jesus slept;—God's dying Son
  Pass'd through the grave, and blest the bed:
Rest here, blest saint, till from his throne
  The morning break, and pierce the shade
4 Break from his throne, illustrious morn,
  Attend, O earth! his sov'reign word;
Restore thy trust—a glorious form—
  Call'd to ascend and meet the Lord.

68 *Disembodied saints.*
1 The saints who die of Christ possess'd,
  Enter into immediate rest;
For them no further test remains,
  Of purging fires and torturing pains.
2 Who trusting in their Lord depart,
  Cleansed from all sin, and pure in heart,
The bliss unmix'd, the glorious prize,
  They find with Christ in Paradise.
3 Yet, glorified by grace alone,
  They cast their crowns before the throne
And fill the echoing courts above
  With praises of redeeming love.

RUSSIA. * L. M.

22 69 READ.

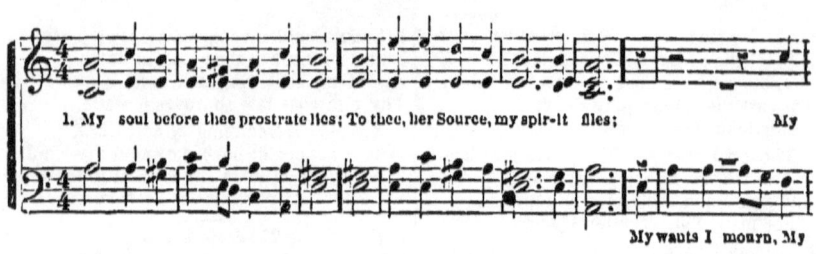

2 Jesus, vouchsafe my heart and will
With thy meek lowliness to fill;
No more her power let nature boast,
But in thy will may mine be lost.

3 Already springing hope I feel,—
God will destroy the power of hell,
And, from a land of wars and pain,
Lead me where peace and safety reign.

4 One only care my soul shall know,—
Father, all thy commands to do;
And feel, what endless years shall prove,
That thou, my Lord, my God, art love.

70   *An Advocate with the Father.*

1 Jesus, my Advocate above,
My Friend before the throne of love,
It' now for me prevails thy prayer,
If now I find thee pleading there,—

2 If thou the secret wish convey,
And sweetly prompt my heart to pray,—
Hear, and my weak petitions join,
Almighty Advocate, to thine.

3 Jesus, my heart's desire obtain;
My earnest suit present, and gain:

My fulness of corruption show;
The knowledge of myself bestow.

4 Save me from death; from hell set free;
Death, hell, are but the want of thee:
My life, my only heaven thou art;—
O might I feel thee in my heart.

71   *For sustaining grace.*

1 My hope, my all, my Savior thou,
To thee, lo, now my soul I bow;
I feel the bliss thy wounds impart,—
I find thee, Savior, in my heart.

2 Be thou my strength,—be thou my way
Protect me through my life's short day;
In all my acts may wisdom guide,
And keep me, Savior, near thy side.

3 In fierce temptation's darkest hour,
Save me from sin and Satan's power;
Tear every idol from thy throne,
And reign, my Savior, reign alone.

4 My suff'ring time shall soon be o'er;
Then shall I sigh and weep no more:
My ransom'd soul shall soar away,
To sing thy praise in endless day.

* See foot note on p. 3d. of Introduction.

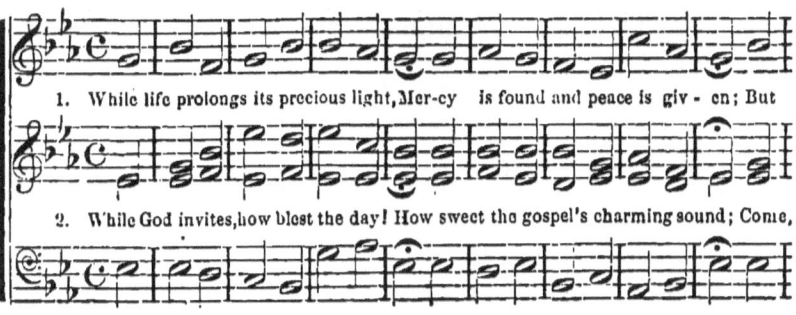

1. While life prolongs its precious light, Mer-cy is found and peace is giv-en; But soon, ah, soon, ap-proaching night Shall blot out eve-ry hope of heaven.

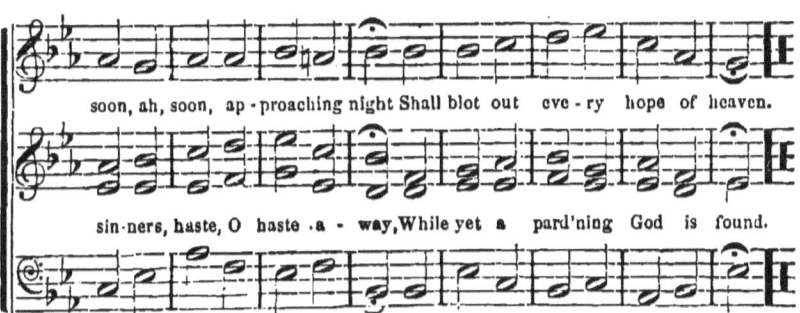

2. While God invites, how blest the day! How sweet the gospel's charming sound; Come, sinners, haste, O haste a-way, While yet a pard'ning God is found.

3 Soon, borne on time's most rapid wing,
   Shall death command you to the grave,
Before his bar your spirits bring,
   And none be found to hear or save.

4 In that lone land of deep despair,
   No Sabbath's heavenly light shall rise,
No God regard your bitter prayer,
   No Savior call you to the skies.

5 Now God invites; how blest the day!
   How sweet the Gospel's charming sound;
Come, sinners, haste, O haste away,
   While yet a pard'ning God is found.

73 *Shut up in unbelief.*

1 Light of the Gentile world, appear;
   Command the blind thy rays to see:
Our darkness chase, our sorrows cheer,
   And set the plaintive pris'ner free.

2 Me, me who still in darkness sit,
   Shut up in sin and unbelief,
Deliver from this gloomy pit,—
   This dungeon of despairing grief.

3 Open mine eyes the Lamb to know,
   Who bears the gen'ral sin away;
And to my ransomed spirit show
   The glories of eternal day.

74. *The inevitable doom.*

1 Tremendous God, with humble fear,
   Prostrate before thy awful throne,
The word unchangeable we hear—
   Thy sov'reign righteousness we own.

2 'Tis fit we should to dust return,
   Since such the will of God Most High;
In sin conceived, to trouble born,
   Born to lament, and toil, and die.

3 Submissive to thy just decree,
   We all shall soon from earth remove,
But when thou sendest, Lord, for me,
   O let the messenger be love.

4 Whisper thy love into my heart;
   Warn me of my approaching end
And then I joyfully depart,
   And then I to thy arms ascend.

MIGDOL. L. M.
Dr. L. MASON

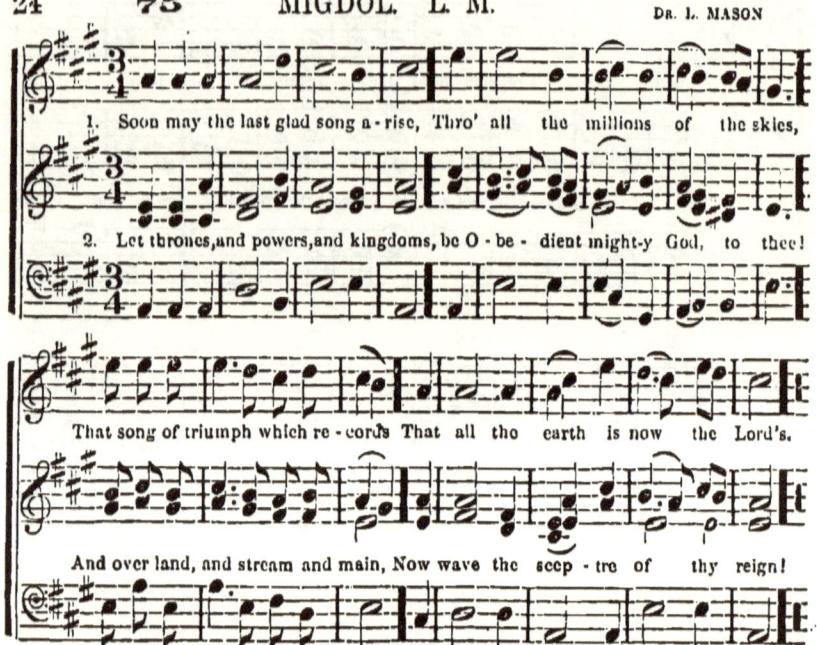

1. Soon may the last glad song a-rise, Thro' all the millions of the skies,
2. Let thrones, and powers, and kingdoms, be O - be - dient mighty God, to thee!
That song of triumph which re - cords That all the earth is now the Lord's.
And over land, and stream and main, Now wave the scep - tre of thy reign!

3 O let that glorious anthem swell;
 Let host to host the triumph tell,
 That not one rebel heart remains,
 But over all the Savior reigns!

76. *The King of glory.*

1 Our Lord is risen from the dead;
 Our Jesus is gone up on high;
 The powers of hell are captive led,—
 Dragg'd to the portals of the sky:

2 There his triumphal chariot waits,
 And angels chant the solemn lay;—
 Lift up your heads, ye heavenly gates;
 Ye everlasting doors give way!

3 Loose all your bars of massy light,
 And wide unfold th' ethereal scene;
 He claims these mansions as his right;
 Receive the King of glory in!

4 Who is the King of glory? Who?
 The Lord, that all our foes o'ercame;—
 The world, sin, death, and hell o'erthrew;—
 And Jesus is the Conqu'ror's name.

5 Lo! his triumphal chariot waits,
 And angels chant the solemn lay;

 Lift up your heads, ye heavenly gates;
 Ye everlasting doors, give way!

6 Who is the King of glory? Who?
 The Lord, of glorious power possess'd;—
 The King of saints and angels too;—
 God over all, forever blest!

77. *The heavenly Zion.*

1 Arm of the Lord, awake, awake!
 Thine own immortal strength put on!
 With terror clothed, hell's kingdom shake,
 And cast thy foes with fury down.

2 As in the ancient days appear!
 (The sacred annals speak thy fame;)
 Be now omnipotently near,
 To endless ages still the same.

3 By death and hell pursued in vain,
 To thee the ransom'd seed shall come
 Shouting, their heavenly Zion gain,
 And pass thro' death triumphant home.

4 The pain of life shall then be o'er,
 The anguish and distracting care;
 There sighing grief shall weep no more,
 And sin shall never enter there.

UXBRIDGE. L. M.
Dr. L. Mason.

1. Arm me with thy whole armor, Lord; Support my weakness with thy might;

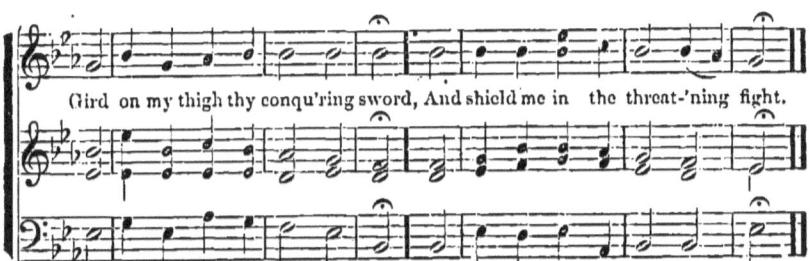

Gird on my thigh thy conqu'ring sword, And shield me in the threat-'ning fight.

2 From faith to faith, from grace to grace,
So in thy strength shall I go on;
Till heaven and earth flee from thy face,
And glory end what grace begun.

79 *True worship everywhere accepted.*
1 O thou, to whom, in ancient time,
The psalmist's sacred harp was strung,
Whom kings adored in song sublime,
And prophets praised with glowing tongue:
2 Not now on Zion's height alone
The favored worshiper may dwell,
Nor where, at sultry noon, thy Son
Sat weary by the patriarch's well.
3 From every place below the skies,
The grateful song, the fervent prayer,
The incense of the heart, may rise
To heaven and find acceptance there.
4 O thou, to whom, in ancient time,
The holy prophet's harp was strung;
To thee, at last, in every clime,
Shall temples rise, and praise be sung.

80 *The plenitude of His grace and power.*
1 O spirit of the living God,
In all thy plenitude of grace,
Where'er the foot of man hath trod,
Descend on our apostate race.
2 Give tongues of fire, and hearts of love,
To preach the reconciling word;

Give power and unction from above,
Where'er the joyful sound is heard.
3 Be darkness, at thy coming, light;
Confusion—order, in thy path:
Souls without strength, inspire with might;
Bid mercy triumph over wrath.
4 Baptize the nations; far and nigh
The triumphs of the cross record;
The name of Jesus glorify,
Till every kindred call him Lord.

81 *Faith reveals God's presence.*
1 Not here, as to the prophet's eye,
The Lord upon his throne appears;
Nor seraph tongues responsive cry,
Holy! thrice holy! in our ears:—
2 Yet God is present in this place,
Veiled in serener majesty;
So full of glory, truth, and grace,
That faith alone such light can see.
3 Nor, as he in the temple taught,
Is Christ within these walls revealed,
When blind, and deaf and dumb were brought,
Lepers and lame—and all were healed
4 Yet here, when two or three shall meet,
Or thronging multitudes are found
All may sit down at Jesus' feet,
And hear from him the joyful sound.

EVENING HYMN.

1. Glo-ry to thee, my God, this night, For all the blessings of the light:
Keep me, O keep me, King of kings, Beneath the shadow of thy wings.

2 Forgive me, Lord, for thy dear Son, The ill which I this day have done;
That with the world, myself, and thee, I, ere I sleep, at peace may be.

3 Teach me to live, that I may dread
The grave as little as my bed;
Teach me to die, that so I may
Rise glorious at the judgment-day.

4 O let my soul on thee repose,
And may sweet sleep mine eyelids close;
Sleep, which shall me more vig'rous make,
To serve my God, when I awake.

5 Lord, let my soul forever share
The bliss of thy paternal care:
'Tis heaven on earth, 'tis heaven above,
To see thy face, and sing thy love.

83 *Your life is hid with Christ in God.*
1 Ye faithful souls, who Jesus know,
If risen indeed with him ye are,
Superior to the joys below,
His resurrection's power declare.

2 Your faith by holy tempers prove:
By actions show your sins forgiven:
And seek the glorious things above,
And follow Christ your head to heaven.

3 There your exalted Savior see,
Seated at God's right hand again,
In all his Father's majesty,
In everlasting pomp to reign.

4 To him continually aspire,
Contending for your native place;
And emulate the angel choir,
And only live to love and praise.

5 For who by faith your Lord receive,
Ye nothing seek or want beside;
Dead to the world and sin ye live;
Your creature-love is crucified.

6 Your real life, with Christ conceal'd,
Deep in the Father's bosom lies;
And glorious as your Head reveal'd,
Ye soon shall meet him in the skies.

84 *Graven on the palms of His hands.*
1 Jesus, the Lamb of God, hath bled;
He bore our sins upon the tree;
Beneath our curse he bow'd his head;—
'Tis finish'd! he hath died for me.

2 See, where before the throne he stands,
And pours the all-prevailing prayer;
Points to his side, and lifts his hands,
And shows that I am graven there.

3 He ever lives for me to pray;
He prays that I with him may reign:
Amen to what my Lord doth say;
Jesus, thou canst not pray in vain.

MONMOUTH. L. M.

3 In robes of judgment, lo! he comes;
Shakes the wide earth and cleaves the tombs;
Before him burns devouring fire;—
The mountains melt, the seas retire.

4 His enemies, with sore dismay,
Fly from the sight, and shun the day:
Then lift your heads, ye saints! on high,
And sing, for your redemption's nigh.

86 *Holiness.*

1 Holy as thou, O Lord, is none;
Thy holiness is all thine own;
A drop of that unbounded sea
Is ours,—a drop derived from thee.

2 And when thy purity we share,
Thine only glory we declare;
And, humbled into nothing, own,
Holy and pure is God alone.

3 Sole, self-existing God and Lord,
By all thy heavenly hosts adored,
Let all on earth bow down to thee,
And own thy peerless majesty:

4 Thy power unparallel'd confess,
Establish'd on the Rock of peace;
The Rock that never shall remove,—
The Rock of pure, almighty love.

87 *Dedication.*

1 When Israel trod the desert way,
God dwelt within the curtain'd tent;
There gath'ring tribes repair'd to pray,
And found his gracious ear attent.

2 But, when fair Salem's towers arose,
And massive walls her hosts surround—
When God had scatter'd Zion's foes,
And peace and plenty reign'd around—

3 Then Lebanon's tall cedars came,
And polished stones majestic rose;
While lofty turrets tipp'd with flame,
Point upward to the saint's repose.

4 But vain were glitt'ring gems and gold;
And blood, in vain, from altars ran;
Till the unfolding glory told,
Jehovah comes to dwell with man.

5 Thus here, O God, our off'ring lies,
Cold in its beauty—cold and dead!
O, living fire—burst from the skies—
On us thy hallowing influence shed.

6 Thy priests shall feel its quick'ning power
Thy people catch the rising flame;
While all confess, to time's last hour,
Jehovah here records his name.

OLD HUNDRED. L. M.

WM. FRANC

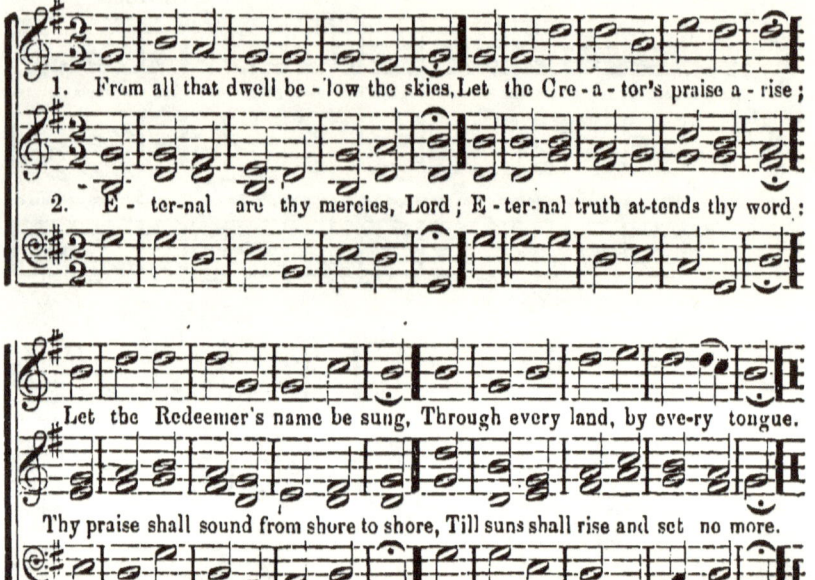

1. From all that dwell be-low the skies, Let the Cre-a-tor's praise a-rise;
2. E-ter-nal are thy mercies, Lord; E-ter-nal truth at-tends thy word:
Let the Redeemer's name be sung, Through every land, by eve-ry tongue.
Thy praise shall sound from shore to shore, Till suns shall rise and set no more.

3 Your lofty themes, ye mortals, bring;
In songs of praise divinely sing;
The great salvation loud proclaim,
And shout for joy the Savior's name.

4 In every land begin the song;
To every land the strains belong:
In cheerful sounds all voices raise,
And fill the world with loudest praise.

89 *Grateful adoration.*

1 Before Jehovah's awful throne
Ye nations bow with sacred joy;
Know that the Lord is God alone,
He can create, and he destroy.

2 His sov'reign power, without our aid,
Made us of clay, and formed us men;
And when like wand'ring sheep we stray'd,
He brought us to his fold again.

3 We'll crowd thy gates with thankful songs,
High as the heavens our voices raise;
And earth, with her ten thousand tongues,
Shall fill thy courts with sounding praise.

4 Wide as the world is thy command;
Vast as eternity thy love;
Firm as a rock thy truth shall stand,
When rolling years shall cease to move.

90 *Solemn reverence.*

1 Eternal Power, whose high abode
Becomes the grandeur of a God:
Infinite lengths, beyond the bounds
Where stars revolve their little rounds:

2 Thee while the first archangel sings,
He hides his face behind his wings:
And ranks of shining thrones around
Fall worshipping, and spread the ground.

3 Lord, what shall earth and ashes do?
We would adore our Maker too;
From sin and dust to thee we cry,
The Great, the Holy, and the High.

4 Earth, from afar, hath heard thy fame,
And worms have learn'd to lisp thy name;
But O! the glories of thy mind
Leave all our soaring thoughts behind.

Doxology.

Praise God, from whom all blessings flow;
Praise him, all creatures here below;
Praise him above, ye heavenly host,
Praise Father, Son, and Holy Ghost.

STONEFIELD. L. M.
S. STANLEY.

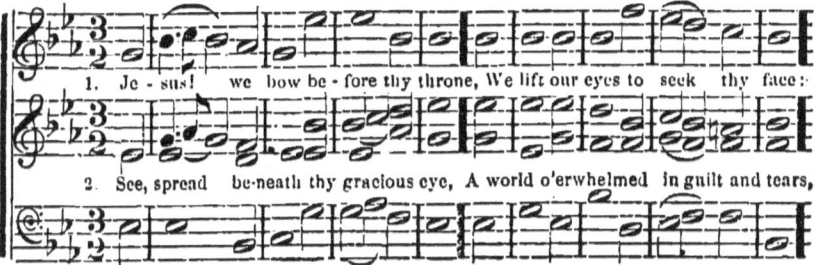

1. Je-sus! we bow be-fore thy throne, We lift our eyes to seek thy face:
2. See, spread be-neath thy gracious eye, A world o'erwhelmed in guilt and tears,

To bleed-ing hearts thy love make known, On contrite souls be-stow thy grace.
Where death-less souls in ru-in lie, And no kind voice dis-pels their fears.

3 Lord! arm thy truth with power divine;
Its conquests spread from shore to shore,
Till suns and stars forget to shine,
And earth and skies shall be no more.

4 O rise! ye ransomed captives, rise!
Peal the loud anthem here below!
Let earth reflect it to the skies,
And heaven with new born rapture glow.

92 *Welcome to Church fellowship.*

1 Brethren in Christ, and well beloved,
To Jesus and his servants dear,
Enter, and show yourselves approved;
Enter, and find that God is here.

2 Welcome from earth: lo, the right hand
Of fellowship to you we give:
With open hearts and hands we stand,
And you in Jesus' name receive.

3 Jesus, attend: thyself reveal;
Are we not met in thy great name?
Thee in the midst we wait to feel;
We wait to catch the spreading flame.

4 Truly our fellowship below
With thee and with the Father is:
In thee eternal life we know,
And heaven's unutterable bliss.

5 Though but in part we know thee here,
We wait thy coming from above;
And we shall then behold thee near,
And be forever lost in love.

93 *God, the nation's guardian.*

1 Great God! beneath whose piercing eye
The earth's extended kingdoms lie;
Whose fav'ring smile upholds them all,
Whose anger smites them, and they fall;—

2 We bow before thy heaven.ly throne;
Thy power we see—thy greatness own;
Yet, cherish'd by thy milder voice,
Our bosoms tremble and rejoice.

3 Thy kindness to our fathers shown
Their children's children long shall own;
To thee, with grateful hearts, shall raise
The tribute of exulting praise.

4 Led on by thine unerring aid,
Secure the paths of life we tread,
And, freely as the vital air,
Thy first and noblest bounties share.

5 Great God, our guardian, guide and friend!
O still thy shelt'ring arm extend;
Preserved by thee for ages past,
For ages let thy kingdom last.

HEBRON. L. M.

Dr. L. Mason.

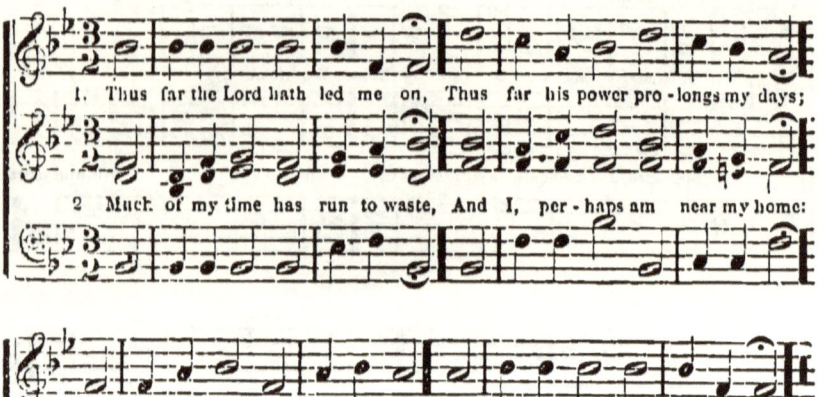

1. Thus far the Lord hath led me on, Thus far his power pro-longs my days;
And eve-ry eve-ning shall make known Some fresh me-mo-rial of his grace.

2 Much of my time has run to waste, And I, per-haps am near my home:
But he for-gives my fol-lies past, And gives me strength for days to come.

3 I lay my body down to sleep;
Peace is the pillow for my head;
While well-appointed angels keep
Their watchful stations round my bed.

4 Thus, when the night of death shall come,
My flesh shall rest beneath the ground,
And wait thy voice to rouse my tomb,
With sweet salvation in the sound.

95 *The Riches of his grace.*

1 What am I, O thou glorious God!
And what my father's house to thee,
That thou such mercy hast bestowed
On me, the vilest sinner, me?

2 Me, in my blood, thy love pass'd by,
And stopp'd my ruin to retrieve;
Wept o'er my soul thy pitying eye;
Thy bowels yearn'd, and sounded,—live!

3 Dying, I heard the welcome sound,
Received the blessing from above,
And pardon in thy mercy found,
Astonish'd at thy boundless love.

4 Honor, and might, and thanks, and praise,
I render to my pard'ning God;
Extol the riches of thy grace,
And spread thy saving name abroad.

5 I magnify thy gracious power,
And all within me shouts thy Name:
Thy Name let every soul adore;
Thy power let every tongue proclaim.

96 *The realizing light of faith.*

1 Author of faith, eternal Word,
Whose Spirit breathes the active flame,
Faith, like its finisher and Lord,
To-day, as yesterday, the same:—

2 To thee our humble hearts aspire,
And ask the gift unspeakable;
Increase in us the kindled fire,
In us the work of faith fulfil.

3 By faith we know thee strong to save:
(Save us, a present Savior thou :)
Whate'er we hope, by faith we have;
Future, and past, subsisting now.

4 To him that in thy Name believes,
Eternal life with thee is given;
Into himself he all receives,—
Pardon, and holiness, and heaven.

5 The things unknown to feeble sense,
Unseen by reason's glimm'ring ray,
With strong commanding evidence,
Their heavenly origin display.

PILESGROVE. L. M.

97   MITCHELL.   **31**

1. Another six day's work is done,
Another Sabbath is begun;
Return, my soul, enjoy thy rest,
Improve the day thy God hath blest.

2 Come, bless the Lord, whose love assigns
So sweet a rest to wearied minds;
Provides an antepast of heaven,
And gives this day the food of seven.

3 O that our thoughts and thanks may rise
As grateful incense to the skies;
And draw from heaven that sweet repose
Which none but he that feels it knows.

4 This heavenly calm within the breast
Is the dear pledge of glorious rest,
Which for the church of God remains,
The end of cares, the end of pains.

5 In holy duties let the day
In holy pleasures pass away;
How sweet a Sabbath thus to spend,
In hope of one that ne'er shall end.

98   *In the sanctuary.*

1 Far from my thoughts, vain world, be gone,
Let my religious hours alone;
Fain would mine eyes my Savior see:
I wait a visit, Lord from thee.

2 O warm my heart with holy fire,
And kindle there a pure desire;
Come, sacred Spirit, from above,
And fill my soul with heavenly love.

3 Blest Savior, what delicious fare!
How sweet thine entertainments are!
Never did angels taste above
Redeeming grace and dying love.

4 Hail, great Immanuel, all divine!
In thee thy Father's glories shine;
Thy glorious name shall be adored,
And every tongue confess thee Lord.

99   *Design of prayer.*

1 Prayer is appointed to convey
The blessings God designs to give:
Long as they live should Christians pray;
They learn to pray when first they live.

2 If pain afflict, or wrongs oppress;
If cares distract, or fears dismay;
If guilt deject; if sin distress:
In every case, still watch and pray.

3 'Tis prayer supports the soul that's weak:
Tho' thought be broken, language lame,
Pray if thou canst, or canst not speak:
But pray with faith in Jesus' name.

4 Depend on him; thou canst not fail;
Make all thy wants and wishes known;
Fear not; his merits must prevail:
Ask but in faith, it shall be done.

Doxology.

Praise God, from whom all blessings flow
Praise him, all creatures here below;
Praise him above, ye heavenly host;
Praise Father, Son, and Holy Ghost.

WARE. L. M.

Geo. Kingsley,
By permission.

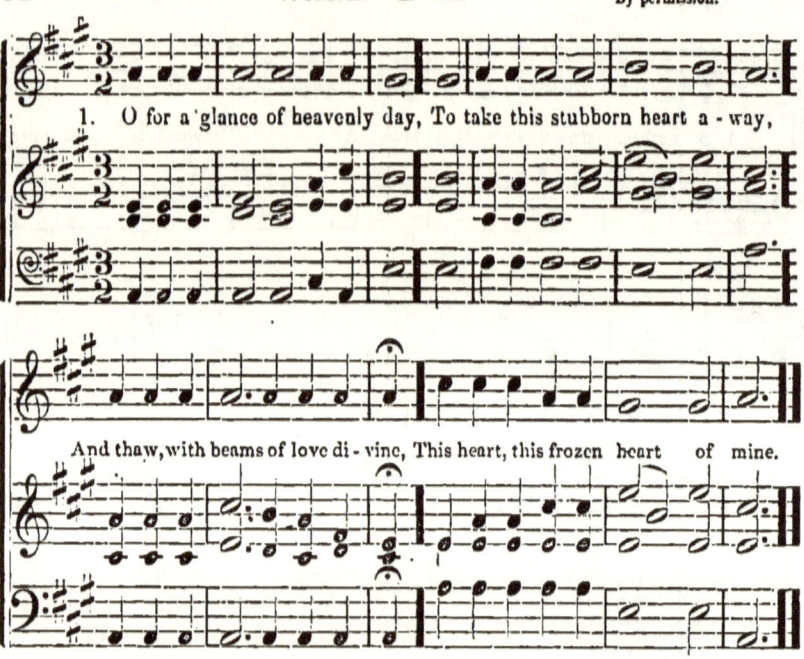

1. O for a glance of heavenly day, To take this stubborn heart a-way, And thaw, with beams of love di-vine, This heart, this frozen heart of mine.

2 The rocks can rend; the earth can quake;
The seas can roar; the mountains shake:
Of feeling, all things show some sign,
But this unfeeling heart of mine.

3 To hear the sorrows thou hast felt,
O Lord, an adamant would melt;
But I can read each moving line,
And nothing moves this heart of mine.

4 Thy judgments too, which devils fear,—
Amazing thought!— unmoved I hear:
Goodness and wrath in vain combine,
To stir this stupid heart of mine.

5 But power divine can do the deed;
And, Lord, that power I greatly need;
Thy Spirit can from dross refine,
And melt and change this heart of mine.

101 *Zeal implored.*

1 O thou, who all things canst control,
Chase this dread slumber from my soul:
With joy and fear, with love and awe,
Give me to keep thy perfect law.

2 O may one beam of thy blest light,
Pierce through, dispel, the shade of night;
Touch my cold breast with heavenly fire;
With holy, conqu'ring zeal inspire.

3 For zeal I sigh, for zeal I pant;
Yet heavy is my soul, and faint:
With steps unwav'ring, undismay'd,
Give me in all thy paths to tread.

4 With outstretch'd hands, and streaming eyes,
Oft I begin to grasp the prize:
I groan, I strive, I watch, I pray;
But ah! my zeal soon dies away.

5 The deadly slumber then I feel
Afresh upon my spirit steal:
Rise, Lord, stir up thy quick'ning power,
And wake me that I sleep no more.

102 *Rejoicing in forgiving love.*

1 My soul, with humble fervor raise
To God the voice of grateful praise,
And all my ransom'd powers combine
To bless his attributes divine.

2 Deep on my heart let mem'ry trace
His acts of mercy and of grace:
Who, with a Father's tender care,
Saved me when sinking in despair;—

3 Gave my repentant soul to prove
The joy of his forgiving love;
Pour'd balm into my bleeding breast,
And led my weary feet to rest.

STERLING. L. M.

Rev. R. HARRISON.

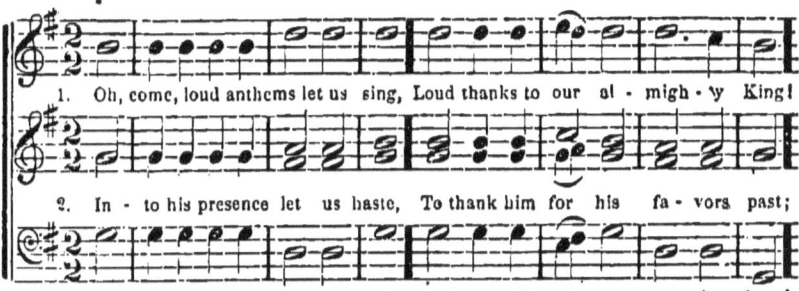

1. Oh, come, loud anthems let us sing, Loud thanks to our almighty King!
2. Into his presence let us haste, To thank him for his favors past;
3. Oh, let us to his courts repair, And bow with adoration there!

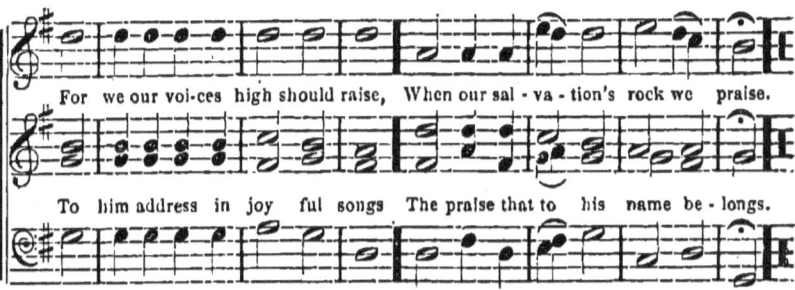

For we our voices high should raise, When our salvation's rock we praise.
To him address in joyful songs The praise that to his name belongs.
Down on our knees, devoutly, all Before the Lord, our Maker fall

---

104

"Justice and judgment are the habitation of thy throne."

1 He reigns! the Lord, the Savior reigns!
  Sing to his name in lofty strains;
  Let the whole earth in songs rejoice,
  And in his praise exalt their voice!

2 Deep are his counsels, and unknown;
  But grace and truth support his throne:
  Tho' gloomy clouds his way surround,
  Justice is their eternal ground.

3 In robes of judgment, lo! he comes,—
  Shakes the wide earth, and cleaves the tombs;
  Before him burns devouring fire!
  The mountains melt, the seas retire!

4 His enemies, with sore dismay,
  Fly from the sight, and shun the day:
  Then lift your heads, ye saints, on high,
  And sing, for your redemption's nigh!

---

105 *"God so loved the world."*

1 Not to condemn the sons of men,
  Did Christ, the Son of God, appear;
  No weapons in his hands are seen,
  No flaming sword, nor thunder there.

2 Such was the pity of our God,
  He loved the race of man so well,
  He sent his Son to bear our load
  Of sins, and save our souls from hell.

---

106 *Christ, the good Physician.*

1 Jesus, thy far-extended fame
  My drooping soul exults to hear;
  Thy Name, thy all-restoring Name,
  Is music in a sinner's ear.

2 Sinners of old thou didst receive
  With comfortable words, and kind;
  Their sorrows cheer, their wants relieve,
  Heal the diseased, and cure the blind.

3 And art thou not the Savior still,
  In every place and age the same?
  Hast thou forgot thy gracious skill,
  Or lost the virtue of thy name?

4 Faith in thy changeless name I have:
  The good, the kind Physician, thou
  Art able now our souls to save,
  Art willing to restore them now.

WARD. L. M.

From a Scotch tune by Dr. L. MASON.

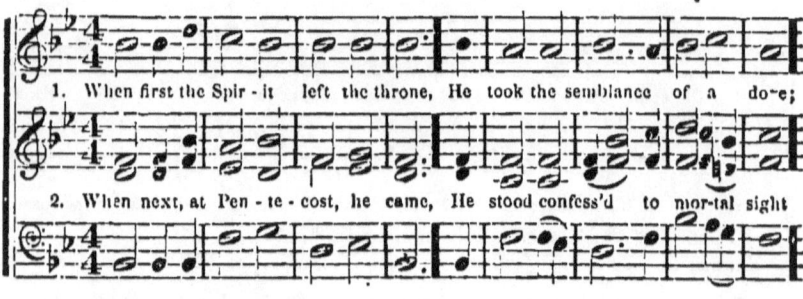

1. When first the Spir-it left the throne, He took the semblance of a dove;
2. When next, at Pen-te-cost, he came, He stood confess'd to mor-tal sight

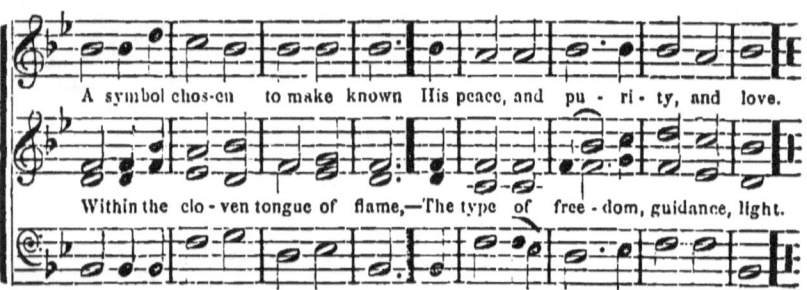

A sym-bol chos-en to make known His peace, and pu-ri-ty, and love.
Within the clo-ven tongue of flame,—The type of free-dom, guidance, light.

3 Vouchsafe, celestial Dove, thy peace,
   That we at perfect peace may be ;
Within our hearts thy love increase,—
   Within our thoughts, thy purity.

4 O Light divine ! direct our feet,
   Which long in error's paths have trod ;
Our prison'd souls with freedom greet,
   Convince of sin, and lead to God.

108   *He careth for you.*
1 Peace, troubled soul, thou need'st not fear,
Thy great Provider still is near ;
Who fed thee last, will feed thee still :
Be calm, and sink into his will.

2 The Lord, who built the earth and sky,
In mercy stoops to hear thy cry;
His promise all may freely claim :
Ask and receive in Jesus' name.

3 Without reserve give Christ your heart ;
Let him his righteousness impart ;
Then all things else he'll freely give ;
With him you all things shall receive.

4 Thus shall the soul be truly blest,
That seeks in God his only rest ;
May I that happy person be,
In time and in eternity.

109   *The evidence of perfect love.*
1 Quicken'd with our immortal Head,
   Who daily, Lord, ascend with thee ;
Redeem'd from sin, and free indeed,
   We taste our glorious liberty.

2 Saved from the fear of hell and death,
   With joy we seek the things above ;
And all thy saints the spirit breathe
   Of power, sobriety, and love.

3 Pure love to God thy members find ;
   Pure love to every soul of man ;
And in thy sober, spotless mind,
   Savior, our heaven on earth we gain.

110   *For the fire of divine love.*
1 O thou who camest from above,
   The pure celestial fire t' impart,
Kindle a flame of sacred love,
   On the mean altar of my heart.

2 Jesus, confirm my heart's desire,
   To work, and speak, and think for thee ;
Still let me guard the holy fire,
   And still stir up thy gift in me.

3 Ready for all thy perfect will,
   My acts of faith and love repeat,
Till death thy endless mercies seal,
   And make the sacrifice complete.

CRUCIFIXION. L. M.

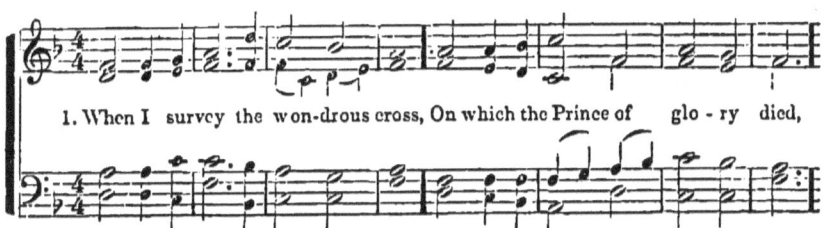

1. When I survey the won-drous cross, On which the Prince of glo-ry died,

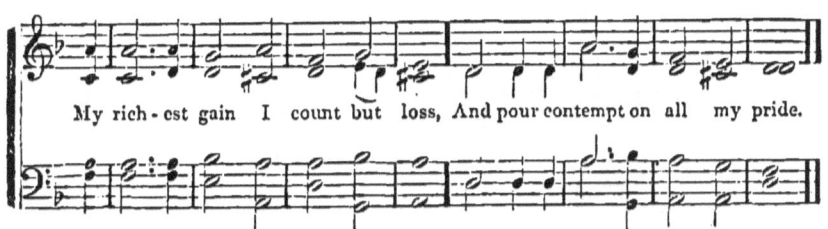

My rich-est gain I count but loss, And pour contempt on all my pride.

2 Forbid it, Lord, that I should boast,
Save in the death of Christ, my God;
All the vain things that charm me most,
I sacrifice them to his blood.

3 See, from his head, his hands, his feet,
Sorrow and love flow mingled down;
Did e'er such love and sorrow meet,
Or thorns compose so rich a crown?

4 Were the whole realm of nature mine,
That were a present far too small;
Love so amazing, so divine,
Demands my soul, my life, my all.

112 *The hidings of the Father's face.*
1 From Calvary a cry was heard,—
A bitter and heart-rending cry;
My Savior! every mournful word
Bespeaks thy soul's deep agony.

2 A horror of great darkness fell
On thee, thou spotless, holy One!
And all the swarming hosts of hell
Conspired to tempt God's only Son.

3 The scourge, the thorns, the deep disgrace,
These thou couldst bear, nor once repine;
But when Jehovah veil'd his face,
Unutterable pangs were thine.

4 Let the dumb world its silence break;
Let pealing anthems rend the sky;
Awake, my sluggish soul, awake!
He died, that we might never die.

5 Lord! on thy cross I fix mine eye;
If e'er I lose its strong control,
O, let that dying, piercing cry,
Melt and reclaim my wand'ring soul.

113 *The only Plea.*
1 Jesus, the sinner's friend, to thee,
Lost and undone, for aid I flee;
Weary of earth, myself, and sin:
Open thine arms, and take me in.

2 Pity and heal my sin-sick soul;
'Tis thou alone canst make me whole:
Dark, till in me thine image shine,
And lost I am, till thou art mine.

3 At last I own it cannot be
That I should fit myself for thee:
Here, then, to thee I all resign;
Thine is the work, and only thine.

4 What shall I say thy grace to move?
Lord, I am sin,—but thou art love:
I give up every plea beside,—
Lord, I am lost—but thou hast died.

114 *I am going the way of all the earth.*
1 Pass a few swiftly fleeting years,
And all that now in bodies live
Shall quit, like me, the vale of tears,
Their righteous sentence to receive.

2 But all, before they hence remove,
May mansions for themselves prepare
In that eternal house above;
And, O my God, shall I be there?

ZEPHYR. L. M.

115 Wm. B. BRADBURY.

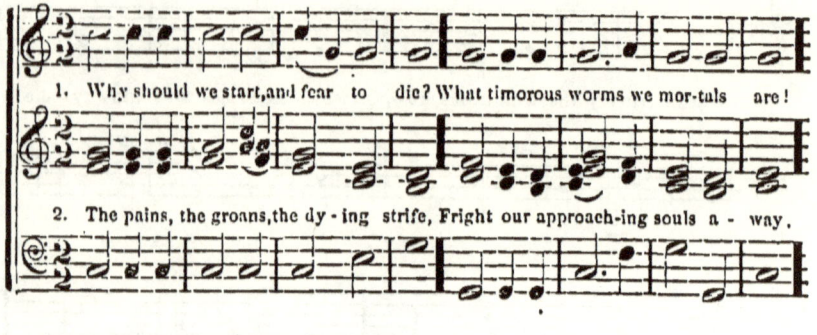

1. Why should we start, and fear to die? What timorous worms we mor-tals are!
2. The pains, the groans, the dy-ing strife, Fright our approach-ing souls a - way.

Death is the gate to end-less joy, And yet we dread to en - ter there.
And we shrink back a - gain to life, Fond of our pris - on and our clay.

3 O would the Lord his servant meet,
My soul would stretch her wings in haste,
Fly fearless through death's iron gate,
Nor feel the terrors as she pass'd.

4 Jesus can make a dying bed
Feel soft as downy pillows are:
While on his breast I lean my head,
And breathe my life out sweetly there.

116 *Hope in God.*

1 God of my strength, in thee alone,
A refuge from distress I see;
O why hast thou thine aid withdrawn?
Why hast thou, Lord, forsaken me?

2 O let thy light my footsteps guide;
Thy love and truth my spirit fill:
That in thy house I may reside,
And worship at thy holy hill.

3 Then will I at thine altar bend;
My harp its softest notes shall raise,
And from my lips to heaven ascend
The song of thankfulness and praise.

4 Why then, my soul, art thou cast down?
Why art thou anxious and distress'd?
Hope thou in God, his mercy own,
For I shall yet enjoy his rest.

117 *It is I; be not afraid.*

1 When power divine, in mortal form,
Hush'd with a word the raging storm,

In soothing accents Jesus said,—
Lo, it is I! be not afraid.

2 So when in silence nature sleeps,
And lonely watch the mourner keeps,
One thought shall every pang remove —
Trust, feeble man, thy Maker's love.

3 God calms the tumult and the storm:
He rules the seraph and the worm:
No creature is by him forgot,
Of those who know, or know him not.

4 And when the last dread hour shall come,
And shudd'ring nature wait her doom,
This voice shall wake the pious dead,—
Lo, it is I! be not afraid.

118 *Jesus every-where present.*

1 Jesus, where'er thy people meet,
There they behold thy mercy-seat;
Where'er they seek thee, thou art found,
And every place is hallow'd ground.

2 For thou, within no walls confined,
Dost dwell with those of humble mind;
Such ever bring thee, where they come,
And, going, take thee to their home.

3 Great Shepherd of thy chosen few,
Thy former mercies here renew:
Here, to our waiting hearts, proclaim
The sweetness of thy saving name.

REFUGE. L. M.

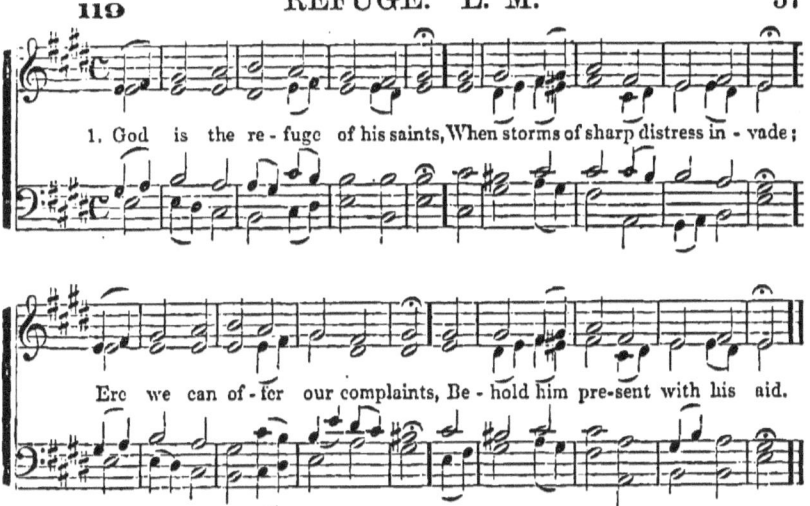

1. God is the re-fuge of his saints, When storms of sharp distress in-vade; Ere we can of-fer our complaints, Be-hold him pre-sent with his aid.

2 Let mountains from their seats be hurled,
   Down to the deep, and buried there;
Convulsions shake the solid world;
   Our faith shall never yield to fear.

3 Loud may the troubled ocean roar—
   In sacred peace our souls abide;
While every nation, every shore,
   Trembles and dreads the swelling tide.

4 There is a stream, whose gentle flow
   Supplies the city of our God;
Life, love, and joy still gliding through,
   And watering our divine abode.

5 That sacred stream, thy holy word,
   Our grief allays, our fear controls;
Sweet peace thy promises afford,
   And give new strength to fainting souls.

6 Zion enjoys her monarch's love,
   Secure against a threatening hour;
Nor can her firm foundation move,
   Built on his truth, and armed with power.

---

120 *Christ's Invitation to Sinners.*

1 " Come hither, all ye weary souls,
   " Ye heavy laden sinners, come;
" I'll give you rest from all your toils,
   " And raise you to my heavenly home.

2 " They shall find rest, who learn of me;
   " I'm of a meek and lowly mind;
" But passion rages like the sea,
   " And pride is restless as the wind.

3 "Blest is the man, whose shoulders take
   "My yoke, and bear it with delight;
"My yoke is easy to his neck,
   "My grace shall make the burden light."

4 Jesus, we come at thy command,
   With faith, and hope, and humble zeal;
Resign our spirits to thy hand,
   To mould and guide us at thy will.

---

121 *How dreadful is this place!*

1 O thou, whom all thy saints adore,
   We now with all thy saints agree,
And bow our inmost souls before
   Thy glorious, awful Majesty.

2 We come, great God, to seek thy face,
   And for thy loving kindness wait;
And O, how dreadful is this place!
   'Tis God's own house, 'tis heaven's gate

3 Tremble our hearts to find thee nigh;
   To thee our trembling hearts aspire;
And lo! we see descend from high
   The pillar and the flame of fire.

4 Still let it on th' assembly stay,
   And all the house with glory fill;
To Canaan's bounds point out the way,
   And lead us to thy holy hill.

5 There let us all with Jesus stand,
   And join the gen'ral Church above,
And take our seats at thy right hand,
   And sing thine everlasting love.

ROTHWELL. L. M.
Arr. by Dr. L. MASON.

1. A-rise, my soul, with rapture rise, And, fill'd with love and fear, a-dore The awful Sov'reign of the skies, Whose mercy lends thee one day more, Whose mercy lends thee one day more.

2. And may this day, In-dul-gent Pow'r, Not I - dly pass, nor fruitless be; But may each swiftly pass-ing hour Still nearer bring my soul to thee, Still near-er bring my soul to thee.

123 *Hosanna to the Son of David.*

1 What are those soul-reviving strains,
Which echo thus from Salem's plains?
What anthems loud, and louder still,
So sweetly sound from Zion's hill?

2 Lo! 'tis an infant chorus sings
Hosanna to the King of kings:
The Savior comes! — and babes proclaim
Salvation, sent in Jesus' name.

3 Nor these alone their voice shall raise,
For we will join this song of praise:
Still Israel's children forward press,
To hail the Lord, their Righteousness.

4 Messiah's name shall joy impart,
Alike to Jew and Gentile heart;
He bled for us, he bled for you,
And we will sing hosanna too.

5 Proclaim hosannas, loud and clear;
See David's Son and Lord appear!
All praise on earth to him be given,
And glory shout through highest heaven.

124 *Infinite in wisdom.*

1 Praise ye the Lord! 'tis good to raise
Your hearts and voices in his praise:
His nature and his works invite
To make this duty our delight.

2 He form'd the stars, those heav'nly flames,
He counts their numbers, calls their names:
His wisdom's vast, and knows no bound,—
A deep where all our thoughts are drown'd

3 Sing to the Lord! exalt him high,
Who spreads the clouds along the sky:
There he prepares the fruitful rain,
Nor lets the drops descend in vain.

4 He makes the grass the hills adorn;
He clothes the smiling fields with corn·
The beasts with food his hands supply,
And the young ravens when they cry.

5 What is the creature's skill or force?
The sprightly man, or war-like horse?
The piercing wit, the active limb?
All are too mean delights for him.

IOSCO. L. M.

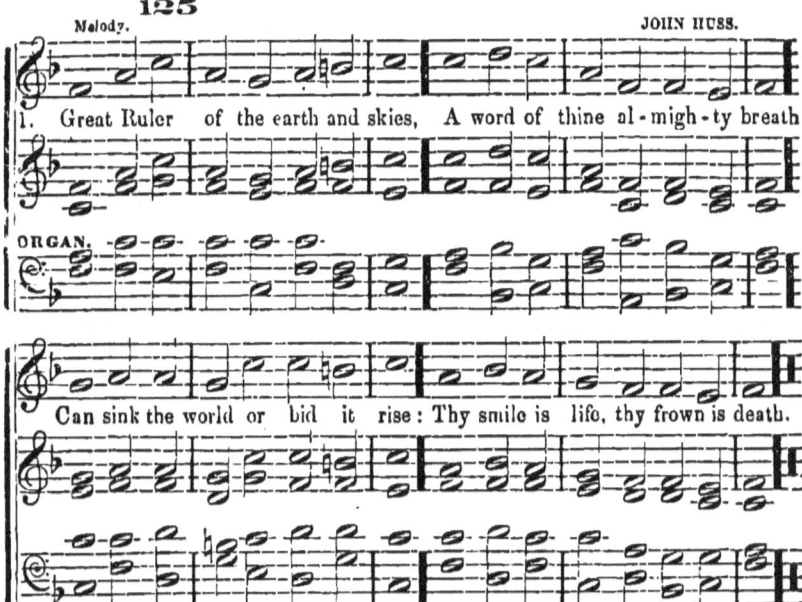

125 — JOHN HUSS.

1. Great Ruler of the earth and skies,
A word of thine al-migh-ty breath
Can sink the world or bid it rise:
Thy smile is life, thy frown is death.

2 When angry nations rush to arms,
And rage, and noise, and tumult reign,
And war resounds its dire alarms,
And slaughter dyes the hostile plain,—

3 Thy sov'reign eye looks calmly down,
And marks their course, and bounds their power;
Thy law the angry nations own,
And noise and war are heard no more.

4 Then peace returns with balmy wing;
Sweet peace, with her what blessings fled!
Glad plenty laughs, the valleys sing,
Reviving commerce lifts her head.

5 To thee we pay our grateful songs;
Thy kind protection still implore:
O may our hearts, and lives, and tongues,
Confess thy goodness, and adore.

126 *Not ashamed of Jesus.*

1 Jesus, and shall it ever be,
A mortal man ashamed of thee!
Ashamed of thee, whom angels praise,—
Whose glories shine through endless days.

2 Ashamed of Jesus!—that dear Friend
On whom my hopes of heaven depend;
No!—when I blush, be this my shame,
That I no more revere his Name.

3 Ashamed of Jesus!—yes I may,
When I've no guilt to wash away;
No tear to wipe, no good to crave,
No fears to quell, no soul to save.

4 Till then—nor is my boasting vain—
Till then, I boast a Savior slain;
And O, may this my glory be,—
That Christ is not ashamed of me

127 *God's presence with his people.*

1 When Israel of the Lord beloved,
Out from the land of bondage came,
Her Father's God before her moved,
An awful guide, in smoke and flame

2 By day, along th' astonished lands
The cloudy pillar glided slow;
By night, Arabia's crimson'd sands
Return'd the fiery column's glow.

3 Thus present, still, tho' now unseen,
When brightly shines the prosperous day
Be thoughts of thee a cloudy screen,
To temper the deceitful ray.

4 And O, when gathers on our path,
In shade and storm, the frequent night,
Be thou, long suff'ring, slow to wrath,
A burning and a shining light.

MISSIONARY CHANT. L. M.
Ch. Zeuner.

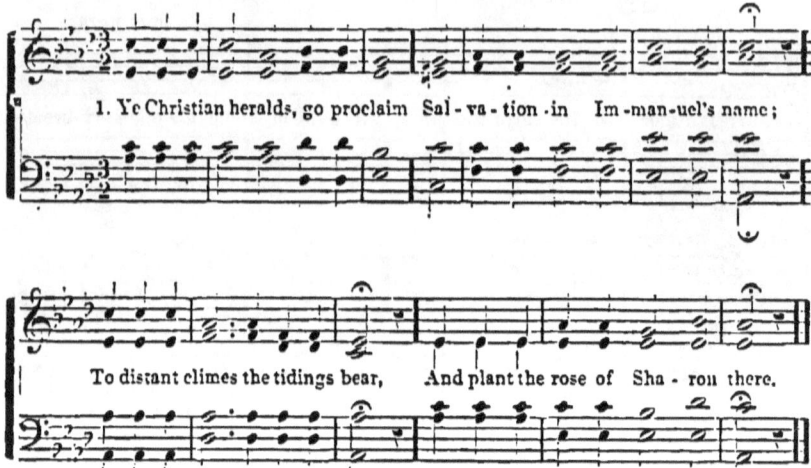

1. Ye Christian heralds, go proclaim Salvation in Immanuel's name; To distant climes the tidings bear, And plant the rose of Sharon there.

2 He'll shield you with a wall of fire,
With holy zeal your hearts inspire;
Bid raging winds their fury cease,
And calm the savage breast to peace.

3 And when our labors all are o'er,
Then we shall meet to part no more:
Meet, with the blood-bought throng, to fall,
And crown our Jesus—Lord of all!

---

129   *His way is in the sea.*

1 Lord of the wide, extensive main,
  Whose power the wind and sea controls,
Whose hand doth earth and heaven sustain,
  Whose Spirit leads believing souls:

2 'Tis here thine unknown paths we trace,
  Which dark to human eyes appear;
While through the mighty waves we pass,
  Faith only sees that God is here.

3 Throughout the deep thy footsteps shine;
  We own thy way is in the sea,
O'erawed by majesty divine,
  And lost in thine immensity.

4 Thy wisdom here we learn t' adore
  Thine everlasting truth we prove;
Amazing heights of boundless power,
  Unfathomable depths of love.

---

130   *Security and safety.*

1 God is our refuge and defence;
  In trouble our unfailing aid:
Secure in his omnipotence,
  What foe can make our souls afraid!

2 Yea, though the earth's foundations rock,
  And mountains down the gulf be hurled,
His people smile amid the shock;
  They look beyond this transient world.

3 There is a river pure and bright, [plains,
  Whose streams make glad the heavenly
Where in eternity of light
  The city of our God remains.

4 Built by the word of his command,
  With his unclouded presence blest,
Firm as his throne the bulwarks stand;
  There is our home, our hope, our rest.

---

131   *The redeemed in heaven.*

1 Lo! round the throne, a glorious band,
  The saints in countless myriads stand;
Of every tongue redeemed to God,
  Arrayed in garments washed in blood.

2 Through tribulation great they came;
  They bore the cross, despised the shame;
But now from all their labors rest,
  In God's eternal glory blest.

3 They see the Savior face to face;
  They sing the triumphs of his grace;
And day and night, with ceaseless praise,
  To him their loud hosannas raise.

4 O, may we tread the sacred road
  That holy saints and martyrs trod;
Wage to the end the glorious strife,
  And win, like them, a crown of life.

FOREST. L. M. CHAPIN.

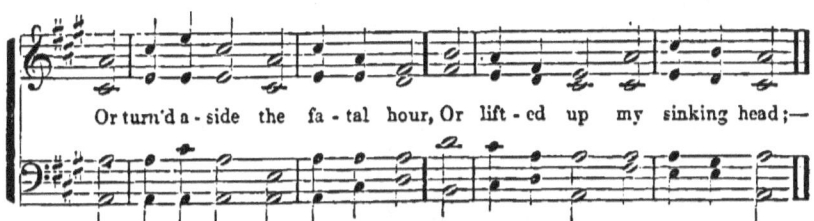

1. God of my life, whose gracious pow'r Thro' va-ried deaths my soul hath led, Or turn'd a-side the fa-tal hour, Or lift-ed up my sinking head;—

2 In all my ways thy hand I own,—
Thy ruling providence I see;
Assist me still my course to run,
And still direct my paths to thee.

3 Whither, O whither should I fly,
But to my loving Savior's breast!
Secure within thine arms to lie,
And safe beneath thy wings to rest.

4 I have no skill the snare to shun,
But thou, O Christ, my wisdom art;
I ever into ruin run,
But thou art greater than my heart.

5 Foolish, and impotent, and blind,
Lead me a way I have not known;
Bring me where I my heaven may find,—
The heaven of loving thee alone.

133 *The Promised Comforter.*

1 Lord, we believe to us and ours
The apostolic promise given;
We wait the pentecostal powers,—
The Holy Ghost sent down from heaven.

2 Assembled here with one accord,
Calmly we wait the promised grace,—
The purchase of our dying Lord;
Come, Holy Ghost, and fill the place.

3 If every one that asks may find,—
If still thou dost on sinners fall,—
Come as a mighty rushing wind;
Great grace be now upon us all.

4 Ah! leave us not to mourn below,
Or long for thy return to pine;
Now, Lord, the Comforter bestow,
And fix in us the Guest divine.

134 *Only Jesus.*

1 When, gracious Lord, when shall it be,
That I shall find my all in thee?
The fulness of thy promise prove,—
The seal of thine eternal love?

2 Thee, only thee, I fain would find,
And cast the world and flesh behind;
Thou, only thou, to me be given,
Of all thou hast in earth or heaven.

3 When from the arm of flesh set free,
Jesus, my soul shall fly to thee;
Jesus, when I have lost my all,
I shall upon thy bosom fall.

135 *The Land of Rest.*

1 Thy loving Spirit, Lord, alone,
Can lead me forth, and make me free;
The bondage break in which I groan,
And set my heart at liberty.

2 Now let thy spirit bring me in,
And give thy servant to possess
The land of rest from inbred sin,—
The land of perfect holiness.

3 Lord, I believe thy power the same;
The same thy truth and grace endure;
And in thy blessed hands I am,
And trust thee for a perfect cure.

4 Come, Savior, come, and make me whole,
Entirely all my sins remove;
To perfect health restore my soul—
To perfect holiness and love.

136 DUKE STREET. L. M. — J. HATTON

1. And will the great eternal God On earth establish his abode?
1. These walls we to thy honor raise; Long may they echo with thy praise:
And will he, from his radiant throne, Accept our temple for his own?
And thou descending fill the place With choicest tokens of thy grace.

3 Here let the great Redeemer reign,
With all the graces of his train;
While power divine his word attends,
To conquer foes, and cheer his friends.

4 And in the great decisive day,
When God the nations shall survey,
May it before the world appear
That crowds were born to glory here.

137
The Savior's coming expected and prayed for.

1 Jesus! thy church, with longing eyes,
For thine expected coming waits:
When will the promised light arise,
And glory beam on Zion's gates?

2 E'en now, when tempests round us fall,
And wintry clouds o'ercast the sky,
Thy words with pleasure we recall,
And deem that our redemption's nigh.

3 O! come, and reign o'er every land;
Let Satan from his throne be hurl'd,—
All nations bow to thy command,
And grace revive a dying world.

4 Teach us, in watchfulness and prayer,
To wait for thine appointed hour;
And fit us, by thy grace, to share
The triumphs of thy conqu'ring power.

138 *Dying, rising, reigning.*

1 He dies! the Friend of sinners dies!
Lo! Salem's daughters weep around;
A solemn darkness veils the skies,
A sudden trembling shakes the ground.

2 Come, saints, and drop a tear or two
For him who groan'd beneath your load;
He shed a thousand drops for you,—
A thousand drops of purer blood.

3 Here's love and grief beyond degree:
The Lord of glory dies for man!
But lo! what sudden joys we see:
Jesus, the dead, revives again.

4 The rising God forsakes the tomb;
(In vain the tomb forbids his rise;)
Cherubic legions guard him home,
And shout him welcome to the skies.

5 Break off your tears, ye saints, and tell
How high your great Deliv'rer reigns,
Sing how he spoil'd the hosts of hell,
And led the monster death in chains:

6 Say, Live forever, wondrous King!
Born to redeem, and strong to save;
Then ask the monster, Where's thy sting
And, Where's thy vict'ry, boasting grave?

PARK ST. L. M.

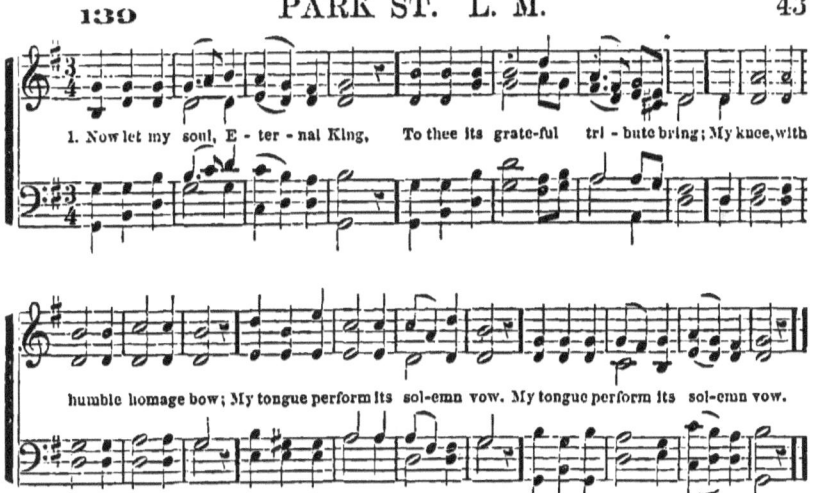

1. Now let my soul, E-ter-nal King, To thee its grate-ful tri-bute bring; My knee, with humble homage bow; My tongue perform its sol-emn vow. My tongue perform its sol-emn vow.

2 All nature sings thy boundless love,
In worlds below, and worlds above;
But in thy blessed word I trace
Diviner wonders of thy grace.

3 There Jesus bids my sorrows cease,
And gives my lab'ring conscience peace;
Raises my grateful thoughts on high,
And points to mansions in the sky.

4 For love like this, O let my song,
Through endless years, thy praise prolong;
Let distant climes thy Name adore,
Till time and nature are no more.

140 *Sacrifice of praise and prayer.*
1 Awake, my soul, and with the sun
Thy daily stage of duty run;
Shake off dull sloth, and joyful rise
To pay thy morning sacrifice.

2 Wake, and lift up thyself, my heart,
And with the angels bear thy part,
Who all night long unwearied sing
High praises to th' eternal King.

3 All praise to Thee, who safe hast kept,
And hast refresh'd me while I slept;
Grant, Lord, when I from death shall wake,
I may of endless life partake.

4 Lord, I my vows to thee renew;
Scatter my sins as morning dew;
Guard my first springs of thought and will,
And with thyself my spirit fill.

5 Direct, control, suggest, this day,
All I design, or do, or say;
That all my powers, with all their might,
In thy sole glory may unite.

141 *Prophet, Priest, and King.*
1 To us a child, of royal birth,
End of the promises, is given;
Th' Invisible appears on earth,—
The Son of man, the God of heaven.

2 A Savior born, in love supreme,
He comes, our fallen souls to raise;
He comes, his people to redeem,
With all his plenitude of grace.

3 The Christ, by raptured seers foretold,
Fill'd with the Holy Spirit's power,
Prophet, and Priest, and King, behold!
And Lord of all the world adore.

4 The Lord of Hosts, the God most high,
Who quits his throne, on earth to live,
With joy we welcome from the sky,
With faith into our hearts receive.

142 *Christ's Universal Kingdom.*
1 Jesus shall reign where'er the sun
Does his successive journeys run;
His kingdom spread from shore to shore,
Till moons shall wax and wane no more.

2 From north to south the princes meet,
To pay their homage at his feet;
While western empires own their Lord,
And savage tribes attend his word.

3 To him shall endless prayer be made,
And endless praises crown his head;
His Name like sweet perfume shall rise
With every morning sacrifice.

4 People and realms of every tongue
Dwell on his love with sweetest song,
And infant voices shall proclaim
Their early blessings on his Name.

143 EFFINGHAM. L. M.

1. My gracious Lord, I own thy right
To every service I can pay,
And call it my supreme delight
To hear thy dictates and obey.

2 What is my being but for thee,—
Its sure support, its noblest end?
'Tis my delight thy face to see,
And serve the cause of such a Friend.

3 I would not sigh for worldly joy,
Or to increase my worldly good;
Nor future days nor powers employ
To spread a sounding name abroad.

4 'Tis to my Savior I would live,—
To him who for my ransom died;
Nor could all worldly honor give
Such bliss as crowns me at his side.

5 His work my hoary age shall bless,
When youthful vigor is no more;
And my last hour of life confess
His saving love, his glorious power.

144 *Rejoicing at return of Sabbath.*
1 My opening eyes with rapture see
The dawn of this returning day;
My thoughts, O God, ascend to thee,
While thus my early vows I pay.

2 I yield my heart to thee alone,
Nor would receive another guest;
Eternal King, erect thy throne,
And reign sole monarch in my breast.

3 O bid this trifling world retire,
And drive each carnal thought away;
Nor let me feel one vain desire,
One sinful thought through all the day.

4 Then, to thy courts when I repair,
My soul shall rise on joyful wing,—
The wonders of thy love declare,
And join the strain which angels sing.

145 *Morning; The Lord is my portion.*
1 O God, my God, my all thou art:
Ere shines the dawn of rising day,

Thy sov'reign light within my heart,
Thy all-enliv'ning power display.

2 For thee my thirsty soul doth pant,
While in this desert land I live;
And, hungry as I am, and faint,
Thy love alone can comfort give.

3 In a dry land, behold, I place
My whole desire on thee, O Lord;
And more I joy to gain thy grace,
Than all earth's treasures can afford.

4 More dear than life itself, thy love
My heart and tongue shall still employ;
And to declare thy praise will prove
My peace, my glory, and my joy.

5 In blessing thee, with grateful songs,
My happy life shall glide away;
The praise that to thy Name belongs,
Hourly, with lifted hands, I'll pay.

146 *The River of Life.*
1 Great Source of being and of love!
Thou wat'rest all the worlds above;
And all the joys which mortals know,
From thine exhaustless fountain flow.

2 A sacred spring, at thy command,
From Zion's mount, in Canaan's land,
Beside thy temple cleaves the ground,
And pours its limpid stream around.

3 Close by its banks, in order fair,
The blooming trees of life appear;
Their blossoms fragrant odors give,
And on their fruit the nations live.

4 Flow, wondrous stream! with glory crown'd
Flow on to earth's remotest bound,
And bear us, on thy gentle wave,
To him who all thy virtues gave.

147 ROSEDALE. L. M. G. F. ROOT. 45

1. Lord, I despair myself to heal; I see my sin, but cannot feel; I cannot, till thy Spirit blow, And bid th' obedient waters flow.

2 'Tis thine a heart of flesh to give;
Thy gifts I only can receive,
Here, then, to thee, I all resign;
To draw, redeem, and seal,— are thine.

3 With simple faith, on thee I call,—
My light, my life, my Lord, my all:
I wait the moving of the pool;
I wait the word that speaks me whole.

4 Speak, gracious Lord—my sickness cure,—
Make my infected nature pure:
Peace, righteousness, and joy impart,
And pour thyself into my heart!

148 *For the Lambs of the flock.*
1 Author of faith, we seek thy face
For all who feel thy work begun;
Confirm, and strengthen them in grace,
And bring thy feeblest children on.

2 Thou seest their wants, thou know'st their names,
Be mindful of thy youngest care;
Be tender of the new-born lambs,
And gently in thy bosom bear.

3 In safety lead thy little flock,—
From hell, the world, and sin, secure;
And set their feet upon the rock,
And make in thee their going sure.

149 *The Atonement completed.*
1 'Tis finished! the Messiah dies,—
Cut off for sins, but not his own;
Accomplish'd is the sacrifice,—
The great redeeming work is done.

2 'Tis finished! all the debt is paid;
Justice divine is satisfied;
The grand and full atonement made:
Christ for a guilty world hath died.

3 The veil is rent; in him alone
The living way to heaven is seen;
The middle wall is broken down,
And all mankind may enter in.

4 The types and figures are fulfill'd;
Exacted is the legal pain;
The precious promises are sealed;
The spotless Lamb of God is slain.

5 Death, hell, and sins are now subdued;
All grace is now to sinners given:
And lo! I plead th' atoning blood,
And in thy right I claim my heaven.

150 *Meekness and Patience.*
1 Thou Lamb of God, thou Prince of peace,
For thee my thirsty soul doth pine;
My longing heart implores thy grace;
O make me in thy likeness shine.

2 With fraudless, even, humble mind,
Thy will in all things may I see;
In love be every wish resign'd,
And hallow'd my whole heart to thee.

3 When pain o'er my weak flesh prevails,
With lamb-like patience arm my breast;
When grief my wounded soul assails,
In lowly meekness may I rest.

4 Close by thy side still may I keep,
Howe'er life's various current flow;
With steadfast eye mark every step,
And follow where my Lord doth go.

5 So, when on Zion thou shalt stand,
And all heaven's host adore their King,
Shall I be found at thy right hand,
And, free from pain, thy glories sing.

151 WARREN. L. M.
V. C. TAYLOR.
By permission.

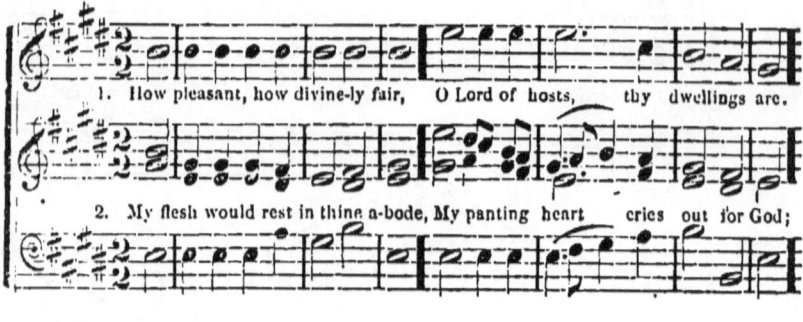

1. How pleasant, how divine-ly fair, O Lord of hosts, thy dwellings are.
2. My flesh would rest in thine a-bode, My panting heart cries out for God;

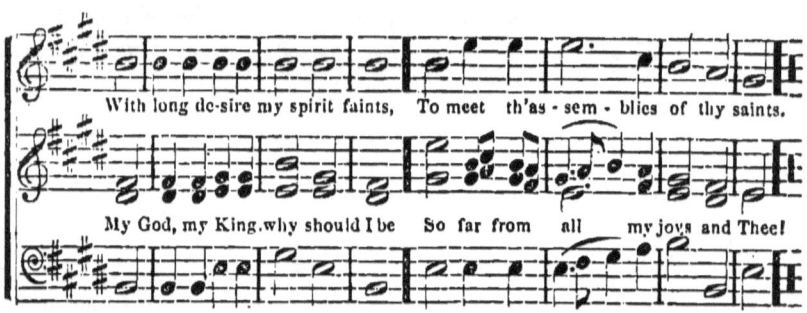

With long de-sire my spirit faints, To meet th'as-sem-blies of thy saints.
My God, my King, why should I be So far from all my joys and Thee!

3 Blest are the souls that find a place
Within the temple of thy grace;
There they behold thy gentler rays,
And seek thy face, and learn thy praise.

4 Blest are the men whose hearts are set
To find the way to Zion's gate:
God is their strength, and through the road
They lean upon their Helper, God.

5 Cheerful they walk with growing strength,
Till all shall meet in heaven at length;
Till all before thy face appear,
And join in nobler worship there.

152 *The joys of the Sabbath.*

1 Sweet is the work, my God, my King,
To praise thy name, give thanks, and sing;
To show thy love by morning light,
And talk of all thy truth by night.

2 Sweet is the day of sacred rest;
No mortal care shall seize my breast;
O may my heart in tune be found,
Like David's harp of solemn sound.

3 When grace has purified my heart,
Then I shall share a glorious part:
And fresh supplies of joy be shed,
Like holy oil to cheer my head.

4 Then shall I see, and hear, and know
All I desired or wish'd below;
And every power find sweet employ
In that eternal world of joy.

153 *Sown in weakness, raised in glory.*

1 The morning flowers display their sweets,
And gay their silken leaves unfold,
As careless of the noontide heats,
As fearless of the evening cold.

2 Nipp'd by the wind's untimely blast,
Parch'd by the sun's directer ray,
The momentary glories waste,
The short-lived beauties die away.

3 So blooms the human face divine,
When youth its pride of beauty shows;
Fairer than spring the colors shine,
And sweeter than the virgin rose.

4 Or worn by slowly-rolling years,
Or broke by sickness in a day,
The fading glory disappears,
The short-lived beauties die away.

5 Yet these, new rising from the tomb
With lustre brighter far shall shine
Revive with ever-during bloom,
Safe from diseases and decline.

GRACE CHURCH. L. M.

Arranged by L. T. DOWNES.
From the "Russian National Air."

1. A-rise, my soul, on wings sub-lime, A-bove the van-i-ties of time:
2. Born by a new, ce-les-tial birth, Why should I grov-el here on earth?
Let faith now pierce the veil, and see The glo-ries of e-ter-ni-ty.
Why grasp at vain and fleet-ing toys, So near to heaven's e-ter-nal joys?

3 Shall aught beguile me on the road,—
The narrow road that leads to God?
Or can I love this earth so well,
As not to long with God to dwell?

4 To dwell with God,—to taste his love,
Is the full heav'n enjoy'd above:
The glorious expectation now
Is heavenly bliss begun below.

155 *For lowliness and purity.*
1 Jesus, in whom the Godhead's rays
Beam forth with mildest majesty;
I see thee full of truth and grace,
And come for all I want to thee.

2 Save me from pride,—the plague expel;
Jesus, thine humble self impart;
O let thy mind within me dwell;
O give me lowliness of heart.

3 Enter thyself, and cast out sin;
Thy spotless purity bestow;
Touch me, and make the leper clean;
Wash me, and I am white as snow.

4 Sprinkle me, Savior, with thy blood,
And all thy gentleness is mine:
And plunge me in the purple flood,
Till all I am is lost in thine.

156 *Constraining love of Christ.*
1 Give me the faith which can remove
And sink the mountain to a plain;

Give me the child-like, praying love,
Which longs to build thy house again:
Thy love let it my heart o'erpower,
And all my simple soul devour.

2 I want an even, strong desire,
I want a calmly fervent zeal,
To save poor souls out of the fire,
To snatch them from the verge of hell,
And turn them to a pard'ning God,
And quench the brands in Jesus' blood.

3 I would the precious time redeem,
And longer live for this alone,
To spend, and to be spent for them,
Whose have not yet my Savior known;
Fully on these my mission prove,
And only breathe, to breathe thy love

4 My talents, gifts, and graces, Lord,
Into thy blessed hands receive;
And let me live to preach thy word;
And let me to thy glory live;
My every sacred moment spend
In publishing the sinner's Friend.

5 Enlarge, inflame, and fill my heart;
With boundless charity divine!
So shall I all my strength exert,
And love them with a zeal like thine
And lead them to thy open side,
The sheep for whom their Shepherd died.

157 ALL SAINTS. L. M.
Wm. Knapp

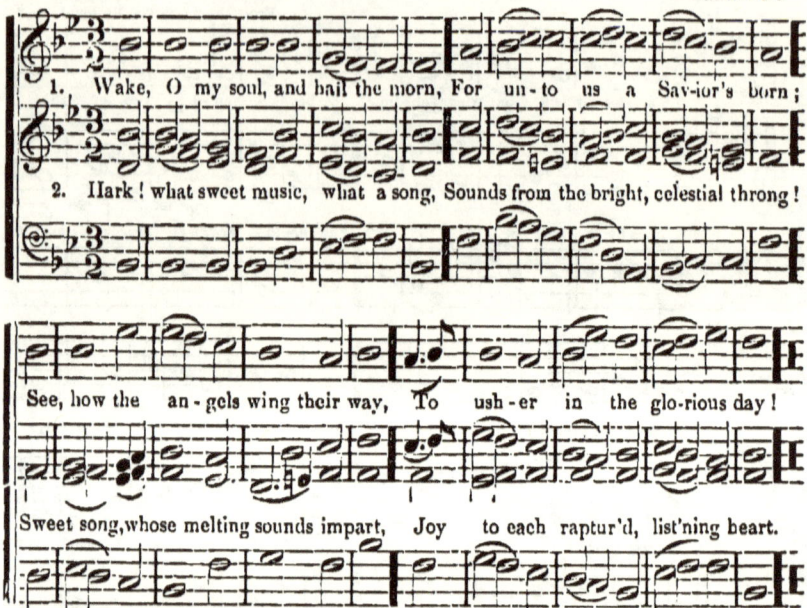

1. Wake, O my soul, and hail the morn, For un-to us a Sav-ior's born;
   See, how the an-gels wing their way, To ush-er in the glo-rious day!
   Sweet song, whose melting sounds impart, Joy to each raptur'd, list'ning heart.

2. Hark! what sweet music, what a song, Sounds from the bright, celestial throng!

3 Come, join the angels in the sky;
Glory to God, who reigns on high;
Let peace and love on earth abound,
While time revolves and years roll round.

158 *Seeking a tabernacle.*
1 When to the exiled seer were given
Those rapt'rous views of highest heaven,
All glorious though the visions were,
Yet he beheld no temple there.

2 The New Jerusalem on high
Hath one pervading sanctity;
No sin to mourn, no grief to mar,—
God and the Lamb its temple are.

3 But we, frail sojourners below,
The pilgrim heirs of guilt and wo,
Must seek a tabernacle where
Our scatter'd souls may blend in prayer.

4 O Thou! who o'er the cherubim
Didst shine in glories veil'd and dim,
With purer light our temple cheer,
And dwell in unveil'd glory here.

159 *The restoration of Israel.*
1 Arise, great God! and let thy grace
Shed its glad beams on Jacob's race;
Restore the long-lost, scatter'd band,
And call them to their native land.

2 Their misery let thy mercy heal;
Their trespass hide, their pardon seal;
O God of Israel! hear our prayer,
And grant them still thy love to share.

3 How long shall Jacob's offspring prove
The sad suspension of thy love?
Lord, shall thy wrath forever burn?
And will thy mercy ne'er return?

4 Thy quick'ning Spirit now impart,
And wake to joy each grateful heart;
While Israel's rescued tribes in thee
Their bliss and full salvation see.

160 *"Glad homage."*
1 With one consent, let all the earth,
To God their cheerful voices raise;
Glad homage pay, with awful mirth,
And sing before him songs of praise.

2 Oh, enter ye his temple gate,
Thence to his courts devoutly press:
And still your grateful hymns repeat,
And still his name with praises bless.

3 For he's the Lord, supremely good,
His mercy is for ever sure;
His truth, which always firmly stood,
To endless ages shall endure.

161   TRURO. L. M.   Dr. C. BURNEY.

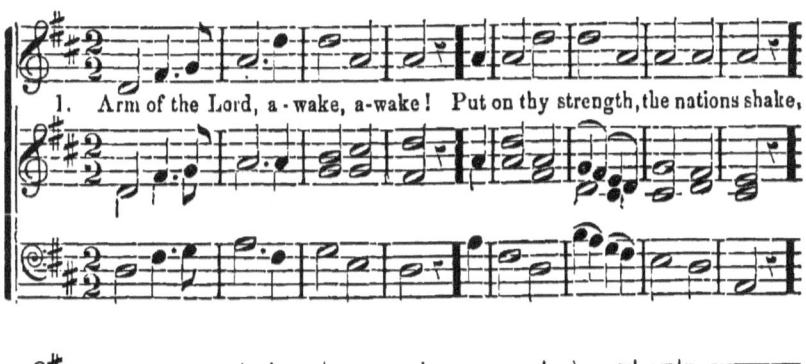

1. Arm of the Lord, a-wake, a-wake! Put on thy strength, the nations shake,

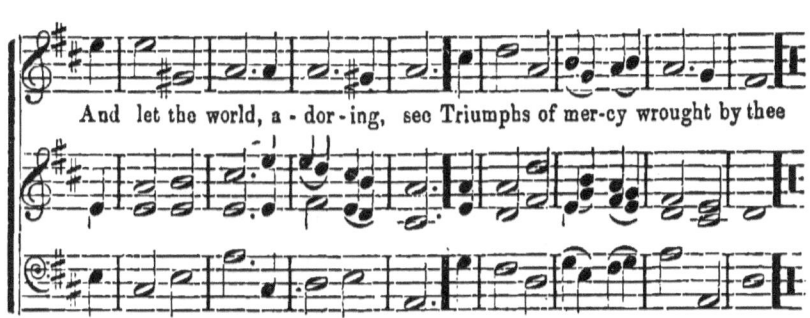

And let the world, a-dor-ing, see Triumphs of mer-cy wrought by thee

2 Say to the heathen, from thy throne,
   I am Jehovah—God alone :
   Thy voice their idols shall confound,
   And cast their altars to the ground.

3 No more let creature blood be spilt—
   Vain sacrifice for human guilt !
   But to each conscience be applied
   The blood that flow'd from Jesus' side.

4 Almighty God, thy grace proclaim,
   In every land, of every name ;
   Let adverse powers before thee fall,
   And crown the Savior Lord of all.

162   *Calm in the storm.*

1 Glory to Thee, whose powerful word
   Bids the tempestuous winds arise ;
   Glory to thee, the sov'reign Lord
   Of air, and earth, and sea, and skies.

2 Let air, and earth, and skies obey,
   And seas thine awful will perform :
   From them we learn to own thy sway,
   And shout to meet the gath'ring storm.

3 What though the floods lift up their voice,
   Thou hearest, Lord, our louder cry ;
   They cannot damp thy children's joys,
   Or shake the soul when God is nigh.

4 Rage, while our faith the Savior tries,
   Thou sea, the servant of his will ;
   Rise, while our God permits thee, rise;
   But fall when he shall say,—Be still.

163   *The bond of love.*

1 Praise waits in Zion, Lord, for thee :
   Thy saints adore thy holy name ;
   Thy creatures bend th' obedient knee,
   And, humbly, now thy presence claim.

2 Eternal Source of truth and light,
   To thee we look, on thee we call ;
   Lord, we are nothing in thy sight,
   But thou to us art all in all.

3 Still may thy children in thy word
   Their common trust and refuge see ;
   O, bind us to each other, Lord,
   By one great bond,—the love of thee.

4 So shall our sun of hope arise,
   With brighter still and brighter ray,
   Till thou shalt bless our longing eyes,
   With beams of everlasting day.

LUTON. L. M.
BURDER.

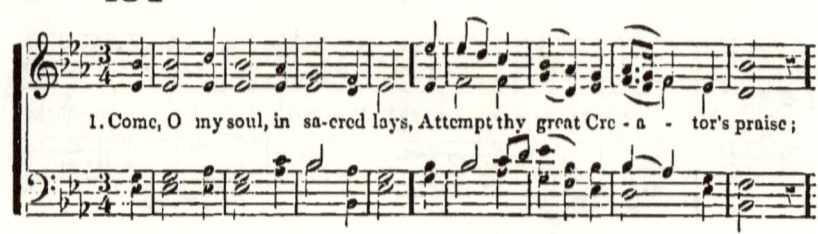

1. Come, O my soul, in sacred lays, Attempt thy great Creator's praise;

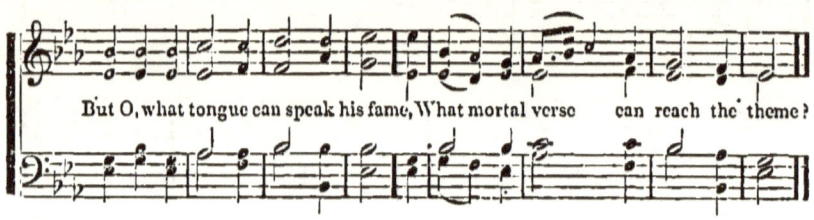

But O, what tongue can speak his fame, What mortal verse can reach the theme?

2 Enthroned amid the radiant spheres,
He glory like a garment wears;
To form a robe of light divine,
Ten thousand suns around him shine.

3 In all our Maker's grand designs,
Omnipotence, with wisdom, shines;
His works, through all this wondrous frame,
Declare the glory of his Name.

4 Raised on devotion's lofty wing,
Do thou, my soul, his glories sing;
And let his praise employ thy tongue,
Till list'ning worlds shall join the song.

---

165 *The Glories of Jehovah.*

1 Servants of God! in joyful lays,
Sing ye the Lord Jehovah's praise;
His glorious Name let all adore,
From age to age, forever more.

2 Blest be that Name, supremely blest,
From the sun's rising to its rest;
Above the heavens his power is known,
Through all the earth his goodness shown.

3 Who is like God? so great, so high,
He bows himself to view the sky;
And yet, with condescending grace,
Looks down upon the human race.

4 He hears the uncomplaining moan
Of those who sit and weep alone;
He lifts the mourner from the dust;
In Him the poor may safely trust.

5 O then, aloud, in joyful lays,
Sing to the Lord Jehovah's praise;
His saving Name let all adore,
From age to age, forever more.

---

166 *The heavens declare his glory.*

1 The spacious firmament on high,
With all the blue ethereal sky,
And spangled heavens, a shining frame,
Their great Original proclaim:

2 Th' unwearied sun, from day to day,
Doth his Creator's power display,
And publishes to every land
The work of an Almighty Hand.

3 Soon as the evening shades prevail,
The moon takes up the wondrous tale,
And nightly, to the list'ning earth,
Repeats the story of her birth;

4 While all the stars that round her burn,
And all the planets in their turn,
Confirm the tidings as they roll,
And spread the truth from pole to pole.

5 What, though in solemn silence all
Move round the dark terrestrial ball;
What, though no real voice nor sound
Amid the radiant orbs be found;

6 In reason's ear they all rejoice,
And utter forth a glorious voice;
Forever singing as they shine,
The Hand that made us is divine.

167 WELTON. L. M.

ARR. BY DR. MASON.
FROM DR. MALAN.

1. Jesus, thy wand'ring sheep behold! See, Lord, with yearning bowels, see, Poor souls that cannot find the fold, Till sought and gathered in by thee.
2. Lost are they now, and scatter'd wide, In pain and weariness, and want: With no kind shepherd near to guide The sick, and spiritless and faint.

3 Thou, only thou, the kind, and good,
  And sheep-redeeming, Shepherd art;
Collect thy flock, and give them food,
  And pastors after thine own heart.

4 Give the pure word of gen'ral grace,
  And great shall be the preachers' crowd;
Preachers who all the sinful race
  Point to the all-atoning blood.

5 Thine only glory let them seek;
  O let their hearts with love o'erflow;
Let them believe, and therefore speak,
  And spread thy mercy's praise below.

168 *Embracing the Savior by faith.*
1 Into thy gracious hands I fall,
  And with the arms of faith embrace;
O King of glory, hear my call;
  O raise me, heal me by thy grace.
Now righteous through thy grace I am;
  No condemnation now I dread;
I taste salvation in thy name,—
  Alive in thee, my living Head.

2 Still let thy wisdom be my guide,
  Nor take thy flight from me away;
Still with me let thy grace abide,
  That I from thee may never stray:
Let thy word richly in me dwell,—
  Thy peace and love my portion be:
My joy to' endure and do thy will,
  Till perfect I am found in thee.

169 *Infinite indebtedness.*
1 Great God, let all our tuneful powers
  Awake, and sing thy mighty Name;
Thy hand revolves the circling hours—
  Thy hand, from whence our being came.

2 Seasons and moons, still rolling round
  In beauteous order, speak thy praise;
And years with smiling mercy crown'd,
  To thee successive honors raise.

3 Our life, and health, and friends, we owe
  All to thy vast, unbounded love;
Ten thousand precious gifts below,
  And hope of nobler joys above.

4 Thus may we sing till nature cease,—
  Till sense and language are no more;
And, after death, thy boundless grace
  Through everlasting years adore.

Doxology.
Praise God, from whom all blessings flow;
Praise him, all creatures here below;
Praise him above, ye heavenly host;
Praise Father, Son, and Holy Ghost.

170 ORTONVILLE. C. M.
Dr. T. Hastings.
By permission.

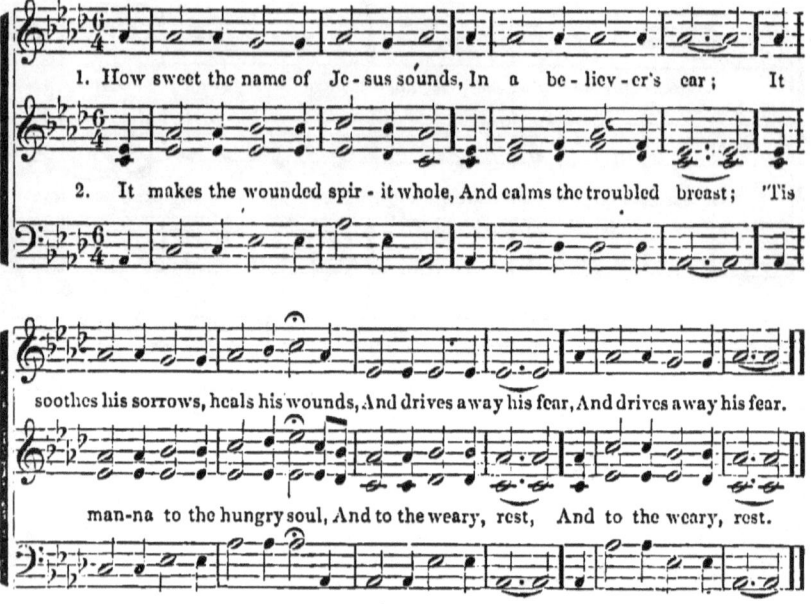

1. How sweet the name of Jesus sounds, In a believer's ear; It soothes his sorrows, heals his wounds, And drives away his fear, And drives away his fear.

2. It makes the wounded spirit whole, And calms the troubled breast; 'Tis manna to the hungry soul, And to the weary, rest, And to the weary, rest.

3 Dear Name, the rock on which I build,
My shield and hiding place;
My never-failing treasure, filled
With boundless stores of grace:

4 Jesus, my Shepherd, Savior, Friend,
My Prophet, Priest, and King,
My Lord, my Life, my Way, my End,
Accept the praise I bring.

5 I would thy boundless love proclaim
With every fleeting breath;
So shall the music of thy name
Refresh my soul in death.

4 Closer and closer let us cleave
To his beloved embrace;
Expect his fulness to receive,
And grace to answer grace.

5 Partakers of the Savior's grace,
The same in mind and heart,
Nor joy, nor grief, nor time, nor place,
Nor life, nor death can part.

6 Then let us hasten to the day
Which shall our flesh restore;
When death shall all be done away,
And bodies part no more.

171 *United—though separated.*

1 Blest be the dear uniting love,
That will not let us part:
Our bodies may far off remove,
We still are one in heart.

2 Joined in one spirit to our Head,
Where he appoints we go;
And still in Jesus' footsteps tread,
And show his praise below.

3 O may we ever walk in him,
And nothing know beside,—
Nothing desire, nothing esteem,
But Jesus crucified.

172 *Light upon the narrow path.*

1 Bright was the guiding-star that led,
With mild, benignant ray,—
The Gentiles to the lowly shed
Where the Redeemer lay.

2 But lo! the Scriptures' clearer light
Now points to his abode;
It shines through sin and sorrow's night
To guide us to our God.

3 O let us tread the narrow path,
While light and grace are given;
And thus escape the coming wrath,
And reign with him in heaven.

173 EMMONS. C. M. Arranged from BURGMULLER.

1. Thou dear Redeemer, dying Lamb, I love to hear of thee; No music's like thy charming name, Nor half so sweet can be, Nor half so sweet can be.

2. Oh, may I ever hear thy voice In mercy to me speak; In thee, my Priest, will I rejoice, And thy salvation seek, And thy salvation seek.

3 While Jesus shall be still my theme,
   While on this earth I stay;
   I'll sing my Jesus' lovely name,
   When all things else decay.

4 When I appear in yonder cloud,
   With all his favored throng,
   Then will I sing more sweet, more loud,
   And Christ shall be my song.

174 *At evening time it shall be light.*

1 We journey through a vale of tears,
   By many a cloud o'ercast;
   And worldly cares, and worldly fears,
   Go with us to the last.

2 Not to the last! Thy word hath said,
   Could we but read aright,—
   Poor pilgrim, lift in hope thy head;
   At eve it shall be light!

3 Though earth-born shadows now may
   Thy thorny path awhile,   [shroud
   God's blessed word can part each cloud,
   And bid the sunshine smile.

4 Only believe, in living faith,
   His love and power divine;
   And ere thy sun shall set in death,
   His light shall round thee shine.

5 When tempest clouds are dark on high,
   His bow of love and peace
   Shines sweetly in the vaulted sky,—
   A pledge that storms shall cease.

6 Hold on thy way, with hope unchill'd,
   By faith and not by sight,
   And thou shalt own his word fulfill'd,—
   At eve it shall be light.

175 *The goodly city in prospect.*

1 Jerusalem! my happy home!
   Name ever dear to me!
   When shall my labors have an end,
   In joy, and peace in thee?

2 O when, thou city of my God,
   Shall I thy courts ascend,
   Where congregations ne'er break up,
   And Sabbath has no end?

3 Why should I shrink at pain and wo?
   Or feel, at death, dismay?
   I've Canaan's goodly land in view,
   And realms of endless day.

4 Apostles, martyrs, prophets, there,
   Around my Savior stand;
   And soon my friends in Christ below
   Will join the glorious band.

5 Jerusalem! my happy home!
   My soul still pants for thee;
   Then shall my labors have an end,
   When I thy joys shall see.

176 ST. MARTIN. C. M.
TANSUR. 1735.

1. How great the wisdom, power, and grace, Which in redemption shine;
The heavenly host with joy confess The work is all divine.
And, with ten thousand thousand tongues, Proclaim his power to save.

2. Before his feet they cast their crowns, Those crowns which Jesus gave,

3 They tell the triumphs of his cross,
The suff'rings which he bore;
How low he stooped, how high he rose,—
And rose to stoop no more.

4 With them let us our voices raise,
And still the song renew;
Salvation well deserves the praise
Of men and angels too.

177 *Thy will be done.*

1 Thy presence, Lord, the place shall fill;
My heart shall be thy throne:
Thy holy, just, and perfect will,
Shall in my flesh be done.

2 I thank thee for the present grace,
And now in hope rejoice,
In confidence to see thy face,
And always hear thy voice.

3 I have the things I ask of thee;
What more shall I require?
That still my soul may restless be,
And only thee desire.

4 Thy only will be done, not mine,
But make me, Lord, thy home:
Come as thou wilt, I that resign,
But O, my Jesus, come!

178 *The Lord, my portion.*

1 Eternal Source of joys divine,
To thee my soul aspires;
O! could I say,— the Lord is mine!
'Tis all my soul desires.

2 My hope, my trust, my life, my Lord,
Assure me of thy love;
O! speak the kind, transporting word,
And bid my fears remove.

3 Then shall my thankful powers rejoice,
And triumph in my God,
Till heavenly rapture tune my voice,
To spread thy praise abroad.

179 *The entire surrender.*

1 O Savior, welcome to my heart;
Possess thy humble throne:
Bid every rival, Lord, depart,
And reign, O Christ, alone.

2 The world and Satan I forsake;
To thee I all resign:
My longing heart, O Savior, take,
And fill with love divine.

3 O may I never turn aside,
Nor from thy bosom flee;
Let nothing here my heart divide:
I give it all to thee.

NORTHFIELD.* C. M.

1. O for a thousand tongues to sing my great Redeemer's praise! The glories of my God and King, The triumphs of his grace.

2 My gracious Master, and my God,
   Assist me to proclaim,—
To spread through all the earth abroad,
   The honors of thy Name.

3 Jesus! the Name that charms our fears,
   That bids our sorrows cease;
'Tis music in the sinner's ears;
   'Tis life, and health, and peace.

4 He breaks the power of cancell'd sin;
   He sets the pris'ner free;
His blood can make the foulest clean:
   His blood availed for me.

5 He speaks,—and, list'ning to his voice,
   New life the dead receive;
The mournful, broken hearts rejoice;
   The humble poor believe.

6 Hear him, ye deaf; his praise, ye dumb,
   Your loosened tongues employ;
Ye blind, behold your Savior come;
   And leap, ye lame, for joy.

181 *God, my all-sufficient portion.*

1 My God, my portion, and my love,
   My everlasting All,
I've none but thee in heaven above,
   Or on this earthly ball.

2 To thee I owe my wealth and friends,
   And health, and safe abode;
Thanks to thy Name for meaner things;
   But they are not my God.

3 How vain a toy is glittering wealth,
   If once compared to thee;

Or what's my safety or my health,
   Or all my friends to me?

4 Were I possessor of the earth,
   And called the stars my own,
Without thy graces and thyself,
   I were a wretch undone.

5 Let others stretch their arms like seas,
   And grasp in all the shore;
Grant me the visits of thy grace,
   And I desire no more.

182 *All-sufficiency of the Gospel.*

1 The gospel! O, what endless charms
   Dwell in that blissful sound;
Its influence every fear disarms,
   And spreads delight around.

2 Here pardon, life, and joy divine,
   In rich effusion flow,
For guilty rebels, lost in sin,
   And doomed to endless woe.

3 Th' Almighty Former of the skies,
   Stoops to our vile abode;
While angels view with wond'ring eyes,
   And hail th' incarnate God.

4 How rich the depths of love divine!
   Of bliss a boundless store!
Redeemer, let me call thee mine,—
   Thy fullness I implore.

5 On thee alone my help relies;
   Beneath thy cross I fall;
My Lord, my life, my sacrifice,
   My Savior, and my all.

* See foot note on p. 3d. of Introduction.

LANESBORO'. C. M.   ENGLISH

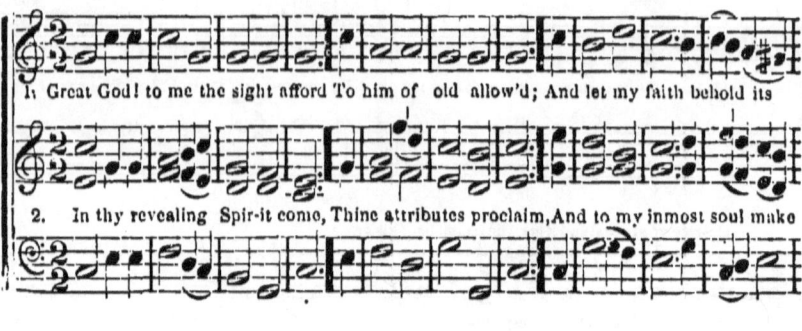

1. Great God! to me the sight afford To him of old allow'd; And let my faith behold its Lord, Descending in a cloud.

2. In thy revealing Spirit come, Thine attributes proclaim, And to my inmost soul make known, The glories of thy Name.

3 Jehovah, Christ, I thee adore,
  Who gav'st my soul to be;
Fountain of being and of power,
  And great in majesty.

4 The Lord, the mighty God, thou art,
  But let me rather prove
That name inspoken to my heart,
  That fav'rite name of love.

184
Strength renewed by waiting upon the Lord.

1 Lord, I believe thy every word,
  Thy every promise true;
And lo! I wait on thee, my Lord,
  Till I my strength renew.

2 If in this feeble flesh I may
  Awhile show forth thy praise,
Jesus, support the tott'ring clay,
  And lengthen out my days.

3 If such a worm as I can spread
  The common Savior's name,
Let him who raised thee from the dead,
  Quicken my mortal frame.

4 Still let me live thy blood to show,
  Which purges every stain;
And gladly linger out below
  A few more years in pain.

185
Joining the song of the Church triumphant.

1 Sing we the song of those who stand
  Around the' eternal throne,
Of every kindred, clime, and land,—
  A multitude unknown.

2 Life's poor distinctions vanish here;
  To-day the young, the old,
Our Savior and his flock, appear,
  One shepherd and one fold.

3 Toil, trial, suff'ring, still await
  On earth the pilgrim throng;
Yet learn we in our low estate
  The Church triumphant's song.

4 Worthy the Lamb for sinners slain,
  Cry the redeem'd above,
Blessing and honor to obtain,
  And everlasting love.

5 Worthy the Lamb, on earth we sing,
  Who died our souls to save;
Henceforth, O Death, where is thy sting?
  Thy victory, O Grave?

6 Then hallelujah! power and praise
  To God in Christ be given;
May all who now this anthem raise,
  Renew the song in heaven.

MARLOW. C. M.

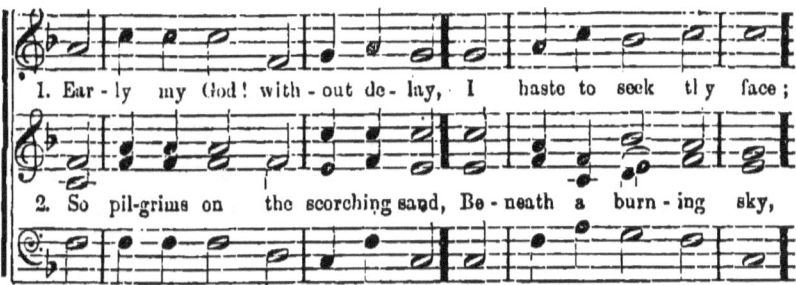

1. Ear-ly my God! with-out de-lay, I haste to seek thy face;
2. So pil-grims on the scorching sand, Be-neath a burn-ing sky,

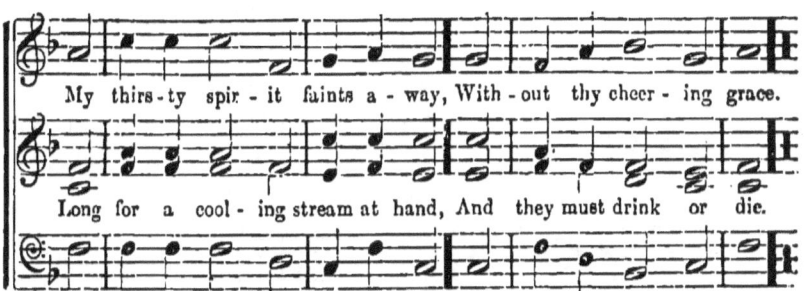

My thirs-ty spir-it faints a-way, With-out thy cheer-ing grace.
Long for a cool-ing stream at hand, And they must drink or die.

3 I've seen thy glory and thy power
   Through all thy temple shine :
  My God, repeat that heavenly hour,
   That vision so divine.

4 Not life itself, with all its joys,
   Can my best passions move,
  Or raise so high my cheerful voice,
   As thy forgiving love.

5 Thus, till my last expiring day,
   I'll bless my God and King;
  Thus will I lift my hands to pray,
   And tune my lips to sing.

187 *Grace implored in baptism.*
Celestial dove, come from on high,
   And on the water brood :
Come, with thy quick'ning power apply
   The water and the blood.

2 I love the Lord, that stoops so low
   To give his word a seal ;
  But the rich grace his hands bestow
   Exceeds the figure still.

3 Almighty God, for thee we call,
   And our request renew ;
  Accept in Christ, and bless withal,
   The work we have to do.

188 *Unwearied earnestness.*
1 Father, I stretch my hands to thee ;
   No other help I know :
  If thou withdraw thyself from me,
   Ah ! whither shall I go ?

2 What did thine only Son endure,
   Before I drew my breath !
  What pain, what labor, to secure
   My soul from endless death !

3 O Jesus, could I this believe,
   I now should feel thy power ;
  And all my wants thou wouldst relieve,
   In this accepted hour.

4 Author of faith ! to thee I lift
   My weary, longing eyes :
  O let me now receive that gift,—
   My soul without it dies.

5 Surely thou canst not let me die ;
   O speak, and I shall live ;
  And here I will unwearied lie,
   Till thou thy Spirit give.

6 How would my fainting soul rejoice,
   Could I but see thy face ;
  Now let me hear thy quick'ning voice,
   And taste thy pard'ning grace.

189 COWPER. C. M.
Dr. L. Mason

1. There is a foun-tain, filled with blood, Drawn from Immanu-el's veins;
2. The dy-ing thief re-joiced to see That foun-tain, in his day;

And sinners, plunged beneath that flood, Lose all their guilty stains, Lose all, &c.
And there may I, though vile as he, Wash all my sins a-way, Wash all my sins a-way.

3 Thou dying Lamb! thy precious blood
    Shall never lose its power,
Till all the ransomed church of God
    Are saved, to sin no more.

4 E'er since, by faith, I saw the stream
    Thy flowing wounds supply,
Redeeming love has been my theme,
    And shall be, till I die.

5 When this poor lisping, stamm'ring tongue,
    Lies silent in the grave,
Then in a nobler, sweeter song,
    I'll sing thy power to save.

190 *Grateful remembrance.*

1 According to thy gracious word,
    In meek humility,
This will I do, my dying Lord,—
    I will remember thee.

2 Thy body, broken for my sake,
    My bread from heaven shall be:
Thy testamental cup I take,
    And thus remember thee.

3 Gethsemane can I forget?
    Or there thy conflict see,
Thine agony and bloody sweat,
    And not remember thee?

4 When to the cross I turn mine eyes,
    And rest on Calvary,
O Lamb of God, my Sacrifice,
    I must remember thee!

5 Remember thee and all thy pains,
    And all thy love to me;
Yea, while a breath, a pulse remains,
    Will I remember thee.

6 And when these failing lips grow dumb,
    And mind and mem'ry flee,
When thou shalt in thy kingdom come,
    Jesus, remember me.

191 *He is faithful that hath promised.*

1 Jesus, the sinner's rest thou art,
    From guilt, and fear, and pain;
While thou art absent from the heart
    We look for rest in vain.

2 O when wilt thou my Savior be?
    O when shall I be clean?
The true eternal Sabbath see,—
    A perfect rest from sin?

3 The consolations of thy word
    My soul have long upheld;
The faithful promise of the Lord
    Shall surely be fulfill'd.

WOODLAND. C. M.

N. D. GOULD

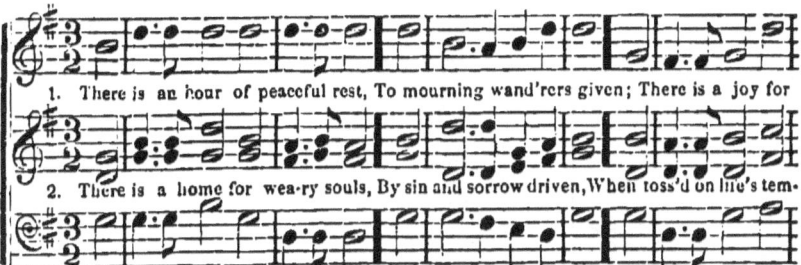

1. There is an hour of peaceful rest, To mourning wand'rers given; There is a joy for souls distress'd, A balm for eve-ry wounded breast,'Tis found a-bove in heaven.

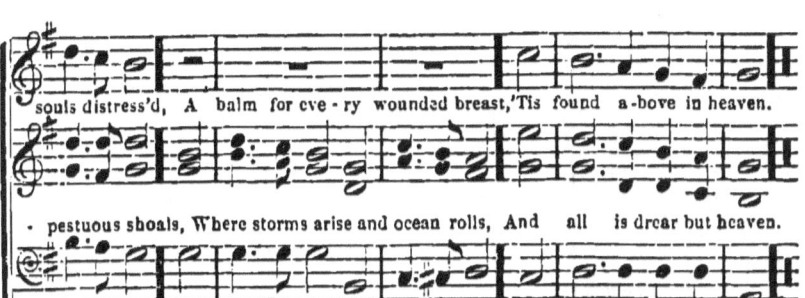

2. There is a home for wea-ry souls, By sin and sorrow driven, When toss'd on life's tem-pestuous shoals, Where storms arise and ocean rolls, And all is drear but heaven.

3 There faith lifts up the tearless eye,
    To brighter prospects given;
And views the tempest passing by,
The evening shadows quickly fly,
    And all serene in heaven.

4 There fragrant flowers immortal bloom,
    And joys supreme are given;
There rays divine disperse the gloom;
Beyond the confines of the tomb
    Appears the dawn of heaven.

193   *Evening.—Solitude.*

1 I love to steal awhile away,
    From every cumb'ring care,
And spend the hours of setting day
    In humble, grateful prayer.

2 I love in solitude to shed
    The penitential tear,
And all his promises to plead
    Where none but God can hear.

3 I love to think on mercies past,
    And future good implore,—
And all my cares and sorrows cast
    On Him whom I adore.

4 I love by faith to take a view
    Of brighter scenes in heaven;
The prospect doth my strength renew,
    While here by tempests driven.

5 Thus, when life's toilsome day is o'er,
    May its departing ray
Be calm as this impressive hour,
    And lead to endless day.

194   *The wanderer recalled.*

1 Return, O wanderer, return,
    And seek thy Father's face;
Those new desires which in thee burn
    Were kindled by his grace.

2 Return, O wanderer, return;
    He bears thy humble sigh:
He sees thy softened spirit mourn,
    When no one else is nigh.

3 Return, O wanderer, return;
    Thy Savior bids thee live:
Come to his cross, and, grateful, learn
    How freely he'll forgive.

4 Return, O wanderer, return,
    And wipe the falling tear:
Thy Father calls,—no longer mourn;
    'Tis love invites thee near.

5 Return, O wanderer, return;
    Regain thy long-sought rest ·
The Savior's melting mercies yearn
    To clasp thee to his breast.

195. NAOMI. C. M.

Dr. L. Mason.

1. Lord, I approach the mercy seat, Where thou dost answer prayer;
There humbly fall before thy feet, For none can perish there.

2. Thy promise is my only plea; With this I venture nigh;
Thou callest burden'd souls to thee, And such, O Lord, am I.

3 Bow'd down beneath a load of sin,
By Satan sorely press'd;
By wars without, and fears within,
I come to thee for rest.

4 Be thou my shield and hiding-place;
That, shelter'd near thy side,
I may rejoice in Jesus' grace,—
In Jesus crucified.

5 O, wondrous love!—to bleed and die,
To bear the cross and shame,
That guilty sinners, such as I,
Might plead thy gracious name.

196 *Fear of hell.*

1 Terrible thought! shall I alone,
Who may be saved, shall I,
Of all, alas! whom I have known,
Through sin forever die?

2 While all my old companions dear,
With whom I once did live,
Joyful at God's right hand appear,
A blessing to receive:—

3 Shall I, amidst a ghastly band,
Dragg'd to the judgment-seat,
Far on the left with horror stand,
My fearful doom to meet?

4 Ah! no;—I still may turn and live,
For still his wrath delays;
He now vouchsafes a kind reprieve,
And offers me his grace.

197 *The leper.*

1 Jesus, if still thou art to-day,
As yesterday, the same,—
Present to heal,—in me display
The virtue of thy Name.

2 Now, Lord, to whom for help I call,
Thy miracles repeat;
With pitying eyes behold me fall
A leper at thy feet.

3 Loathsome, and vile, and self-abhorr'd,
I sink beneath my sin;
But, if thou wilt, a gracious word
Of thine can make me clean.

198 *Self loathed; Christ exalted*

1 O could I lose myself in thee,
Thy depth of mercy prove,—
Thou vast, unfathomable sea
Of unexhausted love.

2 My humbled soul, when thou art near,
In dust and ashes lies:
How shall a sinful worm appear,
Or meet thy purer eyes?

3 I loathe myself when God I see,
And into nothing fall;
Content if thou exalted be,
And Christ be all in all.

BACH. C. M.

A Celebrated German Choral.

1. When rising from the bed of death, O'erwhelm'd with guilt and fear,
I view my Maker face to face, O how shall I appear?
If yet, while pardon may be found, And mercy may be sought,
My soul with inward horror shrinks, And trembles at the thought.

3 When thou, O Lord, shalt stand disclosed
   In majesty severe,
And sit in judgment on my soul,—
   O how shall I appear?

4 O may my broken, contrite heart,
   Timely my sins lament;
And early, with repentant tears,
   Eternal woe prevent.

200 *Knocking at the door of mercy.*

1 Lord, at thy feet we sinners lie,
   And knock at mercy's door;
With heavy heart, and downcast eye
   Thy favor we implore.

2 Without thy grace, we sink oppress'd,
   Down to the gates of hell;
O give our troubled spirits rest,—
   Our gloomy fears dispel.

3 'Tis mercy, mercy, now we plead;
   Let thy compassion move;
Mercy, that led thee once to bleed,
   In tenderness and love.

4 In mercy, now, for Jesus' sake,
   O God, our sins forgive;
Thy grace our stubborn hearts can break,
   And, breaking, bid us live.

201 *Determined Importunity.*

1 Because for me the Savior prays,
   And pleads his death for me,
God hath vouchsafed a longer space,
   And spared the barren tree.

2 Time to repent thou dost bestow;
   Now, Lord, the power impart,
And let mine eyes with tears o'erflow,
   And break my stubborn heart.

3 I now from all my sins would turn,
   To my atoning God;
And look on him I pierced, and mourn,
   And feel the sprinkled blood:—

4 Would nail my passions to the cross,
   Where my Redeemer died;
And all things else account but loss
   For Jesus crucified.

5 Giver of penitential pain,
   Before thy cross I lie;
In grief determined to remain
   Till thou thy blood apply.

6 Forgiveness on my conscience seal;
   Bestow thy promised rest;
With purest love thy servant fill,
   And number with the blest.

* These Hymns are adapted to NAOMI, on opposite page.

202   DUNDEE. C. M.   SCOTCH PSALTER

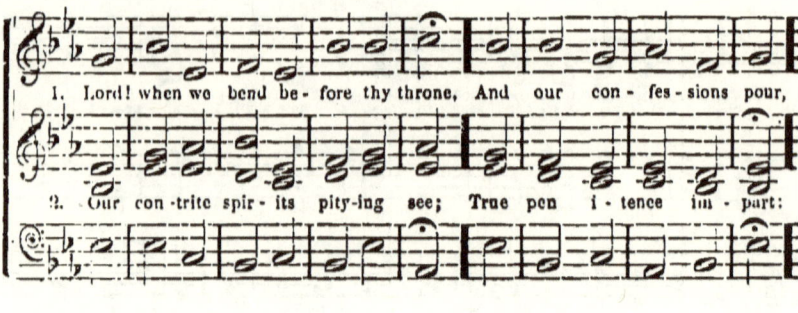

1. Lord! when we bend be-fore thy throne, And our con-fes-sions pour,
2. Our con-trite spir-its pity-ing see; True pen-i-tence im-part:

O! may we feel the sins we own, And hate what we de-plore.
And let a heal-ing ray from thee Beam peace in-to each heart.

3 When we disclose our wants in prayer,
  O let our wills resign;
  And not a thought our bosom share;
  Which is not wholly thine.

4 And when with heart and voice we strive
  Our grateful hymns to raise,
  Let love divine within us live,
  And fill our souls with praise.

5 Then, on thy glories while we dwell,
  Thy mercies we'll review;
  With love divine, transported, tell—
  Thou, God, art Father too.

203   *He justifieth the ungodly.*

1 Lovers of pleasure more than God,
  For you he suffer'd pain;
  For you the Savior spilt his blood:
  And shall he bleed in vain?

2 Sinners, his life for you he paid
  Your basest crimes he bore;
  Your sins were all on Jesus laid,
  That you might sin no more.

3 To earth the great Redeemer came,
  That you might come to heaven;
  Believe, believe in Jesus' name,
  And all your sin's forgiven.

4 Believe in him who died for thee;
  And, sure as he hath died,
  Thy debt is paid, thy soul is free,
  And thou art justified.

204   *Comfort from the Bible.*

1 Lord! I have made thy word my choice,
  My lasting heritage;
  These shall my noblest powers rejoice,
  My warmest thoughts engage.

2 I'll read the hist'ries of thy love,
  And keep thy laws in sight,
  While through the promises I rove,
  With ever-fresh delight.

3 'Tis a broad land of wealth unknown,
  Where springs of life arise;
  Seeds of immortal bliss are sown,
  And hidden glory lies:—

4 The best relief that mourners have;
  It makes our sorrows blest:—
  Our fairest hope, beyond the grave,
  And our eternal rest.

    To Father, Son, and Holy Ghost,
      Who sweetly all agree
    To save a world of sinners lost,
      Eternal glory be.

205 PARSONS. C. M.
Arranged from S. HUBBARD.

1. For-ev-er here my rest shall be, Close to thy bleed-ing side;
This all my hope, and all my plea,— For me the Sa-vior died.

2. My dy-ing Sa-vior, and my God, Fountain for guilt and sin,
Sprinkle me ev-er with thy blood, And cleanse and keep me clean.

3 Wash me, and make me thus thine own;
Wash me, and mine thou art;
Wash me, but not my feet alone,—
My hands, my head, my heart.

4 Th' atonement of thy blood apply,
Till faith to sight improve;
Till hope in full fruition die,
And all my soul be love.

206 *Safety in union.*

1 Jesus, great Shepherd of the sheep,
To thee for help we fly:
Thy little flock in safety keep,
For O! the wolf is nigh.

2 He comes, of hellish malice full,
To scatter, tear, and slay;
He seizes every straggling soul
As his own lawful prey.

3 Us into thy protection take,
And gather with thine arm;
Unless the fold we first forsake,
The wolf can never harm.

4 We laugh to scorn his cruel power,
While by our Shepherd's side;
The sheep he never can devour,
Unless he first divide.

5 O do not suffer him to part
The souls that here agree;
But make us of one mind and heart,
And keep us one in thee.

6 Together let us sweetly live,—
Together let us die;
And each a starry crown receive,
And reign above the sky.

207 *Lord, help my unbelief.*

1 How sad our state by nature is;
Our sin, how deep it stains;
And Satan binds our captive souls
Fast in his slavish chains.

2 But there's a voice of sov'reign grace
Sounds from the sacred word:—
Ho! ye despairing sinners, come,
And trust a faithful Lord.

3 My soul obeys the gracious call,
And runs to this relief;
I would believe thy promise, Lord;
O help my unbelief!

4 To the blest fountain of thy blood,
Incarnate God, I fly;
Here let me wash my guilty soul
From crimes of deepest dye.

5 A guilty, weak, and helpless worm,
Into thine arms I fall;
Be thou my strength and righteousness,
My Jesus, and my all.

208 DEVIZES. C. M. SWAN.

1. Let all in whom the Spir-it glows, In whom God's word hath place, The all-u-nit-ing
2. Then shall the world admiring view The gather'd flock at rest; And own the Son di-

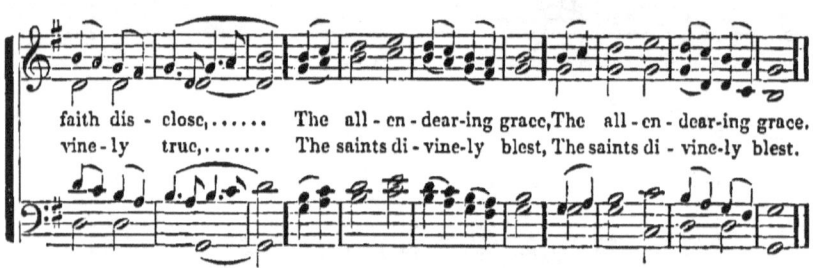

faith dis - close,...... The all-en-dear-ing grace, The all-en-dear-ing grace.
vine-ly true,...... The saints di-vine-ly blest, The saints di-vine-ly blest.

209 *The type of everlasting rest.*

1 Come, let us join with one accord
   In hymns around the throne;
   This is the day our rising Lord
   Hath made and call'd his own.

2 This is the day which God hath blest,
   The brightest of the seven,
   Type of that everlasting rest
   The saints enjoy in heaven.

3 Then let us in his name sing on,
   And hasten to that day
   When our Redeemer shall come down,
   And shadows pass away.

4 Not one, but all our days below,
   Let us in hymns employ;
   And, in our Lord rejoicing, go
   To his eternal joy.

210
The Lamb worshipped on earth and in heaven.

1 Come, let us join our cheerful songs
   With angels round the throne:
   Ten thousand thousand are their tongues,
   But all their joys are one.

2 Worthy the Lamb that died, they cry,
   To be exalted thus:
   Worthy the Lamb, our hearts reply,
   For he was slain for us.

3 Jesus is worthy to receive
   Honor and power divine;
   And blessings more than we can give,
   Be, Lord, forever thine.

4 The whole creation join in one,
   To bless the sacred Name
   Of Him that sits upon the throne,
   And to adore the Lamb.

211 *Praise,—delightful.*

1 My Savior, my almighty Friend,
   When I begin thy praise,
   Where will the growing numbers end,—
   The numbers of thy grace?

2 I trust in thy eternal word;
   Thy goodness I adore:
   Send down thy grace, O blessed Lord,
   That I may love thee more.

3 My feet shall travel all the length
   Of the celestial road;
   And march, with courage in thy strength,
   To see the Lord my God.

4 Awake! awake! my tuneful powers,
   With this delightful song;
   And entertain the darkest hours,
   Nor think the season long.

212 TURNER.* C. M. MAXIM.

2 Look, how we grovel here below,
  Fond of these earthly toys;
  Our souls, how heavily they go,
  To reach eternal joys.

3 In vain we tune our formal songs,—
  In vain we strive to rise;
  Hosannas languish on our tongues,
  And our devotion dies.

4 Father, and shall we ever live
  At this poor dying rate;
  Our love so faint, so cold to thee,
  And thine to us so great?

5 Come, Holy Spirit, Heavenly Dove,
  With all thy quick'ning powers;
  Come, shed abroad a Savior's love,
  And that shall kindle ours.

213 *The race for glory.*

1 Awake, my soul! stretch every nerve,
  And press with vigor on;
  A heavenly race demands thy zeal,
  And an immortal crown.

2 'Tis God's all-animating voice
  That calls thee from on high;
  'Tis he whose hand presents the prize
  To thine aspiring eye.

3 A cloud of witnesses around
  Hold thee in full survey;
  Forget the steps already trod,
  And onward urge thy way.

4 Blest Savior! introduced by thee,
  Our race have we begun;
  And, crown'd with victory, at thy feet
  We'll lay our trophies down.

214 *Life, light, and love.*

1 Enthroned on high, Almighty Lord,
  The Holy Ghost send down;
  Fulfil in us thy faithful word,
  And all thy mercies crown.

2 Though on our heads no tongues of fire
  Their wondrous powers impart,
  Grant, Savior, what we more desire,—
  Thy Spirit in our heart.

3 Spirit of life, and light, and love,
  Thy heavenly influence give;
  Quicken our souls, our guilt remove,
  That we in Christ may live.

4 To our benighted minds reveal
  The glories of his grace,
  And bring us where no clouds conceal
  The brightness of his face.

* See foot note on p. 3d, of Introduction.

CAMBRIDGE. C. M. Dr. RANDALL.

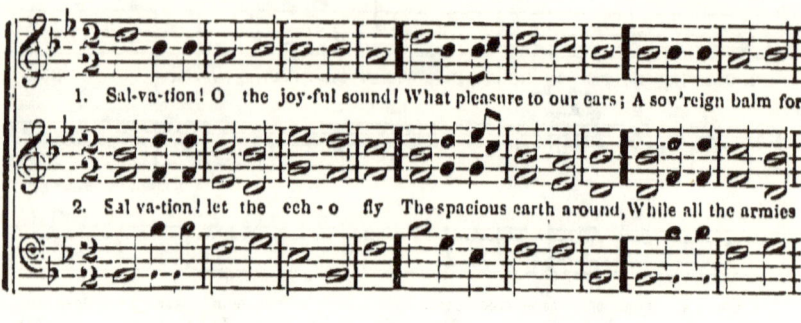

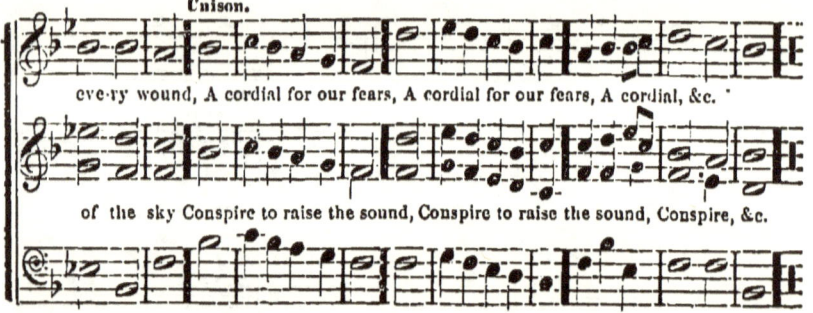

3 Salvation! O thou bleeding Lamb!
To thee the praise belongs:
Salvation shall inspire our hearts,
And dwell upon our tongues.

216 *Returning to Zion with songs of joy.*
1 Daughter of Zion, from the dust
Exalt thy fallen head;
Again in thy Redeemer trust,—
He calls thee from the dead.

2 Awake, awake, put on thy strength,
Thy beautiful array;
The day of freedom dawns at length,—
The Lord's appointed day.

3 Rebuild thy walls, thy bounds enlarge,
And send thy heralds forth;
Say—to the south,—Give up thy charge!
And,—Keep not back, O north!

4 They come, they come: thine exiled bands,
Where'er they rest or roam,
Have heard thy voice in distant lands,
And hasten to their home.

5 Thus, though the universe shall burn,
And God his works destroy,
With songs thy ransomed shall return,
And everlasting joy.

217 *The universal bond of love.*
1 The glorious universe around,
The heavens with all their train,
Sun, moon, and stars, are firmly bound
In one mysterious chain.

2 The earth, the ocean, and the sky,
To form one world agree;
Where all that walk, or swim, or fly,
Compose one family.

3 God in creation thus displays
His wisdom and his might,
While all his works with all his ways
Harmoniously unite.

4 In one fraternal bond of love,
One fellowship of mind,
The saints below and saints above
Their bliss and glory find.

5 Here, in their house of pilgrimage,
Thy statutes are their song;
There, through one bright, eternal age,
Thy praises they prolong.

6 Lord, may our union form a part
Of that thrice happy whole;
Derive its pulse from thee, the heart,
Its life from thee, the soul.

218 PETERBORO'. C. M.

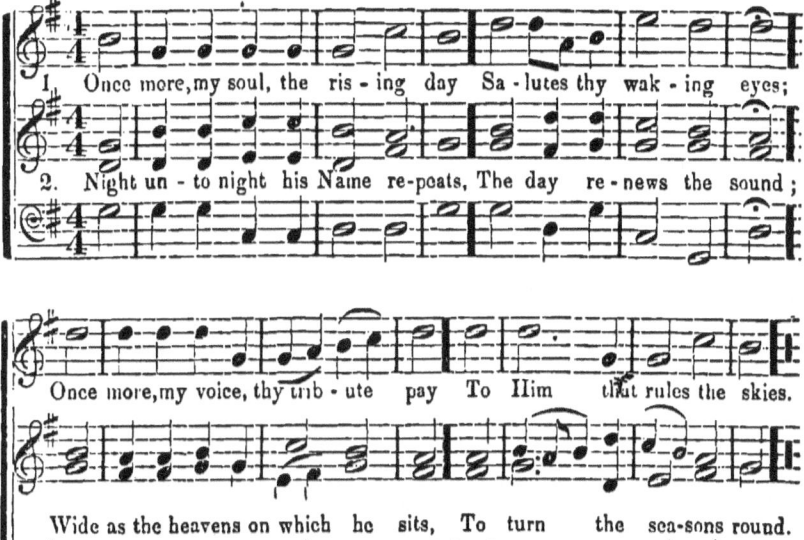

1. Once more, my soul, the rising day
Salutes thy waking eyes;
Once more, my voice, thy tribute pay
To Him that rules the skies.

2. Night unto night his Name repeats,
The day renews the sound;
Wide as the heavens on which he sits,
To turn the seasons round.

3 'Tis he supports my mortal frame;
My tongue shall speak his praise;
My sins might rouse his wrath to flame,
But yet his wrath delays.

4 O God, let all my hours be thine,
Whilst I enjoy the light;
Then shall my sun in smiles decline,
And bring a peaceful night.

219 *The exceeding great reward.*

1 Thy name to me, thy nature grant!
This, only this be given!
Nothing beside my God I want;
Nothing in earth or heaven.

2 Come, O my Savior, come away;
Into my soul descend;
No longer from thy creature stay,
My Author and my End.

3 The bliss thou hast for me prepared,
No longer be delay'd:
Come, my exceeding great Reward,
For whom I first was made.

4 Come, Father, Son, and Holy Ghost,
And seal me thine abode;
Let all I am in thee be lost,
Let all be lost in God.

220 *Source of light and joy.*

1 Great Spirit, by whose mighty power,
All creatures live and move,
On us thy benediction shower;
Inspire our souls with love.

2 Hail! Source of light! arise and shine,
All gloom and doubt dispel;
Give peace and joy, for we are thine;
In us forever dwell.

3 From death to life our spirits raise,
And full redemption bring;
New tongues impart to speak the praise
Of Christ, our God and King.

4 Thine inward witness bear, unknown
To all the world beside;
With joy we then shall feel and own
Our Savior glorified.

221 *The Holy Spirit witnessing with ours.*

1 Eternal Spirit! God of truth!
Our contrite hearts inspire;
Kindle a flame of heavenly love—
The pure celestial fire.

2 'Tis thine to soothe the sorrowing,
With guilt and fear oppress'd;
'Tis thine to bid the dying live,
And give the weary rest.

222. EXHORTATION. C. M. — HIBBARD

1. There is a land of pure delight, Where saints immortal reign; Infinite day excludes the night, And pleasures banish pain.

2 There everlasting Spring abides,
   And never-with'ring flowers;
   Death, like a narrow sea, divides
   This heavenly land from ours.

3 Sweet fields, beyond the swelling flood,
   Stand dress'd in living green;
   So to the Jews old Canaan stood,
   While Jordan roll'd between.

4 Could we but climb where Moses stood,
   And view the landscape o'er,
   Not Jordan's stream, nor death's cold flood
   Should fright us from the shore.

223. *The Promised Land.*

1 On Jordan's stormy banks I stand,
   And cast a wishful eye
   To Canaan's fair and happy land,
   Where my possessions lie.

2 O the transporting, rapturous scene,
   That rises to my sight!
   Sweet fields, array'd in living green,
   And rivers of delight.

3 There generous fruits, that never fail,
   On trees immortal grow;
   There rock, and hill, and brook, and vale,
   With milk and honey flow.

4 O'er all those wide, extended plains,
   Shines one eternal day;
   There God the Son forever reigns,
   And scatters night away.

5 No chilling winds, or pois'nous breath,
   Can reach that healthful shore;
   Sickness and sorrow, pain and death,
   Are felt and fear'd no more.

* See foot note on p. 3d. of Introduction.

6 When shall I reach that happy place,
　　And be forever blest?
　When shall I see my Father's face,
　　And in his bosom rest?

7 Filled with delight, my raptured soul
　　Would here no longer stay,
　Though Jordan's waves around me roll,
　　Fearless I'd launch away.

224　*The Gospel feast.*

1 Let every mortal ear attend,
　　And every heart rejoice;
　The trumpet of the gospel sounds
　　With an inviting voice.

2 Ho! all ye hungry, starving souls,
　　That feed upon the wind,
　And vainly strive with earthly toys
　　To fill an empty mind:—

3 Eternal Wisdom hath prepared
　　A soul-reviving feast,
　And bids your longing appetites
　　The rich provision taste.

4 Ho! ye that pant for living streams,
　　And pine away and die,
　Here you may quench your raging thirst
　　With springs that never dry.

5 Rivers of love and mercy here
　　In a rich ocean join;
　Salvation in abundance flows,
　　Like floods of milk and wine.

6 The happy gates of gospel grace
　　Stand open night and day:
　Lord, we are come to seek supplies,
　　And drive our wants away.

225　*The invitation.*

1 The King of heaven his table spreads,
　　And blessings crown the board;
　Not Paradise, with all its joys,
　　Could such delight afford.

2 Pardon and peace to dying men,
　　And endless life are given,
　Through the rich blood that Jesus shed,
　　To raise our souls to heaven.

3 Millions of souls, in glory now,
　　Were fed and feasted here;
　And millions more, still on the way,
　　Around the board appear.

4 All things are ready, come away,
　　Nor weak excuses frame;
　Crowd to your places at the feast
　　And bless the Founder's name.

226　*The loadstone of His love.*

1 Jesus, united by thy grace,
　　And each to each endeared,
　With confidence we seek thy face,
　　And know our prayer is heard.

2 Still let us own our common Lord,
　　And bear thine easy yoke,
　A band of love, a three-fold cord,
　　Which never can be broke.

3 Make us into one spirit drink;
　　Baptize into thy name;
　And let us always kindly think,
　　And sweetly speak, the same.

4 Touched by the loadstone of thy love,
　　Let all our hearts agree;
　And ever toward each other move,
　　And ever move toward thee.

5 To thee, inseparably joined,
　　Let all our spirits cleave;
　O may we all the loving mind
　　That was in thee receive.

227　*"Jerusalem, my happy home."*

1 Jerusalem, my happy home,
　　O how I long for thee!
　When will my sorrows have an end—
　　Thy joys when shall I see!

2 Thy walls are all of precious stone,
　　Most glorious to behold;
　Thy gates are richly set with pearl,
　　Thy streets are paved with gold.

3 Reach down, O Lord, thine arm of grace
　　And cause me to ascend;
　Where congregations ne'er break up,
　　And Sabbaths never end.

4 Jesus, my Lord, to glory's gone,
　　Him will I go and see,
　And all my brethren here below,
　　Will soon come after me.

5 When we've been there ten thousand
　　Bright shining as the sun,　[years,
　We've no less days to sing God's praise
　　Than when we first begun.

228   DEDHAM. C. M.   WM. GARDINER.

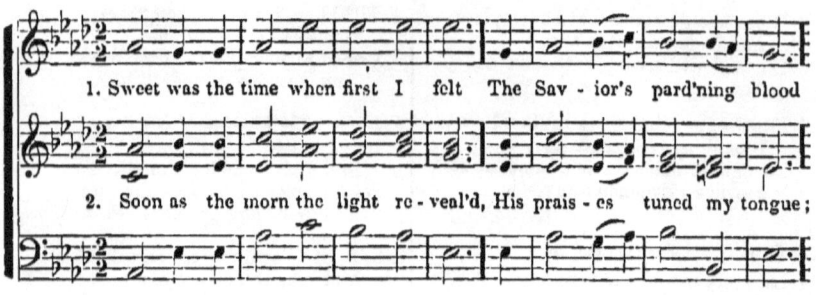

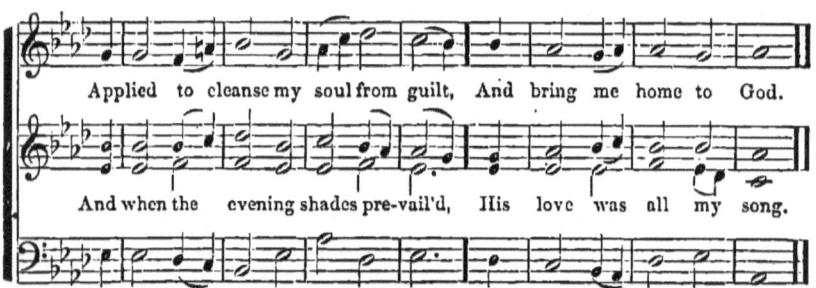

1. Sweet was the time when first I felt The Savior's pard'ning blood Applied to cleanse my soul from guilt, And bring me home to God.

2. Soon as the morn the light reveal'd, His praises tuned my tongue; And when the evening shades prevail'd, His love was all my song.

3 In prayer my soul drew near the Lord,
   And saw his glory shine;
And when I read his holy word,
   I call'd each promise mine.

4 But now when evening shade prevails,
   My soul in darkness mourns;
And when the morn the light reveals,
   No light to me returns.

5 Rise, Lord, and help me to prevail;
   O make my soul thy care;
I know thy mercy cannot fail;—
   Let me that mercy share.

229   *The pastoral office.*

1 Let Zion's watchmen all awake,
   And take th' alarm they give;
Now let them from the mouth of God
   Their awful charge receive.

2 'Tis not a cause of small import,
   The pastor's care demands;
But what might fill an angel's heart,
   And fill'd a Savior's hands.

3 They watch for souls for which the Lord
   Did heavenly bliss forego;
For souls, which must forever live
   In raptures, or in wo.

4 May they in Jesus, whom they preach,
   Their own Redeemer see;
And watch thou daily o'er their souls,
   That they may watch for thee.

230   *Come, Lord Jesus.*

1 O Jesus! at thy feet we wait,
   Till thou shalt bid us rise;
Restored to our unsinning state,—
   To love's sweet paradise.

2 Savior, from sin, we thee receive,
   From all indwelling sin;
Thy blood, we steadfastly believe,
   Shall make us truly clean.

3 Since thou wouldst have us free from sin,
   And pure as those above;
Make haste to bring thy nature in,
   And perfect us in love.

4 The counsel of thy love fulfil;
   Come quickly, gracious Lord!
Be it according to thy will,
   According to thy word.

5 O that the perfect grace were given
   Thy love diffused abroad:
O that our hearts were all a heaven,
   Forever fill'd with God.

231 AZMON.* C. M. From Glaser, by Dr. MASON.

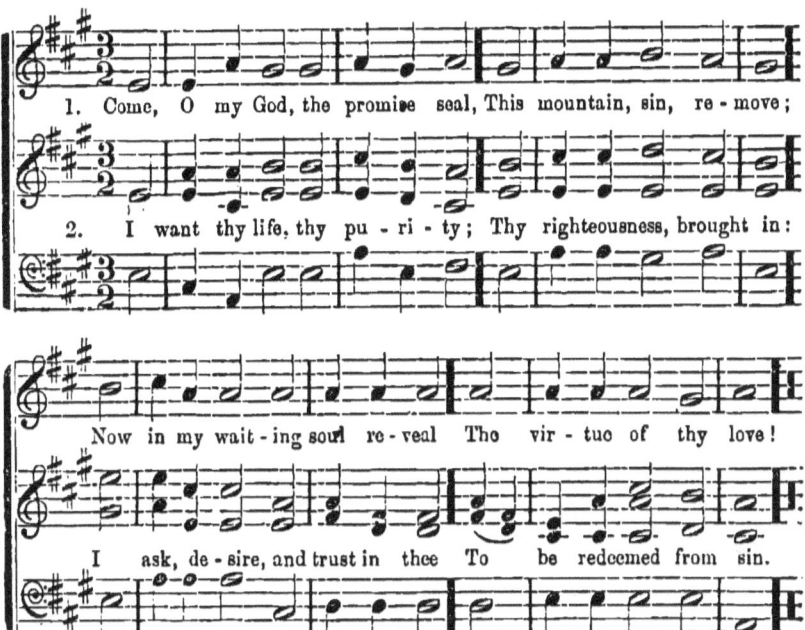

1. Come, O my God, the promise seal, This mountain, sin, remove; Now in my waiting soul reveal The virtue of thy love!

2. I want thy life, thy purity; Thy righteousness, brought in: I ask, desire, and trust in thee To be redeemed from sin.

3 For this, as taught by thee, I pray,
My inbred sin cast out;
Thou wilt, in me, thy power display:
I can no longer doubt.

4 Let anger, sloth, desire, and pride,
This moment be subdued;
Be cast into the crimson tide
Of my Redeemer's blood.

5 Savior, to thee my soul looks up,
My present Savior, thou!
In all the confidence of hope,
I claim the blessing now.

6 'Tis done; thou dost this moment save—
With full salvation bless;
Redemption through thy blood I have,
And spotless love and peace.

232 *Invoking God's presence and blessing.*

1 Within thy house, O Lord our God,
In majesty appear;
Make this a place of thine abode,
And shed thy blessings here.

2 As we thy mercy-seat surround,
Thy Spirit, Lord, impart:
And let thy Gospel's joyful sound,
With power reach every heart.

3 Here let the blind their sight obtain;
Here give the mourner rest;
Let Jesus here triumphant reign,
Enthroned in every breast.

4 Here let the voice of sacred joy
And fervent prayer arise,
Till higher strains our tongues employ,
In bliss beyond the skies.

233 *The blessedness of adoption.*

1 And can my heart aspire so high
To say,—My Father, God?
Lord, at thy feet I fain would lie
And learn to kiss the rod.

2 I would submit to all thy will,
For thou art good and wise;
Let each rebellious thought be still
Nor one faint murmur rise.

3 Thy love can cheer the darkest gloom,
And bid me wait serene,
Till hopes and joys immortal bloom,
And brighten all the scene.

4 My Father, God, permit my heart
To plead her humble claim,
And ask the bliss those words impart,
In my Redeemer's name.

* These tunes can be substituted, the one for the other

234 MELODY. C. M. WESTERN.

1. O for a faith that will not shrink, Though press'd by every foe,
2. That will not murmur or complain Beneath the chast'ning rod,

That will not tremble on the brink Of any earthly wo;
But in the hour of grief or pain, Will lean upon its God;—

3 A faith that shines more bright and clear
  When tempests rage without;
That when in danger knows no fear,
  In darkness feels no doubt;—
4 That bears, unmoved, the world's dread frown,
  Nor heeds its scornful smile;
That seas of trouble cannot drown,
  Or Satan's arts beguile;—
5 A faith that keeps the narrow way
  Till life's last hour is fled,
And with a pure and heavenly ray
  Illumes a dying bed.
6 Lord, give us such a faith as this,
  And then, whate'er may come,
We'll taste, e'en here, the hallow'd bliss
  Of an eternal home.

235   *The garner of God.*

1 Come, thou omniscient Son of man,
  Display thy sifting power;
Come, with thy Spirit's winn'wing fan,
  And thoroughly purge thy floor.
2 The chaff of sin, the accursed thing,
  Far from our souls be driven;
The wheat into thy garner bring,
  And lay us up for heaven.

3 Whate'er offends thy glorious eyes,
  Far from our hearts remove;
As dust before the whirlwind flies,
  Disperse it by thy love.
4 Then let us all thy fulness know,
  From every sin set free;
Saved to the utmost, saved below,
  And perfected in thee.

236   *Easter Sunday.*

1 The Lord of Sabbath let us praise,
  In concert with the blest,
Who, joyful in harmonious lays,
  Employ an endless rest.
2 Thus, Lord, while we remember thee,
  We blest and pious grow;
By hymns of praise we learn to be
  Triumphant here below.
3 On this glad day a brighter scene
  Of glory was display'd,
By the eternal Word, than when
  This universe was made.
4 He rises, who mankind has bought,
  With grief and pain extreme:
'Twas great to speak the world from naught;
  'Twas greater to redeem.

237 HEBER. C. M. — G. KINGSLEY. By permission.

1 When God revealed his gracious name,
　And changed my mournful state,
　My rapture seemed a pleasing dream,
　The grace appeared so great.
2 The world beheld the glorious change,
　And did thy hand confess;
　My tongue broke out in unknown strains,
　And sung surprising grace.
3 " Great is the work!" my neighbors cried,
　And owned thy power divine;
　" Great is the work!" my heart replied,—
　"And be the glory thine.
4 The Lord can clear the darkest skies,
　Can give us day for night;
　Make drops of sacred sorrow rise
　To rivers of delight.
5 Let those who sow in sadness, wait
　Till the fair harvest come:
　They shall confess their sheaves are great,
　And shout the blessings home.

238 *Anniversary.*
1 Hosanna, be the children's song,
　To Christ the children's King;
　His praise, to whom our souls belong,
　Let all the children sing.
2 From little ones to Jesus brought,
　Hosanna now be heard;
　Let little infants now be taught
　To lisp that lovely word.
3 Hosanna, sound from hill to hill,
　And spread from plain to plain,
　While louder, sweeter, clearer, still
　Woods echo to the strain.
4 Hosanna, on the wings of light,
　O'er earth and ocean fly,
　Till morn to eve, and noon to night,
　And heaven to earth, reply.
5 Hosanna, then, our song shall be;
　Hosanna to our King:
　This is the children's jubilee;
　Let all the children sing.

239 *Children in heaven.*
1 There is a glorious world of light,
　Above the starry sky,
　Where saints departed, clothed in white,
　Adore the Lord most high.
2 And hark, amid the sacred songs
　Those heavenly voices raise,
　Ten thousand thousand infant tongues
　Unite in perfect praise.
3 Those are the hymns that we shall know,
　If Jesus we obey;
　That is the place where we shall go,
　If found in wisdom's way.
4 Soon will our earthly race be run—
　Our mortal frame decay;
　Children and teachers, one by one,
　Must die and pass away.
5 Great God, impress this serious thought,
　To-day on every breast;
　That both the teachers and the taught,
　May dwell among the blest.

240. CROSS AND CROWN. C. M. — WESTERN MELODY.

1. Must Jesus bear the cross alone, And all the world go free?
No, there's a cross for every one, And there's a cross for me.

2. How happy are the saints above, Who once went sorrowing here;
But now they taste unmingled love, And joy without a tear.

3. The consecrated cross I'll bear, Till death shall set me free,
And then go home my crown, to wear, For there's a crown for me.

241 *Pleading the promises.*

1 Mercy alone can meet my case;
  For mercy, Lord, I cry:
Jesus, Redeemer, show thy face
  In mercy, or I die:—

2 I perish, and my doom were just;
  But wilt thou leave me?—No:
I hold thee fast, my hope, my trust;
  I will not let thee go.

3 Still sure to me thy promise stands,
  And ever must abide:
Behold it written on thy hands,
  And graven in thy side.

4 To this, this only will I cleave;
  Thy word is all my plea;
That word is truth, and I believe:
  Have mercy, Lord, on me.

242 *Struggling into liberty.*

1 Jesus, Redeemer, Savior, Lord,
  The weary sinner's Friend;
Come to my help, pronounce the word,
  And bid my troubles end.

2 Deliverance to my soul proclaim,
  And life, and liberty;
Shed forth the virtue of thy Name,
  And Jesus prove to me.

3 Faith to be healed thou know'st I have,
  For thou that faith hast given;
Thou canst, thou wilt, the sinner save,
  And make me meet for heaven.

4 Thou canst o'ercome this heart of mine;
  Thou wilt victorious prove;
For everlasting strength is thine,
  And everlasting love.

243 *The shadow of a great rock in a weary land.*

1 Now to the haven of thy breast,
  O Son of man, I fly;
Be thou my refuge and my rest,
  For O! the storm is high.

2 Protect me from the furious blast;
  My shield and shelter be:
Hide me, my Savior, till o'erpast
  The storm of sin I see.

3 As welcome as the water-spring
  Is to a barren place,
Jesus, descend on me, and bring
  Thy sweet, refreshing grace.

4 As o'er a parched and weary land,
  A rock extends its shade,
So hide me, Savior, with thy hand,
  And screen my naked head.

5 In all the times of my distress
  Thou hast my succor been;
And in my utter helplessness,
  Restraining me from sin;

6 How swift to save me didst thou move
  In every trying hour;
O still protect me with thy love,
  And shield me with thy power.

MEAR. C. M.

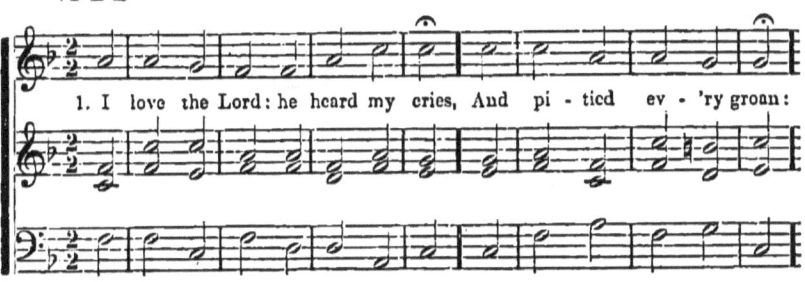

1. I love the Lord: he heard my cries, And pitied ev-'ry groan:
Long as I live, when troubles rise, I'll hasten to his throne.

2 I love the Lord: he bow'd his ear,
  And chas'd my grief away:
  O let my heart no more despair,
  While I have breath to pray.

3 The Lord beheld me, sore, distressed;
  He bade my pains remove:
  Return my soul to God, thy rest,
  For thou hast known his love.

245 *The returning prodigal.*

1 The long-lost son, with streaming eyes,
  From folly just awake,
  Reviews his wand'rings with surprise;
  His heart begins to break.

2 I starve, he cries, nor can I bear
  The famine in this land,
  While servants of my Father share
  The bounty of his hand.

3 With deep repentance I'll return,
  And seek my Father's face;
  Unworthy to be called a son,
  I'll ask a servant's place.

4 Far off the Father saw him move,—
  In pensive silence mourn,—
  And quickly ran, with arms of love,
  To welcome his return.

5 Through all the courts the tidings flew,
  And spread the joy around;
  The angels tuned their harps anew,
  The long-lost son is found.

246 *Light shining out of darkness.*

1 God moves in a mysterious way,
  His wonders to perform;
  He plants his footsteps in the sea,
  And rides upon the storm.

2 Deep in unfathomable mines
  Of never-failing skill,
  He treasures up his bright designs,
  And works his sov'reign will.

3 Ye fearful saints, fresh courage take:
  The clouds ye so much dread
  Are big with mercy, and shall break
  In blessings on your head.

4 Judge not the Lord by feeble sense,
  But trust him for his grace;
  Behind a frowning providence
  He hides a smiling face.

5 His purposes will ripen fast,
  Unfolding every hour:
  The bud may have a bitter taste,
  But sweet will be the flower.

6 Blind unbelief is sure to err,
  And scan his work in vain:
  God is his own interpreter,
  And he will make it plain.

247 BARBY. C. M.
TANSUR.

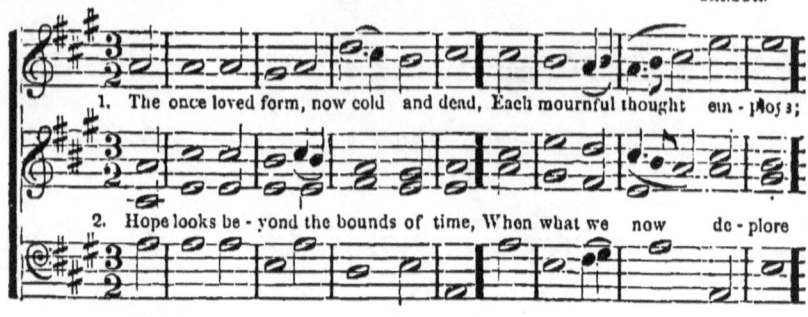

1. The once loved form, now cold and dead, Each mournful thought em-ploys;
2. Hope looks be-yond the bounds of time, When what we now de-plore

And na-ture weeps her com-forts fled, And with-ered all her joys.
Shall rise in full, im-mor-tal prime, And bloom to fade no more.

3 Cease, then, fond nature, cease thy tears!
  Religion points on high;
There everlasting spring appears,
  And joys that can not die.

248 Glory, mercy, grace.

1 Father, how wide thy glory shines,
  How high thy wonders rise!
Known through the earth by thousand signs,
  By thousands through the skies.

2 Those mighty orbs proclaim thy power;
  Their motions speak thy skill:
And on the wings of every hour
  We read thy patience still.

3 Part of thy Name divinely stands,
  On all thy creatures writ;
They show the labor of thy hands,
  Or impress of thy feet:

4 But, when we view thy strange design
  To save rebellious worms,
Where vengeance and compassion join
  In their divinest forms:

5 Here the whole Deity is known,
  Nor dares a creature guess
Which of the glories brighter shone,
  The justice or the grace.

6 Now the full glories of the Lamb
  Adorn the heavenly plains;

Bright seraphs learn Immanuel's name,
  And try their choicest strains.

7 O may I bear some humble part
  In that immortal song!
Wonder and joy shall tune my heart,
  And love command my tongue.

249 National deliverances ascribed to God.

1 O Lord, our fathers oft have told,
  In our attentive ears,
Thy wonders in their days perform'd,
  And in more ancient years.

2 'Twas not their courage, or their sword,
  To them salvation gave;
'Twas not their number, or their strength,
  That did their country save.

3 But thy right hand, thy powerful arm,
  Whose succor they implored,—
Thy providence protected them,
  Who thy great Name adored.

4 As thee their God our fathers own'd,
  So thou art still our King;
O, therefore, as thou didst to them,
  To us deliv'rance bring.

5 To thee the glory we ascribe,
  From whom salvation came;
In God, our shield, we will rejoice,
  And ever bless thy Name.

250 DUNFERMLINE. C. M.

From Ravenscroft's Psalter, 1621.

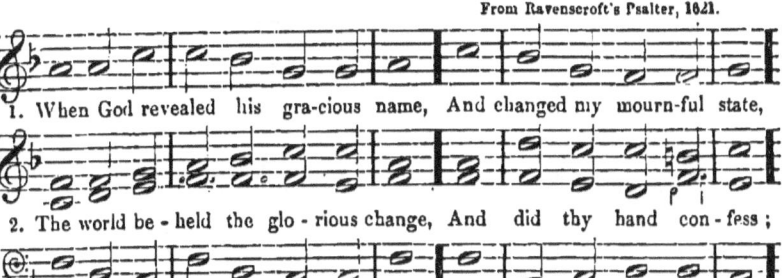

1. When God revealed his gracious name, And changed my mournful state,
My rapture seemed a pleasing dream, The grace appeared so great.

2. The world beheld the glorious change, And did thy hand confess;
My tongue broke out in unknown strains, And sung surprising grace.

3 "Great is the work," my neighbors cried,
And owned thy power divine;
"Great is the work," my heart replied,
"And be the glory thine."

4 The Lord can clear the darkest skies,
Can give us day for night;
Make drops of sacred sorrow rise
To rivers of delight.

5 Let those who sow in sadness, wait
Till the fair harvest come;
They shall confess their sheaves are great,
And shout the blessings home.

6 Though seed lie buried long in dust,
'Twill not deceive their hope;
The precious grain can ne'er be lost,
For grace insures the crop.

251 *God's pavilion.*

1 Grant me within thy courts a place,
Among thy saints a seat,
Forever to behold thy face,
And worship at thy feet:—

2 In thy pavilion to abide,
When storms of trouble blow,
And in thy tabernacle hide,
Secure from every foe.

3 Seek ye my face;—without delay,
When thus I hear thee speak,
My heart would leap for joy, and say,
Thy face, Lord, will I seek.

4 Then leave me not when griefs assail,
And earthly comforts flee;
When father, mother, kindred fail,
My God! remember me.

252 *To God all things are possible.*

1 O that thou wouldst the heavens rend,
In majesty come down,—
Thine arm omnipotent extend,
And seize me for thine own.

2 Descend, and let thy lightnings burn
The stubble of thy foe;
My sins o'erturn, o'erturn, o'erturn,
And make the mountains flow.

3 Thou my impetuous spirit guide,
And curb my headstrong will;
Thou only canst drive back the tide,
And bid the sun stand still.

4 What though I cannot break my chain,
Or e'er throw off my load;
The things impossible to men,
Are possible to God.

WARWICK. C. M.

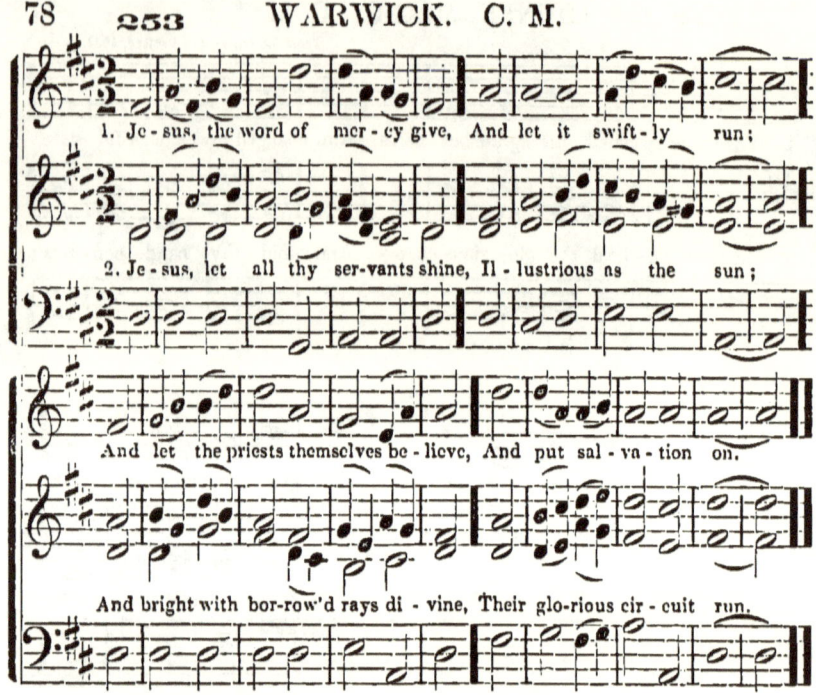

1. Je-sus, the word of mer-cy give, And let it swift-ly run;
And let the priests themselves be-lieve, And put sal-va-tion on.

2. Je-sus, let all thy ser-vants shine, Il-lustrious as the sun;
And bright with bor-row'd rays di-vine, Their glo-rious cir-cuit run.

3 Beyond the reach of mortals, spread
  Their light where'er they go;
And heavenly influences shed
  On all the world below.

4 As giants may they run their race,
  Exulting in their might;
As burning luminaries chase
  The gloom of hellish night.

5 As the bright Sun of righteousness,
  Their healing wings display;
And let their lustre still increase
  Unto the perfect day.

254
Sunday morning: Preparing for worship.

1 Lord, in the morning thou shalt hear
  My voice ascending high:
To thee will I direct my prayer,—
  To thee lift up mine eye:—

2 Up to the hills where Christ is gone,
  To plead for all his saints;
Presenting, at the Father's throne,
  Our songs and our complaints.

3 Thou art a God before whose sight
  The wicked shall not stand;
Sinners shall ne'er be thy delight,
  Nor dwell at thy right hand.

4 Now to thy house will I resort,
  To taste thy mercies there;
I will frequent thy holy court,
  And worship in thy fear.

5 O may thy spirit guide my feet
  In ways of righteousness;
Make every path of duty straight,
  And plain before my face.

255 *On earth as it is in heaven.*

1 Jesus, the Life, the Truth, the Way,
  In whom I now believe,
As taught by thee, in faith I pray,
  Expecting to receive.

2 Thy will by me on earth be done,
  As by the powers above,
Who always see thee on thy throne,
  And glory in thy love.

3 I ask in confidence the grace,
  That I may do thy will,
As angels, who behold thy face,
  And all thy words fulfil.

4 Surely I shall, the sinner I,
  Shall serve thee without fear,
If thou my nature sanctify
  In answer to my prayer.

256 STEPHENS. C. M.

1. Come Holy Ghost, inspire our songs With thine immortal flame;
Enlarge our hearts, unloose our tongues, To praise the Savior's name.

2. How great the riches of his grace! He left his throne above,
And, swift to save our ruin'd race, He flew on wings of love.

3 Now pardon, life, and joys divine,
In rich abundance flow,
For guilty rebels, dead in sin,
And doom'd to endless wo.

4 Th' almighty Former of the skies
Stoop'd to our low abode;
While angels view'd with wond'ring eyes,
And hail'd th' incarnate God.

5 Renew our souls with heavenly strength,
That we may fully prove
The height, and depth, and breadth, and length
Of such transcendent love.

257 *The world has lost its charms.*

1 Let worldly minds the world pursue;
It has no charms for me:
Once I admired its trifles too,
But grace hath set me free.

2 Its pleasures can no longer please,
Nor happiness afford:
Far from my heart be joys like these,
Now I have seen the Lord.

3 As by the light of opening day
The stars are all conceal'd,
So earthly pleasures fade away,
When Jesus is reveal'd.

4 Creatures no more divide my choice;
I bid them all depart:
His name, his love, his gracious voice,
Have fix'd my roving heart.

258
Are they not all ministering spirits?

1 Which of the monarchs of the earth
Can boast a guard like ours,—
Encircled from our second birth
With all the heavenly powers?

2 Myriads of bright, cherubic bands,
Sent by the King of kings,
Rejoice to bear us in their hands,
And shade us with their wings.

3 Angels, where'er we go, attend
Our steps, whate'er betide;
With watchful care their charge defend,
And evil turn aside.

4 Our lives those holy angels keep
From every hostile power;
And, unconcern'd, we sweetly sleep,
As Adam in his bower.

5 And when our spirits we resign,
On outstretch'd wings they bear,
And lodge us in the arms divine,
And leave us ever there.

HYMN. C. M.

From Modern Harp

1. As pants the hart for cooling streams, When heated in the chase, So longs my soul, O God, for thee, And thy refreshing grace.

2 For thee, my God, the living God,
 My thirsty soul doth pine;
O, when shall I behold thy face,
 Thou Majesty divine!

3 I sigh to think of happier days,
 When thou, O Lord, wast nigh;
When every heart was tuned to praise,
 And none more blest than I.

4 Why restless, why cast down, my soul?
 Hope still, and thou shalt sing
The praise of him who is thy God,
 Thy Savior, and thy King.

260 *Longing to be dissolved in love.*

1 Jesus hath died that I might live,
 Might live to God alone;
In him eternal life receive,
 And be in spirit one.

2 Savior, I thank thee for the grace,
 The gift unspeakable;
And wait with arms of faith t' embrace,
 And all thy love to feel.

3 My soul breaks out in strong desire
 The perfect bliss to prove;
My longing heart is all on fire
 To be dissolved in love.

4 Give me thyself; from every boast,
 From every wish set free;
Let all I am in thee be lost,
 But give thyself to me.

5 Thy gifts, alas! cannot suffice,
 Unless thyself be given;
Thy presence makes my paradise,
 And where thou art is Heaven.

261 *The immensity of His grace.*

1 What shall I do my God to love?
 My loving God to praise?
The length, and breadth, and height to prove,
 And depth of sov'reign grace?

2 Thy sov'reign grace to all extends,
 Immense and unconfined;
From age to age it never ends;
 It reaches all mankind.

3 Throughout the world its breadth is known,
 Wide as infinity:
So wide it never pass'd by one,
 Or it had pass'd by me.

4 My trespass was grown up to Heaven;
 But, far above the skies,
Through Christ abundantly forgiven,
 I see thy mercies rise.

5 The depth of all redeeming love,
 What angel tongue can tell?
O may I to the utmost prove
 The gift unspeakable.

EVAN. C. M.

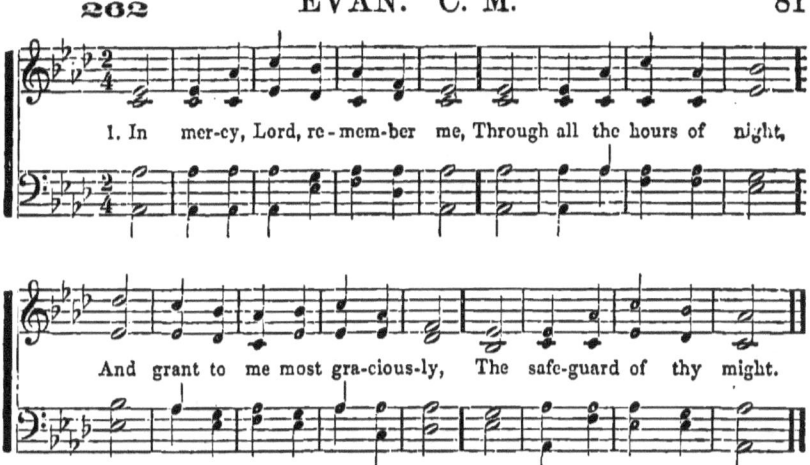

1. In mercy, Lord, remember me, Through all the hours of night, And grant to me most graciously, The safeguard of thy might.

2 With cheerful heart I close mine eyes,
Since thou wilt not remove;
O, in the morning let me rise
Rejoicing in thy love.

3 Or if this night should prove my last,
And end my transient days;
Lord, take me to thy promised rest,
Where I may sing thy praise.

263 *The fullness of God.*

1 Being of beings, God of love,
To thee our hearts we raise;
Thy all sustaining power we prove,
And gladly sing thy praise.

2 Thine, wholly thine, we pant to be;
Our sacrifice receive;
Made, and preserved, and saved by thee,
To thee ourselves we give.

3 Heavenward our every wish aspires,
For all thy mercy's store;
The sole return thy love requires,
Is that we ask for more.

4 For more we ask; we open then
Our hearts t' embrace thy will;
Turn and revive us, Lord, again;
With all thy fullness fill.

5 Come, Holy Ghost, the Savior's love
Shed in our hearts abroad;
So shall we ever live, and move,
And be with Christ in God.

264 *Peace in Believing.*

1 Jesus, to thee I now can fly,
On whom my help is laid:
Oppress'd by sins, I lift mine eye,
And see the shadows fade.

2 Believing on my Lord I find
A sure and present aid:
On thee alone my constant mind
Be every moment stay'd.

3 Whate'er in me seems wise, or good,
Or strong, I here disclaim:
I wash my garments in the blood
Of the atoning Lamb.

4 Jesus, my strength, my life, my rest,—
On thee will I depend,
Till summon'd to the marriage feast,
When faith in sight shall end.

265 *The loadstone of His love.*

1 Jesus, united by thy grace,
And each to each endear'd,
With confidence we seek thy face,
And know our prayer is heard.

2 Still let us own our common Lord,
And bear thine easy yoke,—
A band of love, a three-fold cord,
Which never can be broke.

3 Make us into one spirit drink;
Baptize into thy name;
And let us always kindly think,
And sweetly speak, the same.

4 Touch'd by the loadstone of thy love,
Let all our hearts agree;
And ever toward each other move,
And ever move toward thee.

5 To thee, inseparably join'd,
Let all our spirits cleave;
O may we all the loving mind
That was in thee receive.

BURFORD. C. M. Attributed to PURCELL.

1. Con-sid-'er all my sorrows, Lord, And thy de-liv'-rance send;
My soul for thy sal-va-tion faints; When will my troub-les end?

2. Had not thy word been my de-light When earth-ly joys were fled,
My soul, oppressed with sor-row's weight, Had sunk a-mong the dead.

3 Before I knew thy chastening rod,
My feet were apt to stray;
But now I learn to keep thy word,
Nor wander from thy way.

267   *Impending judgments.*

1 Come, let our souls adore the Lord,
Whose judgments yet delay;
Who yet suspends the lifted sword,
And gives us time to pray.

2 Great is our guilt, our fears are great,
But let us not despair;
Still open is the mercy-seat
To penitence and prayer.

3 Kind Intercessor, to thy love
This blessed hope we owe:
O let thy merits plead above,
While we implore below.

4 Though justice near thy awful throne
Attends thy dread command,
Lord, hear thy servants, hear thy Son,
And save a guilty land.

268   *Overwhelming grief.*

1 O thou, who in the olive shade,
When the dark hour came on,
Didst, with a breath of heavenly aid,
Strengthen thy suff'ring Son,—

2 O, by the anguish of that night,
Send us down blest relief;

Or, to the chasten'd, let thy might
Hallow this whelming grief.

3 And thou, that, when the starry sky
Saw the dread strife begun,
Didst teach adoring faith to cry,—
Father, thy will be done:—

4 By thy meek Spirit, thou, of all
That e'er have mourn'd the chief,
Blest Savior, if the stroke must fall,
Hallow this whelming grief.

269   *The death of a pastor.*

1 To thee, O God, when creatures fail,
Thy flock, deserted, flies;
And on the' eternal Shepherd's care,
Our steadfast hope relies.

2 When o'er thy faithful servant's dust
Thy saints assembled mourn,
In speedy tokens of thy grace,
O Zion's God, return!

3 The powers of nature all are thine,
And thine the aids of grace;
Thine arm has borne thy churches up,
Through each succeeding race.

4 Exert thy sacred influence here,
And here thy suppliants bless;
And change to strains of cheerful praise
Our accents of distress.

270 CHINA. C. M. — SWAN.

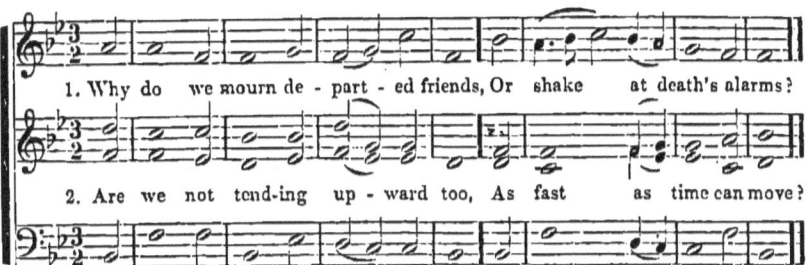

1. Why do we mourn de-part-ed friends, Or shake at death's alarms? 'Tis but the voice that Je-sus sends, To call them to his arms.

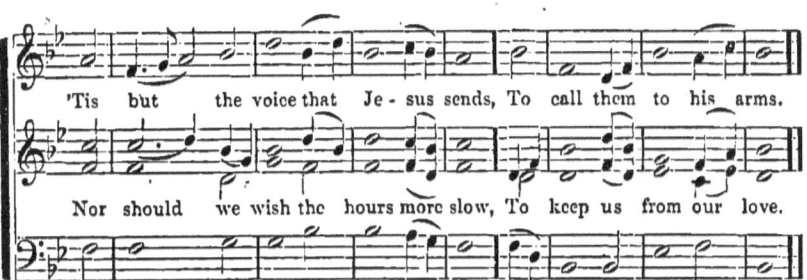

2. Are we not tend-ing up-ward too, As fast as time can move? Nor should we wish the hours more slow, To keep us from our love.

3 Why should we tremble to convey
  Their bodies to the tomb?
 There once the flesh of Jesus lay,
  And left a long perfume.

4 The graves of all his saints he blest,
  And softened every bed:
 Where should the dying members rest,
  But with their dying Head?

5 Thence he arose, ascending high,
  And showed our feet the way:
 Up to the Lord our flesh shall fly,
  At the great rising day.

6 Then let the last, loud trumpet sound,
  And bid our kindred rise:—
 Awake, ye nations under ground;
  Ye saints ascend the skies.

271 *Unwearied earnestness.*

1 Father, I stretch my hands to thee;
  No other help I know:
 If thou withdraw thyself from me,
  Ah! whither shall I go?

2 What did thy only Son endure,
  Before I drew my breath!
 What pain, what labor, to secure
  My soul from endless death!

3 O Jesus, could I this believe,
  I now should feel thy power;
 And all my wants thou wouldst relieve,
  In this accepted hour.

4 Author of faith! to thee I lift
  My weary, longing eyes:
 O let me now receive that gift,—
  My soul without it dies.

272 *The earnest, and pledge, of joys to come.*

1 Why should the children of a King
  Go mourning all their days?
 Great Comforter, descend and bring
  The tokens of thy grace.

2 Dost thou not dwell in all thy saints,
  And seal the heirs of heaven?
 When wilt thou banish my complaints,
  And show my sins forgiven?

3 Assure my conscience of her part
  In the Redeemer's blood;
 And bear thy witness with my heart,
  That I am born of God.

4 Thou art the earnest of his love,—
  The pledge of joys to come;
 May thy blest wings celestial Dove,
  Safely convey me home.

273 WINDSOR. C. M.

From the "SCOTCH PSALTER," 1615.

1. That aw-ful day will sure-ly come, Th' appoint-ed hour makes haste, When I must stand be-fore my Judge, And pass the sol-emn test.

2 Jesus, thou source of all my joys,
Thou ruler of my heart,
How could I bear to hear thy voice
Pronounce the word, Depart!

3 The thunder of that awful word
Would so torment my ear,
'Twould tear my soul asunder, Lord,
With most tormenting fear.

4 What, to be banished from my Lord,
And yet forbid to die;
To linger in eternal pain,
And death forever fly?—

5 O wretched state of deep despair,
To see my God remove,
And fix my doleful station where
I must not taste his love.

---

274 *Secrets of the heart made known.*

1 And must I be to judgment brought,
And answer in that day
For every vain and idle thought,
And every word I say?

2 Yes, every secret of my heart
Shall shortly be made known,
And I receive my just desert
For all that I have done.

3 How careful then ought I to live;
With what religious fear;
Who such a strict account must give
For my behavior here.

275 *Timely Penitence.*

1 When rising from the bed of death,
O'erwhelmed with guilt and fear,
I view my Maker face to face,—
O how shall I appear?

2 If yet, while pardon may be found,
And mercy may be sought,
My soul with inward horror shrinks,
And trembles at the thought:—

3 When thou, O Lord, shalt stand disclosed
In majesty severe,
And sit in judgment on my soul,—
O how shall I appear?

4 O may my broken, contrite heart,
Timely my sins lament;
And early, with repentant tears,
Eternal woe prevent.

5 Behold the sorrows of my heart,
Ere yet it be too late:
And hear my Savior's dying groan,
To give those sorrows weight.

6 For never shall my soul despair
Her pardon to secure,
Who knows thy only Son hath died
To make that pardon sure.

276 *Vain Repentances.*

1 Times without number have I pray'd,—
This only once forgive;
Relapsing when thy hand was stay'd,
And suffer'd me to live:

2 Yet now the kingdom of thy peace,
Lord to my heart restore;
Forgive my vain repentances,
And bid me sin no more.

---

* Dundee is the old name of this tune. The Scotch claim it as a national tune. BURNS has reference to it in the line, "Perhaps DUNDEE'S wild, warbling measures rise;" and another poet said of it, "Could I when being carried to my grave, wake up just to hear what tune would be sung at it, I should like it to be Dundee, or as we call it, Windsor."

277   BROOMSGROVE. C. M.

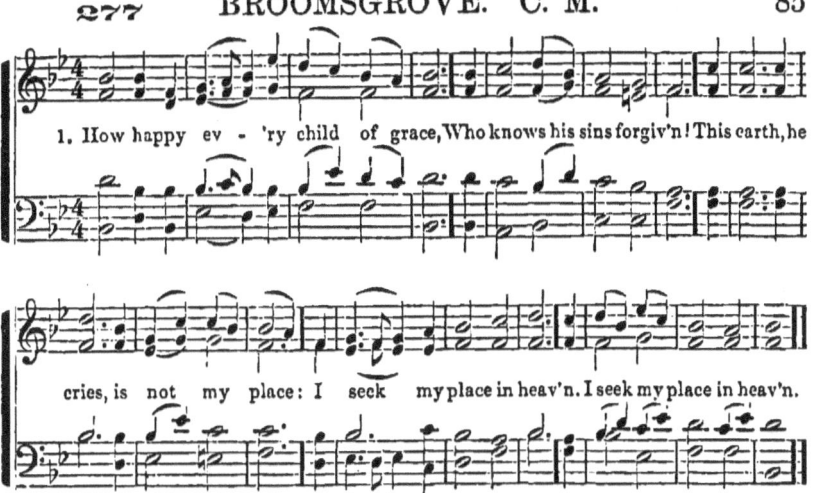

1. How happy ev-'ry child of grace, Who knows his sins forgiv'n! This earth, he cries, is not my place: I seek my place in heav'n. I seek my place in heav'n.

2 A country far from mortal sight,
   Yet, O, by faith I see;
The land of rest, the saints' delight,—
   The heaven prepared for me.

3 O what a blessed hope is ours!
   While here on earth we stay,
We more than taste the heavenly powers,
   And ante-date that day:

4 We feel the resurrection near,—
   Our life in Christ conceal'd,—
And with his glorious presence here
   Our earthen vessels fill'd.

5 O would he more of heaven bestow!
   And when the vessels break,
Let our triumphant spirits go
   To grasp the God we seek;

6 In rapturous awe on him to gaze,
   Who bought the sight for me;
And shout and wonder at his grace,
   To all eternity.

278   *Faith counted for righteousness.*

1 Father of Jesus Christ, my Lord,—
   My Savior, and my Head,—
I trust in thee, whose powerful word
   Hath raised him from the dead.

2 Thou know'st for my offence he died,
   And rose again for me;
Fully and freely justified,
   That I might live to thee.

3 O God! thy record I believe,
   In Abra'm's footsteps tread;
And wait, expecting to receive
   The Christ, the promised Seed.

4 Faith in thy power thou seest I have,
   For thou this faith hast wrought;
Dead souls thou callest from the grave,
   And speakest worlds from naught.

5 Eternal life to all mankind
   Thou hast in Jesus given:
And all who seek, in him shall find
   The happiness of heaven.

279   *Victorious faith.*

1 In hope, against all human hope,
   Self-desp'rate, I believe,—
Thy quick'ning word shall raise me up;
   Thou wilt thy Spirit give.

2 The thing surpasses all my thought;
   But faithful is my Lord;
Through unbelief I stagger not,
   For God hath spoke the word.

3 Faith, mighty faith, the promise sees,
   And looks to that alone;
Laughs at impossibilities,
   And cries,—It shall be done!

4 To thee, the glory of thy power
   And faithfulness I give;
I shall in Christ, at that glad hour,
   And Christ in me shall live.

5 Obedient faith, that waits on thee,
   Thou never wilt reprove;
But thou wilt form thy Son in me,
   And perfect me in love.

CORONATION. C. M.
HOLDEN.

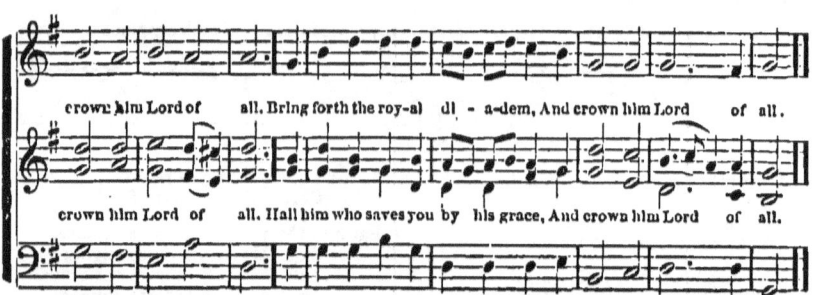

3 Sinners, whose love can ne'er forget,
  The wormwood and the gall;
  Go, spread your trophies at his feet,
  And crown him Lord of all.

4 Let every kindred, every tribe,
  On this terrestrial ball,
  To him all majesty ascribe,
  And crown him Lord of all.

5 O that with yonder sacred throng
  We at his feet may fall;
  We'll join the everlasting song,
  And crown him Lord of all.

281
The refining fire of the Holy Spirit.

1 Jesus, thine all-victorious love
  Shed in my heart abroad:
  Then shall my feet no longer rove,
  Rooted and fixed in God.

2 O that in me the sacred fire
  Might now begin to glow;
  Burn up the dross of base desire,
  And make the mountains flow.

3 O that it now from heaven might fall,
  And all my sins consume:
  Come, Holy Ghost, for thee I call;
  Spirit of burning, come.

4 Refining fire, go through my heart;
  Illuminate my soul;
  Scatter thy life through every part,
  And sanctify the whole.

5 My steadfast soul, from falling free,
  Shall then no longer move;
  While Christ is all the world to me,
  And all my heart is love.

282
Perfect harmony, and joy unspeakable.

1 All praise to our redeeming Lord,
  Who joins us by his grace;
  And bids us, each to each restored,
  Together seek his face.

2 He bids us build each other up;
  And, gather'd into one,
  To our high calling's glorious hope,
  We hand in hand go on.

3 The gift which he on one bestows,
  We all delight to prove;
  The grace through every vessel flows,
  In purest streams of love.

4 E'en now we think and speak the same,
  And cordially agree;
  United all through Jesus' name;
  In perfect harmony.

5 We all partake the joy of one;
　The common peace we feel;
　A peace to sensual minds unknown,—
　A joy unspeakable.

6 And if our fellowship below
　In Jesus be so sweet,
　What height of rapture shall we know
　When round his throne we meet!

283 *Praises to the incarnate Son.*

1 O for a thousand seraph tongues
　To bless the' Incarnate Word!
　O for a thousand thankful songs
　In honor of my Lord!

2 Come, tune afresh your golden lyres,
　Ye angels round the throne;
　Ye saints, in all your sacred choirs,
　Adore th' eternal Son.

284 *Faith sees the final triumph.*

1 Am I a soldier of the cross,—
　A foll'wer of the Lamb,—
　And shall I fear to own his cause,
　Or blush to speak his name?

2 Must I be carried to the skies
　On flowery beds of ease;
　While others fought to win the prize,
　And sailed through bloody seas?

3 Are there no foes for me to face?
　Must I not stem the flood?
　Is this vile world a friend to grace,
　To help me on to God?

4 Since I must fight if I would reign,
　Increase my courage, Lord;
　I 'll bear the toil, endure the pain,
　Supported by thy word.

5 Thy saints in all this glorious war
　Shall conquer, though they die:
　They see the triumph from afar,—
　By faith they bring it nigh.

6 When that illustrious day shall rise,
　And all thy armies shine
　In robes of vict'ry through the skies,
　The glory shall be thine.

285 *The minister's only business.*

1 Jesus, the name high over all,
　In hell, or earth, or sky;
　Angels and men before it fall,
　And devils fear and fly.

2 Jesus, the name to sinners dear,—
　The name to sinners given;
　It scatters all their guilty fear;
　It turns their hell to heaven.

3 Jesus the pris'ner's fetters breaks,
　And bruises Satan's head;
　Power into strengthless souls he speaks,
　And life into the dead.

4 O that the world might taste and see
　The riches of his grace;
　The arms of love that compass me,
　Would all mankind embrace.

5 His only righteousness I show,—
　His saving truth proclaim;
　'Tis all my business here below,
　To cry,—Behold the Lamb!

6 Happy, if with my latest breath
　I may but gasp his name;
　Preach him to all, and cry in death,
　Behold, behold the Lamb.

286 *The good pleasure of His will.*

1 I know that my Redeemer lives,
　And ever prays for me:
　A token of his love he gives,—
　A pledge of liberty.

2 I find him lifting up my head;
　He brings salvation near;
　His presence makes me free indeed,
　And he will soon appear.

3 He wills that I should holy be!
　What can withstand his will?
　The counsel of his grace in me
　He surely shall fulfil.

4 Jesus, I hang upon thy word;
　I steadfastly believe
　Thou wilt return, and claim me, Lord,
　And to thyself receive.

5 When God is mine, and I am his,
　Of paradise possessed,
　I taste unutterable bliss,
　And everlasting rest.

Doxology.

　To Father, Son, and Holy Ghost,
　　Who sweetly all agree,
　To save a world of sinners lost,
　　Eternal glory be.

COMMUNION. C. M.

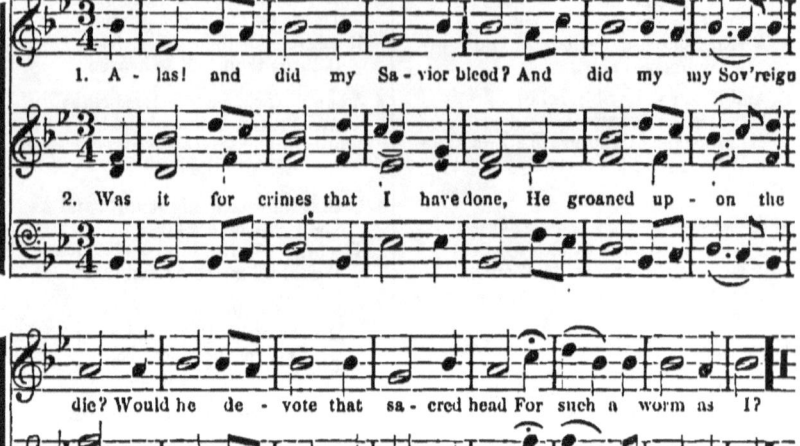

1. Alas! and did my Savior bleed? And did my my Sov'reign die? Would he devote that sacred head For such a worm as I?

2. Was it for crimes that I have done, He groaned upon the tree! Amazing pity! grace unknown! And love beyond degree!

3 Well might the sun in darkness hide,
   And shut his glories in,
When Christ, the mighty Maker, died,
   For man, the creature's sin.

4 Thus might I hide my blushing face
   While his dear cross appears;
Dissolve my heart in thankfulness,
   And melt mine eyes to tears.

5 But drops of grief can ne'er repay
   The debt of love I owe;
Here, Lord, I give myself away,—
   'Tis all that I can do.

288 He died for thee.

1 Behold the Savior of mankind!
   Nail'd to the shameful tree;
How vast the love that him inclined
   To bleed and die for thee!

2 Hark! how he groans, while nature shakes,
   And earth's strong pillars bend:
The temple's veil in sunder breaks,—
   The solid marbles rend.

3 'Tis done! the precious ransom's paid!
   Receive my soul! he cries:
See where he bows his sacred head;
   He bows his head, and dies.

4 But soon he'll break death's envious chain,
   And in full glory shine:
O Lamb of God, was ever pain,
   Was ever love, like thine.

289 Approaching the table.

1 Jesus, at whose supreme command,
   We now approach to God,
Before us in thy vesture stand,
   Thy vesture dipp'd in blood.

2 Now, Savior, now thyself reveal,
   And make thy nature known;
Affix thy blessed Spirit's seal,
   And stamp us for thine own.

3 The tokens of thy dying love,
   O let us all receive,
And feel the quick'ning Spirit move,
   And sensibly believe.

4 The cup of blessing, blest by thee,
   Let it thy blood impart;
The bread thy mystic body be,
   To cheer each languid heart.

5 The living bread sent down from heaven,
   In us vouchsafe to be:
Thy flesh for all the world is given,
   And all may live by thee.

BALERMA. C. M.
WILSON.

1. Come, humble sinner! in whose breast, A thousand thoughts revolve;
Come with your guilt and fear oppressed, And make this last resolve.

2. I'll go to Jesus, though my sin Like mountains round me close;
I know his courts, I'll enter in, Whatever may oppose.

3 Prostrate I'll lie before his throne,
And there my guilt confess;
I'll tell him, I'm a wretch undone
Without his sov'reign grace.

4 Perhaps he will admit my plea,
Perhaps will hear my prayer,
But, if I perish, I will pray,
And perish only there.

5 I can but perish if I go—
I am resolved to try;
For if I stay away, I know
I must forever die.

291
A perfect heart the Redeemer's throne.

1 O for a heart to praise my God,
A heart from sin set free;—
A heart that always feels thy blood,
So freely spilt for me:—

2 A heart resigned, submissive, meek,
My great Redeemer's throne ;
Where only Christ is heard to speak,—
Where Jesus reigns alone.

3 O for a lowly, contrite heart,
Believing, true, and clean ;
Which neither life nor death can part
From him that dwells within :—

4 A heart in every thought renewed,
And full of love divine ;
Perfect, and right, and pure, and good,
A copy, Lord, of thine.

5 Thy nature, gracious Lord, impart;
Come quickly from above ;
Write thy new name upon my heart,—
Thy new, best name of Love.

292
The kingdoms are but one.

1 Happy the souls to Jesus joined,
And saved by grace alone ;
Walking in all his ways, they find
Their heaven on earth begun.

2 The church, triumphant in thy love,
Their mighty joys we know :
They sing the Lamb in hymns above,
And we in hymns below.

3 Thee in thy glorious realm they praise,
And bow before thy throne ;
We in the kingdom of thy grace :
The kingdoms are but one.

4 The holy to the holiest leads,
And thence our spirits rise ;
For he that in thy statutes treads,
Shall meet thee in the skies.

ST. ANN. C. M.

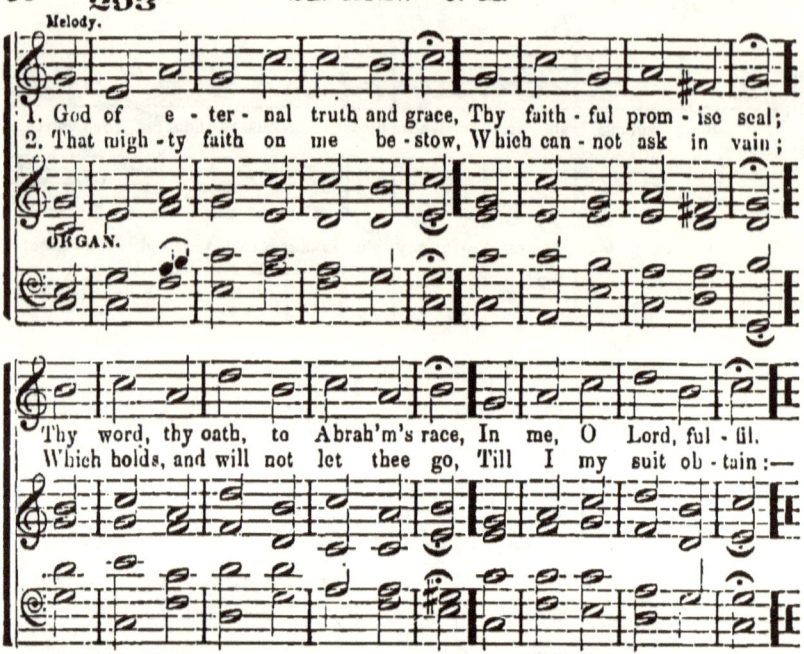

1. God of eternal truth and grace, Thy faithful promise seal;
Thy word, thy oath, to Abrah'm's race, In me, O Lord, fulfil.

2. That mighty faith on me bestow, Which cannot ask in vain;
Which holds, and will not let thee go, Till I my suit obtain:—

3 Till thou into my soul inspire
  The perfect love unknown;
And tell my infinite desire,—
  Whate'er thou wilt, be done.

4 On me the faith divine bestow,
  Which doth the mountain move;
And all my spotless life shall show
  Th' omnipotence of love.

294 *And so fulfil the law of Christ.*
1 Try us, O God, and search the ground
  Of every sinful heart;
Whate'er of sin in us is found,
  O bid it all depart.

2 If to the right or left we stray,
  Leave us not comfortless;
But guide our feet into the way
  Of everlasting peace.

3 Help us to help each other, Lord,
  Each other's cross to bear;
Let each his friendly aid afford,
  And feel his brother's care.

4 Help us to build each other up;
  Our little stock improve;
Increase our faith, confirm our hope,
  And perfect us in love.

5 Up into thee, our living Head,
  Let us in all things grow,
Till thou hast made us free indeed,
  And spotless here below.

6 Then, when the mighty work is wrought,
  Receive thy ready bride:
Give us in heaven a happy lot
  With all the sanctified.

295 *Victory over the fears of death.*
1 O for an overcoming faith,
  To cheer my dying hours,—
To triumph o'er approaching death,
  And all his frightful powers.

2 Joyful, with all the strength I have,
  My quiv'ring lips should sing,
Where is thy boasted vict'ry, Grave?
  And where, O Death, thy sting?

3 If sin be pardon'd, I'm secure;
  Death has no sting beside:
The law gives sin its damning power,
  But Christ, my ransom, died.

4 Now to the God of victory
  Immortal thanks be paid,—
Who makes us conqu'rers, while we die,
  Through Christ, our living Head.

TALLIS. C. M.

296 THOMAS TALLIS, 1565.

1. O God! our help in ages past, Our hope for years to come, Our shelter from the stormy blast, And our eternal home.—

2 Under the shadow of thy throne
Still may we dwell secure;
Sufficient is thine arm alone,
And our defence is sure.

3 Before the hills in order stood,
Or earth received her frame,
From everlasting thou art God,
To endless years the same.

4 A thousand ages, in thy sight,
Are like an evening gone;
Short as the watch that ends the night,
Before the rising sun.

5 Time, like an ever-rolling stream,
Bears all its sons away;
They fly, forgotten, as a dream
Dies at the opening day.

6 The busy tribes of flesh and blood,
With all their cares and fears,
Are carried downward by the flood,
And lost in foll'wing years.

7 O God, our help in ages past,
Our hope for years to come;
Be thou our guide while life shall last,
And our perpetual home!

297 *The affections crucified.*
1 Jesus, my life, thyself apply;
Thy Holy Spirit breathe:
My vile affections, crucify;
Conform me to thy death.

2 Conqu'ror of hell, and earth, and sin,
Still with the rebel strive:
Enter my soul and work within,
And kill and make alive.

3 More of thy life, and more I have,
As the old Adam dies;
Bury me, Savior, in thy grave,
That I with thee may rise.

4 Reign in me, Lord; thy foes control,
That would not own thy sway;
Diffuse thine image through my soul;
Shine to the perfect day.

5 Scatter the last remains of sin,
And seal me thine abode;
O make me glorious all within,—
A temple built by God!

298 *Trusting in the mercy of God.*
1 Why, O my soul, O why depress'd,
And whence thine anxious fears?
Let former mercies fix thy trust,
And check thy rising tears.

2 Affliction is a stormy deep,
Where wave succeeds to wave;
Though o'er my head the billows sweep,
I know the Lord can save.

3 His grace and mercy trust, my soul,
Nor murmur at his rod:
In vain the waves of trouble roll,
While he is still thy God.

299. CHRISTMAS. C. M. — HANDEL.

1. With joy we hail the sacred day
Which God has call'd his own;
With joy the summons we obey,
To worship at his throne.

2 Thy chosen temple, Lord, how fair!
As here thy servants throng
To breathe the humble, fervent prayer,
And pour the grateful song.

3 Spirit of grace! O deign to dwell
Within thy Church below;
Make her in holiness excel,
With pure devotion glow.

4 Let peace within her walls be found—
Let all her sons unite,
To spread with holy zeal around,
Her clear and shining light.

300 *A Blessing on the Word.*

1 Once more we come before our God;
Once more his blessing ask:
O may not duty seem a load,
Nor worship prove a task.

2 Father, thy quick'ning Spirit send
From heaven, in Jesus' name,
And bid our waiting minds attend,
And put our souls in frame.

3 May we receive the word we hear,
Each in an honest heart;
And keep the precious treasure there,
And never with it part.

4 To seek thee, all our hearts dispose;
To each thy blessings suit;
And let the seed thy servant sows,
Produce abundant fruit.

301 *Triumphant Joy.*

1 My God, the spring of all my joys,
The life of my delights;
The glory of my brightest days,
And comfort of my nights.

2 In darkest shades, if thou appear,
My dawning is begun;
Thou art my soul's bright morning star
And thou my rising sun.

3 The opening heavens around me shine
With beams of sacred bliss,
If Jesus shows his mercy mine,
And whispers I am his.

4 My soul would leave this heavy clay
At that transporting word,
Run up with joy the shining way,
To see and praise my Lord.

5 Fearless of hell and ghastly death,
I'd break through every foe;
The wings of love and arms of faith
Would bear me conqu'ror through.

302 *Waiting upon the Lord.*

1 Still, for thy loving kindness, Lord,
I in thy temple wait;
I look to find thee in thy word,
Or at thy table meet.

2 Here, in thine own appointed ways,
I wait to learn thy will;
Silent I stand before thy face,
And hear thee say,— Be still!

3 Be still! and know that I am God;—
'Tis all I live to know;
To feel the virtue of thy blood,
And spread its praise below.

4 I wait my vigor to renew,—
Thine image to retrieve;
The veil of outward things pass through,
And gasp in thee to live.

303 NOTTING HILL. C. M. — C. H. PURDAY. By Permission.

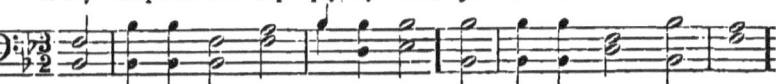
1. My Shepherd will sup-ply my need, Je-ho-vah is his name:

In pas-tures fresh he makes me feed, Be-side the liv-ing stream.

2 He brings my wandering spirit back,
When I forsake his ways;
And leads me for his mercy's sake,
In paths of truth and grace.

3 When I walk through the shades of death,
Thy presence is my stay;
A word of thy supporting breath
Drives all my fears away.

4 Thy hand, in spite of all my foes,
Doth still my table spread;
My cup with blessings overflows,
Thine oil anoints my head.

5 The sure provisions of my God
Attend me all my days;
O may thy house be my abode,
And all my work be praise!

6 There would I find a settled rest,
While others go and come;
No more a stranger or a guest,
But like a child at home

304 *The only solace in sorrow.*

1 O thou who driest the mourner's tear,
How dark this world would be,
If, when deceived and wounded here,
We could not fly to thee.

2 The friends who in our sunshine live,
When winter comes, are flown;
And he who has but tears to give,
Must weep those tears alone.

3 But Christ can heal that broken heart,
Which, like the plants that throw
Their fragrance from the wounded part,
Breathes sweetness out of woe.

4 When joy no longer soothes or cheers,
And e'en the hope that threw
A moment's sparkle o'er our tears
Is dimm'd and vanished too;

5 O who could bear life's stormy doom,
Did not his wing of love,
Come brightly wafting through the gloom,
Our peace-branch from above.

6 Then sorrow touch'd by him, grows bright,
With more than rapture's ray;
As darkness shows us worlds of light,
We never saw by day.

305 *Secret communion with God.*

1 Sweet is the prayer whose holy stream
In earnest pleading flows;
Devotion dwells upon the theme,
And warm and warmer glows.

2 Faith grasps the blessing she desires;
Hope points the upward gaze;
And Love, celestial Love, inspires
The eloquence of praise.

3 But sweeter far the still small voice,
Unheard by human ear,
When God has made the heart rejoice
And dried the bitter tear.

4 No accents flow, no words ascend;
All utt'rance faileth there;
But God himself doth comprehend,
And answer, silent prayer.

HOWARD. C. M.

1. Give me the wings of faith, to rise With-in the veil, and see

The saints a-bove, how great their joys, How bright their glo-ries be!

2 Once they were mourning here below,
   And poured out cries and tears;
They wrestled hard, as we do now,
   With sins, and doubts, and fears.

3 I ask them, whence their victory came;
   They, with united breath,
Ascribe their conquest to the Lamb—
   Their triumph to his death.

4 They marked the footsteps he had trod,
   His zeal inspired their breast;
And following their incarnate God,
   Possessed the promised rest.

5 Our glorious Leader claims our praise,
   For his own pattern given:
While the long cloud of witnesses
   Show the same path to heaven.

307 *Sufficiency and freeness.*

1 O what amazing words of grace
   Are in the gospel found!
Suited to every sinner's case,
   Who knows the joyful sound.

2 Poor, sinful, thirsty, fainting souls,
   Are freely welcome here:
Salvation, like a river, rolls,
   Abundant, free, and clear.

3 Come, then, with all your wants and
     wounds,
   Your every burden bring;

Here love, unchanging love, abounds,—
   A deep, celestial spring.

4 Whoever will — O gracious word!—
   May of this stream partake:
Come, thirsty souls, and bless the Lord,
   And drink, for Jesus' sake.

308 *The refining fire of the
     Holy Spirit.*

1 Jesus, thine all-victorious love
   Shed in my heart abroad;
Then shall my feet no longer rove,
   Rooted and fix'd in God.

2 O that in me the sacred fire
   Might now begin to glow!
Burn up the dross of base desire,
   And make the mountains flow.

3 O that it now from heaven might fall,
   And all my sins consume:
Come, Holy Ghost, for thee I call;
   Spirit of burning, come.

4 Refining fire, go through my heart;
   Illuminate my soul:
Scatter thy life through every part,
   And sanctify the whole.

5 My steadfast soul, from falling free,
   Shall then no longer move;
While Christ is all the world to me,
   And all my heart is love.

309 ZERAH. C. M. Dr. L. Mason. **95**

1. To us a Child of Hope is born, To us a Son is given:
2. His name shall be the Prince of Peace, For-ev-er-more a-dored:
Him shall the tribes of earth o-bey, Him, all the hosts of heav'n.
The Won-der-ful, the Coun-sel-or, The great and mighty Lord.

3 His power increasing, still shall spread;
His reign no end shall know:
Justice shall guard his throne above
And peace abound below.

4 To us a Child of Hope is born,
To us a Son is given —
The Wonderful, the Counselor,
The mighty Lord of Heaven.

310 *The rapture of love.*

1 O, 'tis delight without alloy,
Jesus, to hear thy name:
My spirit leaps with inward joy;
I feel the sacred flame.

2 My passions hold a pleasing reign,
When love inspires my breast,—
Love, the divinest of the train,
The sov'reign of the rest.

3 This is the grace must live and sing,
When faith and hope shall cease,
And sound from every joyful string
Through all the realms of bliss.

4 Swift I ascend the heavenly place,
And hasten to my home;
I leap to meet thy kind embrace,
I come, O Lord, I come.

5 Sink down, ye separating hills;
Let sin and death remove:
'Tis love that drives my chariot wheels,
And death must yield to love.

311 *The desire of nations.*

1 Come, thou Desire of all thy saints,
Our humble strains attend,
While with our praises and complaints,
Low at thy feet we bend.

2 How should our songs, like those above,
With warm devotion rise;
How should our souls, on wings of love,
Mount upward to the skies.

3 Come, Lord, thy love alone can raise
In us the heavenly flame;
Then shall our lips resound thy praise,
Our hearts adore thy name.

4 Now, Savior, let thy glory shine,
And fill thy dwellings here,
Till life, and love, and joy divine,
A heaven on earth appear.

5 Then shall our hearts enraptured say,—
Come, great Redeemer, come,
And bring the bright, the glorious day,
That calls thy children home.

312

ANTIOCH. C. M.

ARR. BY DR. MASON.

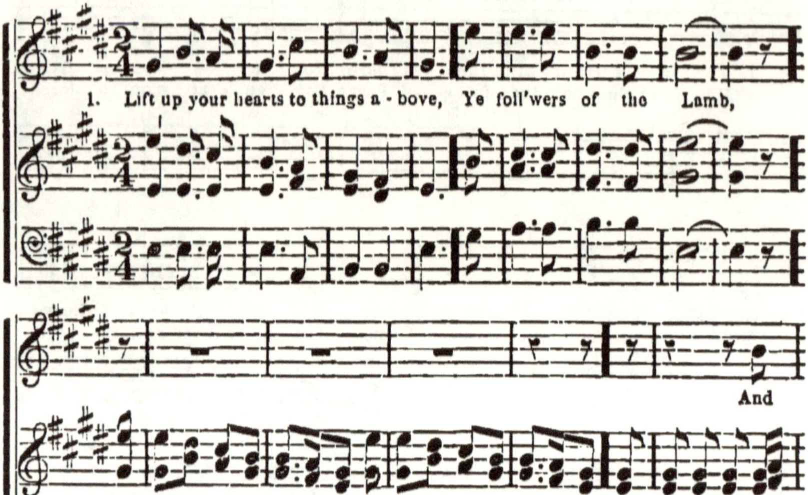
1. Lift up your hearts to things a - bove, Ye foll'wers of the Lamb,
And
And join with us to praise his love, And glo-ri - fy his
glo-ri-fy his name.............................. And glo - ri - fy his name.
name. And glo-ri - fy his name, And glo - ri, glo - ri - fy his name.

2 To Jesus' name give thanks and sing,
Whose mercies never end:
Rejoice! rejoice! the Lord is King;
The King is now our Friend.

3 We for his sake count all things loss;
On earthly good look down;
And joyfully sustain the cross,
Till we receive the crown.

4 O let us stir each other up,
Our faith by works t' approve,—
By holy, purifying hope,
And the sweet task of love.

5 Let all who for the promise wait,
The Holy Ghost receive;
And, raised to our unsinning state,
With God in Eden live:—

6 Live, till the Lord in glory come,
And wait his heaven to share:
He now is fitting up your home;
Go on, we'll meet you there.

313 *Glory to God in the highest.*

1 Mortals, awake, with angels join,
  And chant the solemn lay;
  Joy, love, and gratitude combine,
  To hail th' auspicious day.

2 In heaven the rapt'rous song began,
  And sweet seraphic fire
  Through all the shining legions ran,
  And strung and tuned the lyre.

3 Swift through the vast expanse it flew,
  And loud the echo rolled;
  The theme, the song, the joy, was new,—
  'Twas more than heaven could hold.

4 Down through the portals of the sky
  The impetuous torrent ran;
  And angels flew, with eager joy,
  To bear the news to man.

5 With joy the chorus we repeat,—
  Glory to God on high!
  Good will and peace are now complete—
  Jesus was born to die.

6 Hail, Prince of Life, forever hail!
  Redeemer, Brother, Friend!
  Though earth, and time, and life, shall fail,
  Thy praise shall never end.

314 *Design and object of His advent.*

1 Hark, the glad sound! the Savior comes,
  The Savior, promised long;
  Let every heart prepare a throne,
  And every voice a song.

2 He comes, the pris'ner to release,
  In Satan's bondage held;
  The gates of brass before him burst,
  The iron fetters yield.

3 He comes, from thickest films of vice
  To clear the mental ray,
  And on the eyes oppressed with night
  To pour celestial day.

4 He comes, the broken heart to bind,
  The wounded soul to cure,
  And, with the treasures of his grace,
  T' enrich the humble poor.

5 Our glad hosannas, Prince of peace,
  Thy welcome shall proclaim,
  And heaven's eternal arches ring
  With thy beloved name.

315 *Christ the conqueror.*

1 Jesus, immortal King, arise;
  Assert thy rightful sway;
  Till earth, subdued, its tribute brings,
  And distant lands obey.

2 Ride forth, victorious conqu'ror, ride,
  Till all thy foes submit,
  And all the powers of hell resign
  Their trophies at thy feet.

3 Send forth thy word, and let it fly
  The spacious earth around,
  Till every soul beneath the sun
  Shall hear the joyful sound.

4 O may the great Redeemer's Name
  Through every clime be known,
  And heathen gods, forsaken, fall,
  And Jesus reign alone.

5 From sea to sea, from shore to shore,
  Be thou, O Christ, adored,
  And earth, with all her millions shout,
  Hosannas to the Lord.

316 *Worthy of ceaseless praise from all his creatures.*

1 Praise ye the Lord, ye immortal choirs
  That fill the worlds above;
  Praise him who formed you of his fires,
  And feeds you with his love.

2 Shine to his praise, ye crystal skies,
  The floor of his abode;
  Or veil in shades your thousand eyes
  Before your brighter God.

3 Thou restless globe of golden light,
  Whose beams create our days,
  Join with the silver queen of night,
  To own your borrowed rays.

4 Thunder and hail, and fire and storms,
  The troops of his command,
  Appear in all your dreadful forms,
  And speak his awful hand.

5 Shout to the Lord, ye surging seas,
  In your eternal roar;
  Let wave to wave resound his praise,
  And shore reply to shore.

6 Thus while the meaner creatures sing,
  Ye mortals, catch the sound;
  Echo the glories of your King
  Through all the nations round.

ARLINGTON. C. M.

Dr. ARNE.

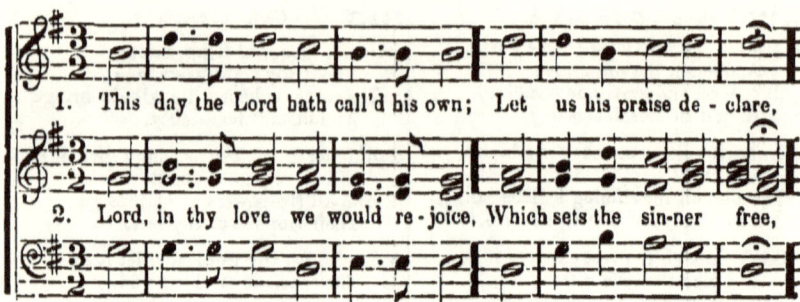

1. This day the Lord hath call'd his own; Let us his praise declare,
Fix our desires on him alone, And seek his face with prayer.

2. Lord, in thy love we would rejoice, Which sets the sinner free,
And, with united heart and voice, Devote these hours to thee.

3 Now let the world's delusive things
   No more our thoughts employ,
But faith be taught to stretch her wings
   Tow'rd heaven's unfailing joy.

4 O let these earthly Sabbaths, Lord,
   Be to our welfare blest;
The purest comfort here afford,
   And fit us for our rest.

318 *Pray without ceasing.*
1 Shepherd Divine, our wants relieve
   In this our evil day;
To all thy tempted followers give
   The power to watch and pray.

2 Long as our fiery trials last,—
   Long as the cross we bear,—
O let our souls on thee be cast
   In never-ceasing prayer.

3 Till thou, thy perfect love impart;
   Till thou thyself bestow,
Be this the cry of every heart,—
   I will not let thee go:—

4 I will not let thee go, unless
   Thou tell thy name to me;
With all thy great salvation bless,
   And make me all like thee.

5 Then let me on the mountain-top
   Behold thy open face;
Where faith in sight is swallowed up,
   And prayer in endless praise.

319 *The covenant with Abraham.*
1 How large the promise, how divine,
   To Abrah'm and his seed,—
I am a God to thee and thine,
   Supplying all their need.

2 The words of his unbounded love
   From age to age endure;
The Angel of the Cov'nant proves
   And seals the blessings sure.

3 Jesus the ancient faith confirms,
   To our great Father given;
He takes our children to his arms,
   And calls them heirs of heaven.

4 O God, how faithful are thy ways!
   Thy love endures the same;
Nor from the promise of thy grace
   Blots out our children's name.

320 *Sweetness of Jesus' name.*
1 Jesus, the very thought of thee
   With sweetness fills my breast;
But sweeter far thy face to see,
   And in thy presence rest.

2 Nor voice can sing, nor heart can frame,
   Nor can the memory find
A sweeter sound than thy blest name,
   O Savior of mankind!

321   CORINTH. C. M.   DR. LOWELL MASON. **99**

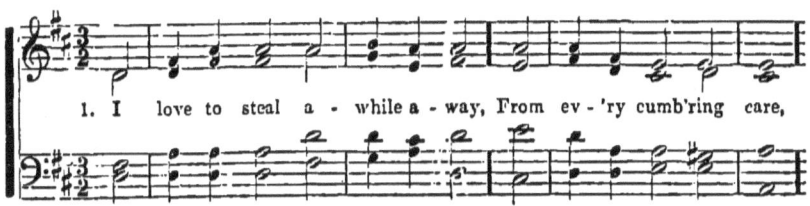

1. I love to steal a-while a-way, From ev-'ry cumb'ring care,

And spend the hours of setting day In humble, grate-ful prayer.

2 I love in solitude to shed
   The penitential tear,
And all his promises to plead
   Where none but God can hear

3 I love to think on mercies past,
   And future good implore,—
And all my cares and sorrows cast
   On him whom I adore.

4 I love by faith to take a view
   Of brighter scenes in heaven;
The prospect doth my strength renew,
   While here by tempests driven.

5 Thus, when life's toilsome day is o'er,
   May its departing ray
Be calm as this impressive hour,
   And lead to endless day.

322   *Sympathy with the afflicted.*

1 Father of mercies, send thy grace,
   All powerful, from above,
To form in our obedient souls
   The image of thy love.

2 O! may our sympathizing breasts
   That generous pleasure know,
Kindly to share in others' joy,
   And weep for others' woe.

3 When poor and helpless sons of grief
   In deep distress are laid,
Soft be our hearts their pains to feel,
   And swift our hands to aid.

4 So Jesus look'd on dying man,
   When, throned above the skies,
And in the Father's bosom blest,
   He felt compassion rise.

5 On wings of love the Savior flew,
   To bless a ruin'd race;
We would, O Lord, thy steps pursue,
   Thy bright example trace.

323   *Godly Sorrow.*

1 O for that tenderness of heart
   Which bows before the Lord,
Acknowledging how just thou art,
   And trembling at thy word;

2 O for those humble, contrite tears,
   Which from repentance flow;
That consciousness of guilt, which fears
   The long-suspended blow.

3 Savior, to me, in pity, give
   The sensible distress;
The pledge thou wilt at last receive.
   And bid me die in peace:

4 Wilt from the dreadful day remove,
   Before the evil come;
My spirit hide with saints above,—
   My body, in the tomb.

Doxology.

To Father, Son, and Holy Ghost,
   Who sweetly all agree
To save a world of sinners lost,
   Eternal glory be.

PHUVAH. C. M.

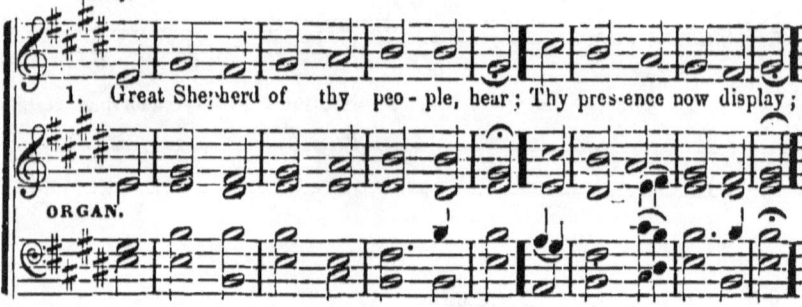

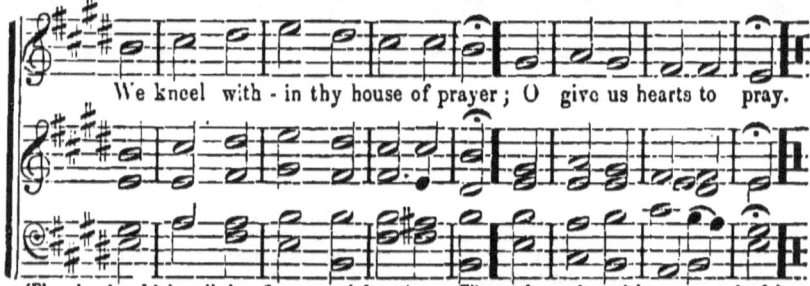

2 The clouds which veil thee from our sight,
In pity, Lord, remove;
Dispose our minds to hear aright
The message of thy love.

3 Help us, with holy fear and joy,
To kneel before thy face;
O make us, creatures of thy power,
The children of thy grace.

325 *Our ever-present Guide.*
1 Jesus, the Lord of glory, died,
That we might never die;
And now he reigns supreme, to guide
His people to the sky.

2 Weak though we are, he still is near,
To lead, console, defend;
In all our sorrow, all our fear,
Our all-sufficient Friend.

3 From His high throne in bliss, he deigns
Our every prayer to heed;
Bears with our folly, soothes our pains,
Supplies our every need.

4 And from his love's exhaustless spring,
Joys like a river come,
To make the desert bloom and sing,
O'er which we travel home.

5 O Jesus, there is none like thee,
Our Savior and our Lord;

Through earth and heaven exalted be,
Beloved, obey'd, adored.

326 *For a tender conscience.*
1 I want a principle within,
Of jealous, godly fear;
A sensibility of sin,—
A pain to feel it near:

2 I want the first approach to feel,
Of pride, or fond desire;
To catch the wand'ring of my will,
And quench the kindling fire.

3 From thee that I no more may part,
No more thy goodness grieve,
The filial awe, the fleshly heart,
The tender conscience, give.

4 Quick as the apple of an eye,
O God, my conscience make;
Awake my soul when sin is nigh,
And keep it still awake.

5 If to the right or left I stray,
That moment, Lord, reprove;
And let me weep my life away,
For having grieved thy love.

6 O may the least omission pain
My well-instructed soul,
And drive me to the blood again,
Which makes the wounded whole.

327 TAMAR. C. M.

1. Come, let us join our friends above, That have obtain'd the prize; And on the eagle wings of love To joys celestial rise.
2. Let all the saints terrestrial sing; With those to glory gone; For all the servants of our King, In earth and heaven, are one.

3 One family we dwell in Him,
   One church above, beneath,
Though now divided by the stream,
   The narrow stream, of death.

4 One army of the living God,
   To his command we bow;
Part of his host have crossed the flood,
   And part are crossing now.

5 Ten thousand to their endless home
   This solemn moment fly;
And we are to the margin come,
   And we expect to die.

6 His militant embodied host,
   With wishful looks we stand,
And long to see that happy coast,
   And reach the heavenly land.

---

328   *The blood of sprinkling.*

1 My God, my God, to thee I cry;
   Thee only would I know;
The purifying blood apply,
   And wash me white as snow.

2 Touch me, and make the leper clean;
   Purge my iniquity:
Unless thou wash my soul from sin,
   I have no part in thee.

3 But art thou not already mine?
   Answer, if mine thou art;
Whisper within, thou love divine,
   And cheer my drooping heart.

4 Behold, for me the Victim bleeds,—
   His wounds are open wide;
For me the blood of sprinkling pleads,
   And speaks me justified.

329   *Thy commandments are exceeding broad.*

1 Deepen the wound thy hands have made
   In this weak, helpless soul:
Till mercy, with its balmy aid,
   Descend to make me whole.

2 The sharpness of thy two-edged sword
   Enable me to' endure;
Till bold to say,—My hall'wing Lord
   Hath wrought a perfect cure.

3 I see th' exceeding broad command,
   Which all contains in one:
Enlarge my heart to understand
   The mystery unknown.

4 O that, with all thy saints, I might
   By sweet experience prove
What is the length, and breadth and hight,
   And depth, of perfect love.

DENNIS. S. M.

Arranged from H. G. NAGELL.

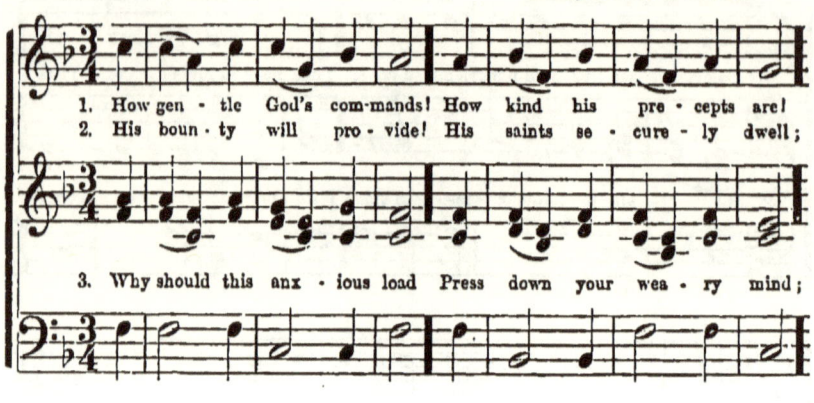

331 *All-sufficient grace.*

1 Grace! 'tis a charming sound,
   Harmonious to the ear;
   Heaven with the echo shall resound,
   And all the earth shall hear.

2 Grace first contrived a way
   To save rebellious man;
   And all the steps that grace display,
   Which drew the wondrous plan.

3 Grace taught my roving feet
   To tread the heavenly road;
   And new supplies each hour I meet,
   While pressing on to God.

4 Grace all the work shall crown,
   Through everlasting days;
   It lays in heaven the topmost stone,
   And well deserves our praise.

332 *The only name given under heaven.*

1 Jesus, thou Source divine,
   Whence hope and comfort flow,—
   Jesus, no other Name than thine
   Can save from endless wo.

2 None else will heaven approve:
   Thou art the only way,
   Ordain'd by everlasting love,
   To realms of endless day.

3 Here let our feet abide,
   Nor from thy path depart:
   Direct our steps, thou gracious Guide!
   And cheer the fainting heart.

4 Safe through this world of night,
   Lead to the blissful plains,—
   The regions of unclouded light,—
   Where joy forever reigns.

333 GOLDEN HILL. S. M. 103

Western Tune, arranged by L. MASON.

1. Thou very present aid In suff'ring and distress: The mind which still on thee is stay'd, Is kept in perfect peace.

2 The soul by faith reclined
On the Redeemer's breast,
'Mid raging storms, exults to find
An everlasting rest.

3 Sorrow and fear are gone,
Whene'er thy face appears;
It stills the sighing orphan's moan,
And dries the widow's tears.

4 It hallows every cross;
It sweetly comforts me;
Makes me forget my every loss,
And find my all in thee.

5 Jesus, to whom I fly,
Doth all my wishes fill;
What though created streams are dry?
I have the fountain still.

6 Stripp'd of each earthly friend,
I find them all in one;
And peace and joy which never end,
And heaven, in Christ, begun.

334 *The Redeemer on his throne.*

1 Enthroned is Jesus now,
Upon his heavenly seat;
The kingly crown is on his brow,
The saints are at his feet.

2 In shining white they stand,—
A great and countless throng;
A palmy sceptre in each hand,
On every lip a song.

3 They sing the Lamb of God,
Once slain on earth for them;
The Lamb, through whose atoning blood,
Each wears his diadem.

4 Thy grace, O Holy Ghost,
Thy blessed help supply,
That we may join that radiant host,
Triumphant in the sky.

335 *Light dawning upon the soul.*

1 Out of the depths of wo,
To thee, O Lord, I cry;
Darkness surrounds me, but I know
That thou art ever nigh.

2 Humbly on thee I wait,
Confessing all my sin;
Lord, I am knocking at the gate,
Open, and take me in.

3 O hearken to my voice,—
Give ear to my complaint;
Thou bidd'st the mourning soul rejoice,
Thou comfortest the faint.

4 Glory to God above.—
The waters soon will cease;
For, lo! the swift returning dove
Brings home the sign of peace.

5 Though storms his face obscure,
And dangers threaten loud;
Jehovah's covenant is sure,—
His bow is in the cloud.

336 KENTUCKY. S. M.

1. Blest be the tie that binds Our hearts in Christian love;
The fellowship of kindred minds Is like to that above.

2. Before our Father's throne, We pour our ardent prayers;
Our fears, our hopes, our aims are one, Our comforts and our cares.

3 We share our mutual woes;
 Our mutual burdens bear;
 And often for each other flows
 The sympathizing tear.

4 When we asunder part,
 It gives us inward pain;
 But we shall still be joined in heart,
 And hope to meet again.

5 This glorious hope revives
 Our courage by the way;
 While each in expectation lives,
 And longs to see the day.

6 From sorrow, toil, and pain,
 And sin we shall be free;
 And perfect love and friendship reign
 Through all eternity.

337
Laborers in the vineyard of the Lord.

1 And let our bodies part,—
 To diff'rent climes repair;
 Inseparably join'd in heart
 The friends of Jesus are.

2 O let us still proceed
 In Jesus' work below;
 And, foll'wing our triumphant Head,
 To further conquests go.

3 The vineyard of the Lord
 Before his lab'rers lies;

And lo! we see the vast reward
 Which waits us in the skies.

4 O let our heart and mind
 Continually ascend,
 That haven of repose to find,
 Where all our labors end.

5 Where all our toils are o'er,
 Our suff'ring and our pain:
 Who meet on that eternal shore,
 Shall never part again.

338 *For diligence and watchfulness.*

1 A charge to keep I have,
 A God to glorify;
 A never-dying soul to save,
 And fit it for the sky.

2 To serve the present age,
 My calling to fulfil,—
 O may it all my powers engage,
 To do my Master's will.

3 Arm me with jealous care,
 As in thy sight to live;
 And O, thy servant, Lord, prepare,
 A strict account to give.

4 Help me to watch and pray,
 And on thyself rely;
 Assured, if I my trust betray,
 I shall forever die.

339 BOYLSTON. S. M. Dr. L. Mason.

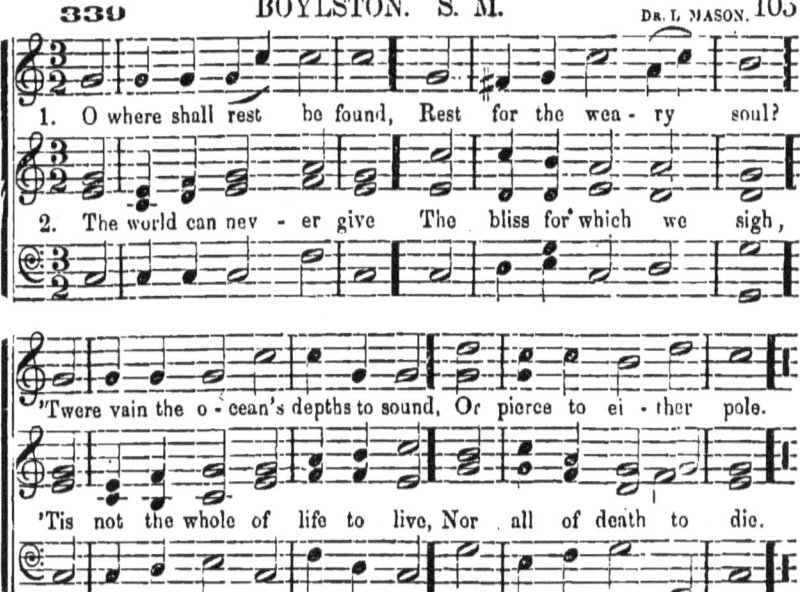

1. O where shall rest be found, Rest for the weary soul? 'Twere vain the ocean's depths to sound, Or pierce to either pole.
2. The world can never give The bliss for which we sigh, 'Tis not the whole of life to live, Nor all of death to die.

3 Beyond this vale of tears
   There is a life above,
 Unmeasured by the flight of years;
   And all that life is love.

4 There is a death, whose pang
   Outlasts the fleeting breath:
 O what eternal horrors hang
   Around the second death!

5 Thou God of truth and grace!
   Teach us that death to shun;
 Lest we be banished from thy face,
   Forevermore undone.

340 *The Redeemer's tears.*

1 Did Christ o'er sinners weep,
   And shall our cheeks be dry?
 Let floods of penitential grief
   Burst forth from every eye.

2 The Son of God in tears
   The wond'ring angels see;
 Be thou astonished, O my soul,
   He shed those tears for thee.

3 He wept that we might weep;
   Each sin demands a tear:
 In heaven alone no sin is found,
   And there's no weeping there.

341 *Embracing the all-sufficient portion.*

1 And can I yet delay—
   My little all to give?
 To tear my soul from earth away
   For Jesus to receive?

2 Nay, but I yield, I yield;
   I can hold out no more:
 I sink, by dying love compelled,
   And own thee conqueror.

3 Though late, I all forsake;
   My friends, my all, resign:
 Gracious Redeemer, take, O take,
   And seal me ever thine.

4 Come, and possess me whole,
   Nor hence again remove;
 Settle and fix my wav'ring soul
   With all thy weight of love.

5 My one desire be this,—
   Thy only love to know;
 To seek and taste no other bliss,—
   No other good below.

6 My life, my portion thou;
   Thou all-sufficient art:
 My hope, my heavenly treasure, now
   Enter, and keep my heart.

Doxology.

Give to the Father praise,
  Give glory to the Son:
And to the Spirit of his grace
  Be equal honor done.

342. MORNINGTON. S. M.
EARL OF MORNINGTON.

1. My Maker and my King, To thee my all I owe;
2. The creature of thy hand, On thee alone I live;

Thy sov'reign bounty is the spring Whence all my blessings flow.

My God, thy benefits demand More praise than I can give.

3 O let thy grace inspire
 My soul with strength divine ;
 Let all my powers to thee aspire,
 And all my days be thine.

343. *The indwelling Spirit.*

1 We by his Spirit prove
 And know the things of God,—
 The things which freely of his love
 He hath on us bestow'd.

2 His Spirit, which he gave,
 Now dwells in us, we know ;
 The witness in ourselves we have,
 And all its fruits we show.

3 The meek and lowly heart,
 That in our Savior was,
 To us his Spirit does impart,
 And signs us with his cross.

4 Our nature's turn'd, our mind
 Transform'd in all its powers ;
 And both the witnesses are joined,—
 Thy Spirit, Lord, with ours.

5 Whate'er our pard'ning Lord
 Commands, we gladly do ;
 And, guided by his sacred word,
 We all his steps pursue.

6 His glory our design,
 We live, our God to please ;
 And rise, with filial fear divine,
 To perfect holiness.

344. *The throne of grace.*

1 Behold the throne of grace ;
 The promise calls us near ;
 There Jesus shows a smiling face,
 And waits to answer prayer.

2 Thine image, Lord, bestow,—
 Thy presence and thy love,—
 That we may serve thee here below,
 And reign with thee above.

3 Teach us to live by faith,—
 Conform our wills to thine ;
 Let us victorious be in death,
 And then in glory shine.

4 If thou these blessings give,
 And thou our portion be,
 All worldly joys we'll gladly leave,
 To find our heaven in thee.

Doxology.

To God, the Father, Son,
 And Spirit, One in Three,
Be glory, as it was, is now,
 And shall forever be.

345 SHIRLAND. S. M. *Stanley.* **107**

1. My God, my life, my love, To thee, to thee I call:
I can-not live, if thou re-move, For thou art all in all.

2. Thy shin-ing grace can cheer This dun-geon where I dwell:
'Tis par-a-dise when thou art here: If thou de-part, 'tis hell.

3 The smilings of thy face,
How amiable they are!
'Tis heaven to rest in thine embrace,
And nowhere else but there.

4 To thee, and thee alone,
The angels owe their bliss;
They sit around thy gracious throne,
And dwell where Jesus is.

5 Not all the harps above
Can make a heavenly place,
If God his residence remove,
Or but conceal his face.

6 Nor earth, nor all the sky,
Can one delight afford,
Nor yield one drop of real joy,
Without thy presence, Lord.

7 Thou art the sea of love,
Where all my pleasures roll:
The circle where my passions move,
And centre of my soul.

346 *Thanks for the unspeakable gift.*

1 Father, our hearts we lift
Up to thy gracious throne,
And thank thee for the precious gift
Of thine incarnate Son.

2 His infant cries proclaim
A peace 'twixt earth and heaven:
Salvation, through his only Name,
To all mankind is given.

3 The gift unspeakable
We thankfully receive,
And to the world thy goodness tell,
And to thy glory live.

4 May all mankind receive
The new-born Prince of peace,
And meekly in his spirit live,
And in his love increase.

347
God's wondrous way among the heathen.

1 To bless thy chosen race,
In mercy, Lord, incline;
And cause the brightness of thy face
On all thy saints to shine;—

2 That so thy wondrous way
May through the world be known,
While distant lands their homage pay
And thy salvation own.

3 Let all the nations join
To celebrate thy fame;
And all the world, O Lord, combine
To praise thy glorious Name

348 THATCHER. S. M. *From HANDEL.*

1. Oh! bless the Lord, my soul! Let all within me join, And aid my tongue to bless his name, Whose favors are divine.

2. Oh! bless the Lord, my soul! Nor let his mercies lie, Forgotten in unthankfulness, And without praises die.

3 'Tis he forgives thy sins,
   'Tis he relieves thy pain,
  'Tis he who heals thy sicknesses,
   And makes thee young again.

4 He crowns thy life with love,
   When ransom'd from the grave ;
  He, who redeem'd my soul from hell,
   Hath sovereign power to save.

5 He fills the poor with good ;
   He gives the sufferers rest :
  The Lord hath judgments for the proud,
   And justice for th' oppress'd.

6 His wondrous works and ways
   He made by Moses known ;
  But sent the world his truth and grace,
   By his beloved Son.

349 *The Spring.*
1 Sweet is the time of spring,
   When nature's charms appear ;
  The birds with ceaseless pleasure sing,
   And hail the opening year ;

2 But sweeter far the spring
   Of wisdom and of grace,
  When children bless and praise their King,
   Who loves the youthful race.

3 Sweet is the dawn of day,
   When light just streaks the sky ;
  When shades and darkness pass away,
   And morning beams are nigh :

4 But sweeter far the dawn
   Of piety in youth ;
  When doubt and darkness are withdrawn,
   Before the light of truth.

5 Sweet is the early dew,
   Which gilds the mountains tops,
  And decks each plant and flower we view,
   With pearly glittering drops :

6 But sweeter far the scene
   On Zion's holy hill,
  When there the dew of youth is seen
   Its freshness to distill.

350 *The opened Fountain.*
1 Call'd from above, I rise,
   And wash away my sin ;
  The stream to which my spirit flies,
   Can make the foulest clean.

2 It runs divinely clear,
   A fountain deep and wide :
  'Twas open'd by the soldier's spear,
   In my Redeemer's side.

351 DOVER. S. M.

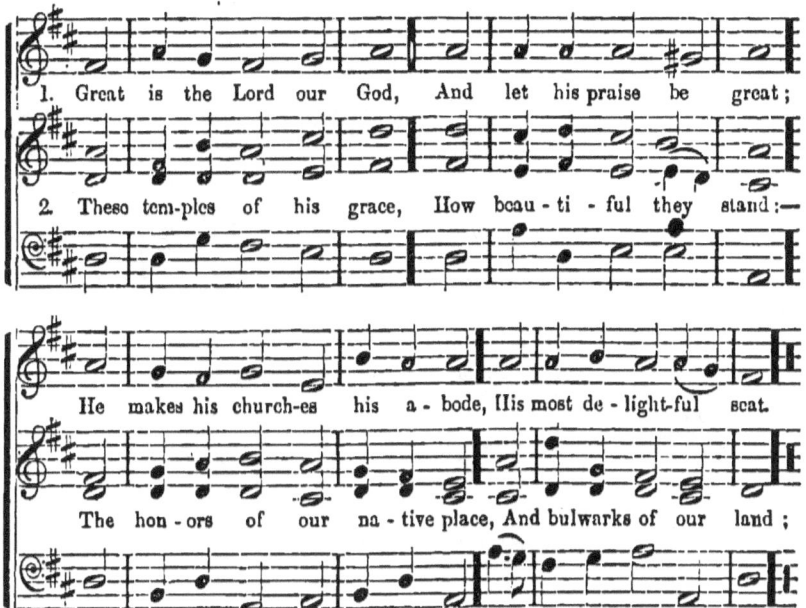

1. Great is the Lord our God, And let his praise be great;
He makes his church-es his a-bode, His most de-light-ful seat.

2. These tem-ples of his grace, How beau-ti-ful they stand:—
The hon-ors of our na-tive place, And bulwarks of our land;

3 In Zion God is known,
  A refuge in distress;
How bright has his salvation shone
  Through all her palaces!

4 In every new distress.
  We'll to his house repair;
We'll think upon his wondrous grace,
  And seek deliv'rance there.

352 *His name is glorious.*

1 Almighty Maker, God,
  How glorious is thy Name;
Thy wonders how diffused abroad,
  Throughout creation's frame.

2 In native white and red
  The rose and lily stand,
And, free from pride, their beauties spread,
  To show thy skilful hand.

3 The lark mounts up the sky,
  With unambitious song;
And bears her Maker's praise on high,
  Upon her artless tongue.

4 Fain would I rise and sing
  To my Creator too;
Fain would my heart adore my King,
  And give him praises due.

5 Let joy and worship spend
  The remnant of my days:
And to my God my soul ascend,
  In sweet perfumes of praise.

353 *Their universal diffusion.*

1 Jesus, the word bestow,—
  The true immortal seed;
Thy gospel then shall greatly grow,
  And all our land o'erspread;

2 Through earth extended wide
  Shall mightily prevail,—
Destroy the works of self and pride,
  And shake the gates of hell.

3 Its energy exert
  In the believing soul;
Diffuse thy grace through every part,
  And sanctify the whole:

4 Its utmost virtue show
  In pure consummate love,
And fill with all thy life below,
  And give us thrones above.

Doxology.

Give to the Father praise,
  Give glory to the Son:
And to the Spirit of his grace
  Be equal honor done.

354 LEBANON. S. M.
J. ZUNDEL

1. I was a wandering sheep, I did not love the fold: I did not love my Shepherd's voice, I would not be controlled; I was a way-ward child, I did not love my home, I did not love my Father's voice, I loved afar to roam.

2 The Shepherd sought His sheep,
  The Father sought His child;
 They followed me o'er vale and hill,
  O'er deserts waste and wild:
 They found me nigh to death,
  Famish'd, and faint, and lone;
 They bound me with the bands of love,
  They saved the wandering one.

3 They spoke in tender love,
  They raised my drooping head;
 They gently closed my bleeding wounds,
  My fainting soul they fed:
 They washed my filth away,
  They made me clean and fair;
 They brought me to my home in peace,
  The long-sought wanderer.

4 Jesus my Shepherd is,
  'T was He that loved my soul,
 'T was He that wash'd me in His blood,
  'T was He that made me whole:
 'T was He that sought the lost,
  That found the wandering sheep,
 'T was He that brought me to the fold—
  'T is He that still doth keep.

5 No more a wand'ring sheep,
  I love to be controll'd,
 I love my tender Shepherd's voice,
  I love the peaceful fold:
 No more a wayward child,
  I seek no more to roam,
 I love my heavenly Father's voice—
  I love, I love His home.

355 EPSILON. S. M. FROM BEETHOVEN.

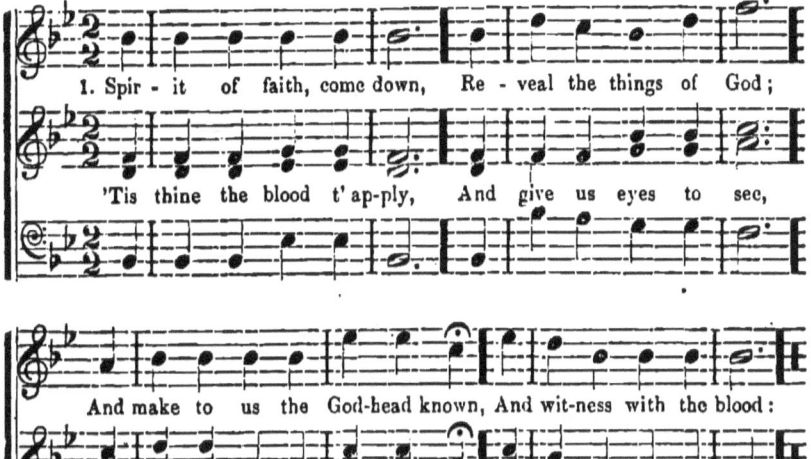

1. Spirit of faith, come down,
Reveal the things of God;
'Tis thine the blood t' apply,
And give us eyes to see,
And make to us the God-head known,
And witness with the blood:
That He who did for sinners die,
Hath surely died for me.

2 No man can truly say
That Jesus is the Lord,
Unless thou take the veil away,
And breathe the living word :
Then, only then we feel
Our int'rest in his blood ;
And cry, with joy unspeakable,—
Thou art my Lord, my God.

3 O that the world might know
The all-atoning Lamb !
Spirit of faith, descend and show
The virtue of his name :
The grace which all may find,
The saving power impart ;
And testify to all mankind,
And speak in every heart.

356 *For entire consecration.*

1 Jesus, my strength, my hope,
On thee I cast my care;
With humble confidence look up,
And know thou hear'st my prayer.
Give me on thee to wait,
Till I can all things do ;
On thee,—almighty to create,
Almighty to renew.

2 I want a sober mind,
A self-renouncing will,
That tramples down, and casts behind,
The baits of pleasing ill :
A soul inured to pain,
To hardship, grief, and loss ;
Bold to take up, firm to sustain,
The consecrated cross.

3 I want a godly fear,
A quick discerning eye,
That looks to thee when sin is near,
And sees the tempter fly :
A spirit still prepared,
And arm'd with jealous care ;
Forever standing on its guard,
And watching unto prayer.

357 *For watchfulness and circumspection.*

1 Bid me of men beware,
And to my ways take heed ;
Discern their every secret snare,
And circumspectly tread.

2 O may I calmly wait
Thy succors from above ;
And stand against their open hate,
And well-dissembled love.

PADDINGTON. S. M.
Rev. Basil Wood.

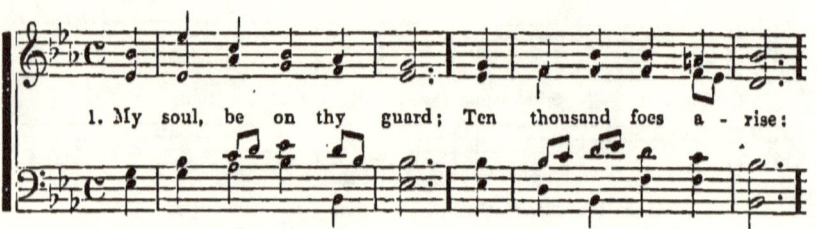

1. My soul, be on thy guard; Ten thousand foes a-rise:

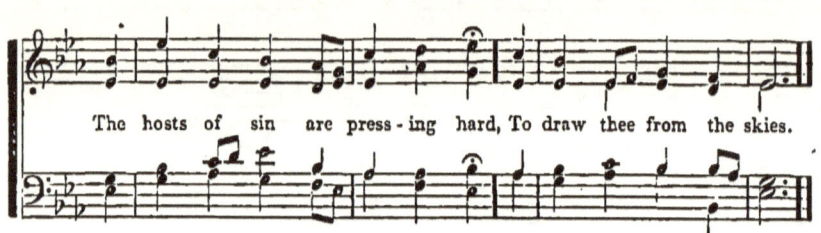

The hosts of sin are pressing hard, To draw thee from the skies.

2 O watch, and fight, and pray;
  The battle ne'er give o'er;
Renew it boldly every day,
  And help divine implore.

3 Ne'er think the vict'ry won,
  Nor lay thine armor down:
The work of faith will not be done,
  Till thou obtain the crown.

4 Then persevere till death
  Shall bring thee to thy God;
He'll take thee, at thy parting breath,
  To his divine abode.

359 *The well-fought day.*
1 Pray, without ceasing, pray,
  (Your Captain gives the word;)
His summons cheerfully obey,
  And call upon the Lord:

2 To God your every want
  In instant prayer display;
Pray always; pray, and never faint;
  Pray, without ceasing, pray.

3 In fellowship,— alone,
  To God with faith draw near;
Approach his courts, besiege his throne
  With all the power of prayer;

4 His mercy now implore,
  And now show forth his praise;

In shouts, or silent awe, adore
  His miracles of grace.

5 From strength to strength go on;
  Wrestle, and fight, and pray;
Tread all the powers of darkness down,
  And win the well-fought day:

6 Still let the Spirit cry,
  In all his soldiers,— Come,
Till Christ the Lord descend from high,
  And take the conqu'rors home.

360 *Spiritual enemies to be encountered.*
1 Angels our march oppose,
  Who still in strength excel,—
Our secret, sworn, eternal foes,
  Countless, invisible;

2 From thrones of glory driven,
  By flaming vengeance hurl'd,
They throng the air, and darken heaven,
  And rule this lower world.

3 But shall believers fear?
  But shall believers fly?
Or see the bloody cross appear,
  And all their powers defy?

4 By all hell's host withstood,
  We all hell's host o'erthrow; [blood,
And, conqu'ring them through Jesus'
  We on to conquer go.

361   LABAN. S. M.   Dr. L. MASON.

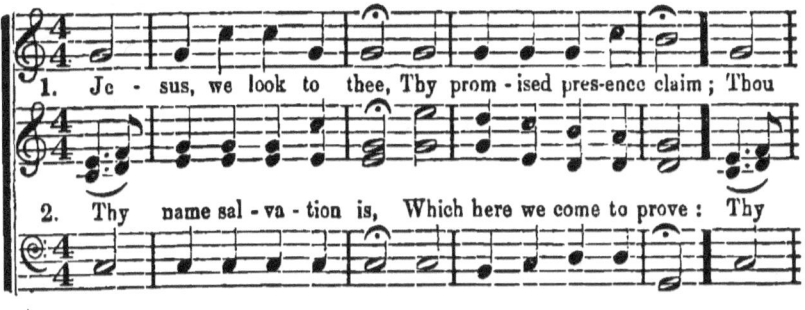

1. Jesus, we look to thee, Thy promised presence claim; Thou in the midst of us shalt be, Assembled in thy name:

2. Thy name salvation is, Which here we come to prove: Thy name is life, and health, and peace, And everlasting love.

3 Not in the name of pride
   Or selfishness we meet;
From nature's paths we turn aside,
   And worldly thoughts forget.

4 We meet the grace to take,
   Which thou hast freely given;
We meet on earth for thy dear sake,
   That we may meet in heaven.

5 Present we know thou art,
   But O, thyself reveal!
Now, Lord, let every bounding heart
   The mighty comfort feel.

6 O may thy quick'ning voice
   The death of sin remove;
And bid our inmost souls rejoice,
   In hope of perfect love.

362   *And yet there is room.*

1 Ye wretched, starving poor,
   Behold a royal feast!
Where mercy spreads her bounteous store
   For every humble guest.

2 See, Christ, with open arms,
   Invites, and bids you come;
O stay not back, though fear alarms;
   For yet there still is room.

3 O come, and with us taste
   The blessings of his love
While hope expects the sweet repast
   Of nobler joys above.

4 There, with united voice,
   Before th' eternal throne,
Ten thousand thousand souls rejoice,
   In ecstasies unknown.

5 Ten thousand thousand more
   Are welcome still to come:
Ye longing souls, the grace adore;
   Approach,—there yet is room.

363
   The word of God, quick and powerful.

1 Thy word, Almighty Lord,
   Where'er it enters in,
Is sharper than a two-edged sword,
   To slay the man of sin,

2 Thy word is power and life;
   It bids confusion cease,
And changes envy, hatred, strife,
   To love, and joy, and peace.

3 Then let our hearts obey
   The Gospel's glorious sound,
And all its fruits from day to day
   Be in us and abound

364 BADEA. S. M. Arr. by Dr. L. Mason.

1. Oh! bless-ed souls are they, Whose sins are cov-er'd o'er;
Divine-ly blest, to whom the Lord Im-putes their sin no more.

2. They mourn their fol-lies past, And keep their hearts with care;
Their lips and lives, with-out de-ceit, Shall prove their faith sin-cere.

3 While I conceal'd my guilt,
　I felt the festering wound!
Till I confess'd my sins to thee,
　And ready pardon found.

4 Let sinners learn to pray,
　Let saints keep near the throne;
Our help in times of deep distress,
　Is found in God alone.

365   *Walking by Faith.*

1 If, on a quiet sea,
　Toward heaven we calmly sail,
With grateful hearts, O God, to thee,
　We'll own the fav'ring gale.

2 But should the surges rise,
　And rest delay to come,
Blest be the sorrow, kind the storm,
　Which drives us nearer home.

3 Soon shall our doubts and fears
　All yield to thy control:
Thy tender mercies shall illume
　The midnight of the soul.

4 Teach us, in every state,
　To make thy will our own;
And when the joys of sense depart,
　To live by faith alone.

366   *The Pillar and the Cloud.*

1 Thou very Paschal Lamb,
　Whose blood for us was shed,
Through whom we out of bondage came,
　Thy ransom'd people lead,

2 Angel of gospel grace,
　Fulfil thy character:
To guard and feed the chosen race,
　In Israel's camp appear.

3 Throughout the desert way,
　Conduct us by the light;
Be thou a cooling cloud by day,
　A cheering fire by night.

4 Our fainting souls sustain
　With blessings from above;
And ever on thy people rain
　The manna of thy love.

367   *Seek Him while he may be found.*

1 My son, know thou the Lord;
　Thy father's God obey;
Seek his protecting care by night,
　His guardian hand by day.

2 Call, while he may be found;
　Seek him while he is near;
Serve him with all thy heart and mind,
　And worship him with fear.

3 If thou wilt seek his face,
　His ear will hear thy cry;
Then shalt thou find his mercy sure,
　His grace forever nigh.

4 But if thou leave thy God,
　Nor choose the path to Heaven;
Then shalt thou perish in thy sins,
　And never be forgiven.

368 BAKER. S. M. W. McDONALD

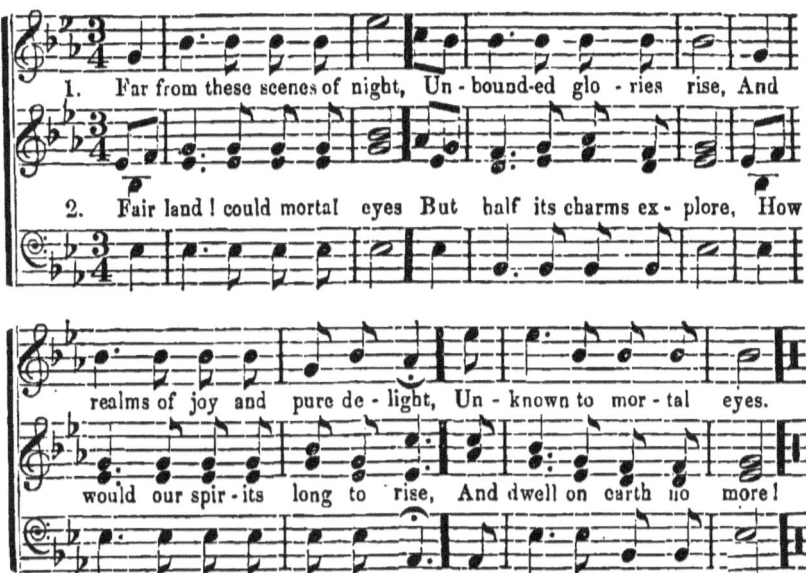

1. Far from these scenes of night, Unbounded glories rise, And realms of joy and pure delight, Unknown to mortal eyes.

2. Fair land! could mortal eyes But half its charms explore, How would our spirits long to rise, And dwell on earth no more!

3 No cloud those regions know,—
 Realms ever bright and fair;
 For sin, the source of mortal wo,
 Can never enter there.

4 O may the prospect fire
 Our hearts with ardent love,
 Till wings of faith, and strong desire,
 Bear every thought above.

5 Prepared, by grace divine,
 For thy bright courts on high,
 Lord, bid our spirits rise and join
 The chorus of the sky.

369 *Seeking the evidence of acceptance.*

1 I listen for the voice
 Which speaks my sins forgiven;
 Speak, Lord, and bid my heart rejoice
 In certain hope of heaven.

2 Thy Name O may I prove,
 Thy Name inscribed on me;
 And triumph in redeeming love
 Through all eternity.

370 *Thy will be done.*

1 This is thy will, I know,
 That I should holy be;
 Should let my sins this moment go,
 This moment turn to thee.

2 O might I now embrace
 Thine all-sufficient power,
 And never more to sin give place,
 And never grieve thee more.

371 *To-day.*

1 All yesterday is gone;
 To-morrow's not our own;
 O sinner, come, without delay,
 And bow before the throne.

2 O hear God's voice to-day,
 And harden not your heart;
 To-morrow, with a frown, he may
 Pronounce the word,—Depart!

372 *A blessing on the ordinance.*

1 Great God, now condescend
 To bless our rising race;
 Soon may their willing spirits bend,
 The subjects of thy grace.

2 O what a pure delight
 Their happiness to see;
 Our warmest wishes all unite,
 To lead their souls to thee.

3 Now bless, thou God of love,
 This ordinance divine;
 Send thy good Spirit from above,
 And make these children thine.

OLMUTZ. S. M. — Arranged by Dr. L. Mason.

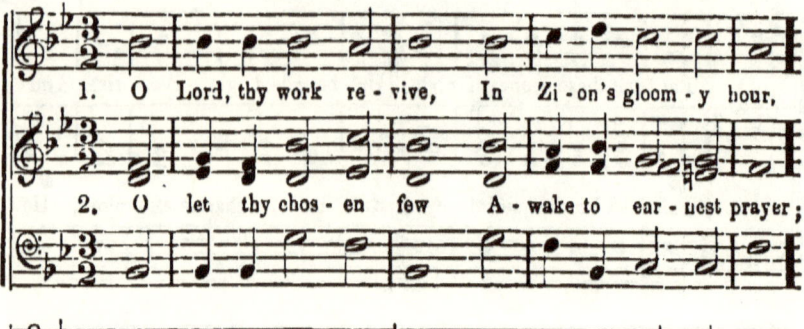

1. O Lord, thy work revive, In Zion's gloomy hour, And let our dying graces live By thy restoring power.

2. O let thy chosen few Awake to earnest prayer; Their covenant again renew, And walk in filial fear.

3 Thy Spirit then will speak
   Through lips of humble clay,
Till hearts of adamant shall break,—
   Till rebels shall obey.

4 Now lend thy gracious ear;
   Now listen to our cry :
O come, and bring salvation near;
   Our souls on thee rely.

---

374   *Accepting the invitation.*

1 Come, weary sinners, come,
   Groaning beneath your load ;
The Savior calls his wand'rers home ;
   Haste to your pard'ning God.

2 Come, all by guilt oppressed,
   Answer the Savior's call—
O come, and I will give you rest,
   And I will save you all.

3 Redeemer, full of love,
   We would thy word obey,
And all thy faithful mercies prove :
   O take our guilt away.

4 We would on thee rely ;
   On thee would cast our care ;
Now to thine arms of mercy fly,
   And find salvation there.

---

375   *For perfect submission.*

1 I want a heart to pray,—
   To pray, and never cease ;
Never to murmur at thy stay,
   Or wish my suff'rings less.
This blessing, above all,—
   Always to pray,—I want ;
Out of the deep on thee to call,
   And never, never faint.

2 I want a true regard,
   A single, steady aim,—
Unmoved by threat'ning or reward,
   To thee and thy great name ;
A jealous, just concern,
   For thine immortal praise ;
A pure desire that all may learn
   And glorify thy grace.

3 I rest upon thy word,—
   The promise is for me ;
My succor and salvation, Lord,
   Shall surely come from thee :
But let me still abide,
   Nor from my hope remove,
Till thou my patient spirit guide
   Into thy perfect love.

376   AYLESBURY. S. M.   Dr. GREEN.   117

1. Ah, how shall fall-en man Be just be-fore his God?

If he con-tend in right-eous-ness, We sink be-neath his rod.

2 If he our ways should mark
   With strict inquiring eyes,
Could we for one of thousand faults,
   A just excuse devise?

3 The mountains, in thy wrath,
   Their ancient seats forsake:
The trembling earth deserts her place,—
   Her rooted pillars shake.

4 Ah, how shall guilty man
   Contend with such a God?
None — none can meet him, and escape,
   But through the Savior's blood.

---

377   *To whom should we go?*

1 Ah! whither should I go,
   Burden'd, and sick, and faint?
To whom should I my trouble show,
   And pour out my complaint?

2 My Savior bids me come;
   Ah! why do I delay?
He calls the weary sinner home,
   And yet from him I stay.

3 What is it keeps me back,
   From which I cannot part,—
Which will not let the Savior take
   Possession of my heart?

4 Searcher of hearts, in mine
   Thy trying power display;
Into its darkest corners shine,
   And take the vail away.

5 I now believe, in thee,
   Compassion reigns alone;
According to my faith, to me
   O let it, Lord, be done!

6 In me is all the bar,
   Which I wouldst fain remove:
Remove it and I shall declare
   That God is only love.

---

378   *The Day-star from on high.*

1 My former hopes are fled;
   My terror now begins:
I feel, alas! that I am dead
   In trespasses and sins.

2 Ah, whither shall I fly?
   I hear the thunder roar;—
The law proclaims destruction nigh,
   And vengeance at the door.

3 When I review my ways,
   I dread impending doom:
But, hark! a friendly whisper says,
   Flee from the wrath to come.

4 With trembling hope, I see
   A glimmering from afar;
A beam of day that shines for me,
   To save me from despair.

5 Forerunner of the sun,
   It marks the pilgrim's way;
I'll gaze upon it while I run,
   And watch the rising day.

379 SEIR. S. M. — Dr. L. Mason.

1. How beauteous are their feet, Who stand on Zion's hill;— Who bring salvation on their tongues, And words of peace reveal.

2 How charming is their voice,
  So sweet the tidings are;
 Zion, behold thy Savior King;
  He reigns and triumphs here.

3 How happy are our ears
  That hear the joyful sound,
 Which kings and prophets waited for,
  And sought, but never found.

4 How blessed are our eyes,
  That see this heavenly light;
 Prophets and priests desired it long,
  But died without the sight.

5 The watchmen join their voice,
  And tuneful notes employ;
 Jerusalem breaks forth in songs,
  And deserts learn the joy.

6 The Lord makes bare his arm
  Through all the earth abroad:
 Let every nation now behold
  Their Savior and their God.

380 *The song of Moses and the Lamb.*

1 Awake, and sing the song
  Of Moses and the Lamb;
 Wake, every heart and every tongue,
  To praise the Savior's Name.

2 Sing of his dying love;
  Sing of his rising power;
 Sing how he intercedes above
  For those whose sins he bore.

3 Ye pilgrims, on the road
  To Zion's city, sing;
 Rejoice ye in the Lamb of God,—
  In Christ th' eternal King.

4 Soon shall we hear him say,—
  Ye blessed children, come;
 Soon will he call us hence away,
  To our eternal home.

5 There shall each raptured tongue
  His endless praise proclaim;
 And sweeter voices tune the song
  Of Moses and the Lamb.

381 *Glorious liberty.*

1 O come, and dwell in me,
  Spirit of power within;
 And bring the glorious liberty
  From sorrow, fear, and sin!

2 The seed of sin's disease,
  Spirit of health, remove,—
 Spirit of finished holiness,
  Spirit of perfect love.

3 Hasten the joyful day
  Which shall my sins consume;
 When old things shall be done away,
  And all things new become.

4 I want the witness, Lord,
  That all I do is right,—
 According to thy will and word,—
  Well pleasing in thy sight.

5 I ask no higher state;
  Indulge me but in this,
 And soon or later then translate
  To my eternal bliss.

382 OLNEY. S. M. Dr. L. MASON.

1. The Spirit in our hearts, Is whispering, "Sinner come:"
2. Let him that heareth say To all about him, "come;"

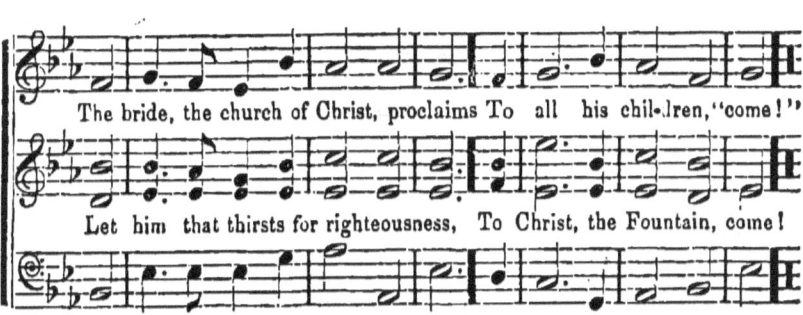

The bride, the church of Christ, proclaims To all his children, "come!"
Let him that thirsts for righteousness, To Christ, the Fountain, come!

3 Yes, whosoever will,
  Oh, let him freely come,
And freely drink the stream of life;
  'Tis Jesus bids him come.

4 Lo! Jesus who invites,
  Declares, " I quickly come;"
Lord, even so; we wait thine hour;
  O blest Redeemer, come!

383 *The mighty God.*

1 Rejoice in Jesus' birth,
  To us a Son is given:
To us a child is born on earth,
  Who made both earth and heaven

2 He reigns above the sky,—
  This universe sustains;—
The God supreme, the Lord most high,
  The king Messiah reigns.

3 The mighty God is He,
  Author of heavenly bliss;
The Father of eternity,
  The glorious Prince of peace.

4 His government shall grow,
  From strength to strength proceed:
His righteousness the church o'erflow,
  And all the earth o'erspread.

384 *Knowledge of forgiveness.*

1 How can a sinner know
  His sins on earth forgiven?
How can my gracious Savior show
  My name inscribed in heaven?

2 What we have felt and seen
  With confidence we tell;
And publish to the sons of men,
  The signs infallible.

3 We who in Christ believe
  That he for us hath died,
We all his unknown peace receive,
  And feel his blood applied.

4 Exults our rising soul,
  Disburden'd of her load,
And swells, unutterably full
  Of glory and of God.

5 His love, surpassing far
  The love of all beneath,
We find within our hearts, and dare
  The pointless darts of death.

6 Stronger than death or hell
  The sacred power we prove;
And, conqu'rors of the world, we dwell
  In heaven, who dwell in love.

385   ST. THOMAS. S. M.   *A. WILLIAMS.*

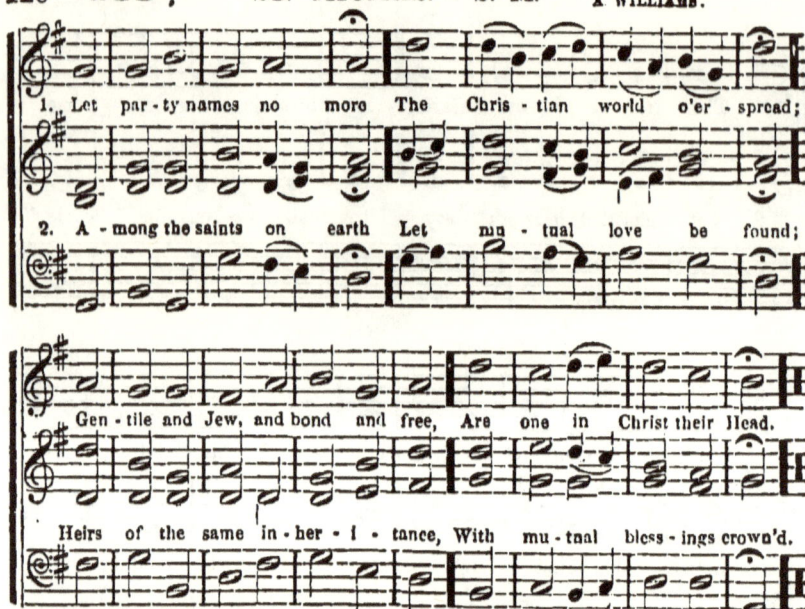

1. Let par-ty names no more The Chris-tian world o'er-spread;
Gen-tile and Jew, and bond and free, Are one in Christ their Head.

2. A-mong the saints on earth Let mu-tual love be found;
Heirs of the same in-her-i-tance, With mu-tual bless-ings crown'd.

3 Thus will the church below
   Resemble that above;
Where streams of bliss forever flow,
   And every heart is love.

386   *The sure foundation.*

1 In every trying hour
   My soul to Jesus flies;
I trust in his almighty power,
   When swelling billows rise.

2 His comforts bear me up;
   I trust the faithful God,
The sure foundation of my hope
   Is in my Savior's blood.

3 Loud hallelujahs sing,
   To our Redeemer's Name;
In joy or sorrow—life or death—
   His love is still the same.

387   *Success certain.*

1 Lord, if at thy command
   The word of life we sow,
Water'd by thy almighty hand,
   The seed shall surely grow:
The virtue of thy grace
   A large increase shall give,
And multiply the faithful race,
   Who to thy glory live.

2 Now, then, the ceaseless shower
   Of gospel blessings send,
And let the soul-converting power
   Thy ministers attend.
On multitudes confer
   The heart renewing love
And by the joy of grace prepare
   For fuller joys above.

388   *The eternal Sabbath.*

1 Hail to the Sabbath-day!
   The day divinely given,
When men to God their homage pay,
   And earth draws near to heaven.

2 Lord, in this sacred hour,
   Within thy courts we bend,
And bless thy love and own thy power,
   Our Father and our Friend.

3 But thou art not alone
   In courts by mortals trod;
Nor only is the day thine own
   When man draws near to God.

4 Thy temple is the arch
   Of yon unmeasured sky;
Thy Sabbath, the stupendous march
   Of vast eternity.

5 Lord, may that holier day
   Dawn on thy servants' sight;
And purer worship may we pay
   In heaven's unclouded light.

ST. MICHAEL. S. M.

380

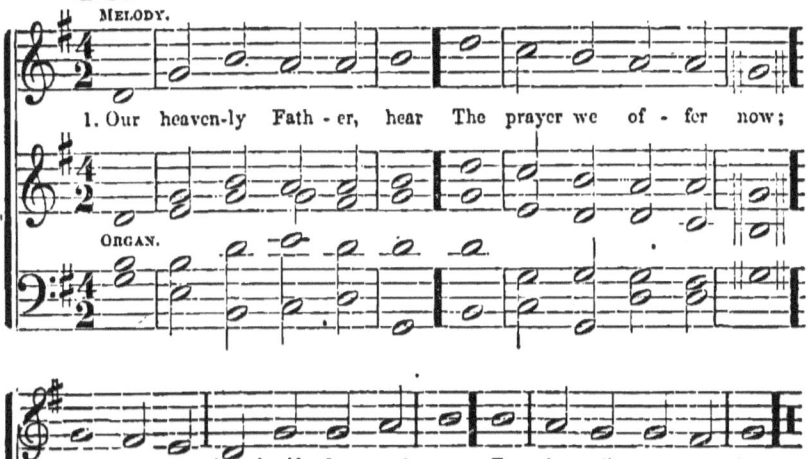

2 Thy kingdom come; thy will
  On earth be done in love,
As saints and seraphim fulfil
  Thy perfect law above.

3 Our daily bread supply,
  While by thy word we live;
The guilt of our iniquity
  Forgive, as we forgive.

4 From dark temptation's power,
  From Satan's wiles, defend;
Deliver in the evil hour,
  And guide us to the end.

5 Thine shall forever be
  Glory and power divine;
The sceptre, throne, and majesty,
  Of heaven and earth are thine.

6 Thus humbly taught to pray
  By thy beloved Son,
Through him we come to thee, and say,
  All for his sake be done.

390 *For fervent zeal.*

1 Jesus, I fain would find
  Thy zeal for God in me;
Thy yearning pity for mankind,—
  Thy burning charity.

2 In me thy Spirit dwell;
  In me thy bowels move;
So shall the fervor of my zeal
  Be the pure flame of love.

391 *Pilgrims and sojourners.*

1 In every time and place,
  Who serve the Lord most high,
Are call'd his sov'reign will t' embrace,
  And still their own deny.

2 To follow his command,
  On earth as pilgrims rove,
And seek an undiscover'd land,
  And house and friends above.

3 Father, the narrow path
  To that far country show;
And in the steps of Abrah'm's faith
  Enable me to go.

4 A cheerful sojourner
  Where'er thou bidd'st me roam,
Till, guided by thy Spirit here,
  I reach my heavenly home.

STAFFORD.* S. M.

READ.

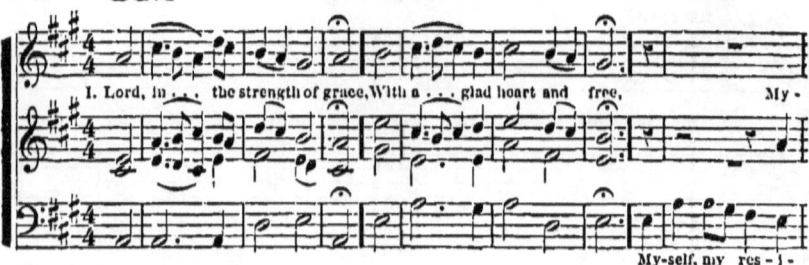

1. Lord, in the strength of grace, With a glad heart and free, Myself, my residue of days, Myself, my residue of days, I consecrate to thee.

2 Thy ransom'd servant, I
Restore to thee thine own;
And from this moment live or die,
To serve my God alone.

393 *A house not made with hands.*

1 We know, by faith we know,
If this vile house of clay,
This tabernacle, sink below,
In ruinous decay—

2 We have a house above,
Not made with mortal hands;
And firm as our Redeemer's love
That heavenly fabric stands.

3 It stands securely high,
Indissolubly sure:
Our glorious mansion in the sky
Shall evermore endure.

4 Full of immortal hope,
We urge the restless strife,
And hasten to be swallow'd up,
Of everlasting life.

5 Lord, let us put on thee
In perfect holiness,
And rise prepared thy face to see,
Thy bright, unclouded face.

6 Thy grace with glory crown,
Who hast the earnest given;
And then triumphantly come down,
And take us up to heaven.

394 *A foretaste of glory.*

1 O what delight is this,
Which now in Christ we know,—
An earnest of our glorious bliss,
Our heaven begun below!

2 When He the table spreads,
How royal is the cheer;
With rapture we lift up our heads,
And own that God is here.

3 The Lamb for sinners slain,
Who died to die no more,
Let all the ransom'd sons of men,
With all his hosts, adore.

4 Let earth and heaven be join'd,
His glories to display,
And hymn the Savior of mankind
In one eternal day.

Doxology.
To God, the Father, Son,
And Spirit, One in Three,
Be glory, as it was, is now,
And shall forever be.

* See foot note on p. 3d, of Introduction.

395 SILVER STREET. S. M. — SMITH

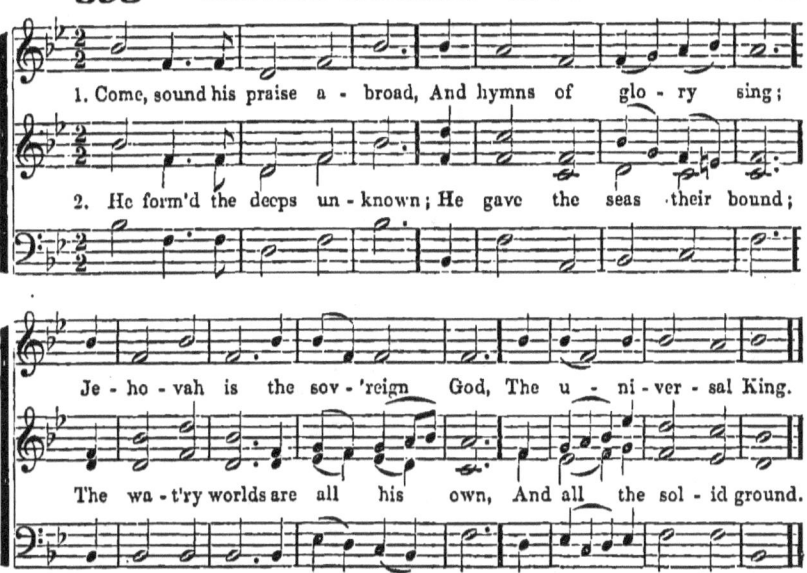

1. Come, sound his praise a-broad, And hymns of glo-ry sing; Je-ho-vah is the sov-'reign God, The u-ni-ver-sal King.

2. He form'd the deeps un-known; He gave the seas their bound; The wa-t'ry worlds are all his own, And all the sol-id ground.

3 Come, worship at his throne,
Come, bow before the Lord;
We are his works, and not our own,
He form'd us by his word.

4 To-day attend his voice,
Nor dare provoke his rod;
Come, like the people of his choice,
And own your gracious God.

396 *The whole armor of God.*

1 Soldiers of Christ, arise,
And put your armor on,
Strong in the strength which God supplies
Through his eternal Son;

2 Strong in the Lord of Hosts,
And in his mighty power,
Who in the strength of Jesus trusts,
Is more than conqueror.

3 Stand then in his great might,
With all his strength endued;
But take, to arm you for the fight,
The panoply of God:

4 That, having all things done,
And all your conflicts past,
Ye may o'ercome, through Christ alone,
And stand entire at last.

5 Leave no unguarded place,—
No weakness of the soul;
Take every virtue, every grace,
And fortify the whole.

6 Indissolubly joined,
To battle all proceed;
But arm youselves with all the mind
That was in Christ, your Head.

397 *The shield of faith.*

1 Soldiers of Christ, lay hold
On faith's victorious shield;
Arm'd with that adamant and gold,
Be sure to win the field:

2 If faith surround your heart,
Satan shall be subdued;
Repell'd his ev'ry fiery dart,
And quench'd with Jesus' blood.

3 Jesus hath died for you;
What can his love withstand?
Believe, hold fast your shield, and who
Shall pluck you from his hand?

4 Believe that Jesus reigns;
All power to him is given;
Believe, till freed from sin's remains;
Believe yourselves to heaven.

398 *The violent take it by force.*

1 O may thy powerful word
Inspire a feeble worm
To rush into thy kingdom, Lord,
And take it as by storm.

2 O may we all improve
The grace already given,
To seize the crown of perfect love,
And scale the mount of heaven.

CONCORD.* S. M. — HOLDEN.

1. Come ye that love the Lord, And let your joys be known; Join in a song, with sweet ac-cord, Join in a song, with sweet ac-cord, While ye surround the throne.

Let those refuse to sing
  Who never knew our God,
But servants of the heavenly King
  May speak their joys abroad.

2 The God that rules on high,
  That all the earth surveys,
That rides upon the stormy sky,
  And calms the roaring seas;
This awful God is ours,
  Our Father and our Love;
He will send down his heavenly powers,
  To carry us above.

3 There we shall see his face,
  And never, never sin;
There, from the rivers of his grace,
  Drink endless pleasures in:
Yea, and before we rise
  To that immortal state,
The thoughts of such amazing bliss
  Should constant joys create.

4 The men of grace have found
  Glory begun below:
Celestial fruit on earthly ground
  From faith and hope may grow:

Then let our songs abound,
  And every tear be dry: [ground,
We're marching through Immanuel's
  To fairer worlds on high.

400 *Love for Zion.*

1 I love thy kingdom, Lord,—
  The house of thine abode,—
The Church our blest Redeemer saved
  With his own precious blood.

2 I love thy Church, O God!
  Her walls before thee stand,
Dear as the apple of thine eye,
  And graven on thy hand.

3 For her my tears shall fall;
  For her my prayers ascend;
To her my cares and toils be given,
  Till toils and cares shall end.

4 Beyond my highest joy
  I prize her heavenly ways;
Her sweet communion, solemn vows,
  Her hymns of love and praise.

5 Sure as thy truth shall last,
  To Zion shall be given
The brightest glories earth can yield,
  And brighter bliss of heaven.

* See foot note on p. 3d. of Introduction.

401 LISBON. S. M.

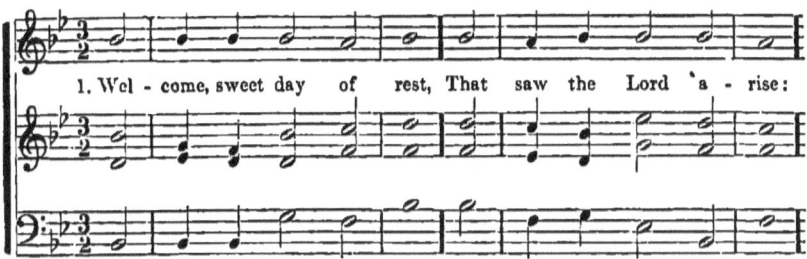

1. Welcome, sweet day of rest, That saw the Lord arise:

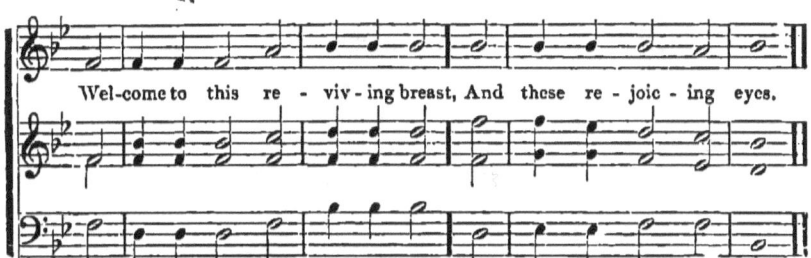

Welcome to this reviving breast, And these rejoicing eyes.

2 The King himself comes near,
    And feasts his saints to-day;
  Here we may sit, and see him here,
    And love, and praise, and pray.

3 One day in such a place,
    Where thou, my God, art seen,
  Is sweeter than ten thousand days
    Of pleasurable sin.

4 My willing soul would stay
    In such a frame as this,
  And sit and sing herself away
    To everlasting bliss.

402 *Laborers rewarded.*

1 O happy, happy place,
    Where saints and angels meet!
  There we shall see each other's face,
    And all our brethren greet.

2 The Church of the first-born,
    We shall with them be blest,
  And, crown'd with endless joy, return
    To our eternal rest.

3 With joy we shall behold,
    In yonder blest abode,
  The patriarchs and prophets old,
    And all the saints of God.

4 Abrah'm and Isaac, there,
    And Jacob, shall receive
The foll'wers of their faith and prayer,
    Who now in bodies live.

5 We shall our time beneath
    Live out, in cheerful hope,
  And fearless pass the vale of death,
    And gain the mountain top.

6 To gather home his own,
    God shall his angels send,
  And bid our bliss, on earth begun,
    In deathless triumphs end.

403
Joy from the certainty of His resurrection.

1 The Lord is risen indeed;
    The grave hath lost its prey;
  With him shall rise the ransom'd seed,
    To reign in endless day.

2 The Lord is risen indeed;
    He lives, to die no more;
  He lives, his people's cause to plead,
    Whose curse and shame he bore.

3 The Lord is risen indeed;
    Attending angels, hear;
  Up, to the courts of heaven, with speed,
    The joyful tidings bear:—

4 Then take your golden lyres,
    And strike each cheerful chord;
  Join, all ye bright celestial choirs,
    To sing our risen Lord.

404 ATHOL. S. M. — Rev. R. Harrison.

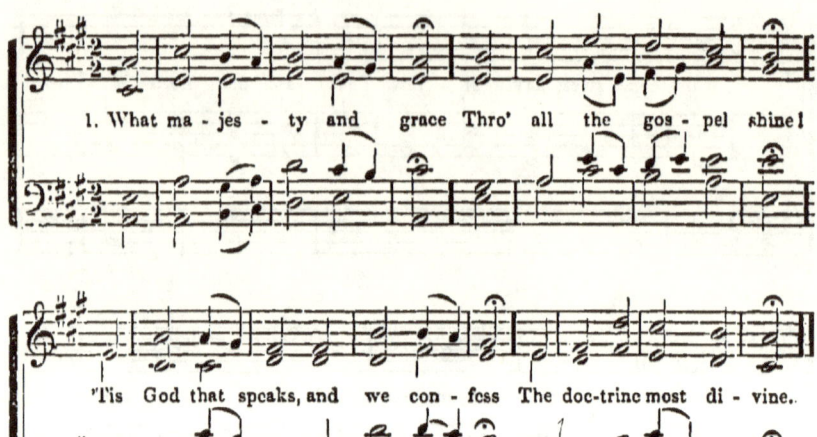

1. What majesty and grace Thro' all the gospel shine!
'Tis God that speaks, and we confess The doctrine most divine.

2 Down from his throne, on high,
 The mighty Savior comes;
Lays his bright robes of glory by,
 And feeble flesh assumes.

3 The debt that sinners owed,
 Upon the cross he pays:
Then thro' the clouds ascends to God,
 'Midst shouts of loftiest praise.

4 There our High Priest appears,
 Before his Father's throne;
Mingles his merits with our tears,
 And pours salvation down.

5 Great Sov'reign, we adore
 Thy justice and thy grace;
And on thy faithfulness and power
 Our firm dependence place.

405 *Waiting at the cross.*

1 Father, I dare believe
 Thee merciful and true:
Thou wilt my guilty soul forgive,—
 My fallen soul renew.

2 Come, then, for Jesus' sake,
 And bid my heart be clean;
An end of all my troubles make,—
 An end of all my sin.

3 I cannot wash my heart,
 But by believing thee,
And waiting for thy blood t' impart
 The spotless purity.

4 While at thy cross I lie,
 Jesus, the grace bestow;
Now thy all-cleansing blood apply,
 And I am white as snow.

406 *Meeting, after absence.*

1 And are we yet alive,
 And see each other's face?
Glory and praise to Jesus give,
 For his redeeming grace.

2 Preserved by power divine,
 To full salvation here,
Again in Jesus' praise we join,
 And in his sight appear.

3 What troubles have we seen!
 What conflicts have we past!
Fightings without, and fears within,
 Since we assembled last!

4 But out of all, the Lord
 Hath brought us by his love;
And still he doth his help afford,
 And hides our life above.

5 Then let us make our boast
 Of his redeeming power,
Which saves us to the uttermost,
 Till we can sin no more.

6 Let us take up the cross
 Till we the crown obtain;
And gladly reckon all things loss,
 So we may Jesus gain.

NASHVILLE. L. P. M.

Arranged by Dr. L. MASON.

1. O God, what off-'ring shall I give, To thee, the Lord of earth and skies?
My spir-it, soul, and flesh re-ceive, A ho-ly, liv-ing sac-ri-fice:
Small as it is, 'tis all my store; More should'st thou have, if I had more.

2 Now, then, my God, thou hast my soul:
   No longer mine, but thine I am:
Guard thou thine own, possess it whole;
   Cheer it with hope, with love inflame.
Thou hast my spirit; there display
Thy glory to the perfect day.

3 Thou hast my flesh, thy hallow'd shrine,
   Devoted solely to thy will:
Here let thy light forever shine —
   This house still let thy presence fill.
O Source of life! live, dwell, and move
In me, till all my life be love.

4 Lord, arm me with thy Spirit's might:
   Since I am call'd by thy great name,
In thee let all my thoughts unite:
   Of all my works be thou the aim:
Thy love attend me all my days,
And my sole business be thy praise.

408 *The prize of our high calling.*

1 Jesus, thy boundless love to me
   No tho't can reach, no tongue declare;
O knit my thankful heart to thee,
   And reign without a rival there:
Thine wholly, thine alone, I am;
Be thou alone my constant flame.

2 O grant that nothing in my soul
   May dwell, but thy pure love alone:
O may thy love possess me whole,—
   My joy, my treasure, and my crown;
Strange flames far from my heart remove;
My every act, word, thought, be love.

3 Unwearied may I this pursue;
   Dauntless to the high prize aspire;
Hourly within my soul renew
   This holy flame, this heavenly fire;
And day and night, be all my care
To guard the sacred treasure there.

4 In suff'ring be thy love my peace;
   In weakness be thy love my power;
And when the storms of life shall cease,
   Jesus, in that important hour,
In death as life be thou my guide,
And save me, who for me hast died.

409 ST. STEPHENS. L. P. M.
Geo. Neumark, 1650.

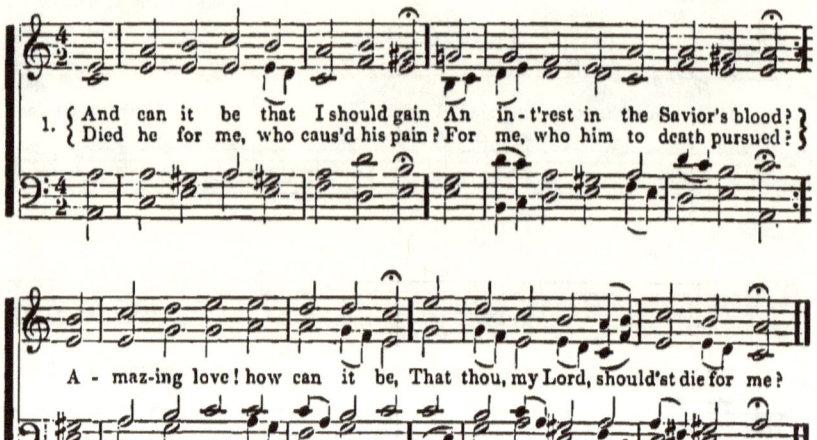

1. And can it be that I should gain An in-t'rest in the Savior's blood?
Died he for me, who caus'd his pain? For me, who him to death pursued?
A-maz-ing love! how can it be, That thou, my Lord, should'st die for me?

2 'Tis myst'ry all,—th' Immortal dies!
  Who can explore his strange design?
  In vain the first-born seraph tries
    To sound the depths of love divine;
  'Tis mercy all! let earth adore:
  Let angel minds inquire no more.

3 He left his Father's throne above;
    (So free, so infinite his grace!)
  Emptied himself of all but love,
    And bled for Adam's helpless race:
  'Tis mercy all, immense and free,
  For, O my God, it found out me!

4 Long my imprison'd spirit lay,
    Fast bound in sin and nature's night;
  Thine eye diffused a quick'ning ray;
    I woke; the dungeon flamed with light;
  My chains fell off, my heart was free,—
  I rose, went forth, and follow'd thee.

5 No condemnation now I dread,—
    Jesus, with all in him, is mine;
  Alive in him, my living Head,
    And clothed in righteousness divine,
  Bold I approach th' eternal throne,
  And claim the crown, thro' Christ my own.

410   *The vail of unbelief.*

1 O thou, whom fain my soul would love,
    Whom only I desire to know:
  This vail of unbelief remove,
    And show me all thy goodness, show;
  Jesus, thyself in me reveal:
  Tell me thy name, thy nature tell.

2 Hast thou been with me, Lord, so long,
    Yet thee, my Lord, have I not known?
  I claim thee with a falt'ring tongue,
    I pray thee, in a feeble groan,
  Tell me, O tell me who thou art,
  And speak thy name into my heart.

3 If now thou talkest by the way
    With me, the abject sinner, me,
  The mystery of grace display;
    Open mine eyes that I may see:
  That I may understand thy word,
  And now cry out,—It is the Lord!

411   *God is in this place.*

1 Lo! God is here! let us adore
    And own how dreadful is this place;
  Let all within us feel his power,
    And silent bow before his face;
  Who know his power, his grace who prove,
  Serve him with awe, with rev'rence, love.

2 Lo! God is here! him, day and night,
    United choirs of angels sing;
  To him, enthroned above all height,
    Heaven's host their noblest praises bring;
  Disdain not, Lord, our meaner song,
  Who praise thee with a stamm'ring tongue.

3 Being of beings! may our praise
    Thy courts with grateful fragrance fill;
  Still may we stand before thy face,
    Still hear and do thy sov'reign will:
  To thee may all our thoughts arise
  Ceaseless, accepted sacrifice.

Immortal honor, endless fame,
    Attend th' Almighty Father's Name:
The Savior Son be glorified,
    Who for lost man's redemption died;
And equal adoration be,
Eternal Comforter, to thee!

412 WRESTLING JACOB. 6 lines 8s. 129

Arranged for this Work.

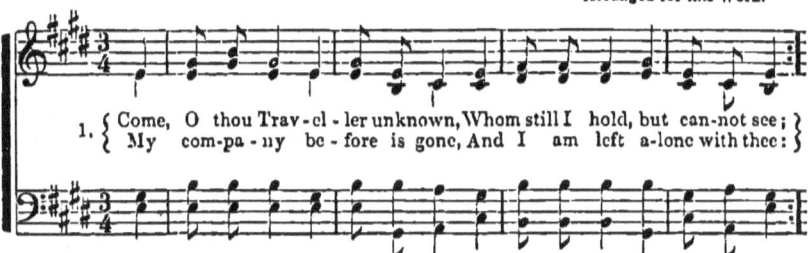

1. Come, O thou Trav-el-ler unknown, Whom still I hold, but can-not see;
My com-pa-ny be-fore is gone, And I am left a-lone with thee:

With thee all night I mean to stay, And wres-tle till the break of day.

2 I need not tell thee who I am;
My sin and misery declare;
Thyself hast call'd me by my name;
Look on thy hands, and read it there:
But who, I ask thee, who art thou?
Tell me thy name, and tell me now.

3 In vain thou strugglest to get free;
I never will unloose my hold;
Art thou the Man that died for me?
The secret of thy love unfold:
Wrestling, I will not let thee go,
Till I thy name, thy nature know.

4 Wilt thou not yet to me reveal
Thy new, unutterable name?
Tell me, I still beseech thee, tell:
To know it now resolved I am:
Wrestling, I will not let thee go,
Till I thy name, thy nature know.

5 What though my shrinking flesh complain,
And murmur to contend so long?
I rise superior to my pain:
When I am weak, then I am strong;
And when my all of strength shall fail,
I shall with the God-man prevail.

Victorious Prayer.

6 Yield to me now, for I am weak,
But confident in self-despair;
Speak to my heart, in blessings speak;
Be conquer'd by my instant prayer;
Speak, or thou never hence shalt move,
And tell me if thy name be Love.

7 'Tis Love! 'tis Love! thou diedst for me;
I hear thy whisper in my heart;
The morning breaks, the shadows flee;
Pure, universal Love thou art:
To me, to all, thy bowels move,—
Thy nature and thy name is Love.

8 My prayer hath power with God; the grace
Unspeakable I now receive;
Through faith I see thee face to face:
I see thee face to face, and live!
In vain I have not wept and strove;
Thy nature and thy name is Love.

9 I know thee, Savior, who thou art,—
Jesus, the feeble sinner's Friend;
Nor wilt thou with the night depart,
But stay and love me to the end:
Thy mercies never shall remove;
Thy nature and thy name is Love.

413 ST. PETERSBURG. L. P. M.

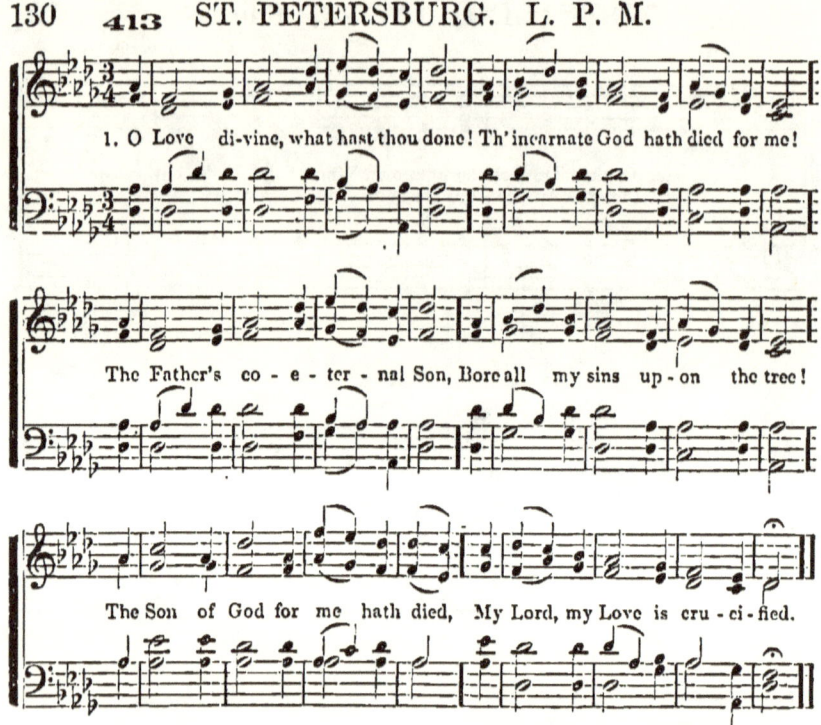

1. O Love divine, what hast thou done! Th' incarnate God hath died for me! The Father's co-eternal Son, Bore all my sins upon the tree! The Son of God for me hath died, My Lord, my Love is crucified.

2 Behold him, all ye that pass by,—
The bleeding Prince of life and peace!
Come see, ye worms, your Savior die,
And say, was ever grief like his?
Come, feel with me his blood applied:
My Lord, my Love, is crucified:—

3 Is crucified for me and you,
To bring us rebels back to God:
Believe, believe the record true,—
Ye all are bought with Jesus' blood:
Pardon for all flows from his side:
My Lord, my Love, is crucified.

4 Then let us sit beneath his cross,
And gladly catch the healing stream;
All things for him account but loss,
And give up all our hearts to him:
Of nothing think or speak beside,—
My Lord, my Love, is crucified.

414. *Dependence and enjoyment.*

1 When streaming from the eastern skies,
The morning light salutes mine eyes,
O Sun of righteousness divine,
On me with beams of mercy shine,
Oh! chase the clouds of guilt away,
And turn my darkness into day.

2 And when to heaven's all glorious King,
My morning sacrifice I bring;
And, mourning o'er my guilt and shame,
Ask mercy in my Savior's name;
Then, Jesus, sprinkle with thy blood,
And be my Advocate with God.

3 As every day thy mercy spares,
Will bring its trials and its cares;
O Savior, till my life shall end,
Be thou my counsellor and friend;
Teach me thy precepts, all divine,
And be thy great example mine.

4 When each day's scenes and labors close,
And wearied nature seeks repose,
With pardoning mercy richly blest,
Guard me, my Savior, while I rest;
And as each morning sun shall rise,
O lead me onward to the skies.

5 And at my life's last setting sun,
My conflicts o'er, my labors done,
Jesus, thy heavenly radiance shed,
To cheer and bless my dying bed:
And from death's gloom my spirit raise,
"To see thy face, and sing thy praise."

415   ARIEL. C. P. M.   Dr. L. Mason.

1. O glorious hope of perfect love, It lifts me up to things above; It bears on eagles' wings; It gives my ravish'd soul a taste, And makes me for some moments feast With Jesus' priests and kings, With Jesus' priests and kings.

2 Rejoicing now in earnest hope,
  I stand, and from the mountain top
    See all the land below:
  Rivers of milk and honey rise,
  And all the fruits of paradise
    In endless plenty grow.

3 A land of corn, and wine, and oil,
  Favor'd with God's peculiar smile,
    With every blessing blest;
  There dwells the Lord our Righteousness,
  And keeps his own in perfect peace,
    And everlasting rest.

4 O that I might at once go up;
  No more on this side Jordan stop,
    But now the land possess;
  This moment end my legal years;
  Sorrows and sins, and doubts and fears,
    A howling wilderness.

416   *Excellency of Christ.*

1 O, could I speak the matchless worth,
  O, could I sound the glories forth,
    Which in my Savior shine,
  I'd soar, and touch the heavenly strings,
  And vie with Gabriel, while he sings
    In notes almost divine.

2 I'd sing the characters he bears,
  And all the forms of love he wears,
    Exalted on his throne;
  In loftiest songs of sweetest praise,
  I would, to everlasting days,
    Make all his glories known.

3 O, the delightful day will come,
  When Christ, my Lord, will bring me home,
    And I shall see his face;
  Then with my Savior, Brother, Friend,
  A blest eternity I'll spend,
    Triumphant in his grace.

HOPE. C. P. M. 417

1. Come on, my part-ners in dis-tress, My comrades thro' the wil-derness, Who still your bo - dies feel; Who still your bo - dies feel; A-while for-get your griefs and fears, And look be - yond this vale of tears, To that ce - les - tial hill, To that ce - les - tial hill.

2. Be-yond the bounds of time and space, Look forward to that heav'nly place, The saints' se - cure a - bode; The saints' se - cure a - bode; On faith's strong ea - gle pin - ions rise, And force your passage to the skies, And scale the mount of God, And scale the mount of God.

3 Who suffer with our master here,
We shall before his face appear,
 And by his side sit down ;
To patient faith the prize is sure ;
And all that to the end endure
 The cross, shall wear the crown.

4 Thrice blessed, bliss-inspiring hope!
It lifts the fainting spirits up ;
 It brings to life the dead :
Our conflicts here shall soon be past,
And you and I ascend at last,
 Triumphant with our Head.

5 That great mysterious Deity,
We soon with open face shall see ;
 The beatific sight
Shall fill the heavenly courts with praise,
And wide diffuse the golden blaze
 Of everlasting light.

418 *The gift of faith.*

1 Author of faith, to thee I cry,
To thee, who wouldst not have me die,
 But know the truth and live :
Open mine eyes to see thy face ;
Work in my heart the saving grace ;
 The life eternal give.

2 Shut up in unbelief, I groan,
And blindly serve a God unknown,
 Till thou the vail remove ;
The gift unspeakable impart,
And write thy Name upon my heart,
 And manifest thy love.

3 I know the work is only thine ;
The gift of faith is all divine ;
 But, if on thee we call,
Thou wilt that gracious gift bestow,
And cause our hearts to feel and know
 That thou hast died for all.

4 Thou bidd'st us knock and enter in,—
Come unto thee, and rest from sin,—
 The blessing seek and find :
Thou bidd'st us ask thy grace, and have;
Thou canst, thou wouldst, this moment save
 Both me and all mankind.

5 Be it according to thy word ;
Now let me find my pard'ning Lord,
 Let what I ask be given :
The bar of unbelief remove :
Open the door of faith and love,
 And let me into heaven.

419 GANGES. C. P. M.

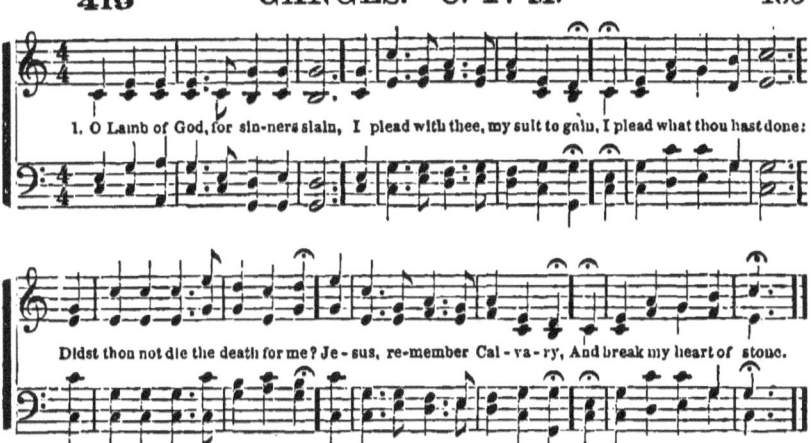

1. O Lamb of God, for sinners slain, I plead with thee, my suit to gain, I plead what thou hast done: Didst thou not die the death for me? Jesus, remember Calvary, And break my heart of stone.

2 Receive the purchase of thy blood,
My Friend, and Advocate with God,—
My ransom and my peace:
My Surety! thou my debt hast paid,
For all my sins atonement made,—
The Lord, my righteousness.

3 O let thy Spirit shed abroad
The love of my redeeming God,
In this cold heart of mine:
O might he now descend, and rest
Forever in this troubled breast,
And keep me ever thine.

420 *The inward Witness.*

1 Thou great mysterious God unknown,
Whose love hath gently led me on,
E'en from my infant days;
Mine inmost soul expose to view,
And tell me if I ever knew
Thy justifying grace.

2 If I have only known thy fear,
And followed with a heart sincere,
Thy drawings from above;
Now, now the further grace bestow,
And let my sprinkled conscience know
Thy sweet forgiving love.

3 Short of thy love I would not stop,
A stranger to the Gospel hope,
The sense of sin forgiven;
I would not, Lord, my soul deceive,
Without the inward witness live,
That ante-past of heaven.

4 If now the witness were in me,
Would he not testify of thee,
In Jesus reconciled?
And should I not with faith draw nigh,
And boldly, Abba, Father, cry,
And know myself thy child?

5 Father, in me reveal thy Son,
And to my inmost soul make known
How merciful thou art;
The secret of thy love reveal,
And by thy hallowing Spirit dwell
Forever in my heart.

421 *The brink of fate.*

1 Lo! on a narrow neck of land,
'Twixt two unbounded seas, I stand,
Secure, insensible:
A point of time, a moment's space,
Removes me to that heavenly place,
Or shuts me up in hell.

2 O God, mine inmost soul convert,
And deeply on my thoughtful heart
Eternal things impress:
Give me to feel their solemn weight,
And tremble on the brink of fate,
And wake to righteousness.

3 Before me place, in dread array,
The pomp of that tremendous day,
When thou with clouds shalt come
To judge the nations at thy bar:
And tell me, Lord, shall I be there,
To meet a joyful doom?

4 Be this my one great business here —
With serious industry and fear,
Eternal bliss t' ensure;
Thine utmost counsel to fulfil,
And suffer all thy righteous will,
And to the end endure.

5 Then, Savior, then my soul receive,
Transported from this vale, to live
And reign with thee above,
Where faith is sweetly lost in sight,
And hope, in full supreme delight,
And everlasting love.

MERIBAH. C. P. M.

Dr. L. MASON.

1. When thou my righteous Judge shalt come, To take thy ransomed people home, Shall I among them stand? Shall such a worthless worm as I, Who sometimes am afraid to die, Be found at thy right hand.

2. I love to meet thy people now, Before thy feet with them to bow, Though vilest of them all; But can I bear the piercing thought, What if my name should be left out, When thou for them shalt call?

3 O Lord, prevent it by thy grace,
Be thou my only hiding place,
In this th' accepted day ;
Thy pardoning voice O let me hear,
To still my unbelieving fear,
Nor let me fall, I pray.

4 Among thy saints let me be found,
Whene'er th' archangel's trump shall sound
To see thy smiling face ;
Then loudest of the crowd I'll sing,
While heaven's resounding mansions ring,
With shouts of sovereign grace.

423 *Entire dependence on Christ.*
1 Except the Lord conduct the plan,
The best concerted schemes are vain,
And never can succeed ; [naught
We spend our wretched strength for
But if our works in thee be wrought,
They shall be blest indeed.

2 In Jesus' name behold we meet,
Far from an evil world retreat,
And all its frantic ways ;
One only thing resolved to know,
And square our useful lives below,
By reason and by grace.

3 Now, Jesus, now thy love impart,
To govern each devoted heart,
And fit us for thy will ;
Deep founded in the truth of grace,
Build up thy rising Church, and place
The city on the hill.

4 O let our love and faith abound
O let our lives, to all around,
With purest lustre shine ;
That all around our works may see,
And give the glory, Lord, to thee,
The heavenly light divine.

MURRAY. C. P. M.

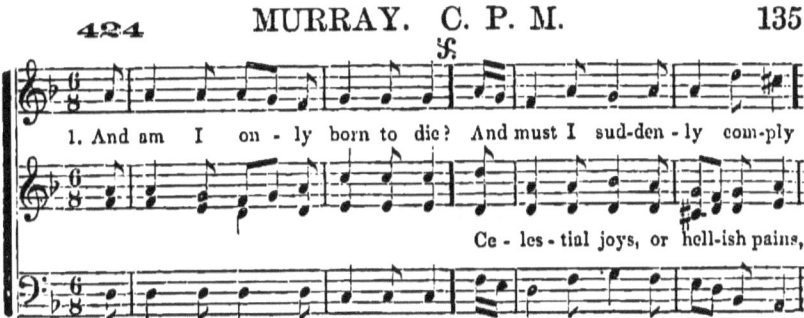

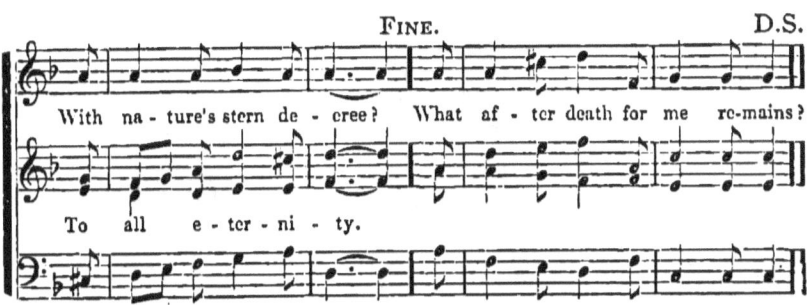

2 How then ought I on earth to live,
While God prolongs the kind reprieve,
And props the house of clay?
My sole concern, my single care,
To watch, and tremble, and prepare
Against that fatal day.

3 No room for mirth or trifling here,
For worldly hope, or worldly fear,
If life so soon is gone;
If now the Judge is at the door,
And all mankind must stand before
The' inexorable throne!

4 No matter which my thoughts employ,
A moment's misery or joy;
But, O! when both shall end,
Where shall I find my destined place?
Shall I my everlasting days
With fiends or angels spend?

5 Nothing is worth a thought beneath,
But how I may escape the death
That never, never dies!
How make mine own election sure:
And when I fail on earth, secure
A mansion in the skies.

6 Jesus, vouchsafe a pitying ray;
Be thou my Guide, be thou my Way
To glorious happiness.
Ah! write the pardon on my heart;
And whensoe'er I hence depart,
Let me depart in peace.

425 *Death of a relative or friend.*

1 If death our friends and us divide,
Thou dost not, Lord, our sorrows chide,
Or frown, our tears to see;
Restrain'd from passionate excess,
Thou bidd'st us mourn in calm distress
For them that rest in thee.

2 We feel a strong immortal hope,
Which bears our mournful spirits up,
Beneath their mountain load;
Redeemed from death, and grief, and pain
We soon shall find our friend again
Within the arms of God.

3 Pass a few fleeting moments more,
And death the blessing shall restore
Which death has snatch'd away;
For us thou wilt the summons send,
And give us back our parted friend,
In that eternal day.

LENOX. H. M. — EDSON.

1. A-rise, my soul, a-rise, Shake off thy guilty fears; The bleeding sacri-fice In my be-half appears.

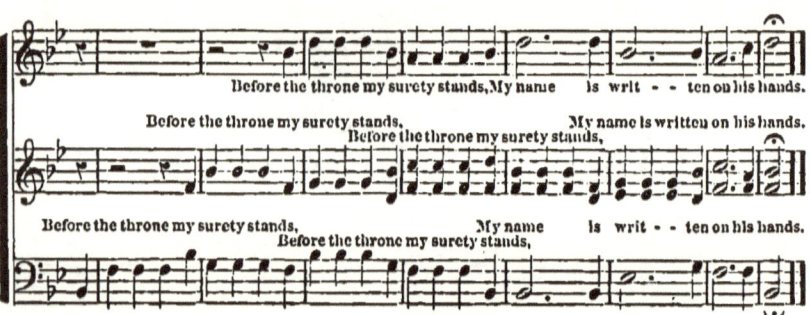

Before the throne my surety stands, My name is writ - - ten on his hands.

2 He ever lives above,
   For me to intercede ;
  His all-redeeming love,
   His precious blood, to plead ;
His blood atoned for all our race,
And sprinkles now the throne of grace.

3 Five bleeding wounds he bears,
   Received on Calvary ;
  They pour effectual prayers,
   They strongly plead for me :—
Forgive him, O forgive, they cry,
Nor let that ransomed sinner die.

4 The Father hears him pray,
   His dear anointed One :
  He cannot turn away
   The presence of his Son :
His Spirit answers to the blood,
And tells me I am born of God.

5 My God is reconciled ;
   His pard'ning voice I hear :
  He owns me for his child ;
   I can no longer fear :
With confidence I now draw nigh,
And Father, Abba, Father, cry.

427 *Bear ye one another's burden.*

1 Thou God of truth and love,
   We seek thy perfect way,
  Ready thy choice t' approve,
   Thy providence t' obey ;
Enter into thy wise design,
And sweetly lose our will in thine.

2 Why hast thou cast our lot
   In the same age and place ?
  And why together brought
   To see each other's face ;—
To join with softest sympathy,
And mix our friendly souls in thee ?

3 Didst thou not make us one,
   That we might one remain ;—
  Together travel on,
   And bear each other's pain ;—
Till all thy utmost goodness prove,
And rise, renewed in perfect love ?

4 Surely thou didst unite
   Our kindred spirits here,
  That all hereafter might
   Before thy throne appear ;—
Meet at the marriage of the Lamb,
And all thy gracious love proclaim.

* See foot note on p. 3d. of the Introduction.

5 Then let us ever bear
  The blessed end in view,
And join with mutual care,
  To fight our passage through;
And kindly help each other on,
Till all receive the starry crown.

6 O may thy Spirit seal
  Our souls unto that day!
With all thy fullness fill,
  And then transport away,
Away to our eternal rest,
Away to our Redeemer's breast.

428 *Parting:—to meet again.*

1 Jesus accept the praise
  That to thy Name belongs;
Matter of all our lays,
  Subject of all our songs;
Through thee we now together came,
And part, exulting in thy Name.

2 In flesh we part awhile,
  But still in spirit joined,
T' embrace the happy toil
  Thou hast to each assigned;
And while we do thy blessed will,
We bear our heaven about us still.

3 O let us thus go on
  In all thy pleasant ways,
And, armed with patience, run
  With joy th' appointed race:
Keep us and every seeking soul,
Till all attain the heavenly goal.

4 There we shall meet again,
  When all our toils are o'er,
And death, and grief, and pain,
  And parting are no more:
We shall with all our brethren rise,
And see thee in the flaming skies.

5 O happy, happy day,
  That calls thy exiles home;
The heavens shall pass away,
  The earth receive its doom:
Earth we shall view, and heaven, destroy'd,
And shout above the fiery void.

6 According to his word,
  His oath, to sinners given,
We look to see restored
  The ruined earth and heaven;
In a new world his truth to prove,
A world of righteousness and love.

7 Then let us wait the sound
  That shall our souls release,
And labor to be found
  Of him in spotless peace:
In perfect holiness renewed,
Adorned with Christ, and meet for God.

429 *The jubilee trumpet.*

1 Blow ye the trumpet, blow
  The gladly-solemn sound;
Let all the nations know,
  To earth's remotest bound,
The year of jubilee is come;
Return, ye ransom'd sinners, home.

2 Jesus, our great High Priest,
  Hath full atonement made:
Ye weary spirits, rest;
  Ye mournful souls, be glad:
The year of jubilee is come;
Return, ye ransom'd sinners, home.

3 Extol the Lamb of God,—
  The all-atoning Lamb;
Redemption in his blood
  Throughout the world proclaim:
The year of jubilee is come;
Return, ye ransom'd sinners, home.

4 Ye slaves of sin and hell,
  Your liberty receive,
And safe in Jesus dwell,
  And blest in Jesus live:
The year of jubilee is come:
Return, ye ransom'd sinners, home.

5 Ye who have sold for naught
  Your heritage above,
Shall have it back unbought,
  The gift of Jesus' love:
The year of jubilee is come;
Return, ye ransom'd sinners, home.

6 The gospel trumpet hear,—
  The news of heavenly grace;
And, saved from earth, appear
  Before your Savior's face:
The year of jubilee is come;
Return, ye ransom'd sinners, home.

LISCHER. H. M.
Dr. L. MASON.

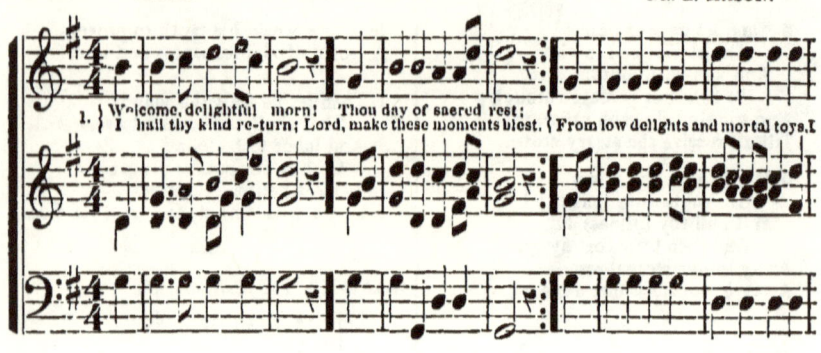

2 Now may the King descend,
  And fill his throne of grace;
Thy sceptre, Lord, extend,
  While saints address thy face;
Let sinners feel thy quick'ning word,
And learn to know and fear the Lord.

3 Descend, celestial dove,
  With all thy quick'ning powers;
Disclose a Savior's love,
  And bless these sacred hours:
Then shall my soul new life obtain,
Nor Sabbaths be indulged in vain.

431 *Joyful homage.*

1 Awake, ye saints, awake!
  And hail this sacred day:
In loftiest songs of praise
  Your joyful homage pay:
Come bless the day that God hath blest,
The type of heaven's eternal rest.

2 On this auspicious morn
  The Lord of life arose;
He burst the bars of death,
  And vanquished all our foes;
And now he pleads our cause above,
And reaps the fruit of all his love.

3 All hail, triumphant Lord!
  Heaven with hosannas rings,
And earth, in humbler strains,
  Thy praise responsive sings:
Worthy the Lamb, that once was slain,
Through endless years to live and reign.

Doxology.

To God, the Father's throne,
  Perpetual honors raise;
Glory to God, the Son,
  And to the Spirit praise:
With all our powers, Eternal King,
Thy everlasting praise we sing.

DARWELL. H. M.
Rev. J. Darwell.

1. Sinners, lift up your hearts, The promise to receive; Jesus himself imparts,—He comes in man to live; The Ho-ly Ghost to man is giv'n; Rejoice in God sent down from heav'n.

2 Jesus is glorified,
  And gives the Comforter
His Spirit, to reside
  In all his members here;
The Holy Ghost to man is given;
Rejoice in God sent down from heaven.

3 To make an end of sin,
  And Satan's works destroy,
He brings his kingdom in,—
  Peace, righteousness, and joy:
The Holy Ghost to man is given;
Rejoice in God sent down from heaven.

4 From heaven he shall once more
  Triumphantly descend,
And all his saints restore
  To joys that never end:
Then, then, when all our joys are given,
Rejoice in God, rejoice in heaven.

433 *Glory to glory's King.*

1 God is gone up on high,
  With a triumphant noise,—
The clarions of the sky
  Proclaim th' angelic joys:
Join all on earth, rejoice and sing;
Glory ascribe to glory's King.

2 All power to our great Lord
  Is by the Father given;
By angel hosts adored,
  He reigns supreme in heaven:
Join all on earth, rejoice and sing;
Glory ascribe to glory's King.

3 High on his holy seat,
  He bears the righteous sway;
His foes beneath his feet
  Shall sink and die away:
Join all on earth, rejoice and sing;
Glory ascribe to glory's King.

4 Till all the earth, renew'd
  In righteousness divine,
With all the hosts of God,
  In one great chorus join,
Join all on earth, rejoice and sing;
Glory ascribe to glory's King.

434 *The barren fig-tree.*

1 The Lord of earth and sky,
  The God of ages praise,
Who reigns enthroned on high,
  Ancient of endless days,—
Who lengthens out our trials here,
And spares us yet another year.

2 Barren and wither'd trees,
  We cumber'd long the ground:
No fruit of holiness
  On our dead souls was found;
Yet doth he us in mercy spare,
Another and another year.

3 When justice bared the sword,
  To cut the fig-tree down,
The pity of the Lord
  Cried,—let it still alone:
The Father mild inclines his ear,
And spares us yet another year.

4 Jesus, thy speaking blood
  From God obtain'd the grace,
Who therefore hath bestow'd
  On us a longer space;
Thou didst in our behalf appear,
And lo! we see another year.

5 Then dig about the root;
  Break up our fallow ground,
And let our gracious fruit
  To thy great praise abound:
O let us all thy praise declare,
And fruit unto perfection bear.

435 PROSPECT. H. M.
Arranged from MICHAEL HAYDN.

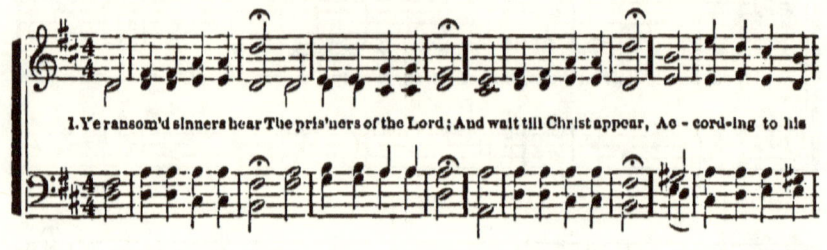

1. Ye ransom'd sinners hear The pris'ners of the Lord; And wait till Christ appear, Ac-cord-ing to his word: Re-joice in hope, re-joice with me; We shall from all our sins be free.

2 In God we put our trust:
  If we our sins confess,
  Faithful is he and just,
  From all unrighteousness
 To cleanse us all, both you and me;
 We shall from all our sins be free.

3 Surely in us the hope
  Of glory shall appear;
  Sinners, your heads lift up,
  And see redemption near:
 Again I say, Rejoice with me;
 We shall from all our sins be free.

4 Who Jesus' suff'rings share,
  My fellow-pris'ners now,
  Ye soon the crown shall wear
  On your triumphant brow:
 Rejoice in hope, rejoice with me;
 We shall from all our sins be free.

5 The word of God is sure,
  And never can remove;
  We shall in heart be pure,
  And perfected in love:
 Rejoice in hope, rejoice with me;
 We shall from all our sins be free.

6 Then let us gladly bring
  Our sacrifice of praise:
  Let us give thanks and sing,
  And glory in his grace:
 Rejoice in hope, rejoice with me;
 We shall from all our sins be free.

436 *God, our preserver.*

1 To heaven I lift mine eyes;
  From God is all my aid—
  The God who built the skies,
  And earth and nature made;
 God is the tower to which I fly;
 His grace is nigh in every hour.

2 My feet shall never slide,
  And fall in fatal snares,
  Since God, my Guard and Guide,
  Defends me from my fears.
 Those wakeful eyes, which never sleep,
 Shall Israel keep when dangers rise.

3 No burning heats by day,
  Nor blasts of evening air,
  Shall take my health away,
  If God be with me there:
 Thou art my sun, and thou my shade,
 To guard my head by night or noon.

4 Hast thou not pledged thy word
  To save my soul from death?
  And I can trust my Lord
  To keep my mortal breath.
 I'll go and come, nor fear to die,
 Till from on high thou call me home.

437. HORTON. 7s. X. Schnyder von Wartensee

1. Come said Jesus' sacred voice; Come, and make my paths your choice; I will guide you to your home, Weary pilgrims! hither come.

2. Hither come, for here is found Balm for every bleeding wound, Peace, which ever shall endure— Rest, eternal, sacred, sure!

438 *Of one heart and of one mind.*

1 Jesus, Lord, we look to thee;
Let us in thy name agree;
Show thyself the Prince of Peace;
Bid our jars forever cease.

2 By thy reconciling love,
Every stumbling-block remove:
Each to each unite, endear;
Come, and spread thy banner here.

3 Make us of one heart and mind,—
Courteous, pitiful, and kind;
Lowly, meek, in thought and word,—
Altogether like our Lord.

4 Let us for each other care;
Each the other's burden bear:
To thy Church the pattern give;
Show how true believers live.

5 Free from anger and from pride,
Let us thus in God abide;
All the depths of love express,—
All the hights of holiness.

6 Let us then with joy remove
To the family above;
On the wings of angels fly;
Show how true believers die.

439 *Perfect submission.*

1 When, my Savior, shall I be
Perfectly resigned to thee?
Poor and vile in my own eyes,
Only in thy wisdom wise?

2 Only thee content to know,
Ignorant of all below?
Only guided by thy light?
Only mighty in thy might?

3 So I may thy Spirit know,
Let him as he listeth blow:
Let the manner be unknown,
So I may with thee be one:—

4 Fully in my life express
All the hights of holiness;
Sweetly let my spirit prove,
All the depths of humble love.

440

1 Thou that dost my life prolong,
Kindly aid my morning song;
Thankful from my couch I rise,
To the God that rules the skies.

2 Gently, with the dawning ray,
On my soul thy beams display;
Sweeter than the smiling morn,
Let thy cheering light return.

HENDON. 7s.
Rev. Dr. Malan

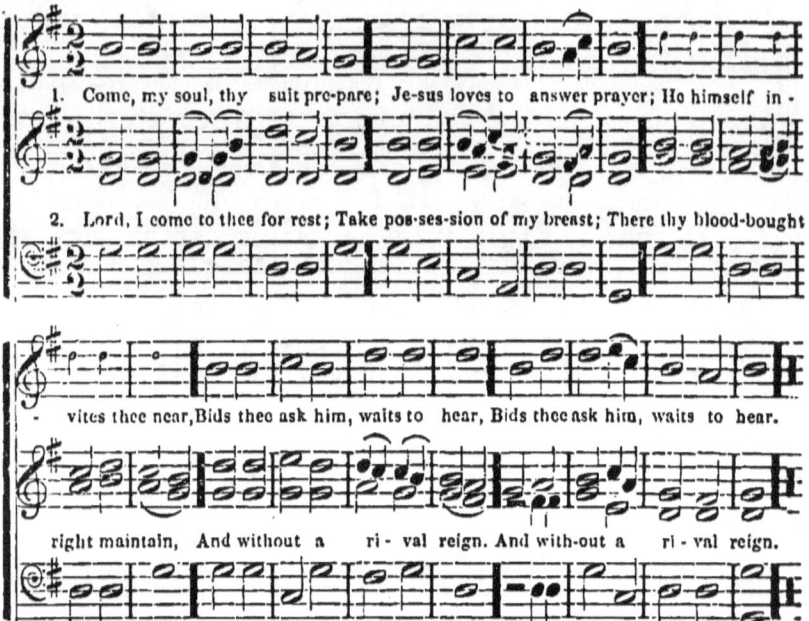

1. Come, my soul, thy suit prepare; Jesus loves to answer prayer; He himself invites thee near, Bids thee ask him, waits to hear, Bids thee ask him, waits to hear.

2. Lord, I come to thee for rest; Take possession of my breast; There thy blood-bought right maintain, And without a rival reign, And without a rival reign.

3 While I am a pilgrim here,
  Let thy love my spirit cheer;
  As my guide, my guard, my friend,
  Lead me to my journey's end.

4 Show me what I have to do;
  Every hour my strength renew;
  Let me live a life of faith,—
  Let me die thy people's death.

442
Life and immortality brought to light.

1 Day of God! thou blessed day,
  At thy dawn the grave gave way
  To the power of Him within,
  Who had, sinless, bled for sin.

2 Thine the radiance to illume
  First, for man, the dismal tomb,
  When its bars their weakness own'd,
  There revealing death dethroned.

3 Then the Sun of righteousness
  Rose, a darken'd world to bless,
  Bringing up from mortal night
  Immortality and light.

4 Day of glory, day of power,
  Sacred be thine every hour,—
  Emblem, earnest, of the rest
  That remaineth for the blest.

443 *Panting for purity.*

1 Holy Lamb, who thee receive,
  Who in thee begin to live,
  Day and night they cry to thee,—
  As thou art, so let us be!

2 Jesus, see my panting breast;
  See, I pant in thee to rest;
  Gladly would I now be clean;
  Cleanse me now from every sin.

3 Fix, O fix my wav'ring mind;
  To thy cross my spirit bind:
  Earthly passions far remove;
  Swallow up my soul in love.

4 Dust and ashes though we be,
  Full of sin and misery,
  Thine we are, thou Son of God;
  Take the purchase of thy blood!

444 *Eternal praises to the Most High.*

1 Thee to laud in songs divine
  Angels in thy presence join:
  We with them our voices raise,
  Echo thine eternal praise.

2 Holy, holy, holy Lord,
  Live, by heaven and earth adored
  Thus, with them, we ever cry,
  Glory be to God most high!

NUREMBERG. 7s.

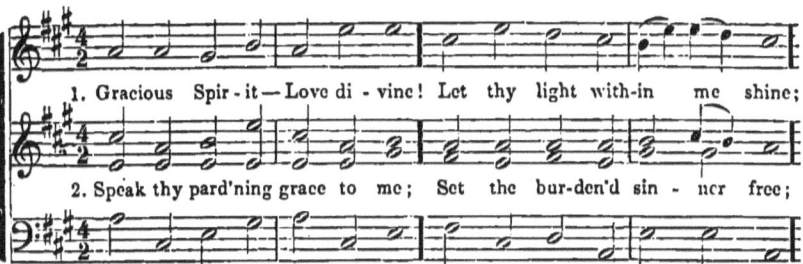

1. Gracious Spir-it—Love di-vine! Let thy light with-in me shine;
2. Speak thy pard'ning grace to me; Set the bur-den'd sin-ner free;

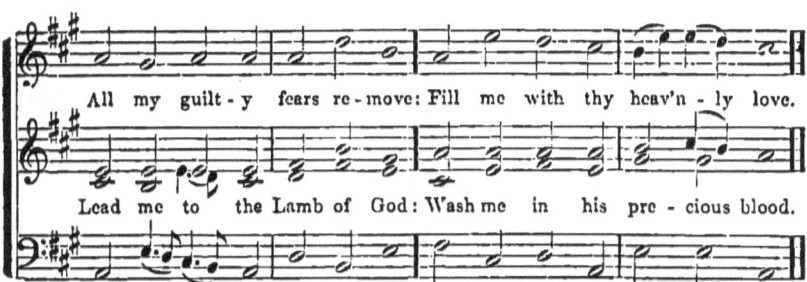

All my guilt-y fears re-move: Fill me with thy heav'n-ly love.
Lead me to the Lamb of God: Wash me in his pre-cious blood.

3 Life and peace to me impart;
Seal salvation on my heart;
Breathe thyself into my breast,—
Earnest of immortal rest.

4 Let me never from thee stray:
Keep me in the narrow way;
Fill my soul with joy divine;
Keep me, Lord, forever thine.

446 *Saints and angels, praising God.*

1 Songs of praise the angels sang,
Heaven with hallelujahs rang,
When Jehovah's work begun,
When he spake, and it was done.

2 Songs of praise awoke the morn,
When the Prince of Peace was born;
Songs of praise arose, when he
Captive led captivity.

3 Heaven and earth must pass away,—
Songs of praise shall crown that day;
God will make new heavens and earth,—
Songs of praise shall hail their birth.

4 And shall man alone be dumb,
Till that glorious morning come?
No!—the church delights to raise
Psalms, and hymns, and songs of praise.

5 Saints below, with heart and voice,
Still in songs of praise rejoice,
Learning here, by faith and love,
Songs of praise, to sing above.

6 Borne upon their latest breath,
Songs of praise shall conquer death;
Then, amid eternal joy,
Songs of praise their powers employ.

447 *Let all the people praise Him.*

1 Thank and praise Jehovah's Name,
For his mercies, firm and sure;
From eternity the same,
To eternity endure.

2 Let the ransomed thus rejoice,
Gathered out of every land;
As the people of his choice,
Plucked from the destroyer's hand.

3 Let the elders praise the Lord,
Him let all the people praise,
When they meet, with one accord,
In his courts on holy days.

4 Praise him, ye who know his love,
Praise him from the depths beneath:
Praise him in the heights above,
Praise your Maker, all that breathe.

5 For his truth and mercy stand,
Past, and present, and to be,
Like the years of his right hand,
Like his own eternity.

PLEYEL'S HYMN. 7s.   PLEYEL.

2 Though unworthy of thine ear,
Deign our humble songs to hear;
Purer praise we hope to bring,
When around thy throne we sing.

3 While on earth ordain'd to stay,
Guide our footsteps in thy way,
Till we come to dwell with thee,
Till we all thy glory see.

4 Then, with angel-harps again,
We will wake a nobler strain;
There, in joyful songs of praise,
Our triumphant voices raise.

449 *Tribute of praise at parting.*

1 Christians, brethren, ere we part,
Every voice and every heart
Join, and to our Father raise,
One last hymn of grateful praise.

2 Though we here should meet no more,
Yet there is a brighter shore;
There, released from toil and pain,
There we all may meet again.

3 Now to thee, thou God of heaven,
Be eternal glory given:
Grateful for thy love divine,
May our hearts be ever thine.

450 *The danger of delay.*

1 Hasten, sinner, to be wise!
Stay not for the morrow's sun:
Wisdom if you still despise,
Harder is it to be won.

2 Hasten mercy to implore!
Stay not for the morrow's sun,
Lest thy season should be o'er
Ere this evening's stage be run.

3 Hasten, sinner, to return!
Stay not for the morrow's sun,
Lest thy lamp should fail to burn
Ere salvation's work is done.

4 Hasten, sinner, to be blest!
Stay not for the morrow's sun,
Lest perdition thee arrest
Ere the morrow is begun.

451 *Little ones brought to Jesus.*

1 Jesus, kind, inviting Lord,
We with joy obey thy word,
And in earliest infancy
Bring our little ones to thee.

2 Born they are, as we, in sin;
Make th' unconsious lepers clean;
Purchase of thy blood they are,—
Let them in thy glory share.

452 *The pilgrim's song.*

1 Children of the heavenly King,
As we journey let us sing;
Sing our Savior's worthy praise,
Glorious in his works and ways.

2 We are trav'ling home to God,
In the way our fathers trod;
They are happy now, and we
Soon their happiness shall see.

3 Fear not, brethren, joyful stand
On the borders of our land;
Jesus Christ, our Father's Son,
Bids us undismayed go on.

4 Lord! obediently we'll go,
Gladly leaving all below:
Only thou our leader be,
And we still will follow thee.

453 *Mercy for the chief of sinners.*

1 Depth of mercy! can there be
Mercy still reserved for me?
Can my God his wrath forbear?
Me, the chief of sinners, spare?

2 I have long withstood his grace;
Long provoked him to his face;
Would not hearken to his calls;
Grieved him by a thousand falls.

3 Now incline me to repent;
Let me now my sins lament;
Now my foul revolt deplore,
Weep, believe, and sin no more.

4 Kindled his relentings are;
Me he now delights to spare;
Cries, How shall I give thee up?—
Lets the lifted thunder drop.

5 There for me the Savior stands;
Shows his wounds, and spreads his hands;
God is love! I know, I feel;
Jesus weeps, and loves me still.

454 *Discerning the Lord's body.*

1 Jesus, all-redeeming Lord,
Magnify thy dying word;
In thine ordinance appear;
Come, and meet thy foll'wers here.

2 In the rite thou hast enjoin'd,
Let us now our Savior find;
Drink thy blood for sinners shed,
Taste thee in the broken bread.

3 Thou our faithful hearts prepare;
Thou thy pard'ning grace declare,
Thou that hast for sinners died,
Show thyself the Crucified!

4 All the power of sin remove;
Fill us with thy perfect love;
Stamp us with the stamp divine;
Seal our souls forever thine.

455 *Why will ye die?*

1 Sinners, turn; why will ye die?
God, your Maker, asks you why?
God, who did your being give,
Made you with himself to live;

2 He the fatal cause demands;
Asks the work of his own hands,—
Why, ye thankless creatures, why
Will ye cross his love, and die?

3 Sinners, turn; why will ye die?
God, your Savior, asks you why?
He, who did your souls retrieve,
Died himself, that ye might live.

4 Will ye let him die in vain?
Crucify your Lord again?
Why, ye ransom'd sinners, why
Will ye slight his grace, and die?

5 Sinners, turn; why will ye die?
God, the Spirit, asks you why?
He, who all your lives hath strove,
Urged you to embrace his love.

6 Will ye not his grace receive?
Will ye still refuse to live?
O ye dying sinners, why,
Why will ye forever die?

456 *Dedication.*

1 Lord of hosts! to thee we raise
Here a house of prayer and praise:
Thou thy people's hearts prepare,
Here to meet for praise and prayer.

2 Let the living here be fed
With thy word, the heavenly bread;
Here, in hope of glory blest,
May the dead be laid to rest.

3 Here to thee a temple stand,
While the sea shall gird the land:
Here reveal thy mercy sure,
While the sun and moon endure.

4 Hallelujah! earth and sky
To the joyful sound reply:
Hallelujah! hence ascend
Prayer and praise till time shall end.

457 TOPLADY. 7s. 6l. DR. THOS. HASTINGS. By permission.

1. Rock of a-ges, cleft for me, Let me hide my-self in thee; Let the wa-ter and the blood, From thy wound-ed side which flow'd, Be of sin the dou-ble cure,—Save from wrath, and make me pure.

2 Could my tears forever flow,—
Could my zeal no languor know,—
These for sin could not atone;
Thou must save, and thou alone:
In my hand no price I bring;
Simply to the cross I cling.

3 While I draw this fleeting breath,
When my eyes shall close in death,
When I rise to worlds unknown,
And behold thee on thy throne,—
Rock of ages, cleft for me,
Let me hide myself in thee.

458 *What sin hath done.*

1 Hearts of stone, relent, relent!
Break, by Jesus' cross subdued;
See his body mangled, rent,
Stain'd and cover'd with his blood!
Sinful soul, what hast thou done?
Crucified th' eternal Son.

2 Yes, thy sins have done the deed;
Driv'n the nails that fix'd him there;
Crown'd with thorns his sacred head;
Plunged into his side the spear;
Made his soul a sacrifice,
While for sinful man he dies.

3 Wilt thou let him bleed in vain?
Still to death thy Lord pursue?
Open all his wounds again,
And the shameful cross renew?
No; with all my sins I'll part;
Savior, take my broken heart.

459 *The Light of Life.*

1 O disclose thy lovely face!
Quicken all my drooping powers:
Gasps my fainting soul for grace,
As a thirsty land for showers;
Hasten, Lord, no more delay;
Come, my Savior, come away.

2 Dark and cheerless is the morn,
Unaccompanied by thee;
Joyless is the day's return,
Till thy mercy's beams I see:
Till thou inward life impart,
Glad my eyes, and warm my Heart.

3 Visit then this soul of mine;
Pierce the gloom of sin and grief;
Fill me, Radiancy divine;
Scatter all my unbelief;
More and more thyself display,
Shining to the perfect day.

460 ROSEFIELD. 7s. 6l.
Rev. Dr. MALAN. Geneva, Switzerland.

1. From the cross up-lift-ed high, Where the Sav-ior deigns to die,
What me-lo-dious sounds we hear Burst-ing on the rav-ished ear:

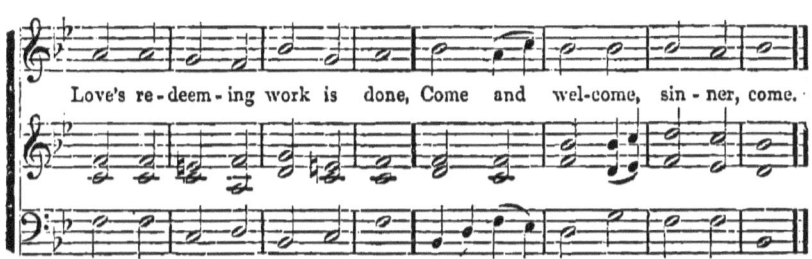

Love's re-deem-ing work is done, Come and wel-come, sin-ner, come.

2 Sprinkled now with blood the throne—
Why beneath thy burdens groan?
On his pierced body laid,
Justice owns the ransom paid;
Bow the knee,—embrace the Son—
Come and welcome, sinner, come!

3 Spread for thee, the festal board,
See with richest bounty stored;
To thy Father's bosom press'd,
Thou shalt be a child confess'd,
Never from his house to roam;
Come and welcome, sinner, come!

461 *Fly to Jesus.*

1 Weary souls, that wander wide
From the central point of bliss;
Turn to Jesus crucified;
Fly to those dear wounds of his:
Sink into the purple flood;
Rise, into the life of God.

2 Find in Christ the way of peace,
Peace unspeakable, unknown;
By his pain he gives you ease,
Life by his expiring groan:
Rise exalted by his fall;
Find in Christ our all in all.

3 O believe the record true,
God to you his Son has given;
Ye may now be happy too,
Find on earth the life of heaven:
Live the life of heaven above,
All the life of glorious love.

4 This the universal bliss,
Bliss for every soul design'd;
God's original promise this,
God's great gift to all mankind:
Blest in Christ this moment be,
Blest to all eternity.

462 *The covenant of grace signed and sealed.*

1 Jesus Christ, who stands between
Angry Heaven and guilty men,
Undertakes to buy our peace;
Gives the covenant of grace;
Ratifies and makes it good;
Signs and seals it with his blood.

2 Life his healing blood imparts,
Sprinkled in our peaceful hearts;
Abel's blood for vengeance cried;
Jesus speaks us justified;
Speaks and calls for better things;
Makes us prophets, priests, and kings.

SABBATH MORN. 7s. 6. Lines.

Dr. L. MASON.

3 Here we come thy name to praise,
   Let us feel thy presence near,
May thy glory meet our eyes,
   While we in thy house appear;
Here afford us, Lord, a taste
Of our everlasting feast.

4 May the gospel's joyful sound,
   Conquer sinners, comfort saints;
Make the fruits of grace abound,
   Bring relief from all complaints:
Thus let all our Sabbaths prove,
Till we join the church above.

464 *Hand in hand to heaven.*

1 Centre of our hopes thou art,
   End of our enlarged desires:
Stamp thine image on our heart;
   Fill us now with heavenly fires:
Join'd to thee by love divine,
Seal our souls forever thine.

2 All our works in thee be wrought,—
   Levell'd at one common aim:
Every word and every thought
   Purge in the refining flame·
Lead us, through the paths of peace,
On to perfect holiness.

3 Let us all together rise,—
   To thy glorious life restored;
Here regain our Paradise,—
   Here prepare to meet our Lord:
Here enjoy the earnest given;
Travel hand in hand to heaven.

465 *Doxology.*

Praise the Name of God most high;
Praise him, all below the sky;
Praise him, all ye heavenly host—
Father, Son, and Holy Ghost:
As through countless ages past,
Evermore his praise shall last.

466. LITANY HYMN. 7s. Double.

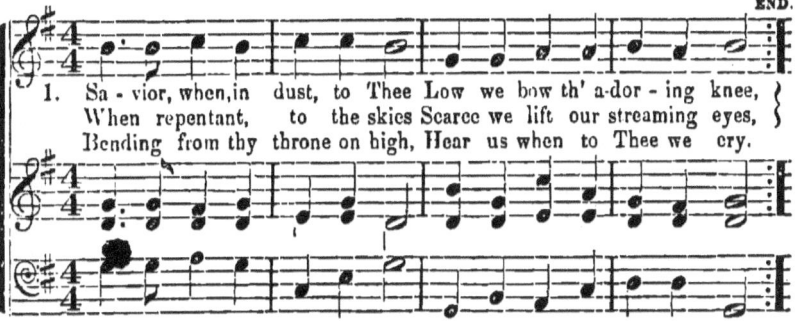

1. Sa-vior, when, in dust, to Thee Low we bow th' ador-ing knee,
   When repentant, to the skies Scarce we lift our streaming eyes,
   Bending from thy throne on high, Hear us when to Thee we cry.

O, by all thy pain and wo Suf-fer'd once for man be-low,

2 By Thy birth and early years,
By Thy human griefs and fears,
By Thy fasting and distress
In the lonely wilderness,
By Thy vict'ry in the hour
Of the subtle tempter's power:
Jesus, look with pitying eye;
Hear our solemn litany.

3 By Thine hour of dark despair,
By Thine agony of prayer;
By the cross, the nail, the thorn,
Piercing spear, and robe of scorn;
By the gloom that vail'd the skies
O'er the perfect sacrifice,—
Jesus, look with pitying eye;
Hear, O hear our humble cry.

3 By Thy deep, expiring groan;
By the seal'd, sepulchral stone;
By Thy triumph o'er the grave,
By Thy power from death to save:
Mighty God, ascended Lord,
To Thy throne in heaven restored,
Prince and Savior, hear our cry,
Hear our solemn litany.

467. *Cut short the work in righteousness.*

1 Savior of the sin-sick soul,
Give me faith to make me whole;
Finish thy great work of grace;
Cut it short in righteousness.
Speak the second time,—Be clean!
Take away my inbred sin;
Every stumbling-block remove;
Cast it out by perfect love.

2 Nothing less will I require;
Nothing more can I desire:
None but Christ to me be given;
None but Christ in earth or heaven.
O that I might now decrease!
O that all I am might cease!
Let me into nothing fall;
Let my Lord be all in all!

Doxology.

Sing we to our God above,
Praise eternal as his love;
Praise the Name of God most high
Praise him, all below the sky;
Praise him, all ye heavenly host,—
Father, Son, and Holy Ghost:
As through countless ages past,
Evermore his praise shall last.

2 As the winged arrow flies
　Speedily the mark to find;
　As the lightning from the skies
　　Darts, and leaves no trace behind,—
　Swiftly thus our fleeting days
　　Bear us down life's rapid stream;
　Upward, Lord, our spirits raise;
　　All below is but a dream.

3 Thanks for mercies past receive;
　　Pardon of our sins renew;
　Teach us henceforth how to live
　　With eternity in view:
　Bless thy word to young and old;
　　Fill us with a Savior's love;
　And when life's short tale is told,
　　May we reign with thee above.

469 *Clothed with immortality.*

1 Spirit, leave thy house of clay;
　　Ling'ring dust, resign thy breath:
　Spirit, cast thy chains away;
　　Dust, be thou dissolved in death:—
　Thus the mighty Savior speaks,
　　While the faithful Christian dies;
　Thus the bonds of life he breaks,
　　And the ransom'd captive flies.

2 Pris'ner, long detain'd below,
　　Pris'ner, now with freedom blest,
　Welcome from a world of wo;
　　Welcome to a land of rest:—
　Thus the choir of angels sing,
　　As they bear the soul on high,
　While with hallelujahs ring
　　All the regions of the sky.

3 Grave, the guardian of our dust,
　Grave, the treasury of the skies,
　Every atom of thy trust
　　Rests in hope again to rise:
　Hark! the judgment trumpet calls—
　　Soul, rebuild thy house of clay;
　Immortality thy walls,
　　And eternity thy day.

470 *The dying believer.*

1 Deathless spirit, now arise;
　Soar, thou native of the skies—
　Pearl of price by Jesus bought,
　To his glorious likeness wrought:—
　Go to shine before the throne;
　Deck the Mediator's crown;
　Go, his triumphs to adorn;
　Made for God, to God return.

2 Angels, joyful to attend,
　Hov'ring round thy pillow bend;
　Wait to catch the signal given,
　And convey thee quick to heaven.
　Burst thy shackles; drop thy clay;
　Sweetly breathe thyself away;
　Singing, to thy crown remove,
　Swift of wing, and fired with love.

3 Shudder not to pass the stream:
　Venture all thy care on Him—
　Him, whose dying love and power
　Still'd its tossing, hush'd its roar.
　Safe is the expanded wave,—
　Gentle as a summer's eve;
　Not one object of his care
　Ever suffer'd shipwreck there.

4 See the haven full in view:
　Love divine shall bear thee through:
　Trust to that propitious gale;
　Weigh thine anchor, spread thy sail.
　Saints in glory, perfect made,
　Wait thy passage through the shade;
　Swiftly to their wish be given;
　Kindle higher joy in heaven.

471
Blessedness of those who die in the Lord.

1 Hark! a voice divides the sky:
　　Happy are the faithful dead!
　In the Lord who sweetly die,
　　They from all their toils are freed;
　Them the Spirit hath declared
　　Blest, unutterably blest;
　Jesus is their great reward,
　　Jesus is their endless rest.

2 Follow'd by their works they go,
　　Where their Head is gone before;
　Reconciled by grace below,
　　Grace hath open'd mercy's door;
　Justified through faith alone,
　　Here they knew their sins forgiven;
　Here they laid their burden down,
　　Hallow'd, and made meet for heaven

472 MARTYN. 7s. Double. S. B. MARSH.

1. Jesus, lover of my soul,
   Let me to thy bosom fly,
   While the nearer waters roll,
   While the tempest still is high;
   Hide me, O my Savior, hide,
   Till the storm of life is past;
   Safe into the haven guide,
   O receive my soul at last.

2 Other refuge have I none;
  Hangs my helpless soul on thee:
Leave, O leave me not alone;
  Still support and comfort me;
All my trust on thee is stay'd;
  All my help from thee I bring;
Cover my defenceless head
  With the shadow of thy wing.

3 Thou, O Christ, art all I want;
  More than all in thee I find:
Raise the fallen, cheer the faint,
  Heal the sick, and lead the blind.
Just and holy is thy name;
  I am all unrighteousness;
False, and full of sin I am;
  Thou art full of truth and grace.

4 Plenteous grace with thee is found,—
  Grace to cover all my sin:
Let the healing streams abound;
  Make and keep me pure within.
Thou of life the fountain art;
  Freely let me take of thee:
Spring thou up within my heart;
  Rise to all eternity.

473 *Tender expostulation.*

1 Sinners, turn, while God is near;
  Dare not think him insincere:
Now, e'en now, your Savior stands;
  All day long he spreads his hands;
Cries, ye will not happy be;
  No, ye will not come to me,—
Me, who life to none deny:
  Why will ye resolve to die?

2 Turn, he cries, ye sinners, turn:
  By his life, your God hath sworn;
He would have you turn and live;
  He would all the world receive.
If your death were his delight,
  Would he you to life invite?
Would he ask, beseech, and cry,—
  Why will ye resolve to die?

3 What could your Redeemer do,
  More than he hath done for you?
To procure your peace with God,
  Could he more than shed his blood?
After all his flow of love,—
  All his drawings from above,
Why will ye your Lord deny?
  Why will ye resolve to die?

474. WATCHMAN. 7s. Double.

1. Watchman, tell us of the night, What its signs of promise are, Trav'ler, o'er yon mountain's height See the glo-ry beam-ing star. Watchman, does its beauteous ray Aught of hope or joy fore-tell? Trav'ler, yes, it brings the day, Promised day of Is-ra-el.

2 Watchman tell us of the night;
Higher yet that star ascends.
Trav'ler, blessedness and light,
Peace and truth, its course portends.
Watchman, will its beams, alone,
Gild the spot that gave them birth?
Trav'ler, ages are its own;
See, it bursts o'er all the earth,

3 Watchman, tell us of the night,
For the morning seems to dawn.
Trav'ler, darkness takes its flight;
Doubt and terror are withdrawn.
Watchman, let thy wand'ring cease;
Hie thee to thy quiet home.
Trav'ler, lo! the Prince of Peace,
Lo! The Son of God is come.

475 *Mutual love the bond of union.*

1 While we walk with God in light,
God our hearts doth still unite;
Dearest fellowship we prove,—
Fellowship in Jesus' love:
Sweetly each, with each combined,
In the bonds of duty joined,
Feels the cleansing blood applied;—
Daily feels that Christ hath died.

2 Still, O Lord, our faith increase;
Cleanse from all unrighteousness:
Thee th' unholy cannot see;
Make, O make us meet for thee:
Every vile affection kill;
Root out every seed of ill;
Utterly abolish sin;
Write thy law of love within.

476 CHRISTMAS HYMN. 7s. Double. MENDELSSOHN.

1. Hark! the herald angels sing Glory to the new-born King; Peace on earth, and mercy mild; God and sinners re-con-cil'd. Joy-ful all ye nations rise,—Join the tri-umph of the skies; With an-gel-ic hosts proclaim Christ is born in Bethlehem. With an-gel-ic hosts proclaim Christ is born in Bethlehem.

2 Veiled in flesh — the Godhead see
Hail th' incarnate Deity;
Pleased as man with men t' appear,
Jesus our Emmanuel here.
Hail the heaven-born Prince of peace!
Hail the Sun of righteousness!
Life and light to all he brings,—
Risen with healing in his wings.

3 Mild, he lays his glory by;
Born, that man no more may die;
Born, to raise the sons of earth;
Born, to give them second birth.
Come, Desire of nations, come!
Fix in us thy humble home:
Second Adam, from above,
Reinstate us in thy love.

---

477 *The word glorified.*

1 See how great a flame aspires,
 Kindled by a spark of grace!
Jesus' love the nations fires,—
 Sets the kingdoms on a blaze.
To bring fire on earth he came;
 Kindled in some hearts it is:
O that all might catch the flame,
 All partake the glorious bliss!

2 When he first the work begun,
 Small and feeble was his day:
Now the world doth swiftly run;
 Now it wins its widening way:
More and more it spreads and grows,
 Ever mighty to prevail;
Sin's strongholds it now o'erthrows,—
 Shakes the trembling gates of hell.

3 Sons of God, your Savior praise!
 He the door hath opened wide;
He hath given the word of grace;
 Jesus' word is glorified.
Jesus, mighty to redeem,
 He alone the work hath wrought;
Worthy is the work of him,—
 Him who spake a world from naught.

4 Saw ye not the cloud arise,
 Little as a human hand?
Now it spreads along the skies,—
 Hangs o'er all the thirsty land:
Lo! the promise of a shower
 Drops already from above;
But the Lord will shortly pour
 All the Spirit of his love.

478 HAYDN'S HYMN. 8s, 7s & 4s.

From J. HAYDN.

1. O thou God of my salvation, My Redeemer from all sin;
Mov'd by thy divine compassion, Who hast died my heart to win,
I will praise thee: I will praise thee, Where shall I thy praise begin?

2 Though unseen I love the Savior;
He hath brought salvation near;
Manifests his pard'ning favor;
And when Jesus doth appear,
Soul and body
Shall his glorious image bear.

3 While the angel choirs are crying,—
Glory to the great I AM,
I with them will still be vying—
Glory! glory to the Lamb!
O how precious
Is the sound of Jesus' name!

4 Angels now are hov'ring round us,
Unperceived amid the throng;
Wond'ring at the love that crown'd us,
Glad to join the holy song:
Hallelujah,
Love and praise to Christ belong!

479 *Worship the new-born Savior.*

1 Angels, from the realms of glory,
Wing your flight o'er all the earth;
Ye who sang creation's story,
Now proclaim Messiah's birth:
Come and worship,—
Worship Christ, the new-born king.

2 Shepherds in the field abiding,
Watching o'er your flocks by night,
God with man is now residing;
Yonder shines the infant light:
Come and worship,—
Worship Christ, the new-born king.

3 Saints, before the altar bending,
Watching long in hope and fear,
Suddenly the Lord descending,
In his temple shall appear:
Come and worship,—
Worship Christ, the new-born king.

4 Sinners, wrung with true repentance,
Doom'd for guilt to endless pains,
Justice now revokes the sentence,—
Mercy calls you,—break your chains:
Come and worship,—
Worship Christ, the new-born king.

480 GREENVILLE. 8s, 7s & 4s.

J. J. ROUSSEAU. 1775.

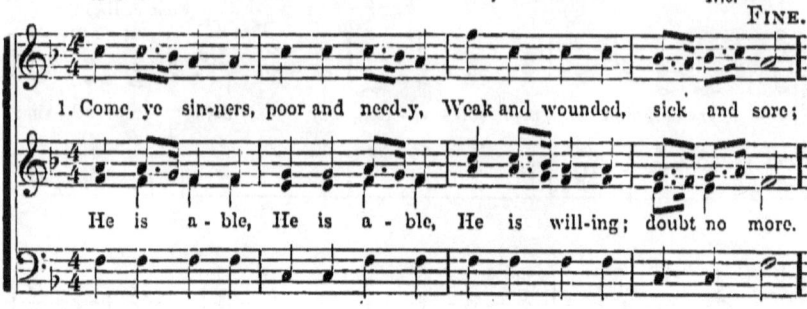

1. Come, ye sinners, poor and needy, Weak and wounded, sick and sore;
He is able, He is able, He is willing; doubt no more.

Jesus ready stands to save you, Full of pity, love, and pow'r:

2 Now, ye needy, come and welcome;
  God's free bounty glorify;
True belief and true repentance,—
Every grace that brings you nigh,—
  Without money,
  Come to Jesus Christ and buy.

3 Let not conscience make you linger;
  Nor of fitness fondly dream:
All the fitness he requireth
Is to feel your need of him:
  This he gives you,—
  'Tis the Spirit's glimm'ring beam.

4 Come, ye weary, heavy-laden,
  Bruised and mangled by the fall;
If you tarry till you're better,
You will never come at all;
  Not the righteous,—
  Sinners Jesus came to call.

5 Agonizing in the garden,
  Your Redeemer prostrate lies;
On the bloody tree behold him!
Hear him cry, before he dies,
  It is finish'd!—
  Sinners, will not this suffice?

6 Lo! th' incarnate God, ascending,
  Pleads the merit of his blood:
Venture on him,—venture freely;
Let no other trust intrude:
  None but Jesus
  Can do helpless sinners good.

7 Saints and angels, join'd in concert,
  Sing the praises of the Lamb;
While the blissful seats of heaven
Sweetly echo with his name:
  Hallelujah!
  Sinners here may do the same.

481 *For the Spirit's influences.*

1 Come, thou soul-transforming Spirit;
  Bless the sower and the seed;
Let each heart thy grace inherit;
Raise the weak,—the hungry feed;
  From the Gospel
  Now supply thy people's need.

2 O may all enjoy the blessing
  Which thy word's design'd to give;
Let us all, thy love possessing,
Joyfully the truth receive,
  And forever
  To thy praise and glory live.

SICILY. 8s, 7s & 4s.

1. Lo! He comes, with clouds descending, Once for favor'd sinners slain;
Thousand, thousand saints, attending, Swell the triumph of his train:
Hallelujah! hallelujah! God appears on earth to reign.

2 Every eye shall now behold him
Robed in dreadful majesty;
Those who set at nought and sold him,
Pierced and nailed him to the tree,
Deeply wailing,
Shall the true Messiah see.

3 All the tokens of his passion
Still his dazzling body bears:
Cause of endless exultation
To his ransomed worshippers;
With what rapture
Gaze we on those glorious scars.

4 Yea, Amen! let all adore thee,
High on thine eternal throne;
Savior, take the power and glory;
Make thy righteous sentence known:
Jah! Jehovah!
Claim the kingdom for thine own.

483 *For the fulness of peace and joy.*

1 Lord dismiss us with thy blessing;
Fill our hearts with joy and peace;
Let us each, thy love possessing,
Triumph in redeeming grace;
O refresh us,
Travelling through this wilderness

2 Thanks we give, and adoration,
For thy Gospel's joyful sound;
May the fruits of thy salvation
In our hearts and lives abound.
May thy presence
With us evermore be found.

3 So, whene'er the signal's given
Us from earth to call away,
Borne on angel's wings to heaven,
Glad the summons to obey,
May we ever
Reign with Christ in endless day.

Doxology.

Great Jehovah! we adore thee,—
God the Father, God the Son,
God the Spirit, joined in glory
On the same eternal throne:
Endless praises
To Jehovah, Three in One.

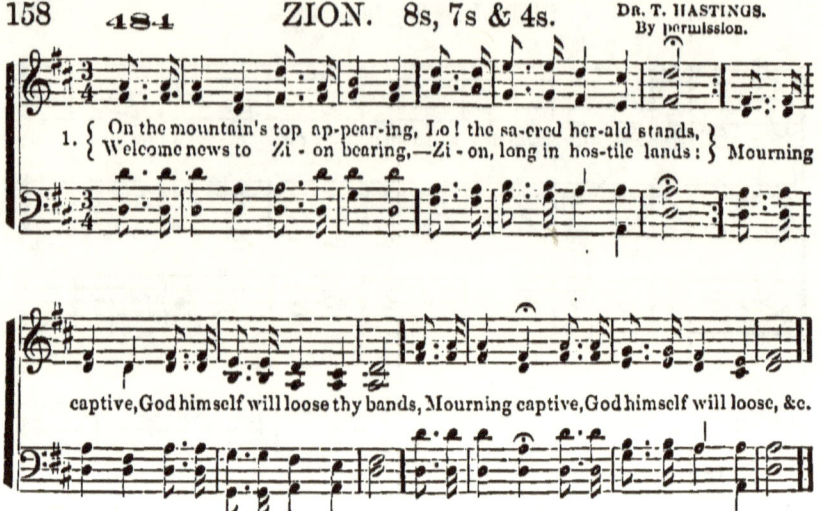

484 ZION. 8s, 7s & 4s. Dr. T. Hastings. By permission.

1. On the mountain's top appearing, Lo! the sacred herald stands, Welcome news to Zion bearing,—Zion, long in hostile lands: Mourning captive, God himself will loose thy bands, Mourning captive, God himself will loose, &c.

2 Has thy night been long and mournful?
Have thy friends unfaithful proved?
Have thy foes been proud and scornful,
By thy sighs and tears unmoved?
Cease thy mourning;
Zion still is well beloved.

3 God, thy God, will now restore thee;
He himself appears thy Friend;
All thy foes shall flee before thee;
Here their boasts and triumphs end:
Great deliverance,
Zion's King will surely send.

4 Peace and joy shall now attend thee;
All thy warfare now is past;
God thy Savior will defend thee;
Victory is thine at last:
All thy conflicts
End in everlasting rest.

485 *We shall appear with him in glory.*

1 Lift your heads, ye friends of Jesus,
Partners in his patience here;
Christ, to all believers precious,
Lord of lords, shall soon appear:
'Mark the tokens
Of his heavenly kingdom near.

2 Sun and moon are both confounded,
Darken'd into endless night,
When, with angel hosts surrounded,
In his Father's glory bright,
Beams the Savior,
Shines the everlasting light.

3 See the stars from heaven falling;
Hark, on earth the doleful cry;
Men on rocks and mountains calling,
While the frowning Judge draws nigh:
Hide us, hide us,
Rocks and mountains, from his eye!

4 With what diff'rent exclamation
Shall the saints his banner see!
By the tokens of his passion,
By the marks received for me:—
All discern him;
All with shouts cry out,—'tis He!

5 Lo! 'tis He! our hearts' Desire,
Come for his espoused below;
Come to join us with his choir,
Come to make our joys o'erflow:
Palms of victory,
Crowns of glory, to bestow.

486 *The pilgrim's guide and guardian.*

1 Guide me, O thou great Jehovah,
Pilgrim through this barren land:
I am weak — but thou art mighty;
Hold me with thy powerful hand:
Bread of heaven,
Feed me till I want no more.

2 Open now the crystal fountain,
Whence the healing waters flow;
Let the fiery, cloudy pillar,
Lead me all my journey through:
Strong Deliv'rer,
Be thou still my strength and shield.

3 When I tread the verge of Jordan,
Bid my anxious fears subside:
Bear me through the swelling current,
Land me safe on Canaan's side:
Songs of praises
I will ever give to thee.

487 ADORATION. 8s & 7s. Double. 159

German Choral.

1. Love divine, all love excelling, Joy of heav'n, to earth come down,
   Fix in us thy humble dwelling: All thy faithful mercies crown.
   Jesus, thou art all compassion, Pure, unbounded love thou art:
   Visit us with thy salvation, Enter ev'ry trembling heart.

2 Breathe, O breathe thy loving Spirit
  Into every troubled breast;
  Let us all in thee inherit,
  Let us find that second rest.
  Take away our bent to sinning;
  Alpha and Omega be:
  End of faith, as its beginning
  Set our hearts at liberty.

3 Come, almighty to deliver,
  Let us all thy life receive:
  Suddenly return, and never,
  Never more thy temples leave.
  Thee we would be always blessing,
  Serve thee as thy hosts above,
  Pray and praise thee without ceasing,
  Glory in thy perfect love.

4 Finish then thy new creation,
  Pure and spotless let us be;
  Let us see thy great salvation,
  Perfectly restored in thee:
  Changed from glory into glory,
  Till in heaven we take our place,—
  Till we cast our crowns before thee,
  Lost in wonder, love, and praise.

488 *Our Paschal Lamb.*

1 Hail, thou once despised Jesus!
  Hail, thou Galilean King!
  Thou didst suffer, to release us;
  Thou didst free salvation bring.
  Hail, thou agonizing Savior,
  Bearer of our sin and shame!
  By thy merits we find favor;
  Life is given through thy name.

2 Jesus, hail! enthroned in glory,
  There forever to abide;
  All the heavenly host adore thee,
  Seated at thy Father's side:
  There for sinners thou art pleading;
  There thou dost our place prepare.
  Ever for us interceding,
  Till in glory we appear.

3 Worship, honor, power, and blessing,
  Thou art worthy to receive;
  Loudest praises, without ceasing,
  Meet it is for us to give.
  Help, ye bright angelic spirits;
  Bring your sweetest, noblest lays;
  Help to sing our Savior's merits;
  Help to chant Immanuel's praise.

AUTUMN. 8s & 7s. Double.

1. Come thou everlasting Spirit, Bring to us a thankful mind;
All the Savior's dying merit, All his suff'rings for mankind:
Now reveal his great salvation Unto every faithful heart.
True recorder of his passion, Now the living faith impart;

2 Come, thou Witness of his dying;
  Come, Remembrancer divine;
Let us feel thy power applying
  Christ to every soul, and mine:
Let us groan thine inward groaning;
  Look on Him we pierced, and grieve;
All partake the grace atoning,—
  All the sprinkled blood receive.

490 *The heavenly banquet.*
1 Jesus spreads his banner o'er us,
    Cheers our famished souls with food;
  He the banquet spreads before us,
    Of his mystic flesh and blood.
  Precious banquet; bread of heaven;
    Wine of gladness, flowing free;
  May we taste it, kindly given,
    In remembrance, Lord, of thee.

2 In thy holy incarnation,
    When the angels sang thy birth;
  In thy fasting and temptation;
    In thy labors on the earth;
  In thy trial and rejection;
    In thy suff'rings on the tree;
  In thy glorious resurrection;
    May we, Lord, remember thee.

Dismission.
Lord, dismiss us with thy blessing
  Bid us now depart in peace;
Still on heavenly manna feeding,
  Let our faith and love increase:
Fill each breast with consolation;
  Up to thee our hearts we raise:
When we reach our blissful station,
  Then we'll give thee nobler praise

491   DURBIN. 3s & 7s. Double.   161

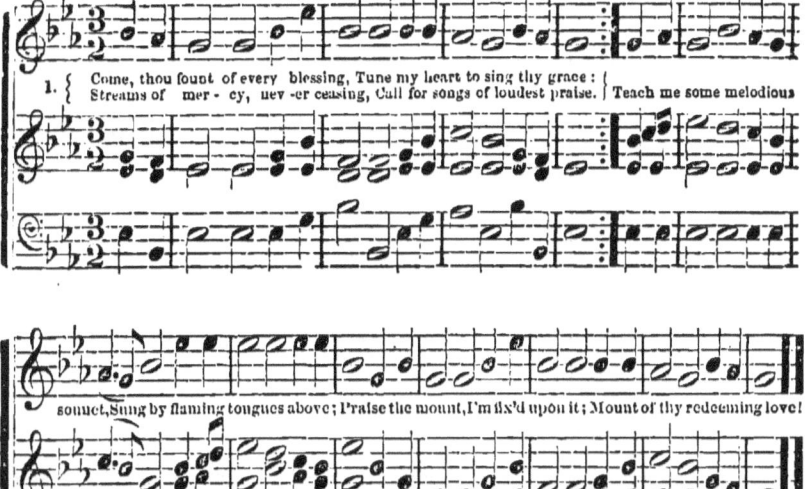

1. Come, thou fount of every blessing, Tune my heart to sing thy grace: Streams of mer—cy, nev-er ceasing, Call for songs of loudest praise. Teach me some melodious sonnet, Sung by flaming tongues above; Praise the mount, I'm fix'd upon it; Mount of thy redeeming love!

2 Here I'll raise mine Ebenezer;
  Hither by thy help I'm come;
And I hope, by thy good pleasure,
  Safely to arrive at home.
Jesus sought me when a stranger,
  Wand'ring from the fold of God;
He, to rescue me from danger,
  Interposed his precious blood.

3 O! to grace how great a debtor
  Daily I'm constrain'd to be!
Let thy goodness, like a fetter,
  Bind my wand'ring heart to thee:
Prone to wander, Lord, I feel it—
  Prone to leave the God I love;
Here's my heart, O take and seal it;
  Seal it for thy courts above.

492   *Guide and Comforter.*

1 Holy Spirit! Fount of blessing,
  Ever watchful, ever kind;
Thy celestial aid possessing,
  Prison'd souls deliverance find.
Seal of truth, and bond of union,
  Source of light, and flame of love,
Symbol of divine communion,
  In the olive-bearing dove;—

2 Heavenly Guide from paths of error,
  Comforter of minds distress'd,
When the billows fill with terror,
  Pointing to an ark of rest:
Promis'd Pledge! eternal Spirit!
  Greater than all gifts below,—
May our hearts thy grace inherit;
  May our lips thy glories show.

493   *Praise to Jehovah.*

1 Praise to thee, thou great Creator!
  Praise to thee from every tongue;
Join, my soul, with every creature,
  Join the universal song.
Father, Source of all compassion,
  Pure, unbounded grace is thine:
Hail the God of our salvation!
  Praise him for his love divine.

2 For ten thousand blessings given,
  For the hope of future joy,
Sound his praise thro' earth and heaven,
  Sound Jehovah's praise on high.
Joyfully on earth adore him,
  Till in heaven our song we raise;
There, enraptured, fall before him,
  Lost in wonder, love and praise.

GRANT. 8s & 7s. Double.

1. Jesus I my cross have taken, All to leave and follow thee;
Naked, poor, despised, forsaken, Thou, from hence, my all shalt be;
Human hearts and looks deceive me, Thou art not like them, untrue;
Perish every fond ambition, All I've sought, or hoped, or known,

2. Let the world despise and leave me; They have left my Savior too;
Yet how rich is my condition! God and heaven are still my own.
Foes may hate, and friends disown me; Show thy face, and all is bright.
And while thou shalt smile upon me, God of wisdom, love, and might,

3 Go, then, earthly fame and treasure,
Come disaster, scorn and pain,
In thy service, pain is pleasure,
With thy favor loss is gain,
I have called thee Abba, Father,
I have set my heart on thee,
Storms may howl, and clouds may gather,
All must work for good to me.

4 Man may trouble and distress me,
'T will but drive me to thy breast;
Life with trials hard may press me,
Heaven will bring me sweeter rest.

Oh! 'tis not in grief to harm me,
While thy love is left to me;
Oh! 't were not in joy to charm me,
Were that joy unmixed with thee.

5 Soul, then know thy full salvation,
Rise o'er sin, and fear, and care;
Joy to find in every station
Something still to do or bear.
Think what Spirit dwells within thee;
Think what Father's smiles are thine
Think that Jesus died to win thee;
Child of heaven, canst thou repine?

495 HARWELL. 8s & 7s. Double. DR. L. MASON. 163

2 Jesus, hail! Whose glory brightens
   All above, and gives it worth;
Lord of life! thy smile enlightens,
   Cheers, and charms thy saints on earth;
When we think of love like thine,
Lord! we own it love divine.
      Hallelujah, &c.

3 Savior! hasten thine appearing,
   Bring,—oh bring the glorious day,
When the awful summons hearing,
   Heaven and earth shall pass away;
Then with golden harps we'll sing—
   "Glory, glory to our King."
      Hallelujah, &c.

496
1 Hark! the notes of angels, singing,
   Glory, glory to the Lamb!
All in heaven their tribute bringing,
   Raising high the Savior's name.
Ye for whom his life was given,
   Sacred themes to you belong:
Come, assist the choir of heaven;
   Join the everlasting song.

2 Fill'd with holy emulation,
   We unite with those above:
Sweet the theme—a free salvation—
   Fruit of everlasting love.
Endless life in him possessing,
   Let us praise his precious name;
Glory, honor, power and blessing,
   Be forever to the Lamb.

497 WILMOT. 8s & 7s. Single.
Arranged from C. M. v. WEBER.

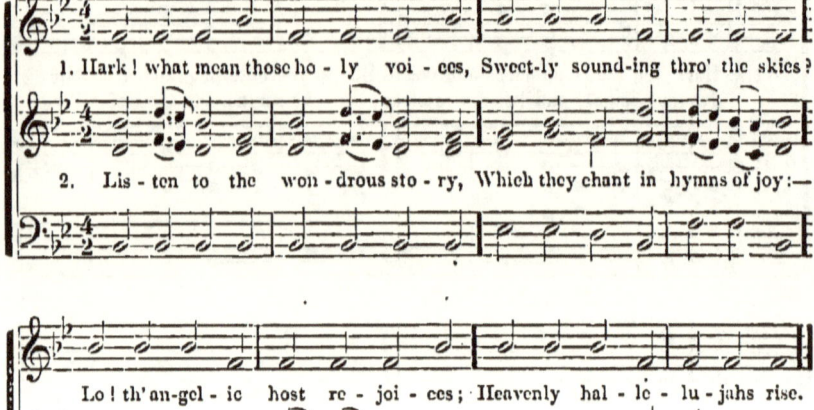

1. Hark! what mean those holy voices, Sweetly sounding thro' the skies?
2. Listen to the wondrous story, Which they chant in hymns of joy:—
   Lo! th' angelic host rejoices; Heavenly hallelujahs rise.
   Glory in the highest, glory, Glory be to God most high!

3 Peace on earth, good-will from heaven,
  Reaching far as man is found;
  Souls redeem'd, and sins forgiven!—
  Loud our golden harps shall sound.

4 Christ is born, the great Anointed,
  Heaven and earth his praises sing;
  O receive whom God appointed,
  For your Prophet, Priest, and King.

5 Hasten, mortals, to adore him;
  Learn his name, and taste his joy;
  Till in heaven ye sing before him,—
  Glory be to God most high!

498 *God is in the midst of her.*

1 Glorious things of thee are spoken,
  Zion, city of our God;
  He, whose word cannot be broken,
  Form'd thee for his own abode;

2 On the Rock of ages founded,
  What can shake thy sure repose?
  With salvation's walls surrounded,
  Thou may'st smile at all thy foes.

3 See, the streams of living waters,
  Springing from eternal love,
  Still supply thy sons and daughters,
  And all fear of want remove:

4 Who can faint while such a river
  Ever flows our thirst t' assuage?
  Grace, which, like the Lord, the giver,
  Never fails from age to age.

5 Round each habitation hov'ring,
  See the cloud and fire appear!
  For a glory and a covering,
  Showing that the Lord is near:

6 He who gives us daily manna,
  He who listens when we cry,
  Let him hear the loud Hosanna
  Rising to his throne on high.

499 *The Triune God glorified.*

1 Glory to th' almighty Father,
  Fountain of eternal love,
  Who, his wand'ring sheep to gather,
  Sent a Savior from above.

2 To the Son all praise be given,
  Who, with love unknown before,
  Left the bright abode of heaven,
  And our sin and sorrows bore.

3 Equal strains of warm devotion
  Let the Spirit's praise employ;
  Author of each pure emotion;
  Source of wisdom, peace, and joy.

4 Thus, while our glad hearts, ascending,
  Glorify Jehovah's Name,
  Heavenly songs with ours are blending
  There the theme is still the same.

500 TALMAR. 8s & 7s. Single.
I. B. W. From Day Spring. By permission.

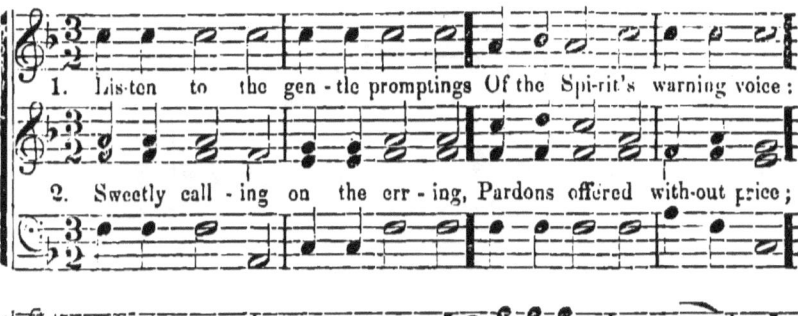

1. Listen to the gentle promptings Of the Spirit's warning voice:
Will ye heed his solemn warnings? Can ye slight his wondrous love?

2. Sweetly calling on the erring, Pardons offered without price;
Come, and round the altar kneeling, O receive the offered grace.

---

501 *The true light.*

1 Light of those whose dreary dwelling
  Borders on the shades of death,
  Come, and, by thyself revealing,
  Dissipate the clouds beneath.

2 Thou, new heaven and earth's Creator
  In our deepest darkness rise;
  Scatt'ring all the night of nature,—
  Pouring day upon our eyes.

3 Still we wait for thine appearing;
  Life and joy thy beams impart,
  Chasing all our fears, and cheering
  Every poor, benighted heart.

4 Come, extend, thy wonted favor
  To our ruin'd, guilty race;
  Come, thou blest, exalted Savior;
  Come, apply thy saving grace.

5 By thine all-atoning merit,
  Every burden'd soul release;
  By the teachings of thy Spirit,
  Guide us into perfect peace.

502
Evening: Confidence in God's protection.

1 Savior, breathe an evening blessing,
  Ere repose our spirits seal;
  Sin and want we come confessing;
  Thou canst save and thou canst heal.

2 Though destruction walk around us,
  Though the arrows past us fly,
  Angel guards from thee surround us;
  We are safe, if thou art nigh.

3 Though the night be dark and dreary,
  Darkness cannot hide from thee;
  Thou art He who, never weary,
  Watchest where thy people be.

4 Should swift death this night o'ertake us,
  And command us to the tomb,
  May the morn in heaven awake us,
  Clad in bright, eternal bloom.

503
Pardon implored for national sins.

1 Dread Jehovah! God of nations,!
  From thy temple in the skies,
  Hear thy people's supplications;
  Now for their deliv'rance rise.

2 Lo! with deep contrition turning,
  In thy holy place we bend;
  Hear us, fasting, praying, mourning;
  Hear us, spare us, and defend.

3 Though our sins, our hearts confounding,
  Long and loud for vengeance call,
  Thou hast mercy more abounding;
  Jesus' blood can cleanse them all.

4 Let that mercy vail transgression;
  Let that blood our guilt efface:
  Save thy people from oppression;
  Save from spoil thy holy place.

MOUNT VERNON. 8s & 7s.
Dr. L. Mason.

1. Sis-ter, thou wast mild and love-ly, Gen-tle as the sum-mer breeze, Pleasant as the air of eve-ning, When it floats a-mong the trees.

2. Peaceful be thy si-lent slumber, Peaceful in the grave so low; Thou no more wilt join our num-ber, Thou no more our songs shalt know.

3 Dearest sister, thou hast left us,
Here thy loss we deeply feel,
But 'tis God that hath bereft us,
He can all our sorrows heal.

4 Yet again we hope to meet thee,
When the day of life is fled,
Then, in heaven with joy to greet thee,
Where no farewell tear is shed.

505 *Adoration.*

1 May I love thee and adore thee,
O thou bleeding, dying Lamb;
Teach my heart to bow before thee,
Kindle there a sacred flame.

2 Teach me what I am by nature,
How to lift my thoughts on high;
Teach me, O thou great Creator!
How to live, and how to die!

506 *The kind Shepherd.*

1 Savior, who thy flock art feeding,
With the Shepherd's kindest care,
All the feeble gently leading,
While the lambs thy bosom share.

2 Now, these little ones receiving,
Fold them in thy gracious arm;
There, we know, thy word believing,
Only there, secure from harm.

3 Never from thy pasture roving,
Let them be the Lion's prey;
Let thy tenderness, so loving,
Keep them all life's dangerous way

4 Then, within thy fold eternal,
Let them find a resting place,
Feed in pastures ever vernal,
Drink the rivers of thy grace.

507 *Jesus our strength.*

1 Jesus, Lord of life and glory,
Friend of children, hear our lays;
Humbly would our souls adore thee,
Sing thy name in hymns of praise.

2 O what debtors to thy kindness
Are we, God of boundless love!
Thousands wander on in blindness,
Strangers to the light above.

3 Jesus, on thy arm relying,
We would tread this earthly vale,
Be our life when we are dying;
Be our strength, when strength shall fail.

4 Let us mount the hills of glory,
Far from sins, and woes, and pains
There, in perfect songs, adore thee,
And in everlasting strains.

508 CONTRAST. 8s, Double.

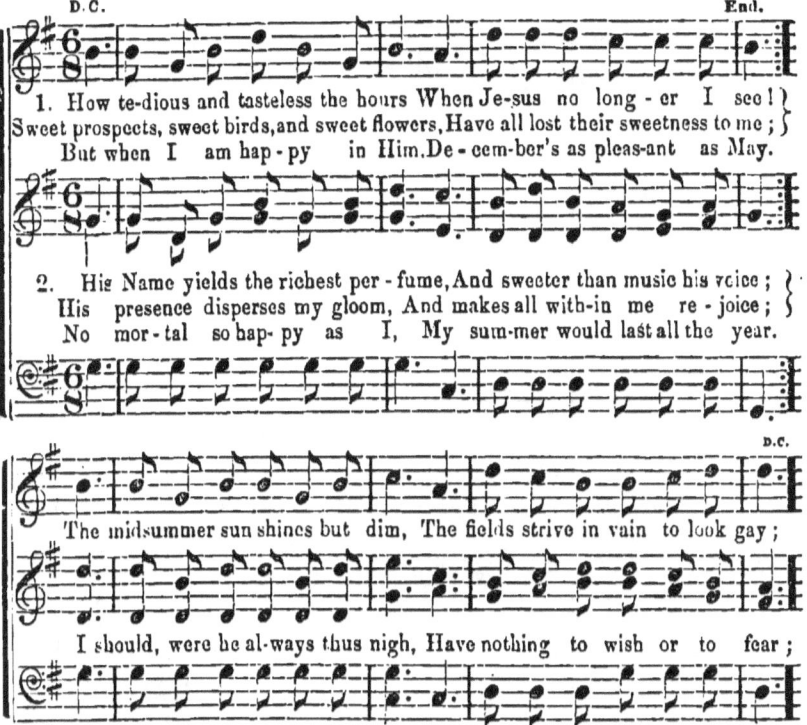

1. How tedious and tasteless the hours When Jesus no longer I see!
Sweet prospects, sweet birds, and sweet flowers, Have all lost their sweetness to me;
But when I am happy in Him, December's as pleasant as May.

2. His Name yields the richest perfume, And sweeter than music his voice;
His presence disperses my gloom, And makes all within me rejoice;
No mortal so happy as I, My summer would last all the year.

The midsummer sun shines but dim, The fields strive in vain to look gay;
I should, were he always thus nigh, Have nothing to wish or to fear;

3 Content with beholding his face,
My all to his pleasure resign'd,
No changes of season or place
Would make any change in my mind:
While blest with a sense of his love,
A palace a toy would appear;
And prisons would palaces prove,
If Jesus would dwell with me there.

4 My Lord, if indeed I am thine,
If thou art my sun and my song,
Say, why do I languish and pine?
And why are my winters so long?
O drive these dark clouds from my sky;
Thy soul-cheering presence restore;
Or take me to thee up on high,
Where winter and clouds are no more.

509 *Following the Lamb.*

What now is my object and aim?
What now is my hope and desire?
To follow the heavenly Lamb,
And after his image aspire:
My hope is all centered in thee;
I trust to recover thy love;
On earth thy salvation to see,
And then to enjoy it above.

510 *Longing for still closer communion.*

1 Thou Shepherd of Israel, and mine,
The joy and desire of my heart,
For closer communion I pine;
I long to reside where thou art:
The pasture I languish to find,
Where all, who their Shepherd obey,
Are fed, on thy bosom reclined,
And screen'd from the heat of the day.

2 Tis there, with the lambs of thy flock,
There only, I covet to rest;
To lie at the foot of the rock,
Or rise to be hid in thy breast:
'Tis there I would always abide,
And never a moment depart,—
Conceal'd in the cleft of thy side,
Eternally held in thy heart.

DAVID. 8s. Single.

1. I long to behold him array'd With glory and light from above;
The king in his beauty display'd His beauty of holiest love.

2 I languish and sigh to be there, Where Jesus hath fix'd his abode;
O, when shall we meet in the air, And fly to the mountain of God.

3 With him I on Zion shall stand,
  For Jesus hath spoken the word;
The breadth of Immanuel's land
  Survey by the light of my Lord:
4 But when, on thy bosom reclined,
  Thy face I am strengthened to see,
My fulness of rapture I find,—
  My heaven of heavens in thee.
5 How happy the people that dwell
  Secure in the city above!
No pain the inhabitants feel,
  No sickness or sorrow shall prove.
6 Physician of souls, unto me
  Forgiveness and holiness give;
And then from the body set free,
  And then to the city receive.

512 *The fountain of living waters.*
1 A fountain of life and of grace
  In Christ, our Redeemer, we see:
For us, who his offers embrace,
  For all, it is open and free:
2 Jehovah, himself doth invite
  To drink of his pleasures unknown:
The streams of immortal delight,
  That flow from his heavenly throne.

3 As soon as in him we believe,
  By faith of his Spirit we take:
And, freely forgiven, receive
  The mercy for Jesus's sake!
4 We gain a pure drop of his love;
  The life of eternity know;
Angelical happiness prove,
  And witness a heaven below.

513 *The Rock that is higher than I.*
1 Encompass'd with clouds of distress,
  And ready all hope to resign,
I long for thy light and thy grace;
  O God, will they never be mine?
2 If sometimes I strive, as I mourn,
  My hold of thy promise to keep,
The billows more fiercely return,
  And plunge me again in the deep.
3 Appear, and my sorrow shall cease;
  The blood of atonement apply;
And lead me to Jesus for peace,—
  The Rock that is higher than I.
4 O enter this desolate heart,—
  Then rule o'er the heart thou hast won;
Nor again in thine anger depart,
  But make it forever thy throne

514 WALMISLEY. 8s. Single.

H. B. WALMISLEY.

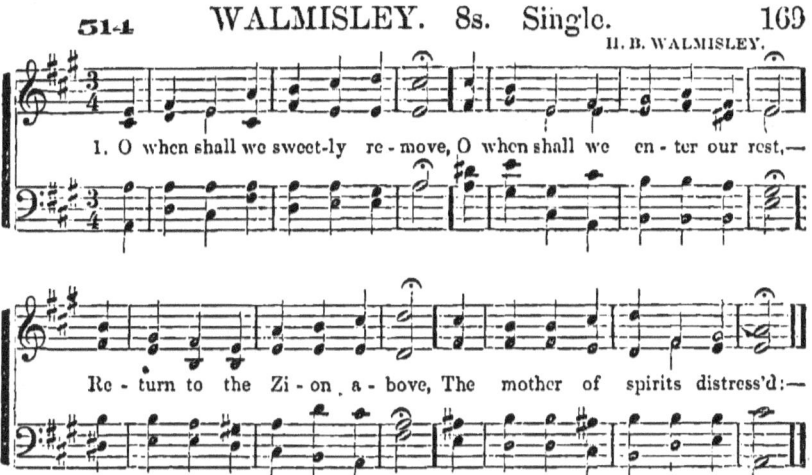

1. O when shall we sweetly remove, O when shall we enter our rest,—
Return to the Zion above, The mother of spirits distress'd:—

2 That city of God, the great King,
   Where sorrow and death are no more,
Where saints our Immanuel sing,
   And cherub and seraph adore?

3 But angels themselves cannot tell
   The joys of that holiest place,
Where Jesus is pleased to reveal
   The light of his heavenly face:

4 When, caught in the rapturous flame,
   The sight beatific they prove;
And walk in the light of the Lamb,
   Enjoying the beams of his love.

5 Thou know'st in the spirit of prayer
   We long thy appearing to see,
Resign'd to the burden we bear,
   But longing to triumph with thee:

6 'Tis good at thy word to be here;
   'Tis better in thee to be gone,
And see thee in glory appear,
   And rise to a share in thy throne.

515 *The Heavenly Jerusalem.*

1 Away with our sorrow and fear,
   We soon shall recover our home;
The city of saints shall appear,
   The day of eternity come.

2 From earth we shall quickly remove,
   And mount to our native abode;
The house of our Father above,—
   The palace of angels and God.

3 Our mourning is all at an end,
   When raised by the life-giving Word,
We see the new city descend,
   Adorned as a bride for her Lord:

4 The city so holy and clean,
   No sorrow can breathe in the air;
No gloom of affliction or sin;
   No shadow of evil is there.

5 By faith we already behold
   That lovely Jerusalem here:
Her walls are of jasper and gold;
   As crystal her buildings are clear:

6 Immovably founded in grace,
   She stands as she ever hath stood,
And brightly her Builder displays,
   And flames with the glory of God.

516 *Praise to Jesus.*

1 My Gracious Redeemer I love,
   His praises aloud I'll proclaim:
And join with the armies above,
   To shout his adorable name.

2 To gaze on his glories divine,
   Shall be my eternal employ;
To see them incessantly shine,
   My boundless, ineffable joy.

3 He freely redeemed with his blood,
   • My soul from the confines of hell,
To live on the smiles of my God,
   And in his sweet presence to dwell:—

4 To shine with the angels in light,
   With saints and with seraphs to sing;
To view, with eternal delight,
   My Jesus, my Savior, my King!

517 AMSTERDAM. 7s & 6s. Peculiar. Dr. Nares.

1. Rise, my soul, and stretch thy wings, Thy better portion trace;
Rise from transitory things, Tow'rd heav'n, thy native place:
Sun, and moon, and stars decay; Time shall soon this earth remove;
Rise, my soul, and haste away To seats prepared above.

2 Rivers to the ocean run,
Nor stay in all their course;
Fire, ascending, seeks the sun;
Both speed them to their source:
So a soul that's born of God,
Pants to view his glorious face;
Upward tends to his abode,
To rest in his embrace.

3 Cease, ye pilgrims, cease to mourn;
Press onward to the prize;
Soon our Savior will return
Triumphant in the skies:
There we'll join the heavenly train,
Welcomed to partake the bliss;
Fly from sorrow, care, and pain,
To realms of endless peace.

518 *Flight of time.*

1 Time is winging us away
To our eternal home;
Life is but a winter's day,—
A journey to the tomb:
Youth and vigor soon will flee,
Blooming beauty lose its charms;
All that's mortal soon shall be
Enclosed in death's cold arms.

2 Time is bearing us away
To our eternal home;
Life is but a winter's day,—
A journey to the tomb:
But the saints shall soon enjoy
Life — immortal life above,
Where no worldly griefs annoy,
Where Jesus reigns in love.

519 *Security and safety.*

1 See the gospel Church secure,
And founded on a Rock;
All her promises are sure:
Her bulwarks who can shock?
Count her every precious shrine:
Tell, to after ages tell,—
Fortified by power divine,
The Church can never fail.

2 Zion's God is all our own,
Who on his love rely;
We his pard'ning love have known,
And live to Christ, and die:
To the New Jerusalem
He our faithful Guide shall be;
Him we claim, and rest in him
Through all eternity.

520 BEETHOVEN. 7s & 6s. Peculiar. 171

Arranged from BEETHOVEN'S 9th Symphony, for this Work.

1. Meet and right it is to sing, In ev-'ry time and place, Glory to our Heav'nly King, The God of truth and grace: Join we then with sweet ac-cord, All in one thanksgiving join: Ho-ly, ho-ly, ho-ly Lord, Eternal praise be thine.

2 Thee the first-born sons of light,
In choral symphonies,
Praise by day, day without night,
And never, never cease;
Angels, and archangels, all
Praise the mystic Three in One;
Sing, and stop, and gaze, and fall
O'erwhelmed before thy throne.

3 Vying with that heavenly choir,
Who chant thy praise above,
We on eagle's wings aspire,—
The wings of faith and love;
Thee they sing, with glory crown'd;
We extol the slaughtered Lamb;
Lower if our voices sound,
Our subject is the same.

4 Father, God, thy love we praise,
Which gave thy Son to die;
Jesus, full of truth and grace,
Alike we glorify:
Spirit, Comforter divine,
Praise by all to thee be given,
Till we in full chorus join,
And earth is turned to heaven.

521 *With the voice of the archangel.*

1 Jesus, faithful to his word,
Shall with a shout descend;
All heaven's host their glorious Lord
Shall joyfully attend:
Christ shall come with dreadful noise;
Lightnings swift, and thunders loud,
With the great archangel's voice,
And with the trump of God.

2 First the dead in Christ shall rise;
Then we that yet remain
Shall be caught up to the skies,
And see our Lord again.
We shall meet him in the air;
All rapt up to heaven shall be;
Find, and love, and praise him there,
To all eternity.

3 Who can tell the happiness
This glorious hope affords?
Joy unutter'd we possess
In these reviving words:
Happy while on earth we breathe;
Mightier bliss ordained to know:
Trampling down sin, hell, and death,
To the third heaven we go.

WEBB. 7s. & 6s.

G. J. WEBB

1. The morning light is breaking, The darkness disappears; The sons of earth are waking To penitential tears. Each breeze that sweeps the ocean Brings tidings from afar Of nations in commotion, Prepared for Zion's war.

2 Rich dews of grace come o'er us
  In many a gentle shower;
And brighter scenes before us
  Are opening every hour:
Each cry to heaven going
  Abundant answer brings;
And heavenly gales are blowing,
  With peace upon their wings.

3 See heathen nations bending
  Before the God we love,
And thousand hearts ascending
  In gratitude above;
While sinners, now confessing,
  The gospel call obey,
And seek the Savior's blessing,—
  A nation in a day.

4 Blest river of salvation,
  Pursue thine onward way;
Flow thou to every nation,
  Nor in thy richness stay:

Stay not till all the lowly
  Triumphant reach their home;
Stay not till all the holy
  Proclaim—" The Lord is come."

523

1 O when shall I see Jesus,
  And reign with him above;
And from that flowing fountain
  Drink everlasting love?
When shall I be delivered
  From this vain world of sin,
And with my blessed Jesus
  Drink endless pleasures in?

2 But now I am a soldier,
  My Captain's gone before;
He's given me my orders,
  And bid me not give o'er:
If I continue faithful,
  A righteous crown he'll give,
And all his valiant soldiers
  Eternal life shall have.

MUNICH. 7s & 6s.

1. We bring no glitt'ring treasures, No gems from earth's deep mine;
We come, with simple measures, To chant thy love divine.
Children, thy favors sharing, Their voice of thanks would raise;
Father, accept our off'ring, Our song of grateful praise.

2 The dearest gift of Heaven,
Love's written word of truth,
To us is early given,
To guide our steps in youth:
We hear the wondrous story,
The tale of Calvary;
We read of homes in glory,
From sin and sorrow free.

3 Redeemer! grant thy blessing!
O! teach us how to pray,
That each, thy fear possessing,
May tread life's onward way;
Then, where the pure are dwelling,
We hope to meet again;
And sweeter numbers swelling,
Forever praise thy Name.

525 *No cause for fear.*

1 God is my strong salvation;
What foe have I to fear?
In darkness and temptation,
My light, my help, is near:
Though hosts encamp around me,
Firm in the fight I stand;
What terror can confound me,
With God at my right hand?

2 Place on the Lord reliance;
My soul, with courage wait:
His truth be thine affiance,
When faint and desolate.
His might thy heart shall strengthen,
His love thy joy increase;
'Mercy thy days shall lengthen:
The Lord will give thee peace.

Conclusion of Hymn 523, on opposite page.

3 Through grace I am determined
To conquer, though I die!
And then away to Jesus,
On wings of love I'll fly.
Farewell to sin and sorrow,
I bid you all adieu;
And O, my friends, be faithful,
And on your way pursue.

4 And if you meet with troubles
And trials on your way,
Then cast your care on Jesus,
And don't forget to pray:
Gird on the heavenly armor
Of faith, and hope, and love;
And when the combat's ended,
He'll carry you above.

526 MISSIONARY HYMN. 7s & 6s.
L. MASON, 1824.

1. From Greenland's icy mountains, From India's coral strand, Where Afric's sunny fountains Roll down their golden sand; From many an ancient river, From many a palmy plain, They call us to deliver Their land from error's chain.

2 What though the spicy breezes
  Blow soft o'er Ceylon's isle;
Though every prospect pleases,
  And only man is vile:
In vain with lavish kindness
  The gifts of God are strown;
The heathen in his blindness
  Bows down to wood and stone.

3 Shall we, whose souls are lighted
  With wisdom from on high,
Shall we to men benighted
  The lamp of life deny?
Salvation!—O salvation!
  The joyful sound proclaim,
Till earth's remotest nation
  Has learn'd Messiah's name.

4 Waft, waft, ye winds, his story,
  And you, ye waters, roll,
Till, like a sea of glory,
  It spreads from pole to pole:

Till o'er our ransom'd nature
  The Lamb for sinners slain,
Redeemer, King, Creator,
  In bliss returns to reign.

527 *The glory of His kingdom.*

1 Hail, to the Lord's anointed,
  Great David's greater Son!
Hail, in the time appointed,
  His reign on earth begun!
He comes to break oppression,—
  To set the captive free;
To take away transgression,
  And rule in equity.

2 He comes, with succor speedy
  To those who suffer wrong;
To help the poor and needy,
  And bid the weak be strong;
To give them songs for sighing,—
  Their darkness turn to light,—

Whose souls, condemn'd and dying,
Were precious in his sight.

3 He shall descend like showers
Upon the fruitful earth,
And love and joy, like flowers,
Spring in his path to birth:
Before him, on the mountains,
Shall peace, the herald, go,
And righteousness, in fountains,
From hill to valley flow.

4 To him shall prayer unceasing,
And daily vows ascend;
His kingdom still increasing,—
A kingdom without end:
The tide of time shall never
His covenant remove;
His name shall stand forever;
That name to us is Love.

528 *Departing missionaries.*

1 Roll on, thou mighty ocean;
And, as thy billows flow,
Bear messengers of mercy
To every land below;
Arise, ye gales, and waft them
Safe to the destined shore;
That man may sit in darkness,
And death's black shade, no more.

2 O thou eternal Ruler,
Who holdest in thine arm
The tempests of the ocean,
Protect them from all harm!
Thy presence, Lord, be with them,
Wherever they may be;
Though far from us who love them,
Still let them be with thee.

529
The comforts, gifts, and graces of the Spirit.

1 God of all consolation,
The Holy Ghost thou art;
Thy secret inspiration
Hath told it to my heart:
The blessing I inherit,
Through Jesus' prayer bestow'd,
The Comforter, the Spirit,
The true eternal God.

2 With God the Son and Savior,
With God the Father one,
The tokens of his favor
Are now to man made known;
An ante-past of heaven
Thou dost in me reveal,
Attest my sins forgiven,
And my salvation seal.

3 Th' indubitable witness
Of thy own Deity,
Thou giv'st my soul its fitness
Thy glorious face to see:
Thy comforts, gifts, and graces,
My largest thoughts transcend,
And challenge endless praises,
When faith in sight shall end.

530 *The universal anthem.*

1 When shall the voice of singing
Flow joyfully along?
When hill and valley, ringing
With one triumphant song,
Proclaim the contest ended,
And Him who once was slain,
Again to earth descended,
In righteousness to reign.

2 Then from the craggy mountains
The sacred shout shall fly;
And shady vales and fountains
Shall echo the reply.
High tower and lowly dwelling
Shall send the chorus round,
All hallelujahs swelling
In one eternal sound!

531

1 Now be the gospel banner
In every land unfurl'd,
And be the shout hosanna
Re-echoed through the world:
Till ev'ry isle and nation,
Till every tribe and tongue,
Receive the great salvation,
And join the happy throng.

2 Yes, Thou shalt reign for ever,
O Jesus, King of kings!
Thy light, Thy love, Thy favor,
Each ransomed captive sings:
The isles for Thee are waiting,
The deserts learn Thy praise,
The hills and vallies greeting,
The song responsive raise.

532 *Doxology.*

To thee be praise forever,
Thou glorious King of kings;
Thy wondrous love and favor
Each ransom'd spirit sings:
We'll celebrate thy glory,
With all thy saints above,
And shout the joyful story
Of thy redeeming love.

JOY. 7s & 6s.

1. To thee, my God, my Savior, My soul, exulting, sings,
Rejoicing in thy favor, Almighty King of kings!
I'll celebrate thy glory, With all the saints above,
And tell the joyful story Of thy redeeming love.

2 Soon as the morn with roses
   Bedecks the dewy east,
And when the sun reposes
   Upon the ocean's breast,
My voice in supplication,
   My Savior, thou shalt hear;
Oh, grant me thy salvation,
   And to my soul draw near!

3 By thee through life supported,
   I pass the dangerous road,
With heavenly hosts escorted
   Up to their bright abode:
There cast my crown before thee,
   And all my conflicts o'er,
Unceasingly adore thee:
   What would an angel more?

534 *"He hath borne our griefs."*

1 I lay my sins on Jesus,
   The spotless Lamb of God;
He bears them all, and frees us
   From the accursed load;
I bring my guilt to Jesus,
   To wash my crimson stains
White in his blood most precious,
   Till not a stain remains.

2 I lay my wants on Jesus;
   All fullness dwells in him;
He heals all my diseases,
   He doth my soul redeem:
I lay my griefs on Jesus,
   My burdens and my cares;
He from them all releases,
   He all my sorrow shares.

3 I rest my soul on Jesus,
   This weary soul of mine;
His right hand me embraces,
   I on his breast recline.
I love the name of Jesus,
   Immanuel, Christ, the Lord;
Like fragrance on the breezes,
   His name abroad is poured.

4 I long to be like Jesus,
   Meek, loving, lowly, mild;
I long to be like Jesus,
   The Father's holy child:
I long to be with Jesus,
   Amid the heavenly throng,
To sing with saints his praises,
   To learn the angels' song

535   EWING. 7s & 6s.   A. EWING.

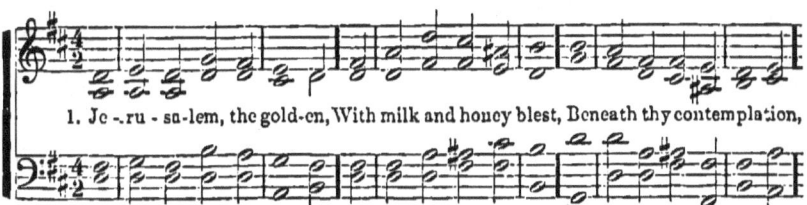

1. Je-ru-sa-lem, the gold-en, With milk and honey blest, Beneath thy contemplation,

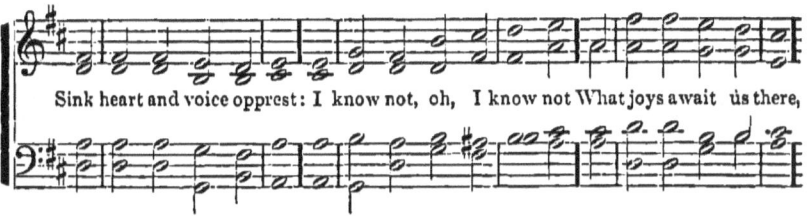

Sink heart and voice opprest: I know not, oh, I know not What joys await us there,

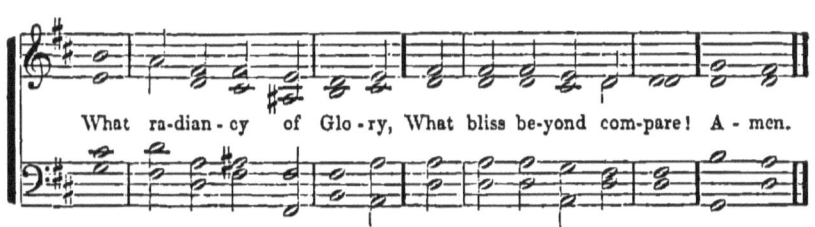

What ra-dian-cy of Glo-ry, What bliss be-yond com-pare! A-men.

2 They stand, those hills of Zion,
   All jubilant with song,
And bright with many an angel,
   And all the martyr throng.
The Prince is ever in them,
   The day-light is serene;
The pastures of the blessed
   Are decked in glorious sheen.

3 There is the Throne of David;
   And there, from care released,
The shout of them that triumph,
   The song of them that feast:
And they who with their Leader
   Have conquered in the fight,
Forever and forever
   Are clad in robes of white.

536 *Contrast of Heaven with earth.*
(An ancient Hymn.)

1 Brief life is here our portion,
   Brief sorrow, short-lived care;
The life that knows no ending,
   The tearless life is there:
Reward of grace, how wondrous!
   Short toil — eternal rest!
Oh! miracle of mercy,
   That rebels should be blest!

2 And now we fight the battle,—
   But then shall wear the crown
Of full and everlasting
   And ever bright renown;
There God, our King and Portion,
   In fullness of his grace,
Shall we behold forever,
   And worship face to face.

3 O sweet and blessed country,
   The home of God's elect!
O sweet and blessed country,
   That eager hearts expect!
Jesu, in mercy bring us
   To that dear land of rest,
Who art with God the Father,
   And Spirit, ever blest. Amen.

YARMOUTH. 7s & 6s.

1. When shall the voice of singing Flow joyfully along? When hill and valley, ringing With one triumphant song, Proclaim the contest ended, And Him who once was slain, Again to earth descended, Again to earth descended, Again to earth descended, In righteousness to reign.

2 Then from the craggy mountains
   The sacred shout shall fly;
And shady vales and fountains
   Shall echo the reply.
High tower and lowly dwelling
   Shall send the chorus round,
All hallelujahs swelling
   In one eternal sound!

---

538 *"Fear not, little flock."*

1 In heavenly love abiding,
   No change my heart shall fear,
And safe is such confiding,
   For nothing changes here:
The storm may roar without me,
   My heart may low be laid,
But God is round about me,
   And can I be dismayed?

2 Wherever he may guide me,
   No want shall turn me back;
My Shepherd is beside me,
   And nothing can I lack:
His wisdom ever waketh,
   His sight is never dim:
He knows the way he taketh,
   And I will walk with him.

3 Green pastures are before me,
   Which yet I have not seen;
Bright skies will soon be o'er me,
   Where darkest clouds have been:
My hope I cannot measure;
   My path to life is free;
My Savior has my treasure,
   And he will walk with me.

MAGDALENA. 7s & 6s.

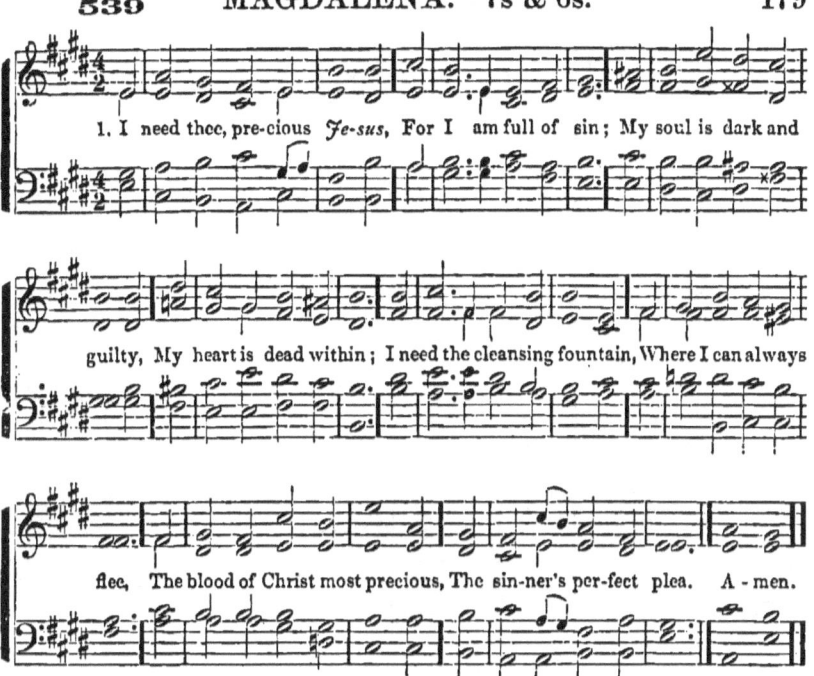

1. I need thee, precious Jesus, For I am full of sin; My soul is dark and guilty, My heart is dead within; I need the cleansing fountain, Where I can always flee, The blood of Christ most precious, The sinner's perfect plea. A-men.

2 I need thee, precious Jesus.
  For I am very poor;
A stranger and a pilgrim,
  I have no earthly store:
I need the love of Jesus,
  To cheer me on my way,
To guide my doubting footsteps,
  To be my strength and stay.

3 I need thee, precious Jesus,
  I need a friend like thee,
A friend to soothe and pity,
  A friend to care for me:
I need the heart of Jesus,
  To feel each anxious care;
To tell my every trial,
  And all my sorrows share.

4 I need thee, precious Jesus,
  I need thee day by day,
To fill me with thy fullness,
  To lead me on my way:
I need thy *Holy Spirit*,
  To teach me what I am;
To show me more of Jesus,
  To point me to the *Lamb*.

5 I need thee, precious Jesus,
  And hope to see thee soon
Encircled with the rainbow,
  And seated on thy throne:
There, with thy blood-bought children,
  My joy shall ever be
To sing thy praises, Jesus,
  To gaze, my *Lord*, on thee. Amen.

540 *The exceeding riches of his grace.*

1 O Lord, thy love's unbounded!
  So full, so sweet, so free!
Our thoughts are all confounded,
  Whene'er we think on thee:
For us, thou cam'st from heaven,
  For us to bleed and die;
That, purchased and forgiven,
  We might ascend on high.

2 Oh, let this love constrain us
  To give our hearts to thee;
Let nothing henceforth pain us,
  But that which paineth thee!
Our joy, our one endeavor,
  Through suffering, conflict, shame,
To serve thee, gracious Savior,
  And magnify thy name.

2 Savior, Prince, enthroned above,
   Repentance to impart,
Give me, through thy dying love,
   The humble contrite heart:
Give what I have long implored,
   A portion of thy grief unknown:
Turn, and look upon me, Lord,
   And break my heart of stone.

3 For thine own compassion's sake,
   The gracious wonder show;
Cast my sins behind thy back,
   And wash me white as snow:
If thy bowels now are stirr'd,
   If now I do myself bemoan,
Turn, and look upon me, Lord,
   And break my heart of stone.

542 Continued.—*The heart broken.*

1 Savior, see me from above,
   Nor suffer me to die;
Life, and happiness, and love,
   Drop from thy gracious eye:
Speak the reconciling word,
   And let thy mercy melt me down;
Turn, and look upon me, Lord,
   And break my heart of stone.

2 Look, as when thine eye pursued
   The first apostate man,—
Saw him welt'ring in his blood,
   And bade him rise again:
Speak my paradise restored;
   Redeem me by thy grace alone:
Turn, and look upon me, Lord,
   And break my heart of stone.

543 *The deceitfulness of sin.*

1 Jesus, friend of sinners, hear
  Yet once again, I pray;
  From my debt of sin set clear,
  For I have naught to pay:
  Speak, O speak the kind release;
  A poor backsliding soul restore;
  Love me freely, seal my peace,
  And bid me sin no more.

2 For my selfishness and pride
  Thou hast withdrawn thy grace;
  Left me long to wander wide,
  An outcast from thy face;
  But I now my sins confess,
  And mercy, mercy, I implore;
  Love me freely, seal my peace,
  And bid me sin no more.

3 Sin's deceitfulness hath spread
  A hardness o'er my heart;
  But if thou thy Spirit shed,
  The stony shall depart:
  Shed thy love, thy tenderness,
  And let me feel thy soft'ning power;
  Love me freely, seal my peace,
  And bid me sin no more.

544 *Tears of joy.*

1 Lord, and is thine anger gone,—
  And art thou pacified?
  After all that I have done,
  Dost thou no longer chide?
  Let thy love my heart constrain,
  And all my restless passions sway:
  Keep me, lest I turn again
  Out of the narrow way.

2 See my utter helplessness,
  And leave me not alone;
  O preserve in perfect peace,
  And seal me for thine own:
  More and more thyself reveal,
  Thy presence let me always find;
  Comfort, and confirm, and heal
  My feeble, sin-sick mind.

3 As the apple of thine eye,
  Thy weakest servant keep;
  Help me at thy feet to lie,
  And there forever weep:
  Tears of joy mine eyes o'erflow,
  That I have any hope of heaven;
  Much of love I ought to know,
  For I have much forgiven.

545 *Determined to know nothing but Jesus.*

1 Vain, delusive world, adieu,
  With all of creature good:
  Only Jesus I pursue,
  Who bought me with his blood:
  All thy pleasures I forego;
  I trample on thy wealth and pride,
  Only Jesus will I know,
  And Jesus crucified.

2 Other knowledge I disdain;
  'Tis all but vanity:
  Christ, the Lamb of God, was slain,—
  He tasted death for me.
  Me to save from endless woe
  The sin-atoning Victim died;
  Only Jesus will I know,
  And Jesus crucified.

3 Him to know is life and peace,
  And pleasure without end;
  This is all my happiness,
  On Jesus to depend;
  Daily in his grace to grow,
  And ever in his faith abide;
  Only Jesus will I know,
  And Jesus crucified.

4 O that I could all invite,
  This saving truth to prove;
  Show the length, the breadth, the hight
  And depth of Jesus' love!
  Fain I would to sinners show
  The blood by faith alone applied;
  Only Jesus will I know,
  And Jesus crucified.

Doxology.

Father, Son, and Holy Ghost,
  Thy Godhead we adore;
Join with the celestial host,
  Who praise thee evermore!
Live by earth and heaven adored,
  The Three in One, the One in Three
Holy, holy, holy Lord,
  All glory be to thee!

LYONS. 5s & 6s. HAYDN.

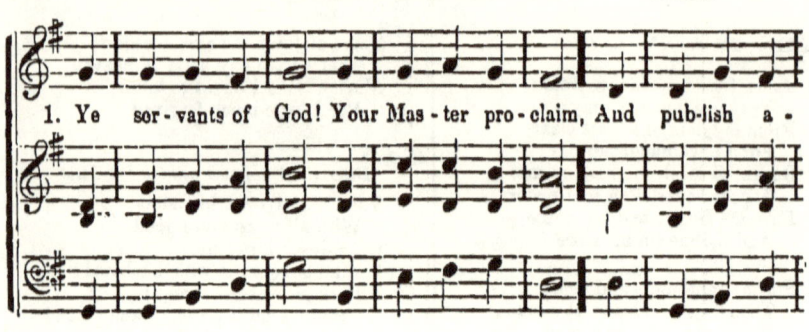

2 God ruleth on high,
   Almighty to save;
And still he is nigh,
   His presence we have:
The great congregation
   His triumph shall sing,
Ascribing salvation
   To Jesus, our King.

3 Salvation to God
   Who sits on the throne;
Let all cry aloud,
   And honor the Son:
The praises of Jesus
   The angels proclaim;
Fall down on their faces,
   And worship the Lamb.

4 Then let us adore,
  And give him his right;
All glory and power,
  And wisdom and might;
All honor and blessing,—
  With angels above,—
And thanks never ceasing,
  And infinite love.

547. *The heavenly Pattern.*

1 Appointed by thee,
  We meet in thy name,
And meekly agree
  To follow the Lamb;
To trace thy example,
  The world to disdain,
And constantly trample
  On pleasure and pain.

2 O what shall we do
  Our Savior to love?
To make us anew,
  Come, Lord, from above:
The fruit of thy passion,
  Thy holiness give;
Give us the salvation
  Of all that believe.

3 O Jesus! appear;
  No longer delay,
To sanctify here,
  And bear us away;
The end of our meeting
  On earth let us see—
Triumphantly sitting
  In glory with thee.

548. *Peace, power, and love.*

1 All thanks to the Lamb,
  Who gives us to meet:
His love we proclaim,
  His praises repeat:
We own him our Jesus,
  Continually near,
To pardon and bless us,
  And perfect us here.

2 In him we have peace,
  In him we have power,
Preserved by his grace
  Throughout the dark hour;
In all our temptation
  He keeps us, to prove
His utmost salvation,
  His fullness of love.

3 Pronounce the glad word,
  And bid us be free.
Ah! hast thou not, Lord,
  A blessing for me?
The peace thou hast given,
  This moment impart,
And open thy heaven,
  O Love, in my heart.

549. *Rejoicing in the freeness of* &c.

1 All glory and praise
  To Jesus our Lord,
So plenteous in grace,
  So true to his word;
To us he hath given
  The gift from above,
The earnest of heaven,
  The Spirit of love.

2 The truth of our God
  We boldly assert;
His love shed abroad,
  And power in our heart,
Ye all may inherit,
  On Jesus who call;
The gift of his Spirit
  Is proffer'd to all.

3 His witness within,
  By faith we receive,
And, ransom'd from sin,
  In righteousness live;
Through Jesus's passion
  We gladly possess
A present salvation,—
  A kingdom of peace.

4 The peace and the power,
  Ye sinners, embrace,
And look for the shower,—
  The Spirit of grace;
The gift and the Giver
  We all may receive,
Forever and ever
  Within us to live.

ROWLEY. 6s & 9s.

Arranged by Dr. L. MASON.

1. Come a-way to the skies, My be-lov-ed a-rise, And re-joice in the day thou wert born; On this fes-ti-val day, Come ex-ult-ing a-way, And with singing to Zi-on re-turn, And with singing to Zi-on re-turn.

2 We have laid up our love,
  And our treasure above,
Though our bodies continue below;
  The redeemed of our Lord,
  We remember his word,
And with singing to Paradise go.

3 With singing we praise
  The original grace,
By our heavenly Father bestowed;
  Our being receive
  From his bounty, and live
To the honor and glory of God.

551 *Rapturous anticipation.*

1 Come, let us ascend,
  My companion and friend,
To a taste of the banquet above;
  If thy heart be as mine,
  If for Jesus it pine,
Come up into the chariot of love.

2 Who in Jesus confide,
  We are bold to outride
The storms of affliction beneath;
  With the prophet we soar
  To the heavenly shore,
And outfly all the arrows of death.

3 By faith we are come
  To our permanent home;
By hope we the rapture improve
  By love we still rise,
  And look down on the skies,
For the heaven of heavens is love.

RAPTURE. 6s & 9s, or 5s, 6s & 9s.

1. O how happy are they Who their Savior obey, And have laid up their treasure above!

Tongue can never express The sweet comfort and peace Of a soul in its ear-li-est love.

4 Who on earth can conceive
  How happy we live,
In the palace of God the great King:
  What a concert of praise,
  When our Jesus's grace
The whole heavenly company sing!

5 What a rapturous song,
  When the glorified throng
In the spirit of harmony join!—
  Join all the glad choirs,
  Hearts, voices, and lyres,
And the burden is,—Mercy divine!

6 Hallelujah, they cry,
  To the King of the sky,—
To the great everlasting I AM;
  To the Lamb that was slain,
  And that liveth again,—
Hallelujah to God and the Lamb!

---

552   *Joy of the young convert.*

1 O how happy are they,
  Who their Savior obey,
And have laid up their treasure above!
  Tongue can never express
  The sweet comfort and peace
Of a soul in its earliest love!

2 That sweet comfort was mine,
  When the favor divine
I first found in the blood of the Lamb;
  When my heart first believed,
  What a joy I received,
What a heaven in Jesus's name!

3 'Twas a heaven below,
  My Redeemer to know:
And the angels could do nothing more,
  Than to fall at his feet,
  And the story repeat,
And the Lover of sinners adore.

4 Jesus all the day long,
  Was my joy and my song;
O that all his salvation might see;
  He hath loved me I cried,
  He hath suffered and died,
To redeem such a rebel as me.

5 On the wings of his love,
  I was carried above,
All my sin, and temptation and pain,
  And I could not believe
  That I ever should grieve,
That I ever should suffer again.

6 O! the rapturous height
  Of that holy delight,
Which I felt in the life-giving blood
  Of my Savior possessed
  I was perfectly blest,
And was fill'd with the fullness of God.

554. AMERICA. 6s & 4s.

National Hymn. Words by S. F. SMITH.

1. My country, 'tis of thee, Sweet land of liberty, Of thee I sing: Land where my fathers died; Land of the pilgrim's pride; From every mountain side Let freedom ring.

2. My native country! thee, Land of the noble free, Thy name I love: I love thy rocks and rills, Thy woods and templed hills; My heart with rapture thrills Like that above.

3 Let music swell the breeze,
And ring from all the trees
  Sweet freedom's song!
Let mortal tongues awake;
Let all that breathe partake;
Let rocks their silence break—
  The sound prolong!

4 Our fathers' God! to thee,
Author of liberty,
  To thee we sing:
Long may our land be bright
With freedom's holy light;
Protect us by thy might,
  Great God, our King!

555

1 My faith looks up to thee,
Thou Lamb of Calvary,
  Savior divine,
Now hear me while I pray;
Take all my guilt away;
O let me from this day
  Be wholly thine.

2 May thy rich grace impart
Strength to my fainting heart;
  My zeal inspire;
As thou hast died for me,
O may my love to thee
Pure, warm and changeless be,
  A living fire.

3 While life's dark maze I tread,
And griefs around me spread,
  Be thou my guide;
Bid darkness turn to day;
Wipe sorrow's tears away,
Nor let me ever stray
  From thee aside.

4 When ends life's transient dream;
When death's cold, sullen stream
  Shall o'er me roll;
Blest Savior, then, in love,
Fear and distress remove;
O, bear me safe above,—
  A ransom'd soul.

556. PORTLAND. 6s, 8s & 4s.
Rev. W. McDonald.

1. Though nature's strength decay, And earth and hell withstand, To Canaan's bounds I urge my way, At his command; The wat'ry deep I pass, With Jesus in my view; And through the howling wilder-ness My way pur-sue.

2. There dwells the Lord our King, The Lord our Righteousness, Triumphant o'er the world of sin, The Prince of peace; On Zi-on's sa-cred hight, His kingdom still maintains; And, glorious, with his saints in light For-ev-er reigns.

3 He keeps his own secure;
  He guards them by his side;
  Arrays in garments white and pure
    His spotless bride;
  With groves of living joys,
    With streams of sacred bliss,
  With all the fruits of Paradise,
    He still supplies.

4 Before the great Three One
    They all exulting stand,
  And tell the wonders he hath done
    Through all their land:
  The list'ning spheres attend,
    And swell the growing fame;
  And sing, in songs which never end,
    The wondrous Name.

557   *Triumphant trust in God.*
1 My Shepherd's mighty aid,
    His dear redeeming love,
  His all-protecting power display'd,
    I joy to prove.
  Led onward by my guide,
    I view the verdant scene,
  Where limpid waters gently glide
    Through pastures green.

2 In error's maze my soul
    Shall wander now no more;
  His Spirit shall, with sweet control,
    The lost restore:
  My willing steps shall lead
    In paths of righteousness;
  His power defend; his bounty feed;
    His mercy bless.

SIMPSON. 6s, 8s & 4s.

Contributed to this work.

1. The God of Abrah'm praise, Who reigns enthroned above; Ancient of everlasting days, And God of love: Jehovah, great I am! By earth and heaven confess'd; I bow and bless the sacred Name, Forever blest.

2 The God of Abrah'm praise,
   At whose supreme command
  From earth I rise, and seek the joys
   At his right hand;
  I all on earth forsake,
   Its wisdom, fame, and power;
  And him my only portion make,
   My shield and tower.

3 The God of Abrah'm praise,
   Whose all-sufficient grace
  Shall guide me all my happy days
   In all his ways;

He calls a worm his friend:
  He calls himself my God!
And he shall save me to the end,
  Through Jesus' blood.

4 He by himself hath sworn:
   I on his oath depend;
  I shall, on eagles' wings upborne,
   To heaven ascend:
  I shall behold his face;
   I shall his power adore,
  And sing the wonders of his grace
   Forever more.

559 THOMPSON. 7s, 8s & 7s.*

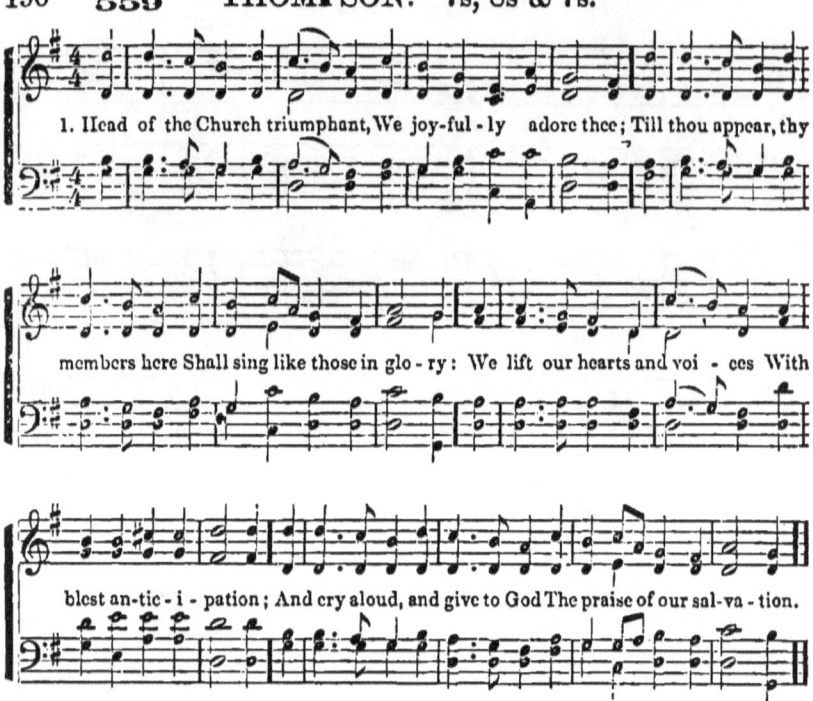

1. Head of the Church triumphant, We joyfully adore thee; Till thou appear, thy members here Shall sing like those in glory: We lift our hearts and voices With blest anticipation; And cry aloud, and give to God The praise of our salvation.

2 Thou dost conduct thy people
   Through torrents of temptation;
Nor will we fear, while thou art near,
   The fire of tribulation:
The world, with sin and Satan,
   In vain our march opposes;
By thee we shall break through them all,
   And sing the song of Moses.

3 By faith we see the glory,
   To which thou shalt restore us:
The cross despise for that high prize
   Which thou hast set before us:
And if thou count us worthy,
   We each, as dying Stephen,
Shall see thee stand, at God's right hand,
   To take us up to heaven.

560 *Triumphing in delivering grace.*
1 Worship, and thanks, and blessing,
   And strength ascribe to Jesus:—
Jesus alone defends his own,
   When earth and hell oppress us:
Jesus, with joy we witness,
   Almighty to deliver;
Our seals set to, that God is true,
   And reigns a King forever.

2 Omnipotent Redeemer,
   Our ransom'd souls adore thee;
Our Savior thou, we find it now,
   And give thee all the glory.
We sing thine arm unshorten'd,
   Brought through our sore temptation:
With heart and voice in thee rejoice,
   The God of our salvation.

3 The world's and Satan's malice,
   Thou, Jesus, hast confounded;
And by thy grace, with songs of praise,
   Our happy souls resounded.
Accepting our deliv'rance,
   We triumph in thy favor;
And for the love which now we prove,
   Shall praise thy Name forever.

Doxology.
To Father, Son, and Spirit,
   Ascribe we equal glory:
One Deity, in Persons Three,
   Let all thy works adore thee:
As was from the beginning,
   Glory to God be given,
By all who know thy Name below,
   And all thy hosts in heaven.

*Or 11s. by uniting the first two parts of each measure.

561   KINGSLEY.. 11s.   G. KINGSLEY. By Permission.

1. I would not live al-way; I ask not to stay Where storm after storm rises dark o'er the way: The few lurid mornings, that dawn on us here, Are enough for life's joys, full enough for its cheer.

2 I would not live alway; no, welcome the tomb!
Since Jesus hath lain there, I dread not its gloom;
There sweet be my rest, till he bid me arise,
To hail him in triumph descending the skies.

3 Who, who would live alway, away from his God—
Away from yon heaven, that blissful abode,
Where rivers of pleasure flow bright o'er the plains,
And the noontide of glory eternally reigns?

4 There saints of all ages in harmony meet,
Their Savior and brethren transported to greet;
While anthems of rapture unceasingly roll,
And the smile of the Lord is the feast of the soul.

562   *"Faint, yet pursuing."*

1 Though faint, yet pursuing, we go on our way;
The Lord is our Leader, his word is our stay:
Though suffering, and sorrow, and trial be near,
The Lord is our refuge, and whom can we fear?

2 He raiseth the fallen, he cheereth the faint;
The weak and oppressed, he will hear their complaint;
The way may be weary, and thorny the road,
But how can we falter? our help is in God!

3 And to his green pastures our footsteps he leads;
His flock in the desert how kindly he feeds!
The lambs in his bosom he tenderly bears,
And brings back the wanderers all safe from the snares.

4 Though clouds may surround us, our God is our light;
Though storms rage around us, our God is our might;
So faint, yet pursuing, still onward we come,
The Lord is our Leader, and heaven is our home!

2 In every condition, in sickness, and health,
In poverty's vale, or abounding in wealth,
At home, or abroad, on the land, on the sea,
" As thy days may demand, shall thy strength ever be."

3 " Fear not, I am with thee, O be not dismay'd;
I now am thy God, and will still give thee aid;
I'll strengthen thee, help thee, and cause thee to stand,
Upheld by my righteous, omnipotent hand.

4 " When through the deep waters I call thee to go,
The rivers of woe shall not thee o'erflow;
For I will be with thee, thy troubles to bless,
And sanctify to thee thy deepest distress.

5 " When through fiery trials thy pathway shall lie,
My grace all-sufficient shall be thy supply;
The flame shall not hurt thee; I only design
Thy dross to consume, and thy gold to refine.

6 " Even down to old age, all my people shall prove
Impartial, eternal, unchangeable love;
And when hoary hairs shall thy temples adorn,
Like lambs they shall still in thy bosom be borne.

7 " The soul that on Jesus doth lean for repose,
I will not, I will not, desert to his foes;
That soul, though all hell should endeavor to shake,
I'll never—no, never—no, never forsake."

---

564 *Rejoicing in the care of the good Shepherd.*

1 The Lord is my Shepherd, no want shall I know;
 I feed in green pastures, safe-folded I rest;
 He leadeth my soul where the still waters flow,
  Restores me when wand'ring, redeems when oppress'd.

2 Through the valley and shadow of death though I stray,
 Since thou art my guardian, no evil I fear;
 Thy rod shall defend me, thy staff be my stay;
  No harm can befall, with my Comforter near.

3 In the midst of affliction my table is spread;
 With blessings unmeasured my cup runneth o'er;
 With oil and perfume thou anointest my head;
  O what shall I ask of thy providence more?

4 Let goodness and mercy, my bountiful God,
 Still follow my steps till I meet thee above;
 I seek—by the path which my forefathers trod,
  Through the land of their sojourn—thy kingdom of love.

HAIL TO THE BRIGHTNESS. 11 & 10s.

Dr. L. Mason. 1830.

2 Hail to the brightness of Zion's glad morning,
Long by the prophets of Israel foretold;
Hail to the millions from bondage returning,
Gentiles and Jews the blest vision behold.

3 Lo! in the desert rich flowers are springing,
Streams ever copious are gliding along:
Loud from the mountain-tops echoes are ringing,
Wastes rise in verdure and mingle in song.

4 See, from all lands—from the isles of the ocean,
Praise to Jehovah ascending on high;
Fallen are the engines of war and commotion,
Shouts of salvation are rending the sky

567 HENLEY. 11s & 10s.

From "The Hallelujah."

1. Come un-to me, when shadows darkly gath-er, When the sad heart is wea-ry and dis-trest, Seek-ing for com-fort from your Heavenly Father, Come un-to me, And I will give you rest!
2. Ye who have mourned when the spring flowers were taken, When the ripe fruit fell rich-ly to the ground, When the loved slept, in brighter homes to waken, Where their pale brows with spirit-wreaths are crowned.
3. Large are the mansions in thy Father's dwelling, Glad are the homes that sor-rows nev-er dim; Sweet are the tones which raise the heavenly hymn.
4. There, like an E-den blossom-ing in gladness, Bloom the fair flowers the earth too rude-ly pressed; Come un-to me, all ye who droop in sadness, Come un-to me, and I will give you rest!

568 THE JUBILEE.

1. What heavenly mu-sic do I hear, Sal-va-tion sound-ing free! Ye souls in bondage lend an ear: This is the Ju-bi-lee!

2 How sweetly do the tidings roll
  All 'round from sea to sea,
From land to land, from pole to pole,
  This is the jubilee.
3 Good news, good news to Adam's race,
  Let Christians all agree
To sing redeeming love and grace,
  This is the jubilee.

4 Jesus is on the mercy seat,
  Before him bend the knee,
Let heaven and earth his praise repeat,
  This is the jubilee.
5 Come, ye redeemed, your tribute bring
  With songs of harmony;
While on the road to Canaan sing
  This is the jubilee.

EVENTIDE. 10s.

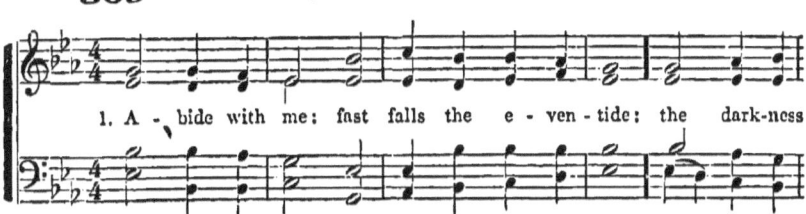

1. A-bide with me: fast falls the e-ven-tide: the dark-ness

deep-ens: Lord, with me a-bide: When oth-er help-ers

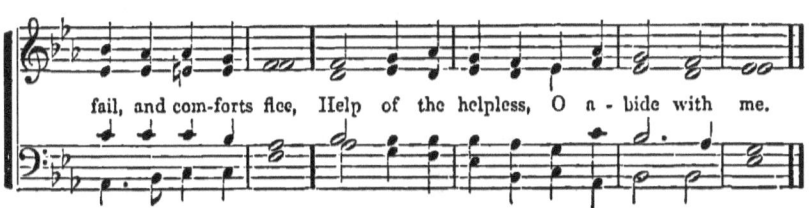

fail, and com-forts flee, Help of the helpless, O a-bide with me.

2 Swift to its close ebbs out life's little day:
Earth's joys grow dim, its glories pass away:
Change and decay in all around I see:
O Thou who changest not, abide with me.

3 I need thy presence every passing hour:
What but thy grace can foil the tempter's power?
Who like thyself my guide and stay can be?
Through cloud and sunshine, Lord, abide with me.

4 I fear no foe, with thee at hand to bless:
Ills have no weight, and tears no bitterness:
Where is death's sting, where, grave, thy victory?
I triumph still, if thou abide with me.

5 Hold thou thy Cross before my closing eyes;
Shine through the gloom, and point me to the skies:
Heaven's morning breaks, and earth's vain shadows flee;
In life, in death, O Lord, abide with me.

570 UNITY. 6s & 5s, (Peculiar.)

Dr. L MASON.

2 When shall love freely flow
  Pure as life's river?
When shall sweet friendship glow,
  Changeless forever?
Where joys celestial thrill,
Where bliss each heart shall fill,
And fears of parting chill,
  Never, no, never!

3 Up to that world of light,
  Take us, dear Savior!
May we all there unite,
  Happy forever!

Where kindred spirits dwell,
There may our music swell,
And time our joys dispel
  Never, no never!

4 Soon shall we meet again,
  Meet ne'er to sever;
Soon will peace wreathe her chain
  Round us forever;
Our hearts will then repose,
Secure from worldly woes;
Our songs of praise shall close
  Never, no, never!

PART SECOND.

THE CROSS. L. M.

571   Rev. G. C. WELLS.
Newly arranged.

1. When I survey the wondrous cross On which the Prince of glory died, My richest gain I count but loss, And pour contempt on all my pride.

The cross, the cross, the precious cross, The wondrous cross of Je-sus, From all our sin, its guilt and pow'r, And ev'ry stain it frees us.

Then I'm clinging, clinging, clinging, O, I'm clinging to the cross, Yes, I'm clinging, clinging, clinging, Clinging to the cross.

2 Forbid it, Lord, that I should boast,
Save in the death of Christ, my God;
All the vain things that charm me most,
I sacrifice them to his blood.

3 See, from his head, his hands, his feet,
Sorrow and love flow mingled down:
Did e'er such love and sorrow meet,
Or thorns compose so rich a crown?

4 Were the whole realm of nature mine,
That were a present far too small;
Love so amazing, so divine,
Demands my soul, my life, my all.

THE OLD, OLD STORY.

W. H. DOANE.

From "Songs of Devotion." By Permission of BIGELOW & MAIN.

1. Tell me the old, old sto-ry, Of unseen things a-bove; Of Je-sus and his glo-ry, Of Je-sus, and his love. Tell me the sto-ry simply, As to a lit-tle child; For I am weak and wea-ry, And helpless, and defiled.

CHORUS.

Tell me the old, old sto-ry, Tell me the old, old sto-ry, Tell me the old, old sto-ry Of Je-sus and his love.

2 Tell me the story slowly,
   That I may take it in —
That wonderful Redemption,
   God's remedy for sin!
Tell me the story often,
   For I forget so soon!
The "early dew" of morning
   Has passed away at noon!—*Cho.*

3 Tell me the story softly,
   With earnest tones and grave;
Remember, I'm the sinner
   Whom Jesus came to save.

Tell me the story always,
   If you would really be,
In any time of trouble,
   A comforter to me.—*Cho.*

4 Tell me the same old story,
   When you have cause to fear
That this world's empty glory
   Is costing me too dear.
Yes, and when that world's glory
   Is dawning on my soul,
Tell me the old, old story,—
   "Christ Jesus makes thee whole."

573 I LOVE TO TELL THE STORY.

3. I love to tell the story;
   'Tis pleasant to repeat
   What seems, each time I tell it,
   More wonderfully sweet.
   I love to tell the story;
   For some have never heard
   The message of salvation
   From God's own holy word.—Cho.

4. I love to tell the story;
   For those who know it best
   Seem hungering and thirsting
   To hear it like the rest.
   And when, in scenes of glory,
   I sing the New, New Song,
   'Twill be the Old, Old Story
   That I have loved so long!—Cho.

574. THE EDEN ABOVE.

Arranged from Revival Melodies, for this work.

1. We're bound for the land of the pure and the ho-ly, The home of the
   Ye wanderers from God in the broad road of fol-ly, O say will you
   hap-py, the king-dom of love, Will you go, will you go, will you
   go to the E-den a-bove?
   go, will you go; O say will you go to the E-den a-bove?

2 In that blessed land neither sighing nor anguish
Can breathe in the fields where the glorified rove ;
Ye heart-burden'd ones, who in misery languish,
O say, will you go to the Eden above?
  Will you go, will you go, &c.
  O say, will you go to the Eden above?

3 No poverty there,—no, the saints are all wealthy,
The heirs of his glory whose nature is love ;
Nor sickness can reach them, that country is healthy;
O say, will you go to the Eden above?
  Will you go, will you go, &c.
  O say will you go to the Eden above?

4 Each saint has a mansion prepared and all furnished,
Ere from this clay house he is summon'd to move ;
Its gates and its towers with glory are burnish'd ;
O say, will you go to the Eden above ?
  Will you go, will you go, &c.
  O say, will you go to this Eden above ?

5 March on, happy pilgrims, that land is before you,
And soon its ten thousand delights we shall prove ;
Yes, soon we shall walk o'er the hills of bright glory,
And drink the pure joys of the Eden above.
  We will go, we will go, &c.
  O yes, we will go to the Eden above.

6 And yet, guilty sinner, we would not forsake thee
We halt yet a moment, as onward we move ;
O come to thy Lord, in his arms he will take thee,
And bear thee along to the Eden above.
  Will you go, will you go, &c.
  O say, will you go to the Eden above?

7 Methinks thou art now in thy wretchedness saying,
O, who can this guilt from my conscience remove?
No other but Jesus ; then come to him praying—
Prepare me, O Lord, for the Eden above.
  Will you go, will you go, &c.
  At last, will you go to the Eden above?

575. THE CHRISTIAN PILGRIM.

Arranged by S. HUBBARD.

1. The Christian pilgrim sings, Heav'n's my home, heav'n's my home; The Christian pilgrim sings, Heav'n's my home. Thro' the tel-es-cope of faith, He looks o'er the riv-er death, And joy-ful-ly exclaims, Heav'n's my home, heav'n's my home; And joy-ful-ly ex-claims, Heav'n's my home.

2. Though poverty's my lot, Heav'n's my home, heav'n's my home; Though pov-er-ty's my lot, Heav'n's my home. Though pov-er-ty's my lot, And the fig-tree blossoms not, I can sing the song of hope, Heav'n's my home, heav'n's my home; I can sing the song of hope, Heav'n's my home.

3 Come ye that love the Lord, unto me, unto me,
Come ye that love the Lord, unto me;
I've something good to say,
About this narrow way,
For Christ the other day saved my soul, saved my soul,
For Christ the other day saved my soul.

4 Some said I'd soon give o'er, you shall see, you shall see,
Some said I'd soon give o'er, you shall see,
Some time has past away,
Since I began to pray,
I love the Lord to-day, bless his name, bless his name,
I love the Lord to-day, bless his name.

576. COME TO JESUS.

1. Come to Je-sus, come to Je-sus, Come to Je-sus, just now, Just now come to Je-sus, Come to Je-sus just now.

2 He will save you, &c.
3 O, believe him, &c.
4 He is able.
5 He is willing.
6 He'll receive you.
7 Call upon him.

8 He will hear you.
9 Look unto him.
10 He'll forgive you.
11 He will cleanse you.
12 Jesus loves you.
13 Only trust him.

3 I will sing for Jesus!
His name alone prevailing,
Shall be my sweetest music,
When heart and flesh are failing.

4 Still I'll sing for Jesus!
O! how will I adore him,
Among the cloud of witnesses,
Who cast their crowns before him.

SAFE WITHIN THE VAIL.

Arranged for this work.

1. Land a-head! Its fruits are waving, O'er the hills of fadeless green;
And the liv-ing waters lav-ing Shores where heavenly forms are seen.

2. Onward, bark! the cape I'm rounding, See, the blessed wave their hands;
Hear the harps of God re-sounding From the bright im-mor-tal bands.

CHORUS.
Rocks and storms, I'll fear no more, When on that e-ter-nal shore.
Drop the anchor! furl the sail! I am safe with-in the vail.

3 There, let go the anchor, riding
  On this calm and silv'ry bay;
  Sea-ward fast the tide is gliding,
  Shores in sunlight stretch away. *Cho.*

4 Now we're safe from all temptation,
  All the storms of life are past;
  Praise the Rock of our Salvation,
  We are safe at home at last! *Cho.*

579. MAGDALEN.

Arr. from "Song Crown," by W. G. F.
By Permission.

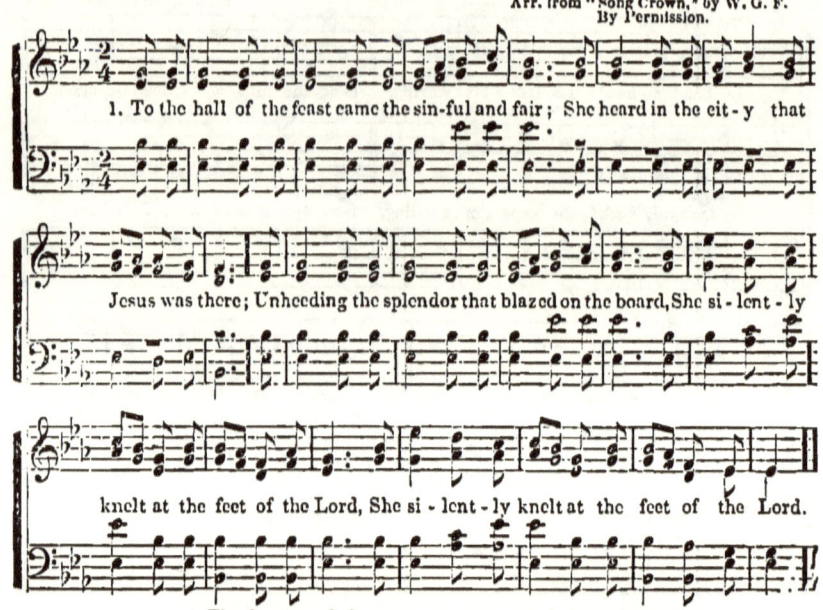

1. To the hall of the feast came the sinful and fair; She heard in the city that Jesus was there; Unheeding the splendor that blazed on the board, She silently knelt at the feet of the Lord, She silently knelt at the feet of the Lord.

2 The frown and the murmur went round thro' them all,
That one so unhallowed should tread in that hall;
No looks save of scorn, the poor outcast did greet,
As the wealth of her perfume she poured on his feet.

3 She saw but the Saviour, she breathed but with sighs;
She dared not look up to the heaven of his eyes:
And the hot tears gush'd forth at each heave of her breast,
As her lips to his feet were so lovingly pressed.

4 In the sky, after tempest, as shineth the bows,
In the glare of the sunbeams, as melteth the snows,
He looked on the lost one: "her sins were forgiven,"
And the mourner went forth in the beauty of heaven.

---

580. *Oh! tell me no more.*

1 Oh tell me no more of this world's vain store,
The time for such trifles with me now is o'er;
A country I've found where true joys abound:
To dwell I'm determined on that happy ground.

2 The souls that believe, in Paradise live,
And me, in that number, will Jesus receive;
My soul, don't delay — he calls thee away:
Rise! follow thy Savior, and bless the glad day.

3 No mortal doth know what he can bestow,
What light, strength and comfort — go after him, go:
Lo! onward I move, to a city above —
None guesses how wondrous my journey will prove.

4 Great spoils I shall win from death, hell and sin,
'Midst outward afflictions shall feel Christ within;
And when I'm to die, "receive me!" I'll cry,
For Jesus hath loved me — I cannot tell why.

581. LIGHTS ALONG THE SHORE.

Words by REV. J. H. STOCKTON.   By Permission.   Arranged by WM. G. FISCHER.

1. I'm a pilgrim and a stranger passing over,
   And a starry crown awaits me o'er the river,
   The road may be rough, but 'tis clear,
   Jesus bids me welcome there.

Chorus.
There are lights along the shore that never grow dim, That never, never grow dim; These souls are all aflame with the love of Jesus' name, They guide us, yes, they guide us unto him.

2 Sometimes I meet with trials on my journey,
   Temptation and sorrow by the way:
  But Jesus speaks, and says, "I'm ever near thee,
   To guide to realms of endless day."
     Chorus.—There are lights along the shore, etc.

3 Friends of Jesus! may your lights be trimm'd and burning,
   And shining along the way of love;
  Soon you'll gain the heights of glory, and be singing
   The happy songs of saints above.
     Chorus.—There are lights along the shore, etc.

4 We're a happy band of Christians, bound for Canaan,
   The land is in view, the wind's fair;
  We will sing redeeming love beyond the Jordan,
   With Jesus dwell forever there.
     Chorus.—There are lights along the shore, etc.

582. JESUS PAID IT ALL.

J. T. Grape.

1. I hear the Saviour say, Thy strength indeed is small; Child of weakness, watch and pray, Find in me thine all in all. Je-sus paid it all: All to him I owe; Sin had left a crim-son stain; He washed it white as snow.

2 O Lord, at last I find
　Thy power, and thine alone,
Can change this heart of mine,
　And make it all thine own.—*Cho.*

3 Then down beneath the cross,
　I lay my sin-sick soul;
Nothing I bring but dross,
　Thy grace must make me whole.—*Cho.*

4 I now in Christ abide —
　In him is perfect rest;
Close sheltered in his side,
　I am divinely blest.—*Cho.*

5 When at my post I fall,
　My ransomed soul shall rise;
And "Jesus paid it all,"
　Shall rend the vaulted skies.—*Cho.*

6 And when, in heaven above,
　At Jesus' feet I fall,
My song shall ever be —
　Jesus hath paid it all.—*Cho.*

583. "OH, BROTHER, BE FAITHFUL."

1. Oh, brother, be faith-ful, Oh, brother, be faith-ful, Oh, brother, be faith-ful, Faith-ful, faith-ful, Till we all ar-rive at home.

2 Oh, sister, be faithful.
3 There we shall see Jesus.
4 There we will shout glory.
5 There'll be no more parting.

584 "LET ME GO."

Words and Music by REV. L. HARTSOUGH. By Permission.

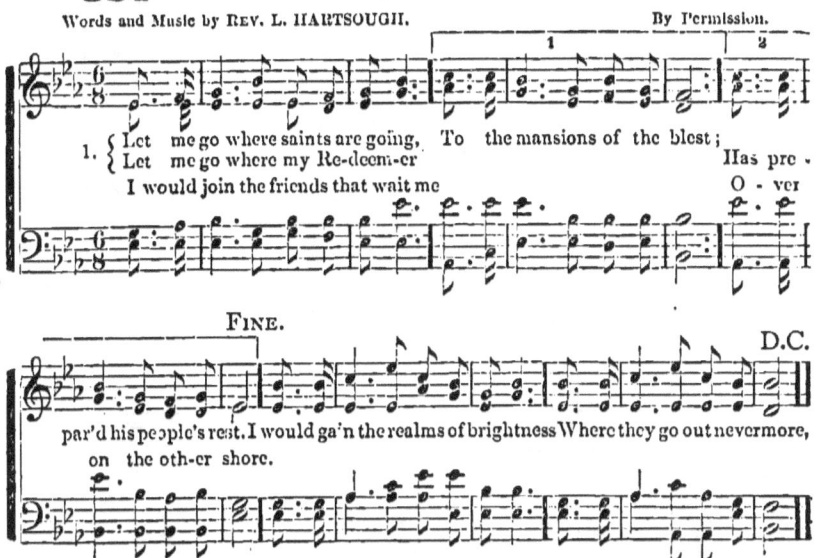

1. Let me go where saints are going, To the mansions of the blest;
   Let me go where my Redeemer Has prepar'd his people's rest.
   I would join the friends that wait me Over on the other shore.
   I would ga'n the realms of brightness Where they go out nevermore,

2 Let me go where none are weary,
  Where is raised no wail of woe.
  Let me go, and bathe my spirit
  In the raptures angels know:
  Let me go, for bliss eternal
  Lures my soul away, away,
  And the victor's song triumphant,
  Thrills my heart, I cannot stay.

3 Let me go, why should I tarry?
  What has earth to bind me here?
  What, but cares, and toils, and sorrows,
  What, but death, and pain and fear?
  Let me go, for hopes most cherish'd,
  Blasted, round me often lie;
  O! I've gathered brightest flowers,
  But to see them fade and die.

4 Let me go where tears and sighing
  Are forever more unknown,
  Where the joyous songs of glory
  Call me to a happier home.
  Let me go, I'd cease this dying,
  I would gain life's fairer plains;
  Let me join the myriad harpers,
  Let me chant their rapturous strains.

5 Let me go, O speed my journey,
  Saints and seraphs lure away;
  O! I almost feel the raptures,
  That belong to endless day.
  Oft methinks I hear the singing
  That is only heard above:
  Let me go, O speed my going,
  Let me go where all is love.

585 CARMARTHEN. H. M.

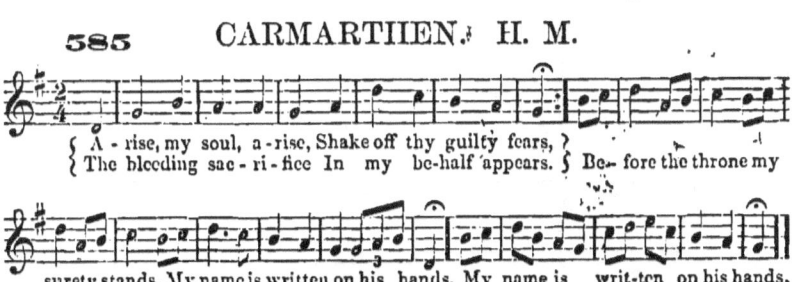

A-rise, my soul, a-rise, Shake off thy guilty fears,
The bleeding sacrifice In my behalf appears. Before the throne my
surety stands, My name is written on his hands, My name is written on his hands.

THE LAND OF BEULAH. C. M.

W. B. BRADBURY. Words by Rev. J. HASKELL.

1. My lat-est sun is sinking fast, My race is near-ly run,
My strongest tri-als now are past, My triumph is be-gun.
2. I know I'm nearing the ho-ly ranks, Of friends and kindred dear,
For I brush the dews on Jordan's banks, The crossing must be near.

REFRAIN.

O come, an-gel band, come and a-round me stand, O hear me a-way on your snow-y wings, To my im-mor-tal home, O bear me a-way on your snow-y wings, To my im-mor-tal home.

3 I've almost gained my heavenly home.
My spirit loudly sings;
The holy ones, behold, they come!
I hear the noise of wings.
O come, angel band, &c.

4 O, bear my longing heart to Him
Who bled and died for me;
Whose blood now cleanses from all sin,
And gives me victory.
O come, angel band, &c.

"JOYFULLY! JOYFULLY!"

Rev. A. D Merrill.

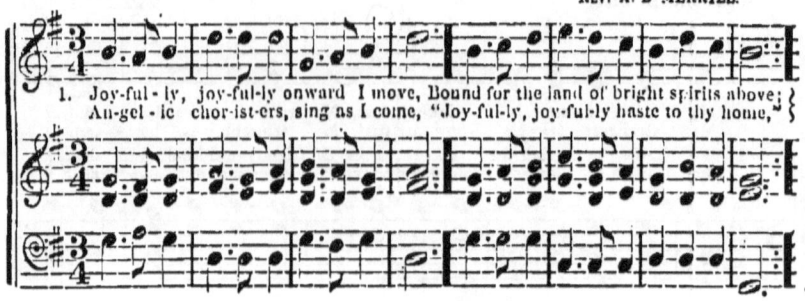
1. Joy-ful-ly, joy-ful-ly onward I move, Bound for the land of bright spirits above;
An-gel-ic chor-ist-ers, sing as I come, "Joy-ful-ly, joy-ful-ly haste to thy home,"

Soon, with my pilgrimage end-ed be-low, Home to the land of bright spirits I'll go,

Pilgrim and stranger no more shall I roam. Joy-ful-ly, joy-ful-ly rest-ing at home.

2 Friends fondly cherished have passed on before, [shore;
Waiting, they watch me approaching the
Singing to cheer me through death's chilling gloom,
"Joyfully, joyfully, haste to thy home."
Sounds of sweet melody fall on my ear;
Harps of the blessed, your voices I hear!
Rings with the harmony heaven's high dome!
"Joyfully, joyfully, haste to thy home."

3 Death, with thy weapons of war lay me low
Strike, King of terrors, I fear not the blow;
Jesus hath broken the bars of the tomb:
Joyfully, joyfully, will I go home.
Bright will the morn of eternity dawn,
Death shall be banished, his sceptre be gone
Joyfully, then shall I witness his doom;
Joyfully, joyfully, safely at home.

THE SHINING SHORE. 8s & 7s.

G. F. ROOT.
By permission.

1. My days are gliding swiftly by, And I, a pilgrim stranger, Would not detain them

as they fly! Those hours of toil and danger. CHORUS. For oh! we stand on Jordan's strand, Our

friends are passing over, And just before the shining shore We may almost dis-cov-er.

2 We'll gird our loins, my brethren dear,
　Our distant home discerning;
　Our absent Lord has left us word,
　Let every lamp be burning—
　　For oh! we stand on Jordan's strand,
　　Our friends are passing over,
　　And just before, the shining shore
　　We may almost discover.

3 Should coming days be cold and dark,
　We need not cease our singing;
　That perfect rest naught can molest,
　Where golden harps are ringing.
　　For oh! we stand on Jordan's strand,
　　Our friends are passing over,
　　And just before, the shining shore
　　We may almost discover.

4 Let sorrow's rudest tempests blow,
　Each chord on earth to sever,
　Our King says come, and there's our home,
　For ever, oh! for ever!
　　For oh! we stand on Jordan's strand,
　　Our friends are passing over,
　　And just before, the shining shore
　　We may almost discover.

214 HOMEWARD BOUND. 10s & 4s.

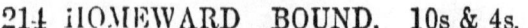
Arranged from REVIVAL MELODIES.

590

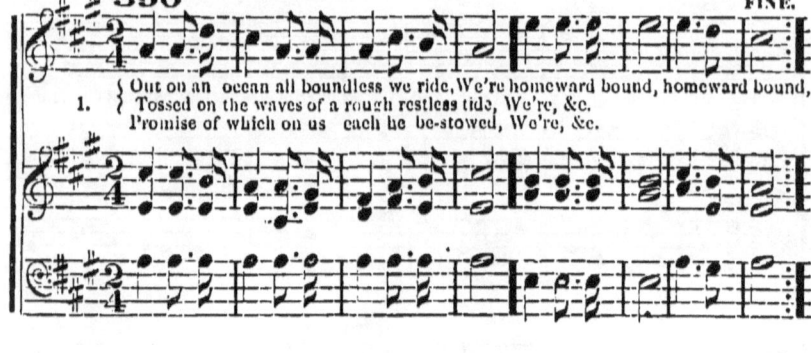

1. Out on an ocean all boundless we ride, We're homeward bound, homeward bound,
Tossed on the waves of a rough restless tide, We're, &c.
Promise of which on us each he bestowed, We're, &c.

Far from the safe, quiet harbor we've rode, Seeking our Father's celestial abode.

2 Wildly the storm sweeps us on as it roars,
    We're homeward bound.
Look ! yonder lie the bright heavenly shores,
    We're homeward bound.
Steady, O pilot ! stand firm at the wheel,
Steady ! we soon shall outweather the gale,
O, how we fly 'neath the loud-creaking sail,
    We're homeward bound.

3 Into the harbor of heaven now we glide,
    We're home at last.
Softly we drift on its bright silver tide,
    We're home at last.
Glory to God ! all our dangers are o'er,
We stand secure on the glorified shore,
Glory to God ! we will shout evermore,
    We're home at last.

591   *Home at last.*

1 We live as pilgrims and strangers below,
    We're homeward bound ;
Though often tempted, yet onward we go,
    We're homeward bound.
Trials and crosses we cheerfully bear,
Toils and temptations expecting to share,
We hasten forward, content with the fare,
    We're homeward bound.

2 Earth, with its trifles, we all have resign'd,
    We're homeward bound.
Heaven, with its glories, we shortly shall find,
    We're homeward bound.
Sinful amusements no longer are dear,
O, how delusive and vain they appear,
While to our home we are drawing so near,
    We're homeward bound.

3 We'll tell the world, as we journey along,
    We're homeward bound ;
Try to persuade them to enter our throng,
    We're homeward bound.
Come, trembling sinner, forlorn and oppress'd,
Join in our number, O come and be blest,
Journey with us to the mansions of rest,
    We're homeward bound.

4 Soon we'll be singing, if faithful we prove,
    We're home at last!
Sounding in triumph, in mansions above,
    We're home at last.
Soon as our toils and temptations are o'er,
Up to our home with the blest we shall soar,
O how we'll shout as we enter the door,
    We're home at last.

OUR LOVED ONES IN HEAVEN.

Words by REV J. W. DADMUN. By permission. Music by LESSUR.

1. Come all ye saints to Pisgah's mountain, Come view your home beyond the tide.
Hear now the voices of your loved ones, What they sing on the other side,—
Some are singing of bright crowns of glory; Some of dear ones who stand near the shore;
CHO. O the prospect! it is so transporting, And no danger I fear from the tide;
For the fond heart must ever be clinging To the faithful we love evermore.
Let me go to the home of the Christian, Let me stand robed in white by their side.

2 There endless springs of life are flowing,
 There are the fields of living green;
 Mansions of beauty are provided,
 And the King of the saints is seen.
 Soon my conflicts and toils will be ended;
 I shall join those who've passed on before;
 For my loved ones, O how I do miss them!
 I must press on and meet them once more.

3 Faith now beholds the flowing river,
 Coming from underneath the throne;
 There, too, the Saviour reigns forever,
 And he'll welcome the faithful home.
 Would you sit by the banks of the river
 With the friends you have loved by your side?
 Would you join in the song of the angels?
 Then be ready to follow your guide.

3 While here a stranger, far from home,
Affliction's waves may round me foam;
We'll wait till Jesus comes, &c.

4 And tho' like Lazarus, sick and poor,
My heavenly mansion is secure.
We'll wait till Jesus comes, &c.

5 Let others seek a home below,
Which flames devour, or waves o'erflow;
We'll wait till Jesus comes, &c.

6 Be mine the happier lot to own,
A heavenly mansion near the throne.
We'll wait till Jesus comes, &c.

7 Then fail this earth, let stars decline,
And sun and moon refuse to shine,
We'll wait till Jesus comes, &c.

8 All nature sink and cease to be,
That heavenly mansion stands for me.
We'll wait till Jesus comes, &c.

HOME BEYOND THE TIDE.

HAPPY DAY. L. M.

1. O happy day that fixed my choice On thee, my Saviour and my God!
Well may this glowing heart rejoice, And tell its raptures all abroad.
Happy day, happy day, When Jesus washed my sins away;
He taught me how to watch and pray, And live rejoicing every day.

2 O happy bond, that seals my vows
  To him who merits all my love ;
Let cheerful anthems fill his house,
  While to that sacred shrine I move.
    Happy day, &c.

3 'Tis done, the great transaction's done ;
  I am my Lord's, and he is mine ;
He drew me, and I followed on,
  Charmed to confess the voice divine.
    Happy day, &c.

4 Now rest, my long-divided heart ;
  Fixed on this blissful centre, rest :
* Nor ever from thy Lord depart :
  With him of every good possessed.
    Happy day, &c.

5 High Heaven, that heard the solemn vow,
  That vow renewed shall daily hear,
Till in life's latest hour I bow,
  And bless in death a bond so dear.
    Happy day, &c.

SHALL WE GATHER AT THE RIVER?

2 On the margin of the river,
  Washing up its silver spray,
  We will walk and worship ever,
  All the happy golden day.—Cho.

3 Ere we reach the shining river,
  Lay we every burden down;
  Grace our spirits will deliver,
  And provide a robe and crown.—Cho.

4 At the smiling of the river,
  Mirror of the Savior's face,
  Saints whom death will never sever
  Lift their songs of saving grace—Cho

5 Soon we'll reach the silver river,
  Soon our pilgrimage will cease;
  Soon our happy hearts will quiver
  With the melody of peace.—Cho.

SWEET HOUR OF PRAYER. L. M. Double.

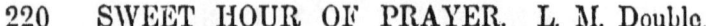

WM. B. BRADBURY.

597

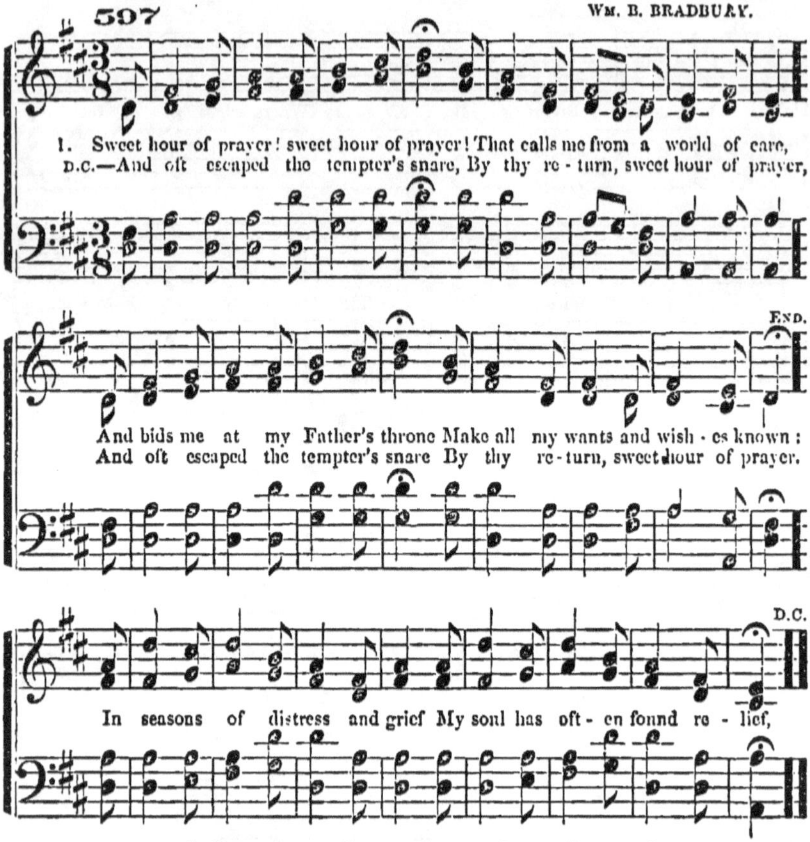
1. Sweet hour of prayer! sweet hour of prayer! That calls me from a world of care,
D.C.—And oft escaped the tempter's snare, By thy re - turn, sweet hour of prayer,
END.
And bids me at my Father's throne Make all my wants and wish - es known:
And oft escaped the tempter's snare By thy re - turn, sweet hour of prayer.
D.C.
In seasons of distress and grief My soul has oft - en found re - lief,

2 Sweet hour of prayer! sweet hour of prayer!
Thy wings shall my petition bear
To him whose truth and faithfulness
Engage the waiting soul to bless;
And since he bids me seek his face,
Believe his word, and trust his grace,
I'll cast on him my every care,
And wait for thee, sweet hour of prayer!

3 Sweet hour of prayer! sweet hour of prayer!
May I thy consolation share,
Till, from Mount Pisgah's lofty height,
I view my home, and take my flight!
This robe of flesh I'll drop and rise,
To seize the everlasting prize;
And shout, while passing through the air,
Farewell, farewell, sweet hour of prayer!

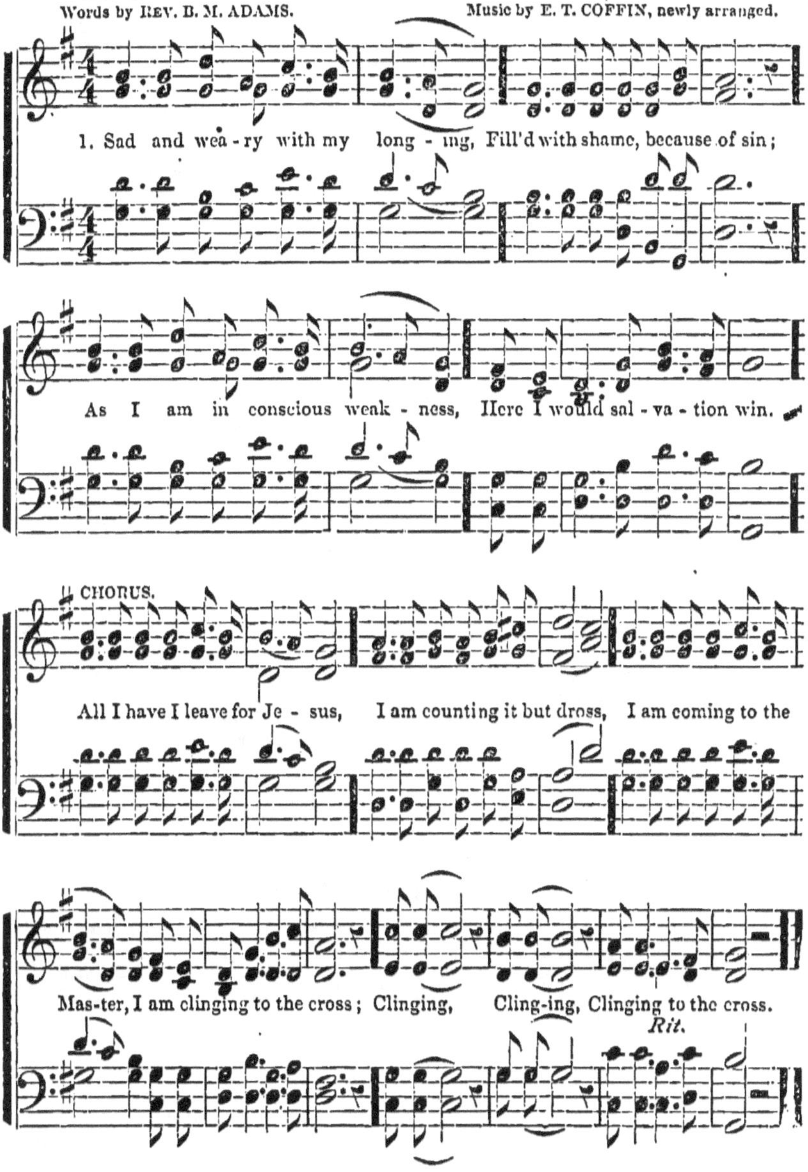

2 O the joy of knowing Jesus,
  It is dawning on my soul;
  I am finding his salvation,
  And the power that makes me whole.

3 O refine me by thy spirit,
  Make my earthly life sublime,
  With my heart a home for Jesus,
  Till I'm done with earth and time.

THE PILGRIMS. C. M.
Rev. B. W. Gorham.

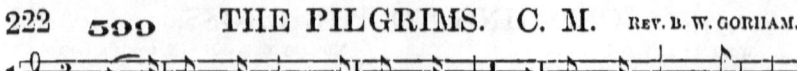

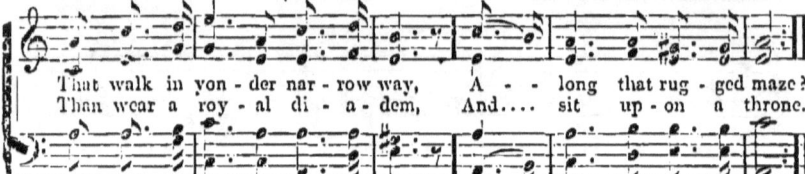

1. What poor despised company Of travelers are these,
Chorus. O, I'd rather be the least of them That are the Lord's alone,

That walk in yonder narrow way, Along that rugged maze?
Than wear a royal diadem, And.... sit upon a throne.

2 Ah! these are of a royal line,
All children of a King:
Heirs of immortal crowns divine,
And lo! for joy they sing.

3 Why do they then appear so mean?
And why so much despised?
Because of their rich robes unseen
The world is not apprised.

4 But some of them seem poor, distressed,
And lacking daily bread;
Ah! they're of boundless wealth possess'd
With heavenly manna fed.

5 Why do they shun the pleasing path
That worldlings love so well?
Because it is the way to death,
The open road to hell.

6 But why keep they the narrow road,
That rugged, thorny maze?
Why, that's the way their leader trod,
They love and keep his ways.

7 What, is there then no other road
To Salem's happy ground?
Christ is the only way to God,
None other can be found.

GLORY TO THE LAMB.
Rev. B. W. Gorham.

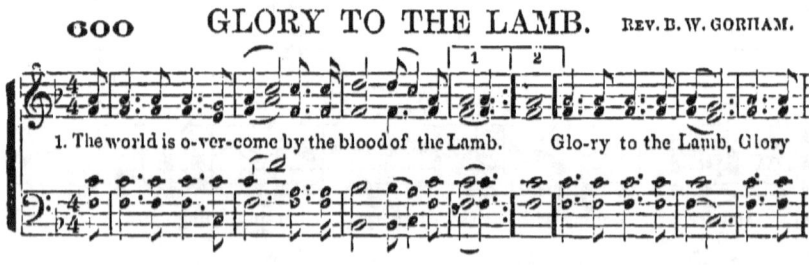
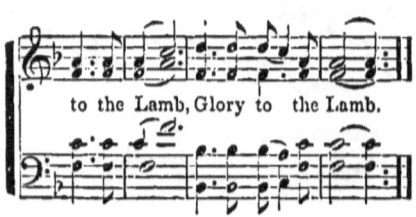

1. The world is overcome by the blood of the Lamb. Glory to the Lamb, Glory to the Lamb, Glory to the Lamb.

2 My sins are washed away
In the blood of the Lamb.

3 I've washed my garments white,
In the blood of the Lamb.

4 The martyrs overcame,
By the blood of the Lamb.

5 I soon shall gain the skies,
Through the blood of the Lamb.

601. WORLD OF LIGHT.

Poetry and Music by O. SNOW. By Permission.

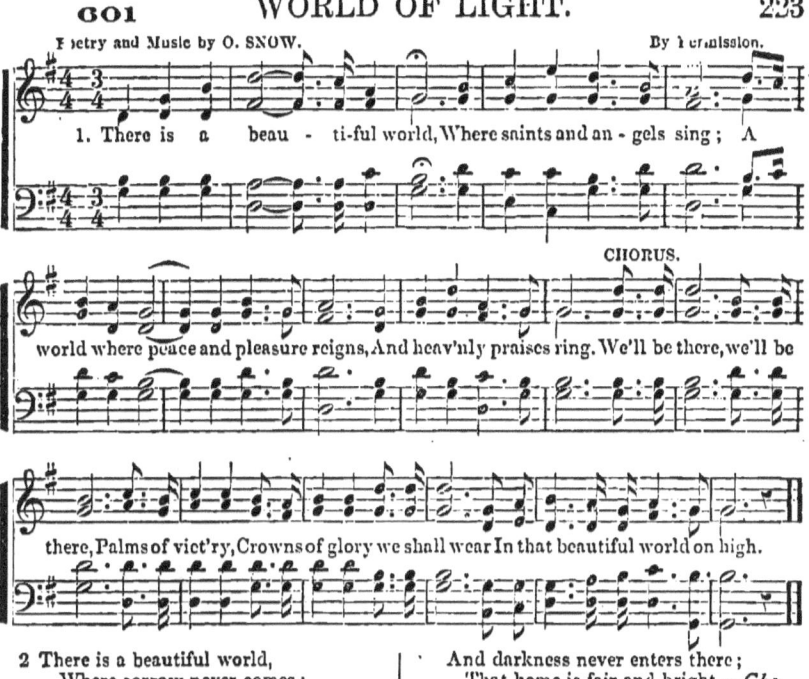

1. There is a beautiful world, Where saints and angels sing; A world where peace and pleasure reigns, And heav'nly praises ring. We'll be there, we'll be there, Palms of vict'ry, Crowns of glory we shall wear In that beautiful world on high.

2 There is a beautiful world,
 Where sorrow never comes;
A world where tears shall never fall,
 In sighing for our home.—*Cho.*

3 There is a beautiful world,
 Unseen to mortal sight;
And darkness never enters there;
 That home is fair and bright.—*Cho.*

4 There is a beautiful world,
 Of harmony and love;
O may we safely enter there,
 And dwell with God above.—*Cho.*

602. "COME, YE DISCONSOLATE."

1. Come, ye dis-con-so-late! Where'er you languish, Come to the mer-cy-seat, Fer-vent-ly kneel; Here bring your wounded hearts, Here tell your anguish; Earth has no sorrow That heav'n cannot heal.

2 Joy of the desolate, light of the straying,
 Hope of the penitent, fadeless and pure,—
Here speaks the Comforter, tenderly saying,—
 Earth has no sorrow that Heaven cannot cure.

3 Here see the bread of life: see waters flowing
 Forth from the throne of God, pure from above;
Come to the feast of love; come, ever knowing
 Earth has no sorrow but Heaven can remove.

603. THE SINNER INVITED. 6s & 7s
Arranged by W. McDonald.

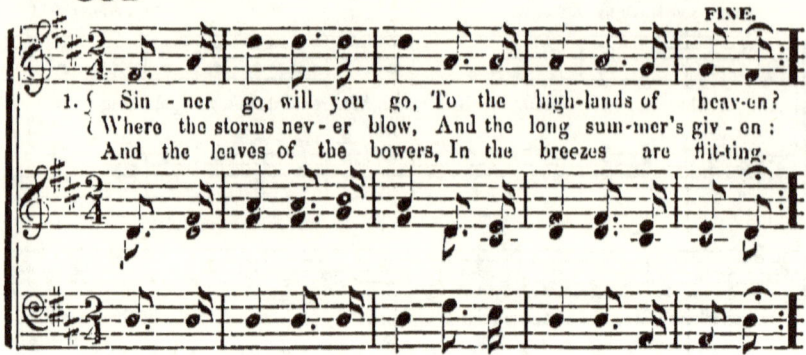

1. Sinner go, will you go, To the high-lands of heav-en?
Where the storms nev-er blow, And the long summer's giv-on:
And the leaves of the bowers, In the breezes are flit-ting.

Where the bright blooming flowers, Are their odors e-mit-ting;

2 Where the saints robed in white—
Cleansed in life's flowing fountain ;
Shining beauteous and bright,
They inhabit the mountain,
Where no sin, nor dismay,
Neither trouble nor sorrow,
Will be felt for a day,
Nor be feared for the morrow.

3 He's prepared thee a home—
Sinner canst thou believe it?
And invites thee to come,
Sinner wilt thou receive it?
O come, sinner, come,
For the tide is receding,
And the Savior will soon,
And forever cease pleading.

604. ANGELS HOVERING ROUND.

1. There are an-gels hov-'ring round, There are an-gels hov-'ring round, There are an - - gels, an - - gels hov-'ring round.

2 To carry the tidings home.
3 To the New Jerusalem.
4 Poor sinners are coming home.
5 And Jesus bids them come.
6 Let him that heareth come.
7 We are on our journey home.

605 DEPTH OF MERCY.

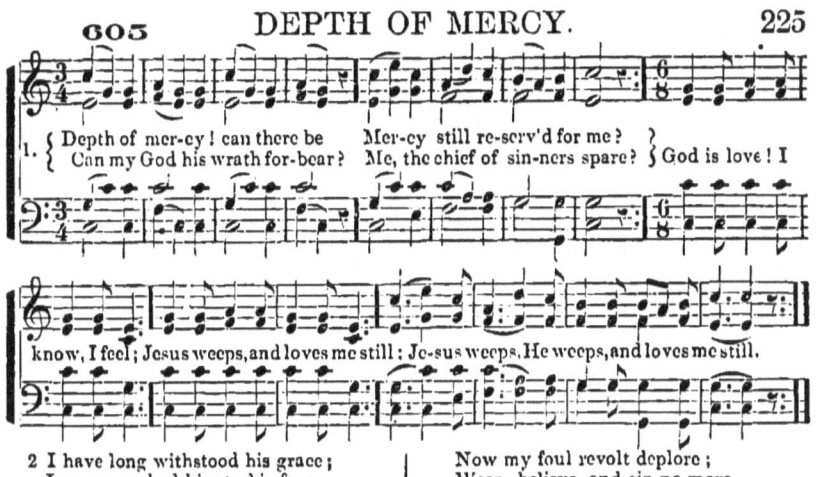

1. Depth of mer-cy! can there be Mer-cy still re-serv'd for me? Can my God his wrath for-bear? Me, the chief of sin-ners spare? God is love! I know, I feel; Jesus weeps, and loves me still: Je-sus weeps, He weeps, and loves me still.

2 I have long withstood his grace;
Long provoked him to his face;
Would not hearken to his calls:
Grieved him by a thousand falls.
God is love! &c.

3 Now incline me to repent;
Let me now my sins lament;
Now my soul revolt deplore;
Weep, believe, and sin no more.
God is love! &c.

4 There for me the Savior stands: [hands;
Shows his wounds, and spreads his
God is love! I know, I feel;
Jesus weeps, and loves me still.
God is love! &c.

606 ALAS! AND DID MY SAVIOR BLEED? S. J. VAIL.

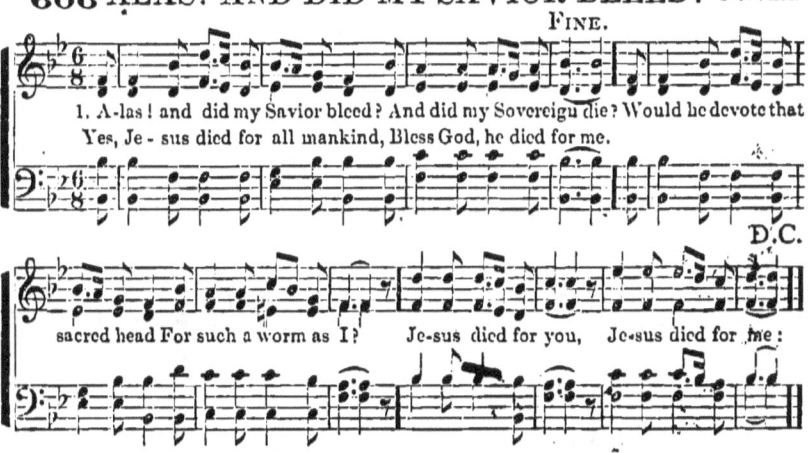

1. A-las! and did my Savior bleed? And did my Sovereign die? Would he devote that sacred head For such a worm as I? Je-sus died for you, Je-sus died for me: Yes, Je-sus died for all mankind, Bless God, he died for me.

2 Was it for crimes that I had done,
He groaned upon the tree?
Amazing pity! grace unknown!
And love beyond degree!

3 Well might the sun in darkness hide,
And shut his glories in,
When Christ the mighty Maker died
For man, the creature's sin.

4 Thus might I hide my blushing face,
While his dear cross appears;
Dissolve my heart in thankfulness,
And melt mine eyes to tears.

5 But drops of grief can ne'er repay
The debt of love I owe:
Here, Lord, I give myself away;
'Tis all that I can do.

HOME OF THE SOUL.

From "Singing Pilgrim," by permission.
PHILIP PHILLIPS.

1. I will sing you a song of that beau-ti-ful land, The far a-way home of the soul, Where no storms ev-er beat on the glittering strand, While the years of e-ter-ni-ty roll, While the years of e-ter-ni-ty roll.

2. O, that home of the soul in my visions and dreams, Its bright Jasper walls I can see, Till I fan-cy but thin-ly the vale inter-venes Be-tween the fair ci-ty and me, Be-tween the fair ci-ty and me.

3 That unchangeable home is for you and for me,
   Where Jesus of Nazareth stands;
The King of all kingdoms forever is he,
   And he holdeth our crowns in his hands.

4 O how sweet will it be in that beautiful land,
   So free from all sorrow and pain ;
With songs on our lips and with harps in our hands,
   To meet one another again.

608. GO WORK IN MY VINEYARD.

1. If you cannot on the ocean
Sail among the swiftest fleet,
Rocking on the highest billows
Laughing at the storms you meet;
You can stand among the sailors;
Anchored yet within the bay,
You can lend a hand to help them,
As they launch their boats away.

2 If you are too weak to journey,
Up the mountain, steep and high;
You can stand within the valley,
While the multitudes go by;
You can chant in happy measure,
As they slowly pass along,
Though they may forget the singer,
They will not forget the song.

3 If you cannot in the harvest
Garner up the richest sheaves,
Many a grain, both ripe and golden
May the careless reapers leave.
Go and glean among the briers,
Growing rank against the wall,
For it may be that their shadow
Hides the heaviest wheat of all.

4 If you cannot be the watchman,
Standing high on Zion's wall,
Pointing out the path to heaven,
Offering life and peace to all:
With your prayers and with your bounties,
You can do what heaven demands,
You can be like faithful Aaron,
Holding up the prophet's hands.

5 Do not, then, stand idly waiting,
For some greater work to do;
Time moves on with rapid motion,
Life and death are both in view;
Go and toil in any vineyard,
Do not fear to do or dare,
If you want a field of labor.
You can find it any where.

228 ROYAL WAY OF THE CROSS.

Music by Rev. L. Hartsough.

1. We may spread our couch with ro-ses, And sleep thro' the sum-mer day;
But the soul that in sloth re-po-ses, Is not in the nar-row way.
For the roy-al way to heaven, Is the roy-al way of the cross.

If we fol-low the chart that is gi-ven, We need not be at a loss,

2 To one who is reared in splendor,
  The cross is a heavy load;
And the feet that are soft and tender,
  Will shrink from the thorny road:
But the chains of the soul must be riven,
  And wealth must be as dross;
For the royal way to heaven,
  Is the royal way of the cross.

3 We say we will walk to-morrow,
  The path we refuse to-day;
And still, with our luke-warm sorrow,
  We shrink from the narrow way.
What heeded the chosen eleven,
  How the fortunes of life might toss,
As they followed their Master to heaven,
  By the royal way of the cross.

610 "I LOVE THEE."

1. I love thee, I love thee, I love thee, my God;
I love thee, my Sa-vior, I love thee,........ my Lord; I love thee, I
But how much I love thee, I nev-er........... can show.

love thee, and that thou dost know,

2 I'm happy, I'm happy, O wondrous account!
My joys are immortal, I stand on the mount!
I gaze on my treasure, and long to be there,
With Jesus and angels, my kindred so dear.

3 O, who's like my Savior? He's Salem's bright King;
He smiles, and he loves me, and learns me to sing;
I'll praise him, I'll praise him, with notes loud and shrill,
While rivers of pleasure my spirit doth fill.

611. DUNBAR. S. M.
REV. E. W. DUNBAR.

1. Through this cold world, a-lone, With none to care for me, I jour-ney to my heaven-ly home, And sing, sal-va-tion's free.
2. Sal-va-tion's free and full— O let the ti-dings roll! In me, I feel it burn-ing now, Like fire all through my soul.
3. Come, breth-ren, help me sing, One song of vic-to-ry; For with-out mon-ey, with-out price, I've found sal-va-tion free.

CHO. I'm glad sal-va-tion's free, I'm glad sal-va-tion's free, Sal-va-tion's free for you and me, I'm glad sal-va-tion's free.

612. TURN TO THE LORD.

1. Come, ye sin-ners, poor and need-y, Weak and wounded, sick and sore;
   Je-sus read-y stands to save you, Full of pi-ty, love and pow'r.
   Turn to the Lord, and seek sal-va-tion, Sound the praise of his dear name;
   Glo-ry, hon-or, and sal-va-tion, Christ the Lord is come to reign.

2 Now, ye needy, come and welcome,
  God's free bounty glorify;
  True belief, and true repentance,
  Every grace that brings you nigh.

3 Let not conscience make you linger,
  Nor of fitness fondly dream;
  All the fitness he requireth,
  Is to feel your need of him.

4 Come, ye weary, heavy laden,
  Bruised and mangled by the fall,
  If you tarry till your better,
  You will never come at all.

5 Agonizing in the garden,
  Lo! your Maker prostrate lies!
  On the bloody tree behold him—
  Hear him cry before he dies.

613. "WILL YOU GO?"

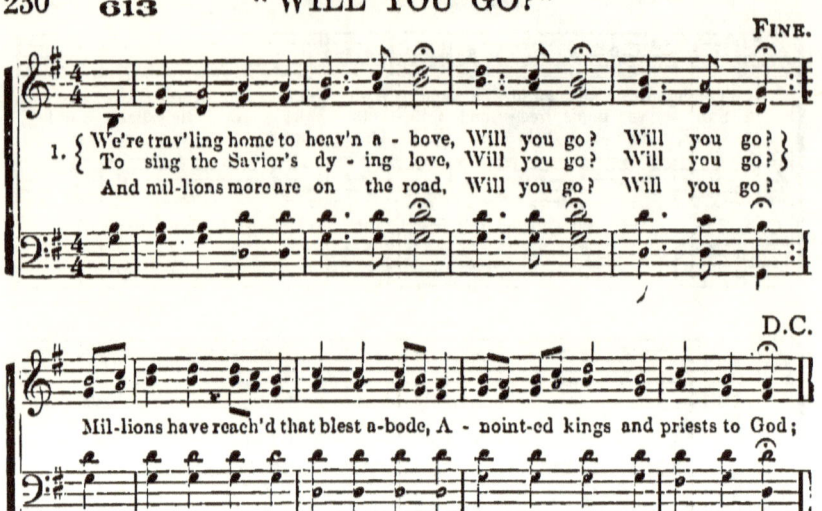

1. We're trav'ling home to heav'n a-bove, Will you go? Will you go? Will you go?
To sing the Savior's dy-ing love, Will you go? Will you go? Will you go?
And mil-lions more are on the road, Will you go? Will you go? Will you go?
Mil-lions have reach'd that blest a-bode, A-noint-ed kings and priests to God;

2 We're going to see the bleeding Lamb,
   Will you go? Will you go?
In rapturous strains to praise his name;
   Will you go? Will you go?
The crown of life we there shall wear,
The conqueror's palms our hands shall bear,
And all the joys of heaven we'll share.
   Will you go? Will you go?

3 The way to heaven is straight and plain,
   Will you go? Will you go?
Repent, believe, be born again,
   Will you go? Will you go?

The Savior cries aloud to thee,
Take up thy cross, and follow me,
And thou shalt my salvation see.
   Will you go? Will you go?

4 Oh, could I hear some sinner say,
   I will go! I will go!
I'll start this moment, clear the way,
   Let me go! Let me go!
My old companions, fare you well,
I will not go with you to hell!
I mean with Jesus Christ to dwell,
   Let me go! Let me go!

614. "I'M GOING HOME."

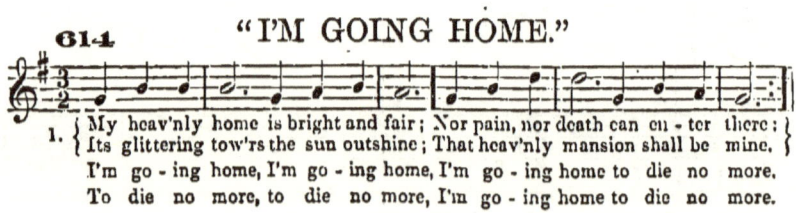

1. My heav'nly home is bright and fair; Nor pain, nor death can en-ter there;
Its glittering tow'rs the sun outshine; That heav'nly mansion shall be mine.
I'm go-ing home, I'm go-ing home, I'm go-ing home to die no more.
To die no more, to die no more, I'm go-ing home to die no more.

2 My Father's house is built on high,
Far, far above the starry sky:
When from this earthly prison free,
That heavenly mansion mine shall be.
   I'm going home, &c.

3 While here, a stranger far from home,
Affliction's waves may round me foam;
And, though like Lazarus, sick and poor,
My heavenly mansion is secure.
   I'm going home, &c.

4 Let others seek a home below,
Which flames devour, or waves o'erflow;
Be mine a happier lot to own
A heavenly mansion near the throne.
   I'm going home, &c.

5 Then fail this earth, let stars decline,
And sun and moon refuse to shine;
All nature sink, and cease to be,
That heavenly mansion stands for me.
   I'm going home, &c.

615. BARTIMEUS. 8s & 7s.

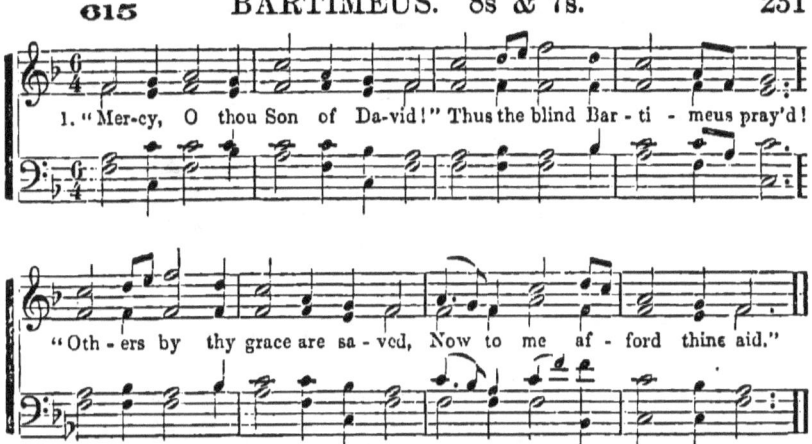

1. "Mer-cy, O thou Son of Da-vid!" Thus the blind Bar-ti-meus pray'd! "Oth-ers by thy grace are sa-ved, Now to me af-ford thine aid."

2 Many for his crying chide him,
  But he called the louder still!
  Till the gracious Savior bid him
  Come, and ask me what you will.
3 Money was not what he wanted!
  Though by begging used to live;
  But he asked, and Jesus granted, [give.
  Alms which none but Christ would
4 Lord, remove this grievous blindness,
  Turn my darkness into day;

Straight he saw, and won by kindness,
  Followed Jesus in the way.
5 Now methinks I hear him praising,
  Publishing to all around,
  Friends, is not my case amazing?
  What a Savior I have found.
6 O that all the blind but knew him,
  And would be advised by me;
  Surely, they would hasten to him,
  He would cause them all to see.

616. JESUS WAITS FOR THEE.

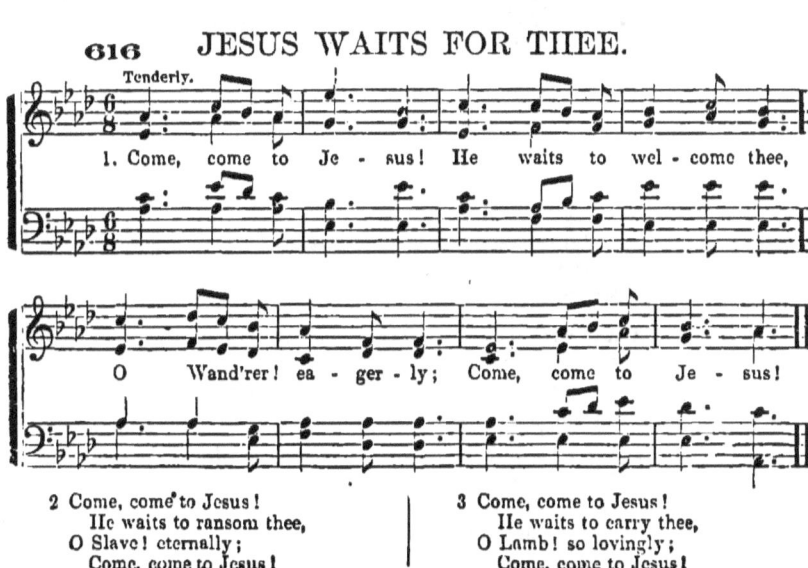

Tenderly.

1. Come, come to Je-sus! He waits to wel-come thee, O Wand'rer! ea-ger-ly; Come, come to Je-sus!

2 Come, come to Jesus!
  He waits to ransom thee,
  O Slave! eternally;
  Come, come to Jesus!

3 Come, come to Jesus!
  He waits to carry thee,
  O Lamb! so lovingly;
  Come, come to Jesus!

THE FOUNTAIN OF MERCY.

2 And when I was willing with all things to part,
He gave me my bounty,— his love in my heart;
So now I am joined with the conqu'ring band
Who are marching to glory at Jesus' command.—*Cho.*

3 Though round me the storms of adversity roll,
And the waves of destruction encompass my soul,
In vain this frail vessel the tempest shall toss;
My hopes rest secure on the blood of the cross.—*Cho.*

4 And when the last trumpet of judgment shall sound,
And wake all the nations that sleep in the ground,
Then, when heaven and earth shall be melting away,
I'll sing of the blood of the cross in that day.—*Cho.*

5 And when with the ransomed by Jesus, my Head,
From fountain to fountain I then shall be led;
I'll fall at his feet, and his mercy adore,
And sing of the blood of the cross evermore -*Cho.*

618 CLEANSING FOUNTAIN.

1. There is a fountain, fill'd with blood, Drawn from Immanuel's veins, And sinners plung'd beneath that flood, Lose all their guilty stains, Lose all their guilty stains, Lose all their guilty stains,

2 The dying thief rejoiced to see
That fountain in his day;
And there may I, though vile as he,
Wash all my sins away.

3 Thou dying Lamb! thy precious blood
Shall never lose its power,
Till all the ransom'd Church of God
Are saved, to sin no more.

4 E'er since by faith I saw the stream
Thy flowing wounds supply,
Redeeming love has been my theme,
And shall be, till I die.

5 When this poor lisping, stamm'ring tongue
Lies silent in the grave,
Then in a nobler, sweeter song,
I'll sing thy power to save.

619 I AM TRUSTING, LORD, IN THEE.

Words by REV. WM. MCDONALD. Music by WM. G. FISCHER.

1. I am coming to the cross; I am poor, and weak, and blind; I am counting all but dross; I shall full salvation find.

Cho.—I am trusting, Lord, in thee, Dear Lamb of Calvary; Humbly at thy cross I bow; Save me, Jesus, save me now.

2 Long my heart has sighed for thee;
Long has evil dwelt within;
Jesus sweetly speaks to me,
I will cleanse you from all sin.—Cho.

3 Here I give my all to thee,—
Friends, and time, and earthly store;
Soul and body thine to be—
Wholly thine forevermore.—Cho.

4 In the promises I trust;
Now I feel the blood applied;
I am prostrate in the dust;
I with Christ am crucified.—Cho.

5 Jesus comes! he fills my soul!
Perfected in love I am:
I am every whit made whole;
Glory, glory to the Lamb!—Cho.

3 Farewell, ye dreams of night,
  Jesus is mine!
Lost in this dawning bright,
  Jesus is mine!
All that my soul has tried
Left but a dismal void;
Jesus has satisfied,
  Jesus is mine!

4 Farewell, mortality;
  Jesus is mine!
Welcome, eternity;
  Jesus is mine!
Welcome, O loved and blest;
Welcome, sweet scenes of rest;
Welcome, my Saviour's breast;
  Jesus is mine!

ZION'S PILGRIM. L. M.

622   235

By Permission of Bigelow & Main.   WM. B. BRADBURY.

1. Pilgrims we are to Canaan bound, Our journey lies along this road;
This wilderness we travel round, To reach the city of our God.
Our robes are wash'd in Jesus' blood, And we are trav'ling home to God.
O happy pilgrims, spotless fair, What makes your robes so white appear?

2 O blessed land! O happy land!
   When shall we reach thy golden shore?
   And one redeemed, unbroken band
   United be forevermore.
     O happy Pilgrims, &c.

3 And if our robes are pure and white,
   May we all reach that blest abode?
   O yes, they all shall dwell in light,
   Whose robes are washed in Jesus' blood.
     O happy Pilgrims, &c.

4 We all shall reach that golden shore,
   If here we watch, and fight, and pray;
   Straight is the way, and straight the door,
   And none but Pilgrims find the way.
     O happy Pilgrims, &c.

5 O may we meet at last above,
   Amid the holy blood-washed throng,
   And sing forever Jesus' love,
   While saints and angels join the song.
     O happy Pilgrims, &c.

HAPPY DYING. 8s & 7s.

O. SNOW.

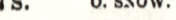
Arranged for this Work.

1. Softly sing, when I am going From the scenes of earth away;

May my soul, 'mid loving voices, Rise to realms of fairest day.

Softly sing of Jesus waiting, When my closing eyes are dim;

When my home I'm drawing nearer, Softly sing to me of him.

2 Softly sing of joyful meetings,
   In the hallowed land above;
Tell me then of peaceful greetings,
   With the missing ones I love:
Softly sing of angels praising
   God around his glorious throne,
There that I may hope to join them,
   When I've cross'd the stream alone.

3 Softly sing of sweet forgiveness,
   Thro' the Lamb that died for me,
May his cross, in radiance beaming,
   Be my last, my only plea:
Softly sing, when I am passing
   From the scenes of earth away;
May my soul, 'mid loving voices,
   Rise to realms of fairest day.

MERCY'S FREE.

Arr. by Rev. W. McDONALD.

1. By faith I view my Savior dying, On the tree, on the tree; He bids the guilty now draw near, Soon as I in his name believed, Hark! hark! what precious words I hear, Mercy's free, mercy's free.

2. Jesus, the mighty God, hath spoken, Peace to me, peace to me; To every nation he is crying, Look to me, look to me: Repent, believe, dismiss thy fear; The Holy Spirit I received, And Christ from death my soul relieved, Mercy's free, mercy's free.

   Now all my chains of sin are broken, I am free, I am free;

3 Jesus my weary soul refreshed,
　Mercy's free, mercy's free;
And every moment Christ is precious,
　Unto me, unto me:
None can describe the bliss I prove,
While through this wilderness I rove;
All may enjoy the Savior's love,
　Mercy's free, mercy's free.

4 Long as I live I'll still be crying,
　Mercy's free, mercy's free;
And this shall be my theme when dying,
　Mercy's free, mercy's free :
And when the vale of death I've passed,
When lodged above the stormy blast,
I'll sing while endless ages last.
　Mercy's free, mercy's free.

625. BETHANY. 6s & 4s.
L. MASON.

1. Nearer, my God, to thee, Nearer to thee; E'en tho' it be a cross That raiseth me, Still all my song shall be, Nearer, my God, to thee, Nearer, my God, to thee, Nearer to thee.

2 Though like a wanderer,
  Day-light all gone,
 Darkness be over me,
  My rest a stone,
 Yet in my dreams I'd be
 Nearer, my God, to thee.—*Nearer, &c.*

3 There let the way appear
  Steps up to heaven;
 All that thou sendest me,
  In mercy given,
 Angels to beckon me
 Nearer, my God, to thee.—*Nearer, &c.*

4 Then with my waking thoughts,
  Bright with thy praise,
 Out of my stony griefs,
  Bethel I'll raise;
 So by my woes to be
 Nearer, my God, to thee.—*Nearer, &c.*

5 Or if on joyful wing,
  Cleaving the sky,
 Sun, moon, and stars forgot,
  Upward I fly,
 Still all my song shall be,
 Nearer, my God, to thee.—*Nearer, &c.*

626. ENTREATY. 8s & 7s.

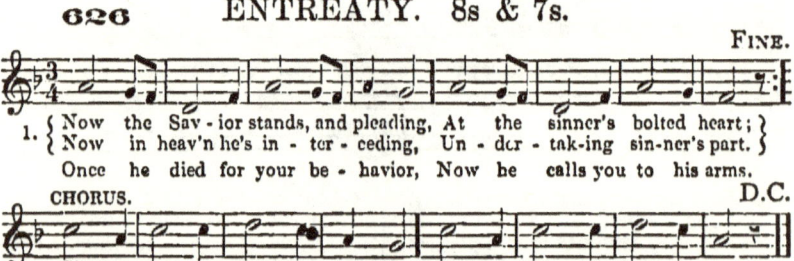

1. Now the Saviour stands, and pleading, At the sinner's bolted heart;
   Now in heav'n he's interceding, Undertaking sinner's part.
   Once he died for your behavior, Now he calls you to his arms.

CHORUS.
Sinner, can you hate the Saviour? Can you thrust him from your arms?

2 Jesus stands, oh, how amazing,
  Stands and knocks at every door;
 In his hand ten thousand blessings,
 Proffer'd to the wretched poor.—*Cho.*

3 See him bleeding, dying, rising,
  To prepare you heavenly rest;
 Listen, while he kindly calls you,
 Hear, and be forever blest.—*Cho.*

627. THE SAINT'S HOME.

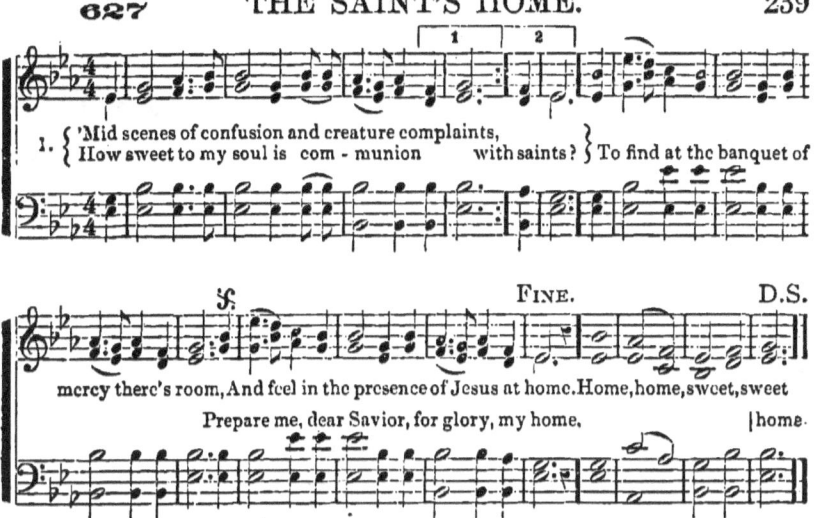

1. 'Mid scenes of confusion and creature complaints,
How sweet to my soul is com-munion with saints? To find at the banquet of mercy there's room, And feel in the presence of Jesus at home. Home, home, sweet, sweet home.

Prepare me, dear Savior, for glory, my home.

2 An alien from God, and a stranger to grace,
I wandered through earth, its gay pleasures to trace;
In the pathway of sin I continued to roam,
Unmindful, alas! that it led me from home.—*Home, &c.*

3 The pleasures of earth, I have seen fade away;
They bloom for a season, but soon they decay:
But pleasures more lasting, in Jesus are given,
Salvation on earth, and a mansion in heaven.—*Home, &c.*

4 Allure me no longer, ye false glowing charms!
The Savior invites me, I'll go to his arms;
At the banquet of mercy, I hear there is room,
O there may I feast with his children at home.—*Home, &c.*

628. *I've started for Canaan.*

1 I have started for Canaan, must I leave you behind?
Will you not go up with me? come, make up your mind:
The land lies before us, 'tis pleasant to view;
Its fruits are abundant, they are offered for you.
    Come, come, friends, friends, come,
    I've started for Canaan, oh, will you not come?

2 What can tempt you to linger, or turn from the way?
The fields are all blooming, as blooming as May:
The music is charming, the harmony pure;
The joys there are lasting, they ever endure.—*Come, &c.*

3 You have friends in that country, most dear to your heart,
Do you not wish to meet them, where friends never part?
Then start in a moment, no longer delay;
While you stop to consider, the night ends the day.—*Come, &c.*

4 'Tis the last call of mercy, oh! turn, lest you die!
Give your heart to the Savior, to-day he is nigh:
While his arms are extended, while his children all pray,
Will you not join our number? come, join us to-day.—*Come, &c.*

"HE LEADETH ME." — Wm. B. Bradbury.

By Permission of Bigelow & Main.

2 Sometimes, 'mid scenes of deepest gloom,
Sometimes where Eden's bowers bloom,
By waters still, o'er troubled sea—
Still 'tis his hand that leadeth me!
   Refrain.—He leadeth me! &c.

3 Lord, I would clasp thy hand in mine,
Nor ever murmur nor repine—
Content, whatever lot I see,
Since 'tis my God that leadeth me.
   Refrain.—He leadeth me! &c.

4 And when my task on earth is done,
When by thy grace the victory's won,
E'en death's cold wave I will not flee,
Since God through Jordan leadeth me.
   Refrain.—He leadeth me! &c.

630. SWEET REST IN HEAVEN.

By Permission of Bigelow & Main.   WM. B. BRADBURY.

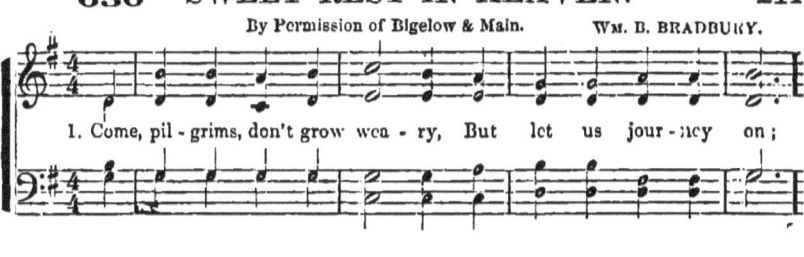

1. Come, pil-grims, don't grow wea-ry, But let us jour-ney on;

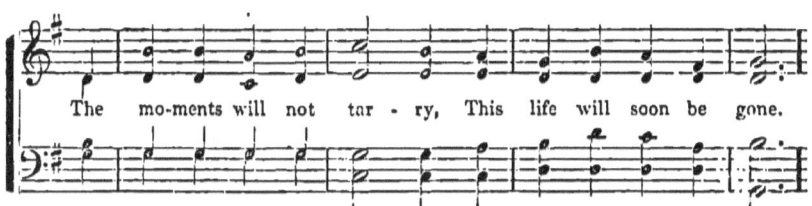

The mo-ments will not tar-ry, This life will soon be gone.

CHORUS.

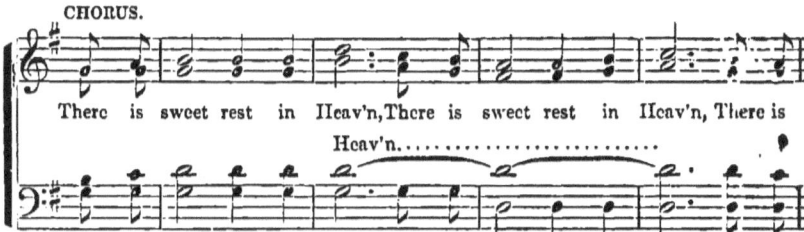

There is sweet rest in Heav'n, There is sweet rest in Heav'n, There is Heav'n............

sweet rest, There is sweet rest, There is sweet rest in Heav'n.

2 We've 'listed for the army,
   We've 'listed for the war;
   We'll fight until we conquer,
   By faith and humble prayer.
Chorus.—There is sweet rest in Heav'n.

3 Our Captain's gone before us,
   He bids us all to come;
   High up, in endless glory,
   He's fitted up our home.
Chorus.—There is sweet rest in Heav'n.

4 And Jesus will be with us,
   E'en to our journey's end;
   In every sore affliction,
   His present help to lend.
Chorus.—There is sweet rest in Heav'n.

5 Then glory be to Jesus,
   Who bought us with his blood;
   And glory be to Jesus,
   Who gives us every good.
Chorus.—There is sweet rest in Heav'n.

LOVE AT HOME.

2 In the cottage there is joy,
   When there's love at home;
Hate and envy ne'er annoy,
   When there's love at home.
Roses blossom 'neath our feet,
All the earth's a garden sweet,
Making life a bliss complete,
   When there's love at home.

3 Kindly heaven smiles above,
   When there's love at home;
All the earth is filled with love,
   When there's love at home.

Sweeter sings the brooklet by,
Brighter beams the azure sky:
Oh, there's one who smiles on high,
   When there's love at home.

4 Jesus, show thy mercy mine,
   Then there's love at home;
Sweetly whisper I am thine,
   Then there's love at home.
Source of love, thy cheering light
Far exceeds the sun so bright—
Can dispel the gloom of night;
   Then there's love at home.

OUTSIDE THE GATE.

By Permission. — PHILLIP PHILLIPS.

1. I stood outside the gate, A poor wayfaring child;
Within my heart there beat
A tempest loud and wild;
A fear oppress'd my soul,—
That I might be *too late;*
And oh! I trembled sore,
And pray'd outside the gate,
And pray'd outside the gate.

2 "Mercy," I loudly cried;
"Oh give me rest from sin!"
"I will," a voice replied,
And Mercy let me in.
She bound my bleeding wounds,
And carried all my sin;
She eased my burdened soul,
Then Jesus took me in.

3 In Mercy's guise, I knew
The Savior long abused;
Who often sought my heart,
And wept when I refused.
Oh! what a blest return
For ignorance and sin!
I stood outside the gate,
And Jesus let me in.

633 O HOW I LOVE JESUS.

1. Jesus, the Name high o-ver all, In hell, or earth, or sky;
Angels and men be-fore it fall, And de-vils fear and fly.
Oh! how I love Jesus, Oh! how I love Jesus,
Oh! how I love Jesus, Because he first loved me.
I'll nev-er for-get thee, I'll nev-er for-get thee, Lord!
I'll nev-er for-get thee, Dear Lord, re-mem-ber me.

2 Jesus, the Name to sinners dear,—
  The name to sinners given;
  It scatters all their guilty fear;
  It turns their hell to heaven.

3 Jesus the pris'ner's fetters breaks,
  And bruises Satan's head;
  Power into strengthless souls he speaks,
  And life into the dead.

4 O that the world might taste and see
  The riches of his grace:
  The arms of love that compass me,
  Would all mankind embrace.

634 *Invitation to praise the Redeemer.*

1 O for a thousand tongues, to sing
  My great Redeemer's praise;
  The glories of my God and King,
  The triumphs of his grace.

2 My gracious Master and my God,
  Assist me to proclaim,—
  To spread, through all the earth abroad,
  The honors of thy Name.

3 Jesus!— the name that charms our fears,
  That bids our sorrows cease;
  'Tis music in the sinner's ears,
  'Tis life, and health, and peace.

4 He breaks the power of cancell'd sin,
  He sets the pris'ner free;
  His blood can make the foulest clean;
  His blood avail'd for me.

WE'LL WALK THROUGH THE VALLEY IN PEACE.

635 Arr. by W. McDONALD.

1. A-rise, my soul to Pisgah's height, And view the promised land,
And see, by faith, the glorious sight, Our her-i-tage at hand.
If Je-sus himself will be our Guide, We shall walk thro' the valley in peace.

Chorus.
We shall walk thro' the val-ley in peace, We shall walk thro' the val-ley in peace,

2 Fair Salem's dazzling gates are seen,
 Just o'er the narrow flood,
And fields adorned in living green,
 The residence of God.

3 My conflicts here will soon be past,
 Where wild distraction reigns;
Through toil and death I'll reach at last
 Fair Canaan's happy plains.

4 O could I cross rough Jordan's wave,
 No danger would I fear;
My bark would every tempest brave,
 For O! my Captain's near.

5 My lamp of life will soon grow pale,
 The spark will soon decay;
And then my happy soul will sail
 To everlasting day.

636 PRECIOUS JESUS.

Music by WM. G. FISCHER.
By Permission.

1. I am but a poor way-far-er, Bearing oft a heavy load; Yet there's One who journeys with me,—Jesus cheers the weary road.

CHORUS.
Precious Jesus, precious Jesus, Thou art all in all to me, Precious Jesus, precious Jesus, Thou art all in all to me.

2 When the noon-day sun is burning,
  And my soul athirst is made,
Lo! appears the cloudy pillar,
  And I rest within the shade.—*Cho.*

3 When the night seems long and dreary,
  And the path is clouded o'er,
Comes the shining of his presence,
  Lighting all the gloom before.—*Cho.*

4 Blessed presence! dear companion!
  Be the journey what it may,
All my needs are met in Jesus,—
  Jesus is my life and way!—*Cho.*

637 *Confidence in God's protection.*

1 Savior, breathe an evening blessing,
  Ere repose our spirits seal;
Sin and want we come confessing;
  Thou canst save and thou canst heal!—
    Cho.

2 Though destruction walk around us,
  Though the arrows past us fly,
Angel guards from thee surround us:
  We are safe if thou art nigh.—*Cho.*

3 Though the night be dark and dreary,
  Darkness cannot hide from thee;
Thou art he who, never weary,
  Watchest where thy people be.—*Cho.*

4 Should swift death this night o'ertake us,
  And command us to the tomb,
May the morn in heaven awake us,
  Clad in bright, eternal bloom.—*Cho.*

LONELY TRAVELLER.

1. I'm a lonely trav-'ler here, Weary, oppress'd;
But my journey's end is near— Soon I shall rest!
Dark and dreary is the way, Toiling I've come;
Ask me not with you to stay, Yonder's my home.

2. I'm a weary trav-'ler here, I must go on,
For my journey's end is near, I must be gone.
Brighter joys than earth can give, Win me away;
Pleasures that forever live— I cannot stay.

3 I'm a traveller to a land
 Where all is fair;
Where is seen no broken band—
 All, all are there.
Where no tear shall ever fall,
 Nor heart be sad:
Where the glory is for all,
 And all are glad.

4 I'm a traveller, and I go
 Where all is fair;
Farewell, all I've loved below,
 I must be there.
Worldly honors, hopes, and gain,
 All I resign;
Welcome sorrow, grief, and pain,
 If heaven be mine.

SALVATION.

250. "ONE MORE DAY'S WORK FOR JESUS."

By Permission of BIGELOW & MAIN.   Rev. R. LOWRY.

1. One more day's work for Je-sus, One less of life for me! But heav'n is nearer, And Christ is dear-er Than yes-ter-day to me; His love and light Fill all my soul to-night.

CHORUS.
One more day's work for Je-sus, One more day's work for Je-sus, One more day's work for Je-sus, One less of life for me.

2 One more day's work for Jesus!
How glorious is my King!
'Tis joy, not duty,
To speak his beauty;
My soul mounts on the wing,
At the mere thought
How Christ my life has bought.—*Cho.*

3 One more day's work for Jesus!
How sweet the work has been,
To tell the story,
To show the glory,
Where Christ's flock enter in!
How it did shine
In this poor heart of mine!—*Cho.*

4 One more day's work for Jesus!
Oh, yes, a weary day;
But heaven shines clearer,
And rest comes nearer,
At each step of the way;
And Christ in all,
Before his face I fall.—*Cho.*

5 O, blessed work for Jesus!
Oh! rest at Jesus' feet!
There toil seems pleasure,
My wants are treasure,
And pain for him is sweet.
Lord, if I may,
I'll serve another day.—*Cho.*

"I WILL FOLLOW THEE."

Words and Music by JAS. L. ELGINBURG. Arranged for this Work.

1. I will fol-low thee, my Savior, Where-so-e'er my lot may be;
Where thou go-est, I will fol-low, Yes, my Lord, I'll fol-low thee.

CHORUS.
I will fol-low thee, my Sav-ior, Thou didst shed thy blood for me;
And tho' all men should forsake thee, By thy grace I'll fol-low thee.

2 Though the road be rough and thorny,
  Trackless as the foaming sea,
  Thou hast trod this way before me,
  And I gladly follow thee.—*Cho.*

3 Though 'tis lone, and dark, and dreary,
  Cheerless though my path may be,
  If thy voice I hear before me,
  Fearlessly I'll follow thee.—*Cho.*

4 Though I meet with tribulations,
  Sorely tempted though I be,
  I remember thou wast tempted,
  And rejoice to follow thee.—*Cho.*

5 Though thou leadest me thro' affliction,
  Poor, forsaken, though I be,
  Thou wast destitute, afflicted,
  And I only follow thee.—*Cho.*

6 Though to Jordan's rolling billows,
  Cold and deep, thou leadest me,
  Thou hast crossed its waves before me,
  And I still will follow thee.—*Cho.*

643 VALLEY OF BLESSING.

Words by Mrs. Annie Wittenmyre. By permission. *Music by W. G. FISCHER.*

1. I have entered the valley of blessing so sweet, And Jesus abides with me there.
And his spirit and blood make my cleansing complete, And his perfect love casteth out fear.

CHORUS.
Oh come to this valley of blessing so sweet, Where Jesus will fullness bestow—
And be-lieve, and re-ceive, and confess him, That all his sal-va-tion may know.

2. There is peace in the valley of blessing so sweet,
   And plenty the land doth impart;
   And there's rest for the weary-worn traveler's feet,
   And joy for the sorrowing heart.—*Chorus.*

3. There is love in the valley of blessing so sweet,
   Such as none but the blood-washed may feel;
   When heaven comes down redeemed spirits to greet,
   And Christ sets his covenant seal.—*Chorus.*

4. There's a song in the valley of blessing so sweet,
   That angels would fain join the strain—
   As, with rapturous praises, we bow at his feet,
   Crying, "Worthy the Lamb that was slain!"—*Chorus.*

NONE BUT JESUS.

By Permission of BIGELOW & MAIN.   REV. R. LOWRY.

1. Weeping will not save me, Tho' my face were bath'd in tears; That could not al-lay my fears, Could not wash the sins of years:

CHORUS.

Weeping will not save me Je-sus wept and died for me; Je-sus suffer'd on the tree. Je-sus waits to make me free, He a-lone can save me.

2 Working will not save me —
 Purest deeds that I can do,
 Holiest thoughts and feelings, too,
 Cannot form my soul anew;
 Working will not save me.
  Chorus.—Jesus wept, &c.

3 Waiting will not save me —
 Helpless, guilty, lost I lie;
 In my ear is mercy's cry;
 If I wait I can but die —
 Waiting will not save me.
  Chorus.—Jesus wept, &c.

4 Faith in Christ will save me —
 Let me trust thy weeping Son;
 Trust the work that he has done:
 To his arms, Lord, help me run —
 Faith in Christ will save me.
  Chorus.—Jesus wept, &c.

646 LIFE'S BATTLE-FIELD.

From "Pilgrim's Harp," By Permission.

1. Soldiers on life's battle-field, Be ye valiant, bold, and strong: In the strife, with cheerful zeal, Urge the Savior's cause along.

CHORUS. Onward, onward to glory! Yield not to the wily foe; Vict'ry and heav'n are before thee; Shout your triumphs as you go.

2 Hark! the battle is begun!
 Rally, Christians, for your King;
Forward, till the vict'ry's won,
 Till the shouts of triumph ring!—*Cho.*

3 Jesus calls us to the field!
 He will lead us ever more;
'Neath his banner ne'er to yield,
 Till the mighty conflict's o'er.—*Cho.*

4 Then, in yonder world of light,
 We will lay our armor down,
And, 'mid throngs of angels bright,
 Each receive a starry crown.—*Cho.*

647 *Second Hymn.*
1 Hasten, sinner, to be wise!
 Stay not for the morrow's sun;
 Wisdom, if you still despise,
 Harder is it to be won.—*Cho.*

2 Hasten mercy to implore!
 Stay not for the morrow's sun,
 Lest thy season should be o'er,
 Ere this evening's stage be run.—*Cho.*

3 Hasten, sinner, to return!
 Stay not for the morrow's sun;
 Lest thy lamp should fail to burn
 Ere salvation's work is done.—*Cho.*

4 Hasten, sinner, to be blest!
 Stay not for the morrow's sun,
 Lest perdition thee arrest,
 Ere the morrow is begun.—*Cho.*

THE HALLOWED SPOT.

From "Pilgrim's Harp," By Permission.

1. There is a spot to me more dear Than native vale or mountain;
A spot for which affection's tear Springs grateful from its fountain;
'Tis not where kindred souls abound, Tho' that on earth is heaven,
But where I first my Savior found, And felt my sins forgiven.

2 Hard was my toil to reach the shore,
  Long toss'd upon the ocean:
Above me was the thunder's roar;
  Beneath, the waves' commotion.
Darkly the pall of night was thrown
  Around me, faint with terror;
In that dark hour, how did my groan
  Ascend for years of error.

3 Sinking and panting, as for breath,
  I knew not help was near me,
And cried, Oh, save me, Lord, from death,
  Immortal Jesus, hear me!

Then quick as thought I felt him mine,—
  My Savior stood before me;
I saw his brightness round me shine,
  And shouted, Glory! glory!

4 O sacred hour! O hallowed spot!
  Where love divine first found me;
Wherever falls my distant lot,
  My heart shall linger round thee:
And when from earth I rise to soar,
  Up to my home in heaven,
Down will I cast mine eyes once more,
  Where I was first forgiven.

I LONG TO BE THERE.

From "Pilgrim's Harp," By Permission.

1. When I think of that ci-ty of light, And of crowns which the glorified wear, And of garments so pure and so white, Then I long, oh, I long to be there.

CHORUS.

Oh, I long with the saints in light To be cloth'd in the gar-ments of white, And in songs with the angels u-nite, Singing, Glory, hal-le-lu-jah to the Lamb.

2 It is not that I'm weary of pain,
Or impatient in trials and cares;
For I know that to die would be gain,
And I long, oh, I long to be there.
Oh, I long with the saints in light
To be clothed in the garments of white,
And in songs with the angels unite,
Singing, Glory, hallelujah to the Lamb.

3 To that city my Savior has gone,
A rich mansion and crowns to prepare
For the hosts that are following on;
And I long, oh, I long to be there.

Oh, I long with the saints in light
To be cloth'd in the garments of white,
And in songs with the angels unite,
Singing, Glory, hallelujah to the Lamb.

4 When I read of the saints gather'd home
To that city of jewels most rare,
I with joy hail the message to "Come,"
For I long, oh, I long to be there.
Oh, I long with the saints in light
To be clothed in the garments of white,
And in songs with the angels unite,
Singing, Glory, hallelujah to the Lamb.

2 O the transporting, rapturous scene,
  That rises to my sight!
Sweet fields arrayed in living green,
  And rivers of delight.—*Cho.*

3 There generous fruits that never fail,
  On trees immortal grow;
There rock, and hill, and brook, and vale,
  With milk and honey flow.—*Cho.*

4 O'er all those wide, extended plains,
  Shines one eternal day;
There God, the Son, forever reigns,
  And scatters night away.—*Cho.*

5 No chilling winds, or pois'nous breath,
  Can reach that healthful shore;
Sickness and sorrow, pain and death,
  Are felt and feared no more.—*Cho.*

RESTING BY AND BY.

Words by REV. SYDNEY DYER. Music by REV. R. LOWRY. By Permission.

1. When faint and weary toil-ing, The sweat drops on my brow, I long to rest from la-bor, To drop the burden now—
   There comes a gen-tle chiding, To quell each mourning sigh; (OMIT.) "Work while the day is shin-ing, There's resting by and by."

CHORUS.
Rest-ing by and by, There's resting by and by,—We shall not always la-bor, We shall not al-ways cry; The end is drawing near-er, The end for which we sigh; We'll lay our heavy burdens down, There's resting by and by.

2 This life to toil is given,
  And he improves it best
  Who seeks by patient labor
   To enter into rest;
  Then, pilgrim, worn and weary,
   Press on! the goal is nigh;
  The prize is straight before thee,
   There's resting by and by.—CHO.

3 Nor ask, when, overburdened,
   You long for friendly aid,—
  "Why idle stands my brother,
   No yoke upon him laid?"
  The Master bids him tarry,
   And dare you ask him why?
  "Go, labor in my vineyard;
   There's resting by and by."—CHO.

4 Wan reaper in the harvest,
  Let this thy strength sustain,—
  Each sheaf that fills the garner
   Brings you eternal gain,
  Then bear the cross with patience,
   To fields of duty hie;
  'Tis sweet to work for Jesus—
   There's resting by and by.—CHO.

260. "WORK, FOR THE NIGHT IS COMING."

Dr. L. Mason.

1. Work, for the night is coming, Work through the morning hours;
Work, for the dew is sparkling, Work 'mid springing flow'rs;
Work, when the day grows brighter, Work in the glowing sun;
Work, for the night is coming, When man's work is done.

2 Work, for the night is coming,
Work through the sunny noon;
Fill brightest hours with labor,—
Rest comes sure and soon:
Give ev'ry flying minute
Something to keep in store;
Work, for the night is coming,
When man works no more.

3 Work, for the night is coming,
Under the sunset skies;
While their bright tints are glowing,
Work, for the daylight flies:
Work till the last beam fadeth,
Fadeth to shine no more;
Work while the night is dark'ning,
When man's work is o'er.

4 Work, for the night is coming,
Work while the fields are white;
Work, for thy sands are running,
Work while hopes are bright;
Gather thy sheaves at morning;
Rest not thy hand at noon;
Labor and strive till ev'ning;
Rest when daylight's gone.

653. WHO'LL STAND UP FOR JESUS?

WORDS AND MUSIC BY REV. L. HARTSOUGH, by permission.

1. O who'll stand up for Jesus, The lowly Nazarene?
And raise the blood-stained banner, Amid the hosts of sin?

2. O who will follow Jesus, Amid reproach and shame?
Where others shrink or falter, Who'll glory in HIS NAME?

CHORUS.
The Cross for Christ I'll cherish, Its crucifixion bear;
All hail! reproach or sorrow, If Jesus leads me there.

3 My *all* to Christ I've *giv'n*,
My *talents, time* and *voice,*
Myself, my *reputation,*
The *lone way* is my choice.

4 O Jesus, Jesus, Jesus,
My all-sufficient Friend!
Come, fold me to thy bosom,
E'en to the journey's end.

654. *Ashamed to be a Christian.*

1 Ashamed to be a Christian,
Afraid the world should know
I'm on the way to Zion,
Where joys eternal flow.

Forbid it blessed Saviour,
That I should ever be
Afraid the cross to cherish,
Or blush to follow thee.

2 Ashamed to be a Christian,
To love my God and King;
The fire of zeal is burning,
My soul is on the wing.
I want a faith made perfect,
That all the world may see,
I stand a living witness,
Of mercy, rich and free.

655 UNION. C. M.

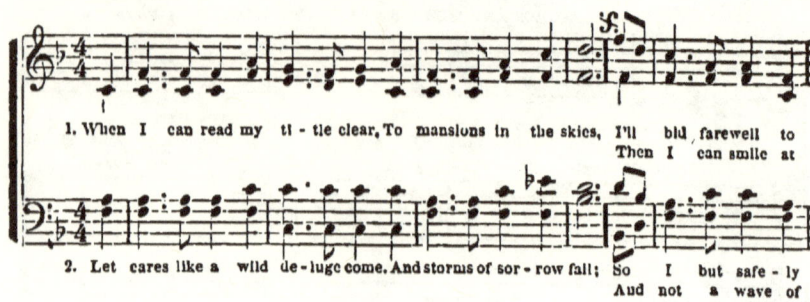

1. When I can read my ti-tle clear, To mansions in the skies, I'll bid farewell to ev'ry fear, And wipe my weeping eyes. Should earth against my soul engage, And fi'ry darts be hurl'd, Then I can smile at Satan's rage, And face a frowning world.

2. Let cares like a wild de-luge come, And storms of sor-row fall; So I but safe-ly reach my home, my God, My heav'n, my all. There I shall bathe my weary soul In seas of heav'nly rest, And not a wave of trou-ble roll A-cross my peaceful breast.

656 *Grateful praise for delivering mercy.*

1 O thou, who, when we did complain,
  Didst all our griefs remove;
  O Savior, do not now disdain
  Our humble praise and love.

2 Since thou a pitying ear didst give,
  And hear us when we pray'd,
  We'll call upon thee while we live,
  And never doubt thy aid.

3 Pale death, with all his ghastly train,
  Our souls encompass'd round;
  Anguish, and fear, and dread, and pain,
  On every side we found.

4 To thee, O Lord of life, we pray'd,
  And did for succor flee:
  O save,—in our distress we said,—
  The souls that trust in thee.

5 How good thou art! how large thy grace!
  How ready to forgive!
  Thy mercies crown our fleeting days;
  And by thy love we live.

6 Our eyes no longer drown'd in tears,
  Our feet from falling free;
  Redeem'd from death and guilty fears,
  O Lord, we'll live to thee.

657 *Perpetual praise.*

1 Yes, I will bless thee, O my God,
  Through all my fleeting days;
  And to eternity prolong
  Thy vast, thy boundless praise.

2 Nor shall my tongue alone proclaim
  The honors of my God;
  My life, with all its active powers,
  Shall spread thy praise abroad.

3 Nor will I cease thy praise to sing,
  When death shall close mine eyes,
  My thoughts shall then to nobler hights,
  And sweeter raptures rise.

4 Then shall my lips, in endless praise,
  Their grateful tribute pay;
  The theme demands an angel's tongue,
  And an eternal day.

To Father, Son, and Holy Ghost,
  Who sweetly all agree
To save a world of sinners lost,
  Eternal glory be.

658   CHORAL. 6s.

1. Now thank we all our God, With heart, and hands, and voices, Who wondrous things hath done, In whom this world rejoices; Who from our mother's arms Hath bless'd us on our way With countless gifts of love, And still is ours to-day.

2 Oh may this bounteous God,
  Through all our life be near us,
With ever joyful hearts,
  And blessed peace to cheer us;
And keep us in his grace,
  And guide us when perplexed,
And free us from all ills
  In this world and the next.

3 All praise and thanks to God,
  The Father, now be given;
The Son, and Him who reigns
  With Them in highest heaven:
The One Eternal God,
  Whom earth and heaven adore;
For this it was, is now,
  And shall be ever-more. Amen

659   *"Thy will be done."*

1 My Jesus, as thou wilt!
  Oh! may thy will be mine;
Into thy hand of love,
  I would my all resign;
Through sorrow or through joy,
  Conduct me as thy own,
And help me still to say,
  My Lord, "Thy will be done."

2 My Jesus, as thou wilt!
  Though seen through many a tear,
Let not my star of hope
  Grow dim, or disappear:
Since thou on earth hast wept,
  And sorrowed oft alone,
If I must weep with thee,
  My Lord, "Thy will be done."

3 My Jesus, as thou wilt!
  All shall be well for me;
Each changing future scene
  I gladly trust to thee;
Straight to my home above
  I travel calmly on,
And sing, in life or death,
  My Lord, "Thy will be done!"

SELECTIONS FOR CHANTING.

No. 1. — *Boyce.*

PSALM XCV.

1 Oh come, let us sing un-| to the | Lord;
  Let us heartily rejoice in the | strength of | our sal-| vation.
2 Let us come before his presence | with thanks-| giving,
  And show ourselves | glad in | him with | psalms.
3 For the Lord is a | great.. | God,
  And a great | King a-| bove all | gods.
4 In his hand are all the corners | of the | earth;
  And the strength of the | hills is | his — | also.
5 The sea is his, | and he | made it,
  And his hands pre-| pared the | dry— | land.
6 Oh come, let us worship, | and fall | down,
  And *kneel* be-| fore the | Lord our | Maker;
7 For he is the | Lord our | God,
  And we are the people of his pasture, | and the | sheep of his | hand.
8 Oh worship the Lord in the | beauty of | holiness;
  Let the whole earth | stand in | awe of | him.
* 9 For he cometh, for he cometh to | judge the | earth,   [truth.
  And with righteousness to judge the world, and the | peo—ple | with his |

Gloria Patri.
Glory be to the Father, and | to the | Son,
And | to the | Holy | Ghost;
As it was in the beginning, is now, and | ev—er | shall be,
World | with-out | end. A— | MEN.

* Begin at middle of the Chant.

No. 2. — *Mornington.*

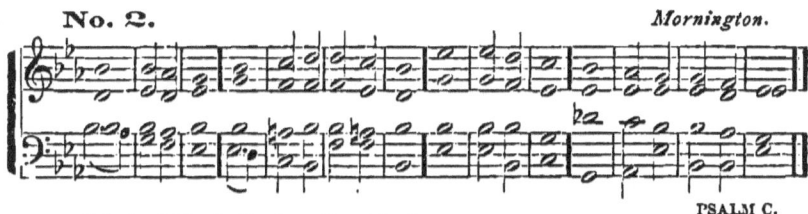

PSALM C.

1 O be joyful in the Lord, | all ye | lands;
  Serve the Lord with gladness, and come before his | presence | with a | song.
2 Be ye sure that the Lord | he is | God;
  It is he that hath made us, and not we ourselves; We are his people.. | and the | sheep of.. his | pasture.
3 O go your way into his gates with thanksgiving, and into his | courts with | praise;
  Be thankful unto him, and | speak good | of his | name.
4 For the Lord is gracious, his mercy is | ever-| lasting:
  And his truth endureth from gene-| ration..to | gene-| ration.
    Glory be to the Father, &c.

No. 3. *Gregorian.*

ST. LUKE, I. 68.

1 Blessed be the Lord | God of | Israel,
  For he hath visited, | and re-| deemed his | people;
2 And hath raised up a mighty sal-| vation | for us,
  In the | house of his | ser-vant | David;
3 As he spake by the mouth of his | ho-ly | Prophets,
  Which have been | since the | world be- |gan;
4 That we should be saved | from our | enemies,
  And from the | hand of | all that | hate us.
    Glory be to the Father, &c.

No. 4. *Jackson.*

PSALM XCVIII.

1 O sing unto the | Lord a new | song,
  For he | hath done | marvellous | things.
2 With his own right hand, and with his | holy | arm,
  Hath he | gotten him-| self the | victory.
3 The Lord declared | his sal-| vation,
  His righteousness hath he openly showed | in the | sight of the | heathen.
4 He hath remembered his mercy and truth toward the | house of | Israel,
  And all the ends of the world have seen the sal-| vation | of our | God.
5 Show yourselves joyful unto the Lord, | all ye | lands;
  Sing, re-| joice, and | give — | thanks.
6 Praise the Lord up-| on the | harp;
  Sing to the harp with a | psalm of | thanks— | giving.
7 With trumpets also, and | shawms,
  O show yourselves joyful be-| fore the | Lord, the | King.
8 Let the sea make a noise, and all that | therein | is;
  The round world, and | they that | dwell there-| in.
9 Let the floods clap their hands, and let the hills be joyful together be-| fore the | Lord.
  For he | cometh to | judge the | earth.
10 With righteousness shall he | judge the | world,
  And the | people | with— | equity.
    Glory be to the Father, &c.

No. 5. — Robinson.

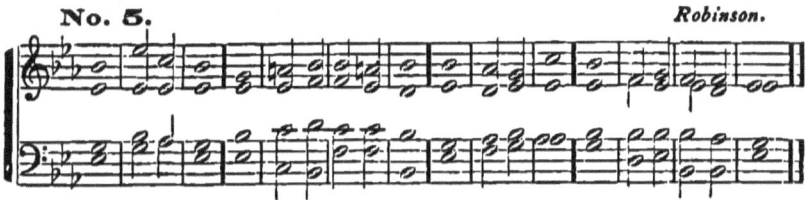

PSALM XCII.

1 It is a good thing to give thanks un-| to the | Lord,
And to sing praises unto thy | name, O | Most — | Highest.

2 To tell of thy loving kindness early | in the | morning,
And of thy | truth in the | night — | season.

3 Upon an instrument of ten strings, and up-| on the | lute;
Upon a loud instrument, | and up-| on the | harp.

4 For thou, Lord, hast made me glad | through thy | works,
And I will rejoice in giving praise for the ope-| rations | of thy | hands.

Glory be to the Father, &c.

No. 6. — Downes.

PSALM LXVII.

1 God be merciful unto | us, and | bless us;
And show us the light of his countenance, and be | merciful | unto | us:

2 That thy way may be | known upon | earth,
Thy saving | health a-| mong all | nations.

3 Let the people praise | thee, O | God;
Yea, let | all the | peo-| ple | praise thee.

4 O let the nations rejoice | and be | glad,
For thou shalt judge the folk right-eously, and govern the | nations |up-on|earth.

5 Let the people praise | thee, O | God,
Yea, let | all the | peo-ple | praise thee.

6 Then shall the earth bring | forth her | increase,
And God, even our own | God, shall | give us his | blessing.

7 God | shall — | bless us,
And all the ends of the | world shall | fear — | him.

Glory be to the Father, &c.

No. 7. Gloria in Excelsis.

PART I. — *PART II.* — A-men. — *PART III.*

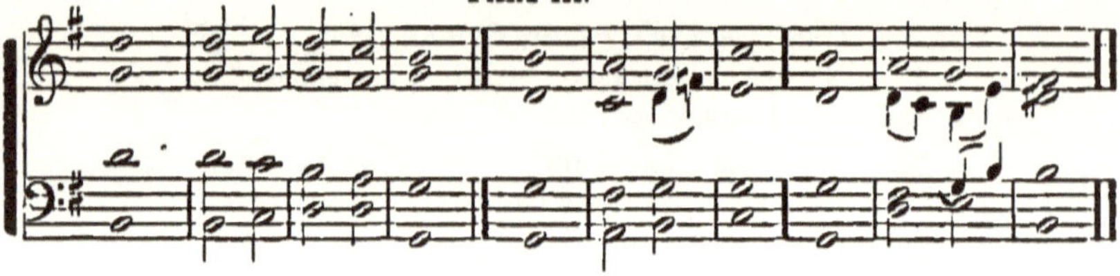

Part I. { 1 Glory be to | God on | high,
And on earth | peace, good | will towards | men.
2 We praise thee, we bless thee, we | worship | thee;
We glorify thee, we give thanks to | thee for | thy great | glory.

Part II. { 3 O Lord God, | heavenly | King, ‖ God the | Father, | Al— | mighty!
4 O Lord, the only-begotten Son, | Jesus | Christ;
O Lord God, Lamb of | God, Son | of the | Father!

Part III. { 5 That takest away the | sins..of the | world, ‖ have mercy | up-on | us.
6 Thou that takest away the | sins..of the | world, ‖ have mercy | up-on | us.
7 Thou that takest away the | sins..of the | world, ‖ re-| ceive our | prayer.
8 Thou that sitteth at the right hand of | God the | Father, ‖ have mercy up-on | us.

Part I. { 9 For thou | only art | holy, ‖ thou | only | art the | Lord.
10 Thou only, O Christ, with the | Holy | Ghost, ‖ art Most High in the | glory..of | God, the | Father. ‖ A-| MEN.

No. 8. Atwood.

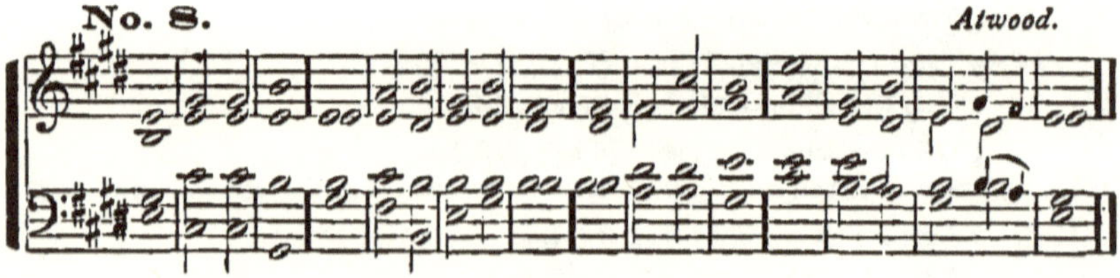

PSALM CIII.

1 Praise the Lord, | O my | soul,
And all that is within me | praise his | holy | name.
2 Praise the Lord, | O my | soul,
And for-| get not | all his | benefits;

Conclusion of Chant No. 8, on opposite page.

No. 9. *Gregorian.*

PSALM XLII.

1. *Minister.* As the hart panteth after the water brooks,
   So panteth my soul after thee, O God.

2. *Choir.* My soul thirsteth for God, for the | liv-ing | God!
   When shall I come and ap-| pear be-| fore — | God?

3. *M.* My tears have been my meat day and night,
   While they continually say unto me, Where is thy God?

4. *C.* When I re-| member these | things,
   I pour ! out my | soul in | me;

5. *M.* For I had gone with the multitude;
   I went with them to the house of God,
   With the voice of joy and praise, with a multitude that kept holy day.

6. *C.* Why art thou cast down, | O my ! soul,
   And why art thou dis-| quiet-ed | in — | me?

7. *M.* Hope thou in God:
   For I shall yet praise him for the help of his countenance.

8. *C.* Glory be to the Father, and | to the | Son,
   And | to the | Holy | Ghost.
   As it was in the beginning, is now, and | ev-er | shall be,
   World | with-out | end.   A-| MEN.

Remainder of Chant No. 8, on opposite page.

3 Who forgiveth | all thy | sin,
  And | heal-eth | all thine in-| firmities.

4 Who saveth thy | life..from de-| struction,
  And crowneth thee with | mercy and | lov-ing | kindness.

5 O praise the Lord, ye angels of his, ye that ex-| cel in | strength;
  Ye that fulfil his commandments, and hearken unto the | voice of | his · | word

6 O praise the Lord, all | ye his | hosts;
  Ye servants of | his that | do his | pleasure.

* 7 O speak good of the Lord, all ye works of his, in all places of | his do-| minion;
  Praise thou the | Lord,— | O my | soul.
    Glory be to the Father, &c.

* **Begin at middle of the Chant.**

No. 10. *Gregorian.*

PSALM XXVII.

1. *Min.*   The Lord is my light and my salvation; whom shall I fear?
         The Lord is the strength of my life; of whom shall I be afraid?

2. *Choir.* When the wicked, even mine enemies and my foes came upon me to eat | up my | flesh,
         They | stum — | bled and | fell.

3. *M.*   Though an host should encamp against me, my heart shall not fear;
         Though war should rise against me, in this will I be confident.

4. *C.*   One thing have I desired of the Lord, that will I | seek — | after;
         That I may dwell in the house of the Lord, all the days of my life, to behold the beauty of the Lord, and to in-| quire — | in his | temple.

5. *M.*   For in the time of trouble, he shall hide me in his pavilion;
         In the secret of his tabernacle shall he hide me: he shall set me up upon a rock.

6. *C.*   And now shall mine head be lifted up above mine enemies | round a-|bout me;
         Therefore will I offer in his tabernacle sacrifices of joy; I will sing, yea, I will sing | prais-es | to the | Lord.

7. *M.*   Hear, O Lord, when I cry with my voice;
         Have mercy also upon me, and answer me.

8. *C.*   When thou saidst, Seek | ye my | face,
         My heart said unto thee, Thy | face, Lord, | will I | seek.

9. *M.*   Hide not thy face far from me; Put not thy servant away in anger.

10. *C.* Thou hast | been my | help;
         Leave me not, neither forsake me, O | God of | my sal-| vation.
         Glory be to the Father, &c.

PSALM XXIV.

1. *M.*   The earth is the Lord's, and the fullness thereof;
         The world, and they that dwell therein.

2. *C.*   For he hath founded it up-| on the | seas,
         And established | it up-| on the | floods.

3. *M.*   Who shall ascend into the hill of the Lord?
         Or who shall stand in his holy place?

4. *C.*   He that hath clean hands and a | pure — | heart;
         Who hath not lifted up his soul unto vanity, | nor — | sworn de-| ceitfully;
         He shall receive the blessing | from the | Lord,
         And righteousness from the | God of | his sal-| vation.

For Conclusion of Psalm xxiv. (for Chant No. 10.) see opposite page.

No. 11. *Farrant.*

PSALM CIII.

1. *Min.* The Lord is merciful and gracious,
   Slow to anger, and plenteous in mercy.

2. *Choir.* He will not | always | chide;
   Neither will he keep his | an — | ger for-| ever.

3. *M.* He hath not dealt with us after our sins,
   Nor rewarded us according to our iniquities.

4. *C.* For as the heaven is high a-| bove the | earth,
   So great is his mercy toward | them that | fear — | him.

5. *M.* As far as the east is from the west,
   So far hath he removed our transgressions from us.

6. *C.* Like as a father | pitieth his | children,
   So the Lord pitieth | them that | fear | him.

7. *M.* For he knoweth our frame;
   He remembereth that we are dust.

8. *C.* Glory be to the Father, and | to the | Son,
   And | to the | Holy | Ghost.
   As it was in the beginning, is now, and | ev-er | shall be,
   World | with-out | end.   A-| MEN.

Remainder of Chant No. 10, on opposite page.

5. *M.* This is the generation of them that seek him;
   That seek thy face, O Jacob.

6. *C.* Lift up your heads, | O ye | gates!
   And be ye lifted up, ye everlasting doors; and the King of | Glo-ry | shall come | in!

7. *M.* Who is this King of Glory?

8. *C.* The Lord, | strong and | mighty;
   The Lord, | might-y | in — | battle.
   Lift up your heads, | O ye | gates!
   Even lift them up, ye everlasting doors; and the King of | Glo-ry | shall come | in!

9. *M.* Who is this King of Glory?

10. *C.* The | Lord of | hosts,
    He | is the | King of | Glory.

   Glory be to the Father, &c.

No. 12. *Gregorian.*

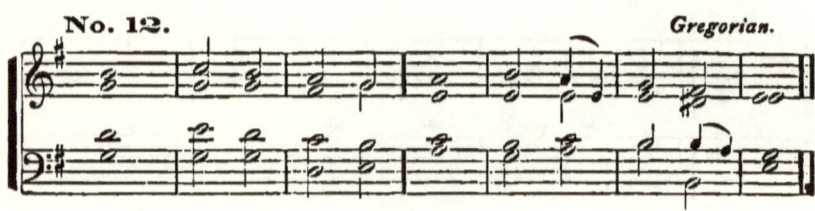

PSALM XCVII.

1. *Min.* The Lord reigneth; let the earth rejoice;
   Let the multitude of isles be glad thereof!
2. *Choir.* Clouds and darkness are | round a-| bout him,
   Righteousness and judgment are the habi-| tation | of his | throne.
3. *M.* A fire goeth before him,
   And burneth up his enemies round about.
4. *C.* His lightnings en-| lightened the | world;
   The | earth — | saw and | trembled.
5. *M.* The hills melted like wax at the presence of the Lord;
   At the presence of the Lord of the whole earth.
6. *C.* The heavens declare his | righteous-| ness,
   And all the | people | see his | glory.
7. *M.* Confounded be all they that serve graven images,
   That boast themselves of idols! Worship him, all ye gods!
8. *C.* Zion heard, | and was | glad;
   And the daughters of Judah rejoiced because of thy | judgments, | O-| Lord!
9. *M.* For thou, Lord, art high above all the earth;
   Thou art exalted far above all gods.
10. *C.* Ye that love the | Lord, hate | evil:
    He preserveth the souls of his saints; he delivereth them out of the | hand — | of the | wicked.
11. *M.* Light is sown for the righteous,
    And gladness for the upright in heart.
12. *C.* Rejoice in the | Lord, ye | righteous,
    And give thanks at the re-| membrance | of his | holiness.

   Glory be to the Father, &c.

PSALM XCVI.

1. *M.* Oh sing unto the Lord a new song;
   Sing unto the Lord, all the earth.
2. *C.* Sing unto the Lord, | bless his | name;
   Shew forth his sal-| vation · from | day to. | day.
3. *M.* Declare his glory among the heathen,
   His wonders among all people..
4. *C.* For the Lord is great, and greatly | to be | praised;
   He is to be | fear-ed a-| bove all | gods.

For Conclusion of Psalm xcvi. see opposite page.

273

No. 13.

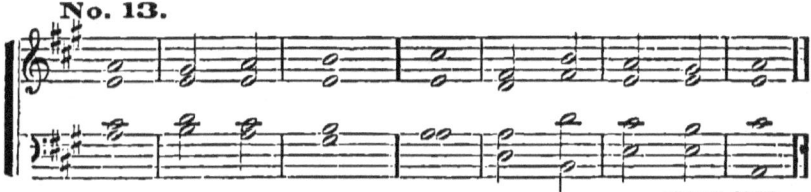

PSALM CXXI.

1. *Min.* I will lift up mine eyes unto the hills,
From whence cometh my help.

2. *Choir.* My help cometh | from the | Lord,
Who | made — | heaven and | earth.

3. *M.* He will not suffer thy foot to be moved!
He that keepeth thee will not slumber.

4. *C.* Behold, he that keepeth | Is-ra-| el,
Shall not | slum — | ber nor | sleep.

5. *M.* The Lord is thy keeper;
The Lord is thy shade upon thy right hand.

6. *C.* The sun shall not smite | thee by | day,
Nor the | moon — | by — | night.

7. *M.* The Lord shall preserve thee from all evil;
He shall preserve thy soul.

8. *C.* The Lord shall preserve thy going out, and thy | coming | in,
From this time forth, and | even for-| ev-er | more.

Glory be to the Father, &c.

Remainder of Psalm xcvi. on opposite page.

5. *M.* For all the gods of the nations are idols;
But the Lord made the heavens.

6. *C.* Honor and majesty | are be-| fore him;
Strength and beauty are | in his | sanctu-| ary.

7. *M.* Give unto the Lord, O ye kindreds of the people,
Give unto the Lord glory and strength.

8. *C.* Give unto the Lord the glory due un-| to his | name:
Bring an offering, and | come in-| to his | courts.

9. *M.* Oh worship the Lord in the beauty of holiness;
Fear before him all the earth.

10. *C.* Say among the heathen that the | Lord — | reigneth:
The world also shall be established, that it shall not be moved; he shall |
judge the | people | righteously.

11. *M.* Let the heavens rejoice, and let the earth be glad;
Let the sea roar, and the fullness thereof.

12. *C.* Let the field be joyful, and all that | is there- | in:
Then shall all the trees of the wood re-| joice be-| fore the | Lord;

13. *M.* For he cometh, for he cometh to judge the earth:
He shall judge the world with righteousness, And the people with his truth.

Glory be to the Father, &c.

No. 14.   Dr. Blow.

Funeral.

1. *Min.*   Lord, let me know mine end, and the number of my days.
   That I may be certified how long I have to live.

2. *Choir.*   Behold, thou hast made my days, as it were, a span long, and mine age is even as nothing in re-| spect of | thee;
   And verily every man living, is | alto-| geth-er | vanity.

3. *M.*   For man walketh in a vain shadow, and disquieteth himself in vain;
   He heapeth up riches, and cannot tell who shall gather them.

4. *C.*   And now Lord, what | is my | hope?
   Truly, my | hope is | even in | thee.

5. *M.*   Deliver me from all mine offences;
   And make me not a rebuke unto the foolish.

6. *C.*   When thou with rebukes doth chasten man for sin, thou makest his beauty to consume away, like as it were a moth | fretting a | garment:
   Every man | therefore | is but | vanity.

7. *M.*   Hear my prayer, O Lord, and with thine ears consider my calling:
   Hold not thy peace at my tears.

8. *C.*   For I am a | stranger with | thee,
   And a sojourner, as | all my | fath-ers | were.

9. *M.*   O spare me a little, that I may recover my strength,
   Before I go hence, and be no more seen.

10. *C.*   Lord, thou hast | been our | refuge,
    From one gene-| ra-tion | to an- | other.

11. *M.*   Before the mountains were brought forth, or ever the earth and the world were made,
    Thou art God from everlasting, and world without end.

12. *C.*   Thou turnest man | to de-| struction;
    Again thou sayest, Come a-| gain, ye | children of | men.

13. *M.*   For a thousand years in thy sight are but as yesterday;
    Seeing that it is past as a watch in the night.

14. *C.*   As soon as thou scatterest them, they are even | as a | sleep;
    And fade away | sudden-ly | like the | grass.

For Conclusion of above Selections, see opposite page.

No. 15.

Funeral.

1. *Min.* Blessed are the dead, who die in the Lord from henceforth;
Yea, saith the Spirit, that they may rest from their labors, and their works do follow them.

2. *Choir.* Our days on earth are as a shadow, and there is | none a-| biding;
We are but of yesterday; there is but a | step be-tween | us and | death:

3. *M.* Man's days are as grass: as a flower of the field so he flourisheth;
He appeareth for a little time, then vanisheth away.

4. *C.* Watch! for ye know not what hour your | Lord doth | come;
Be ye also ready; for in such an hour as ye think not, the | Son of | Man — | cometh.

5. *M.* It is the Lord; let him do what seemeth him good;
The Lord gave, and the Lord hath taken away,
And blessed be the name of the Lord.

6. *C.* Blessed are the dead, who die in the Lord | from hence-| forth;
Yea, saith the Spirit, that they may rest from their labors, and their | works do | fol-low | them.

Glory be to the Father, &c.

Remainder of Selections on opposite page.

15. *M.* In the morning it is green, and groweth up;
But in the evening it is cut down, dried up, and withered.

16. *C.* For we consume away in | thy dis-| pleasure
And are afraid at thy | wrath-ful | in-dig-| nation.

17. *M.* Thou hast set our misdeeds before thee;
And our secret sins in the light of thy countenance.

18. *C.* For when thou art angry, all our | days are | gone:
We bring our years to an end, as it | were a | tale that is | told.

19. *M.* The days of our age are threescore years and ten;
And though men be so strong that they come to fourscore years, yet is their strength then but labor and sorrow; so soon passeth it away, and we are gone.

20. *C.* So teach us to | number our | days,
That we may ap-| ply our | hearts unto | wisdom.

Glory be to the Father, &c.

No. 16.   Jacobs.

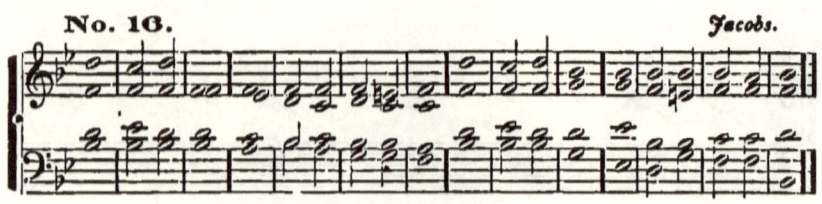

PSALM XLVII.

1 O clap your hands, | all ye | people;
  Shout unto God, | with the | voice of | triumph.
2 For the Lord most | high is | terrible;
  He is a great King | o-ver | all the | earth.
3 He shall subdue the people | under | us,
  And the nations | under | our — | feet.
4 He shall choose our in-| heri-tance | for us,
  The excellency of | Jacob | whom he | loved.
5 God is gone up | with a | shout,
  The Lord, with the | sound of a | trum — | pet,
6 Sing praises to | God, sing | praises,
  Sing praises unto our | King, sing | prais — | es,
7 For God is the King of | all the | earth;
  Sing ye praises with | under-| stand— | ing.
8 God reigneth over the | hea — | then;
  God sitteth upon the | throne of his | ho-li-| ness.
9 The princes of the people are | gathered to-| gether,
  Even the people of the | God of | A-bra-| ham.
10 For the shields of the earth belong | un-to | God:
  He is | great-ly ex- | alt — | ed.
      Glory be to the Father, &c.

ISAIAH XII.

1 O Lord, I will praise thee, though thou wast | angry with | me;
  Thine anger is turned away, | and thou | comfortest | me.
2 Behold, God is | my sal-| vation;
  I will | trust, and | not be a-| fraid.
3 For the Lord Jehovah is my | strength and | song;
  He also is be-| come — | my sal-| vation.
4 Therefore, with joy shall ye draw water out of the | wells of..sal-| vation.
  And in that day shall ye say, Praise the Lord, | call up-| on his | name.
5 Declare his doings among the people, make mention that his name | is ex-| alted.
  Sing unto the Lord, for he hath done excellent things; this is | known in | all the | earth.
6 Cry out and shout, thou in-| habitant of | Zion;
  For great is the Holy One of Israel | in the | midst of | thee.
      Glory be to the Father, &c.

277

No. 17.   Flintoft.

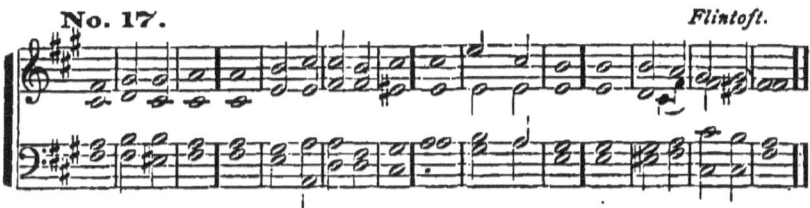

ISAIAH LIII.

1. *Min.*   Who hath believed our report?
        And to whom is the arm of the Lord revealed?
        For he shall grow up before him as a tender plant, and as a root out of dry ground;
        He hath no form nor comeliness; and when we shall see him, there is no beauty, that we should desire him.

2. *C.*   He is despised and re-| jected of | men ;
       A man of sorrows, | and ac-| quainted with | grief.
       And we hid, as it were, our | faces from | him ;
       He was despised, and | we es-| teemed him | not.

3. *M.*   Surely he hath borne our grief, and carried our sorrows ;
       Yet we did esteem him stricken, smitten of God, and afflicted.

4. *C.*   But he was wounded for | our trans-| gressions ;
       He was bruised for | our in-| iqui-| ties ;
       The chastisement of our peace | was upon | him ;
       And by his stripes | we are | heal — | ed.

5. *M.*   All we like sheep have gone astray ;
       We have turned every one to his own way ;
       And the Lord hath laid on him the iniquity of us all.

6. *C.*   He was oppressed, and he | was af-| flicted,
       Yet he | open-ed | not his | mouth :
       He is brought as a | lamb to the | slaughter,
       And as a sheep before her shearers is dumb, so he | open-eth | not his | mouth.

7. *M.*   He was taken from prison and from judgment;
       And who shall declare his generation ?
       For he was cut off out of the land of the living;
       For the transgression of my people was he stricken.

8. *C.*   And he made his grave | with the | wicked,
       And with the | rich in | his — | death.
       Because he had | done no | violence,
       Neither was any | deceit — | in his | mouth.

9. *M.*   Yet it pleased the Lord to bruise him ; he hath put him to grief:
       When thou shalt make his soul an offering for sin, he shall see his seed;
       He shall prolong his days, and the pleasure of the Lord shall prosper in h hands:
       He shall see of the travail of his soul, and shall be satisfied.

        Glory be to the Father, &c.

No. 18.

PSALM XXIII.

1 The Lord is my Shepherd, I | shall not | want;
He maketh me to lie down in green pastures; he leadeth me be-| side the | still — | waters.

2 He restoreth my soul; he leadeth me in the paths of righteousness for his | name's — | sake.
Yea, though I walk through the valley of the shadow of death, I will fear no evil, for thou art with me; thy rod and thy | staff they | comfort | me.

3 Thou preparest a table before me, in the presence | of my | enemies;
Thou anointest my head with oil; my | cup — | runneth | over.

4 Surely goodness and mercy shall follow me all the | days ·· of my | life;
And I will dwell in the house of the | Lord for-| ev --| er.

    Glory be to the Father, &c.

No. 19.

PSALM CXLV.

1 I will extol thee, my | God, O | King;
And I will bless thy | name for-| ever and | ever

2 Every day will I | bless — | thee,
And I will praise thy | name for-| ever and | ever.

3 Great is the Lord, and greatly | to be | praised;
And his greatness | is un-| scarcha-| ble.

4 One generation shall praise thy works | to an-| other,
And shall de-| clare thy | mighty | acts.

5 I will speak of the glorious honor of thy | majes-| ty,
And | of thy | wondrous | works.

6 And men shall speak of the might of thy | terrible | acts,
And I will de-| clare thy | great — | ness.

7 They shall abundantly utter the memory of thy | great — | goodness,
And shall sing | of thy | righteous | ness.

    Glory be to the Father, &c.

279

NOTE.—The following Tunes are selected chiefly for use in the Family and Social Circle. They may, however, be introduced in place of the Anthem or other Select Pieces usually sung by the Choir. When the Hymns are to be sung by the Congregation, they should be adapted to familiar tunes, which should always be announced by the Minister.

DRESDEN. L. M. — BEETHOVEN.

1. How blest the sa-cred tie... that binds In u-nion sweet, ac-cord-ing minds! How swift the heav'n-ly course they run, Whose hearts, and faith, and hopes are one.

2 To each the soul of each how dear!
  What jealous care, what holy fear!
  How doth the generous flame within,
  Refine from earth, and cleanse from sin!
3 Together oft they seek the place
  Where God reveals his awful face;

How high, how strong their raptures swell,
There's none but kindred minds can tell.
4 Nor shall the glowing flame expire,
  'Mid nature's drooping, sickening fire:
  Soon shall they meet in realms above,
  A heaven of joy, because of love.

OSGOOD. L. M. — R. TAYLOR.

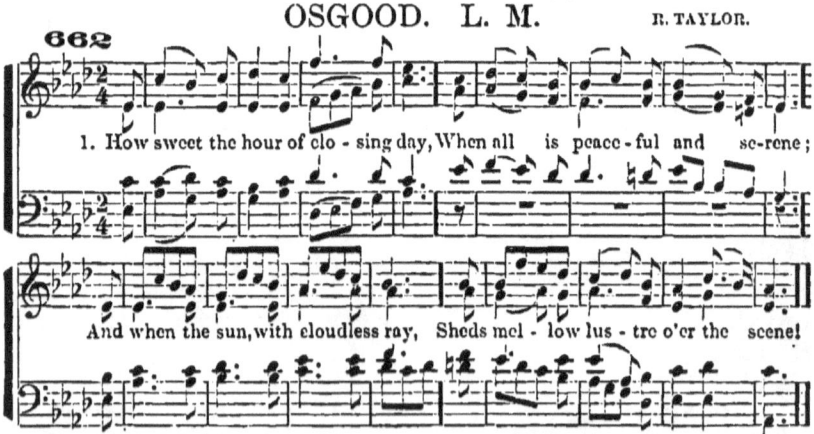

1. How sweet the hour of clo-sing day, When all is peace-ful and se-rene; And when the sun, with cloudless ray, Sheds mel-low lus-tre o'er the scene!

2 Such is the Christian's parting hour;
  So peacefully he sinks to rest;
  When faith, endued from heav'n with pow'r,
  Sustains and cheers his languid breast.
3 Mark but that radiance of his eye,
  That smile upon his wasted cheek;
  They tell us of his glory nigh,
  In language that no tongue can speak.

4 A beam from heaven is sent to cheer
  The pilgrim on his gloomy road;
  And angels are attending near,
  To bear him to their bright abode.
5 Who would not wish to die like those
  Whom God's own Spirit deigns to bless?
  To sink into that soft repose,
  Then wake to perfect happiness?

"UNVEIL THY BOSOM, FAITHFUL TOMB." 281

2 Nor pain, nor grief, nor anxious fear,
Invade thy bounds: no mortal woes
Can reach the peaceful sleeper here,
While angels watch the soft repose.

3 So Jesus slept; — God's dying Son
Pass'd through the grave, and blest the bed:
Rest here, blest saint, till from his throne
The morning break, and pierce the shade.

MESSIAH. C. M.
HANDEL.

1. With joy we med-i-tate the grace Of our High Priest a-bove; His heart is made of ten-der-ness, His bowels melt with love, His bowels melt with love, His bowels melt with love.

2 Touched with a sympathy within,
  He knows our feeble frame;
  He knows what sore temptations mean,
  For he has felt the same.

3 He, in the days of feeble flesh,
  Poured out his cries and tears;
  And, in his measure, feels afresh
  What every member bears.

4 (He'll never quench the smoking flax,
  But raise it to a flame;
  The bruised reed he never breaks,
  Nor scorns the meanest name.)

5 Then let our humble faith address
  His mercy and his power;
  We shall obtain delivering grace,
  In the distressing hour.

665 *The beauty and love of Jesus.*

1 Majestic sweetness sits enthroned
  Upon the Savior's brow;
  His head with radiant glories crowned,
  His lips with grace o'erflow.

2 No mortal can with him compare,
  Among the sons of men;
  Fairer is he than all the fair
  That fill the heavenly train.

3 He saw me plunged in deep distress,
  He flew to my relief;
  For me he bore the shameful cross,
  And carried all my grief.

4 To him I owe my life and breath,
  And all the joys I have;
  He makes me triumph over death,
  He saves me from the grave.

5 To heaven, the place of his abode,
  He brings my weary feet;
  Shows me the glories of my God,
  And makes my joy complete.

6 Since from his bounty I receive
  Such proofs of love divine,
  Had I a thousand hearts to give,
  Lord! they should all be thine.

666 MANOAH. C. M.

1. Let ev-'ry tongue thy goodness speak, Thou Sov-'reign Lord of all:
Thy strength'ning hands up-hold the weak, And raise the poor that fall.

2 When sorrows bow the spirit down,
  When virtue lies distressed,
  Beneath the proud oppressor's frown,
  Thou giv'st the mourner rest.

3 Thou know'st the pains thy servants feel,
  Thou hear'st thy children's cry;
  And their best wishes to fulfil,
  Thy grace is ever nigh.

4 Thy mercy never shall remove
  From men of heart sincere:
  Thou sav'st the souls whose humble love
  Is joined with holy fear.

5 My lips shall dwell upon thy praise,
  And spread thy fame abroad;
  Let all the sons of Adam raise
  The honors of their God.

667 EWER. S. M. — WM. MASON.

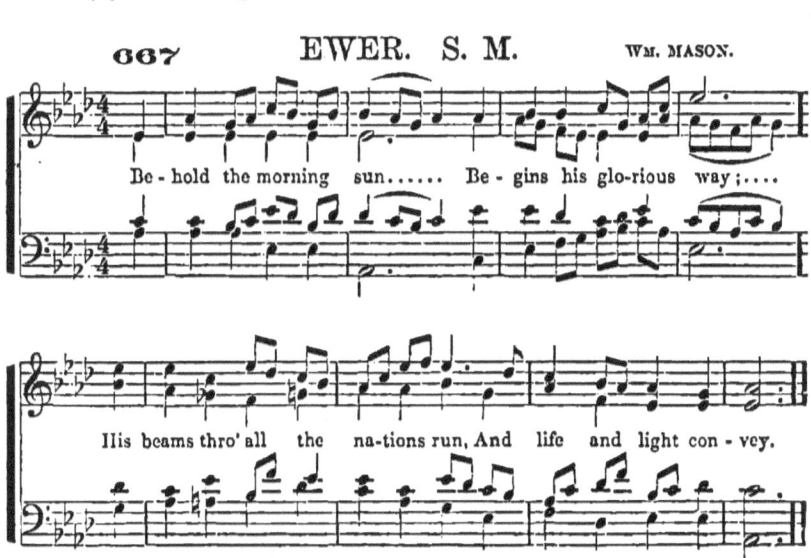

Be-hold the morning sun...... Be-gins his glo-rious way;....
His beams thro' all the na-tions run, And life and light con-vey.

HAYDN. S. M.

1. Lord! I delight in thee,.... And on thy care depend;
To thee, in ev-'ry trou-ble flee, My best, my on-ly Friend.

2 When nature's streams are dried,
Thy fullness is the same;
With this will I be satisfied,
And glory in thy Name.

3 Who made my heaven secure,
Will here all good provide:

While Christ is rich, can I be poor?
What can I want beside?

4 I cast my care on thee!
I triumph and adore:
Henceforth my great concern shall be,
To love and please thee more.

GABRIEL. S. M.

1. Ye pray-ing souls, re-joice, And bless your Father's name;
With joy to him lift up your voice, And all his love pro-claim.

2 Your mournful cry he hears;
He marks your feeblest groan,
Supplies your wants, dispels your fears,
And makes his mercy known.

3 To all his praying saints
He ever will attend,

And to their sorrows and complaints
His ear in mercy bend.

4 Then let us still go on
In his appointed ways,
Rejoicing in his Name alone,
In prayer and humble praise.

672 LUDWIG. 7s.
BEETHOVEN.

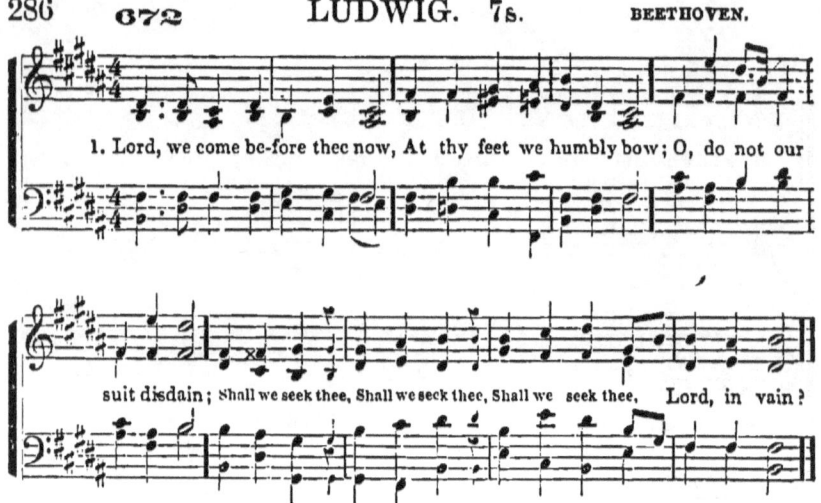

1. Lord, we come before thee now, At thy feet we humbly bow; O, do not our suit disdain; Shall we seek thee, Shall we seek thee, Shall we seek thee, Lord, in vain?

2 Lord, on thee our souls depend;
In compassion now descend;
Fill our hearts with thy rich grace,
Tune our lips to sing thy praise.

3 Send some message from thy word,
That may joy and peace afford;
Let thy Spirit now impart
Full salvation to each heart.

4 Comfort those who weep and mourn;
Let the time of joy return;
Those that are cast down lift up;
Make them strong in faith and hope.

5 Grant that all may seek and find
Thee, a gracious God, and kind:
Heal the sick, the captive free;
Let us all rejoice in thee.

673 SEYMOUR. 7s.

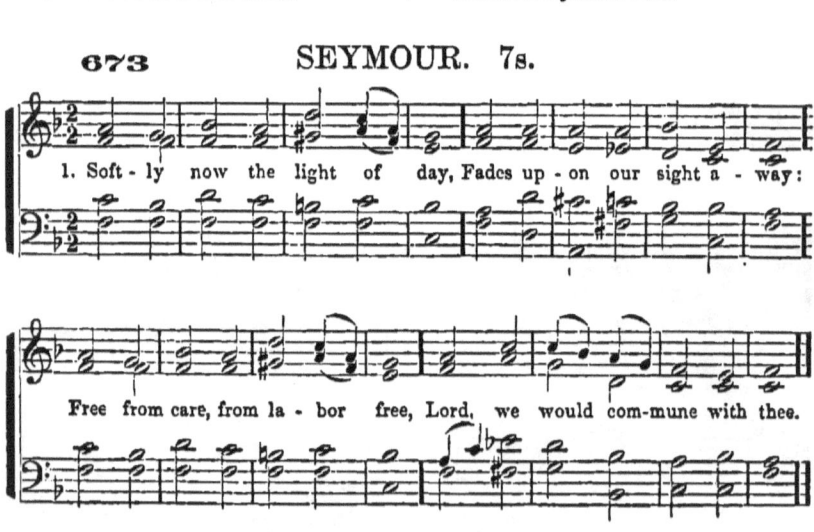

1. Softly now the light of day, Fades upon our sight away: Free from care, from labor free, Lord, we would commune with thee.

2 Soon from us the light of day
Shall forever pass away;
Then, from sin and sorrow free,
Take us, Lord, to dwell with thee.

674 WEBER. 8s & 7s.

1. Sweet the moments, rich in blessing, Which before the cross I spend; Life, and health, and peace possessing, From the sinner's dying Friend.

2 Truly blessed is this station,
  Low before his cross to lie;
  While I see divine compassion
  Beaming in his gracious eye.
3 Love and grief my heart dividing,
  With my tears his feet I'll bathe;
  Constant still, in faith abiding,
  Life deriving from his death.
4 May I still enjoy this feeling,
  In all need to Jesus go;
  Prove his wounds each day more healing,
  And himself more fully know.

675 TRUTH. 8s & 7s.

From "Voice of Praise."
By Permission.

1. Sweet the moments, rich in blessing, Which before the cross I spend; Life, and health, and peace possessing, From the sinner's dying Friend.

676 ITALIAN HYMN. 6s & 4s.

1. Glory to God on high! Let heav'n and earth reply!
"Praise ye his name!" His love and grace adore,
Who all our sorrows bore;
Sing aloud for evermore, Worthy the Lamb!

2 While they around the throne
Cheerfully join in one,
  Praising his name,—
Ye who have felt his blood
Sealing your peace with God,
Sound his dear name abroad,
  "Worthy the Lamb!"

3 Join, all ye ransomed race,
Our Lord and God to bless:
  Praise ye his name!
In him we will rejoice,
And make a joyful noise,
Shouting with heart and voice,
  "Worthy the Lamb!"

4 Soon we must change our place,
Yet will we never cease
  Praising his name:
To him our songs we bring;
Hail him, our gracious King;
And through all ages sing,
  "Worthy the Lamb!"

677 *"Let every thing that hath breath, praise the Lord."*

1 Praise ye Jehovah's name,
Praise through his courts proclaim;
  Rise and adore:
High o'er the heavens above
Sound his great acts of love,
While his rich grace we prove,
  Vast as his power.

2 Now let the trumpet raise
Sounds of triumphant praise,
  Wide as his fame:
There let the harp be found;
Organs, with solemn sound,
Roll your deep notes around,
  Filled with his name.

3 While his high praise ye sing,
Strike every sounding string;
  Sweet the accord!
He vital breath bestows;
Let every breath that flows,
His noblest fame disclose:
  Praise ye the Lord.

DOXOLOGIES.

L. M.
Praise God, from whom all blessings flow,
Praise him, all creatures here below;
Praise him above, ye heavenly host;
Praise Father, Son, and Holy Ghost.

L. M.
To God the Father, God the Son,
And God the Spirit, Three in One,
Be honor, praise, and glory given,
By all on earth, and all in heaven!

C. M.
To Father, Son, and Holy Ghost,
One God, whom we adore,
Be glory as it was, is now,
And shall be evermore!

C. M.
To Father, Son, and Holy Ghost,
Who sweetly all agree
To save a world of sinners lost,
Eternal glory be.

S. M.
To God, the Father, Son,
And Spirit, One in Three,
Be glory as it was, is now,
And shall forever be.

L. M. 6 lines.
Immortal honor, endless fame,
Attend th' Almighty Father's Name:
The Savior Son be glorified,
Who for lost man's redemption died;
And equal adoration be,
Eternal Comforter, to thee!

C. P. M.
To Father, Son, and Holy Ghost,
The God whom heaven's triumphant host,
And saints on earth adore;
Be glory as in ages past,
And now it is, and so shall last,
When time shall be no more.

H. M.
To God, the Father's throne,
Perpetual honors raise;
Glory to God, the Son,
And to the Spirit praise:
With all our powers, Eternal King,
Thy everlasting praise we sing.

7s.
Sing we to our God above
Praise eternal as his love;
Praise him, all ye heavenly host—
Father, Son, and Holy Ghost!

7s. 6 lines.
Praise the name of God most high;
Praise him all below the sky;
Praise him all ye heavenly host—
Father, Son, and Holy Ghost!
As through countless ages past,
Evermore his praise shall last.

8s & 7s.
Praise the God of our salvation,
Praise the Father's boundless love;
Praise the Lamb, our expiation;
Praise the Spirit from above;
Praise the Fountain of Salvation,
Him by whom our spirits live;
Undivided adoration
To the one Jehovah give!

8s, 7s & 4.
Great Jehovah, we adore thee,
God the Father, God the Son,
God the Spirit, joined in glory
On the same eternal throne;
Endless praises
To Jehovah, Three in One!

7s & 6s. Iambic.
To thee be praise forever,
Thou glorious King of kings;
Thy wond'rous love and favor
Each ransom'd spirit sings:
We'll celebrate thy glory,
With all thy saints above,
And shout the joyful story
Of thy redeeming love.

6s & 4s.
To God, the Father, Son,
And Spirit, Three in One,
All praise be given!
Crown him in every song;
To him your hearts belong:
Let all his praise prolong
On earth, in heaven!

INDEX OF FIRST LINES OF HYMNS.

	Page.
Abide with me fast falls the eventide	197
A charge to keep I have	104
According to thy gracious word	58
A fountain of life and of grace	168
Ah, whither should I go	117
Ah, how shall fallen man	117
Alas and did my Savior bleed	88, 225
All glory and praise	183
All hail the power of Jesus' name	86
All praise to our redeeming Lord	86
All thanks to the Lamb	183
All yesterday is gone	115
Almighty Maker, God	109
Am I a soldier of the cross	87
A mighty fortress is our God	264
And am I only born to die	135
And are we yet alive	126
And can it be that I should gain	128
And can I yet delay	105
And can my heart aspire so high	71
And let our bodies part	104
And must I be to judgment brought	84
And will the great Eternal	42
Angels from the realms of glory	155
Angels our march oppose	112
Another six days work is done	31
Appointed by thee we meet	183
Arise great God! and let thy grace	48
Arise, my soul, arise	136, 209
Arise, my soul, on wings sublime	47
Arise, my soul, to Pisgah's height	245
Arise, my soul, with rapture	38
Arm of the Lord, awake, awake	49
Arm me with thy whole armor	25
Ashamed to be a Christian	261
As pants the heart for cooling streams	80
As when the weary traveller gains	8
Author of faith, eternal Word	30
Author of faith, to Thee I cry	132
Author of faith, we seek Thy face	45
Awake and sing the song	118
Awake, my soul, and with the sun	43
Awake, my soul, stretch every nerve	65
Awake, ye saints, awake	138

	Page.
Awaked from sin's delusive sleep	7
Away with our sorrow and fear	169
Because for me the Savior prays	61
Before Jehovah's awful throne	28
Behold the morning sun	283
Behold the Savior of mankind	88
Behold the throne of grace	106
Being of beings, God of love	81
Bid me of men beware	111
Blest be the dear uniting love	52
Blest be the tie that binds	104
Blow ye the trumpet, blow	137
Brethren in Christ, and well beloved	29
Brief life is here our portion	177
Bright was the guiding star that led	52
Brightest and best of the sons of the morning	194
Broad is the road that leads to death	20
By faith I view my Savior	237
Called from above, I rise	108
Celestial dove come from on high	57
Centre of our hopes thou art	148
Children of the heavenly king	145
Christians, brethren, ere we part	144
Come all ye saints to Pisgah's	215
Come away to the skies	184
Come, come to Jesus	231
Come, Father, Son and Holy Ghost	3
Come hither all ye weary souls	37
Come Holy Ghost, inspire our songs	79
Come Holy Spirit, Heavenly dove	65
Come humble sinner in whose breast	89
Come let our souls adore the Lord	82
Come let us anew, our journey	186
Come let us ascend	184
Come let us join our cheerful songs	64
Come let us join our friends	101
Come let us join with one accord	64
Come let us tune our loftiest song	3
Come my soul thy suit prepare	142
Come, O my God the promise seal	71
Come O my soul in sacred lays	50

INDEX OF FIRST LINES OF HYMNS.   291

	Page.
Come, O thou greater than our heart	19
Come O thou traveller unknown	129
Come on my partners in distress	132
Come pilgrims, don't grow weary	241
Come said Jesus' sacred voice	141
Come Savior Jesus from above	9
Come sound his praise abroad	123
Come sinners, to the gospel feast	5
Come thou desire of all thy saints	95
Come thou everlasting Spirit	160
Come thou fount of every blessing.	161
Come thou omniscient Son of Man.	72
Come thou soul transforming Spirit	156
Come to Jesus	203
Come unto me when shadows	196
Come, weary sinners	116
Come, ye disconsolate	223
Come, ye sinners, poor and	156, 229
Come, ye that love the Lord	124
Consider all my sorrows, Lord	82
Daughter of Zion, from the dust	66
Day of God! thou blessed day	142
Dear Savior, if these lambs	8
Deathless spirit, now arise	151
Deepen the wound thy hands have	101
Depth of mercy! can there be	145, 225
Did Christ o'er sinners weep	105
Dread Jehovah! God of nations	165
Drooping souls no longer grieve	249
Early my God, without delay	57
Encompassed with clouds of distress	168
Enthroned on high, Almighty Lord	65
Enthroned is Jesus now	103
Eternal power whose high abode	28
Eternal source of joys divine	54
Eternal Spirit, God of truth	67
Except the Lord conduct the plan	134
Except the Lord our labor bless	14
Extended on a cursed tree	6
Fade, fade, each earthly joy	234
Far from my thoughts vain world	31
Far from these scenes of night	115
Father, how wide thy glory shines	76
Father, I dare believe	126
Father, I stretch my hands to thee	57, 83
Father, if I may call thee so	20
Father of Jesus Christ, my Lord	85
Father of mercies, send thy grace	99
Father, our hearts we lift	107
Forever here, my rest shall be	63
From all that dwell below the skies	28
From Calvary a cry was heard	16, 35
From every stormy wind that blows	13

	Page.
From Greenland's icy mountains	174
From the cross uplifted high	147
Give me the faith which can remove	47
Give me the wings of faith to rise	94
Give to the Father praise	105
Glorious things of Thee are spoken	164
Glory to God on high	288
Glory to the Almighty Father	164
Glory to Thee, my God, this night	26
Glory to thee, whose powerful	49
God in his earthly temple lays	19
God is gone up on high	139
God is my strong salvation	173
God is our refuge and defence	40
God is the refuge of his saints	37
God moves in a mysterious way	75
God of all consolation	175
God of eternal truth and grace	90
God of my life through all my days.	15
God of my life to thee belong	9
God of my life whose gracious	41
God of my strength, in thee	36
Grace, 'tis a charming sound	102
Gracious Spirit, love divine	143
Grant me within thy courts a place	77
Great God attend while Zion sings	5
Great God, beneath whose piercing	29
Great God, indulge my humble claim	10
Great God, let all our tuneful powers	51
Great God, now condescend	115
Great God, to me the sight afford	56
Great is the Lord our God	109
Great Jehovah, we adore thee	157
Great Ruler of the earth and skies	39
Great Shepherd of thy people, hear	100
Great source of being and of love	44
Great Spirit, by whose mighty power	67
Guide me, O thou great Jehovah	158
Hail thou once despised Jesus	159
Hail to the brightness of	195
Hail to the Lord's anointed	174
Hail to the Sabbath day	120
Happy the man who finds the grace.	11
Happy the souls to Jesus joined	89
Hark, a voice divides the sky	151
Hark, ten thousand harps and voices	163
Hark, the glad sound! the Savior.	97
Hark, the herald angels sing	154, 285
Hark, the notes of angels singing	163
Hark, what mean those holy voices.	164
Hasten, sinner, to be wise	144, 255
Head of the church triumphant	190
Hearts of stone, relent, relent!	146
Heavenly Father, sovereign Lord	144
He dies! the friend of sinners dies.	42

INDEX OF FIRST LINES OF HYMNS.

	Page
He leadeth me	240
He reigns, the Lord, the Savior	27, 33
Ho, every one that thirsts	14
Holy as thou, O Lord	27
Holy Lamb who thee receive	142
Holy Spirit, fount of blessing	161
Hosanna be the children's song	73
How beauteous are their feet.—Who stand	118
How blest the sacred tie that binds	280
How can a sinner know	119
How firm a foundation, ye saints	192
How gentle God's commands	102
How great the wisdom, power, and	54
How large the promise, how divine	85
How happy every child of grace	85
How pleasant, how divinely fair	46
How sad our state by nature is	63
How sweet the hour of closing day	280
How sweet the name of Jesus sounds	52
How sweetly flowed the gospel	14
How tedious and tasteless the hours	167
I am but a poor wayfarer	246
I am coming to the cross	233
If death our friends and us divide	135
If Lord, I have acceptance found	16
If on a quiet sea	114
If you cannot on the ocean	227
I have entered the valley	252
I hear the Saviour say	208
I know that my Redeemer lives	87
I lay my sins on Jesus	176
I listen for the voice	115
I long to behold him arrayed	168
I love thee, I love thee	228
I love the Lord: he heard my cries	75
I love thy kingdom, Lord	124
I love to steal awhile away	59, 99
I love to tell the story	201
I'm a lonely traveller here	247
I'm a pilgrim and a stranger	207
I'm but a stranger here	234
I need thee, precious Jesus	179
In every time and place	121
In every trying hour	120
In heavenly love abiding	178
In hope against all human hope	85
In mercy Lord remember me	81
In the Christian's home in glory	210
Into thy gracious hands I fall	51
I stood outside the gate	243
I want a heart to pray	116
I want a principle within	100
I was a wandering sheep	110
I will follow thee, my Saviour	251
I will sing for Jesus	204

	Page
I will sing you a song	226
I would not live alway	191
I have started for Canaan	239
Jerusalem, my happy home, Name ever	58
Jerusalem, my happy home, O how	69
Jerusalem, the golden	177
Jesus accept the praise	137
Jesus, all redeeming Lord	145
Jesus, and shall it ever be	39
Jesus, at whose supreme command	88
Jesus Christ, who stands between	117
Jesus, faithful to his word	171
Jesus, friend of sinners, hear	181
Jesus, great Shepherd of the sheep	63
Jesus hath died, that I might live	80
Jesus, I fain would find	121
Jesus, I fain would walk in thee	13
Jesus, if still thou art to-day	60
Jesus, I my cross have taken	162
Jesus, immortal king arise	97
Jesus, in whom but thee above	8
Jesus, in whom the God-head's	47
Jesus, kind, inviting Lord	144
Jesus, let thy pitying eye	180
Jesus, Lord of life and glory	166
Jesus, Lord we look to thee	141
Jesus, lover of my soul	152, 285
Jesus, my advocate above	22
Jesus my all to heaven is gone	11
Jesus, my life thyself apply	91
Jesus, my strength, my hope	111
Jesus, Redeemer, Saviour, Lord	74
Jesus shall reign where'er the sun	43
Jesus spreads his banner o'er us	160
Jesus, the Lamb of God	26
Jesus, the life, the truth, the way	78
Jesus, the Lord of glory died	100
Jesus, the name high over all	87, 244
Jesus, the sinner's friend to thee	7, 35
Jesus, the sinner's rest thou art	58
Jesus, the word bestow	109
Jesus, the word of mercy give	78
Jesus, the very thought of thee	98
Jesus, thine all victorious love	86, 94
Jesus, thou source divine	102
Jesus, thy boundless love to me	127
Jesus, thy church with longing eyes	42
Jesus, thy far extended fame	33
Jesus, thy wandering sheep	51
Jesus, to thee I now can fly	81
Jesus, united by thy grace	69, 81
Jesus, we bow before thy throne	29
Jesus, we look to thee	113
Jesus, where'er thy people meet	36
Joyfully, joyfully onward I move	212

INDEX OF FIRST LINES OF HYMNS.

	Page
Just as I am, without one plea	9
Land ahead its fruits are waving	205
Let all in whom the Spirit glows	64
Let every mortal ear attend	69
Let every tongue thy goodness speak	283
Let me go where saints are going	209
Let party names no more	120
Let worldly minds the world pursue	79
Let Zion's watchmen all awake	70
Lift up your hearts to things above	96
Lift your heads ye friends of Jesus	158
Light of the Gentile world appear	23
Light of those whose dreary dwelling	165
Listen to the gentle promptings	165
Lo! God is here, let us adore	128
Lo! he comes with clouds descending	157
Lo! on a narrow neck of land	133
Lo! round the throne	40
Lord, and is thine anger gone	181
Lord, at thy feet we sinners lie	61
Lord dismiss us with thy blessing	157, 160
Lord, how secure and blest are they	18
Lord, I am thine, entirely thine	4, 12
Lord, I approach the mercy seat	60
Lord, I believe thy every word	56
Lord, I delight in thee	284
Lord, I despair myself to heal	45
Lord, I have made thy word	62
Lord, if at thy command	120
Lord, in the morning thou shalt hear	78
Lord, in the strength of grace	122
Lord of hosts! to thee we raise	145
Lord of the Sabbath hear us pray	10
Lord of the wide extensive	40
Lord, we are vile, conceived in sin	6
Lord, we believe to us and ours	41
Lord, we come before thee now	286
Lord, when we bend before thy throne	62
Love divine, all love excelling	159
Lovers of pleasure more than God	62
Majestic sweetness sits enthroned	282
May I love thee, and adore thee	166
Meet and right it is to sing	171
Mercy alone, can meet my case	74
Mercy, O thou son of David	231
Mild scenes of confusion	239
Mortals awake	97
Must Jesus bear the cross alone	74
My country, 'tis of thee	187
My days are gliding swiftly by	213
My former hopes are fled	117
My faith looks up to thee	187
My God, how endless is thy love	16
My God, my God to thee	101
My God, my life, my love	107
My God, my portion, and my love	55
My God, the spring of all my joys	92
My gracious Lord, I own thy right	44
My gracious Redeemer, I love	169
My heavenly home is bright	216, 230
My hope, my all, my Savior thou	22
My Jesus, as thou wilt	263
My latest sun is sinking fast	211
My Maker, and my King	106
My opening eyes with rapture	44
My Saviour, my Almighty Friend	64
My Shepherd's mighty aid	188
My Shepherd will supply my need	93
My son, know thou the Lord	114
My soul before thee prostrate lies	22
My soul, be on thy guard	112
My soul, with humble fervor raise	32
Nearer, my God to thee	238
No mortal eye that land hath seen	254
Not here, as to the prophet's eye	25
Not to condemn the sons	33
Now be my heart inspired to sing	14
Now be the gospel banner	175
Now let my soul eternal King	43
Now thank we all our God	263
Now the Savior stands and pleading	238
Now to the haven of thy breast	74
O brother be faithful	208
O come and dwell in me	118
O come, loud anthems	33
O could I lose myself in thee	60
O could I speak the matchless	131
O deem not they are blest alone	17
O disclose thy lovely face	146
Of him who did salvation bring	18
O for a faith that will not shrink	72
O for a glance of heavenly day	32
O for a heart to praise my God	89
O for a thousand seraph tongues	87
O for a thousand tongues to sing	55, 244
O for an overcoming faith	90
O for that flame of living fire	4
O for that tenderness of heart	99
O glorious hope of perfect love	131
O God most merciful and true	11
O God, my God, my all thou art	44
O God, our help in ages past	91
O God, thou art my God alone	13
O God, what offering shall I give	127
O happy day that fixed my choice	17, 218
O happy, happy place	125
Oh blessed souls are they	114
Oh bless the Lord my soul	108
O how happy are they who	185

INDEX OF FIRST LINES OF HYMNS.

	Page.
O Jesus, at thy feet we wait	70
O King of glory, thy rich grace	19
O Lamb of God for sinners slain	133
O Lord, our fathers oft have told	76
O Lord, thy heavenly grace impart	10
O Lord, thy love's unbounded	179
O Lord, thy work revive	116
O Love divine, what hast thou done	130
O may thy powerful word	123
Once more my soul, the rising day	67
Once more we come before our God	92
One more day's work for Jesus	250
On Jordan's stormy banks I stand	68, 258
On the mountain's top appearing	158
O Savior welcome to my heart	54
O Spirit of the living God	25
O tell me no more of this world's vain store	206
O that my load of sin were gone	12
O that thou wouldst the heavens rend	77
O thou God of my salvation	155
O thou to whom in ancient time	25
O thou who all things canst control	32
O thou who camest from above	34
O thou who driest the mourner's tear	93
O thou who in the olive shade	82
O thou whom all thy saints adore	37
O thou whom fain my soul would	128
O thou who when we did complain	262
O 'tis delight without alloy	95
Our Heavenly Father, hear	121
Our Lord is risen from the dead	24
Out of the depths of woe	103
Out on an ocean all boundless	214
O what amazing words of grace	94
O what delight is this	122
O when shall I see Jesus	172
O when shall we sweetly remove	169
O where shall rest be found	105
O who'll stand up for Jesus	261
Pass a few swiftly fleeting years	35
Peace, troubled soul thou	34
Pilgrims, we are to Canaan bound	235
Praise the name of God most high	148
Praise to thee thou great Creator	161
Praise waits in Zion, Lord for thee	49
Praise ye Jehovah's name	288
Praise ye the Lord, 'tis good	38
Praise ye the Lord, ye immortal	97
Prayer is appointed to convey	31
Pray without ceasing, pray	112
Quickened with our immortal	34
Rejoice in Jesus' birth	119
Return my soul, enjoy thy rest	18

	Page
Return, O wanderer, return	59
Rise my soul, and stretch thy wings	170
Rock of ages, cleft for me	146
Roll on thou mighty ocean	175
Sad and weary with my longing	221
Safely through another week	148
Salvation! O the joyful sound	66
Savior, breathe an evening blessing	165, 246
Savior of all, to thee we bow	4
Savior of the sin-sick soul	149
Savior, see me from above	180
Savior, when in dust to thee	149
Savior, who thy flock art feeding	166
See how great a flame aspires	154
See the gospel Church secure	170
Servants of God, in joyful lays	50
Shall we gather at the river	219
Shepherd divine, our wants	98
Shepherd of souls, with pitying eye	12
Show pity, Lord, O Lord, forgive	21
Sing we the song of those who stand	56
Sing we, to our God above	149
Sinner, go, will you go	224
Sinners, lift up your hearts	139
Sinners, obey the gospel word	19
Sinners turn, while God is near	152
Sinners, turn, why will ye die	145
Sister thou wast mild and lovely	166
Softly now, the light of day	286
Softly sing when I am going	236
Soldiers of Christ, arise	123
Soldiers of Christ, lay hold	123
Soldiers on life's battle-field	255
Songs of praise the angels sang	143
Soon may the last glad song arise	24
Spirit, leave thy house of clay	151
Spirit of faith, come down	111
Stay, thou insulted Spirit, stay	21
Still for thy loving kindness, Lord	92
Sun of my soul, thou Saviour	7
Sweet hour of prayer	220
Sweet is the prayer, whose holy	93
Sweet is the time of spring	108
Sweet is the work, my God	5, 46
Sweet the moments, rich in	237
Sweet was the time when first I felt	70
Taught by our Lord, we will not	6
Tell me the old, old, story	200
Terrible thought, shall I alone	
Thank and praise Jehovah's name	
That awful day will surely come	
The Christian pilgrim sings	1
The day of wrath, that dreadful day	

INDEX OF FIRST LINES OF HYMNS.

First line	Page
Thee to laud, in songs divine	142
The glorious universe around	66
The God of Abraham, praise	189
The gospel, O what endless charms	55
The King of heaven, his table spreads	69
The King of saints, how fair his face	15
The long lost son with streaming	75
The Lord is my shepherd	193
The Lord is risen indeed	125
The Lord of earth and sky	139
The Lord of Sabbath let us praise	72
The morning flowers display	46
The morning light is breaking	172
The once loved form now cold	76
The saints who die of Christ	21
The spacious firmament on high	50
The Spirit in our hearts	119
The world is overcome	222
There are angels hovering round	224
There is a beautiful world	223
There is a fountain filled	58, 233
There is a glorious world of light	73
There is an hour of peaceful rest	59
There is a land of pure delight	68
There is a spot to me more dear	256
There is beauty all around	242
This day the Lord hath called his	98
This is thy will, I know	115
Thou art gone to the grave	248
Thou dear Redeemer, dying Lamb	53
Thou God of truth and love	136
Thou great mysterious God unknown	133
Though faint yet pursuing	191
Though I have grieved thy Spirit	20
Though nature's strength decay	188
Though now the nations sit	10
Thou Lamb of God, thou Prince	45
Thou Shepherd of Israel and mine	167
Thou that dost my life prolong	141
Thou very present aid	103
Thou very paschal Lamb	114
Thou whom my soul admires	15
Through this cold world alone	229
Thus far the Lord hath led me on	30
Thy loving Spirit, Lord	41
Thy name to me thy nature grant	67
Thy presence gracious God afford	3
Thy presence, Lord, the place	54
Thy word Almighty Lord	113
Time is winging us away	170
Times without number have I prayed	84
'Tis finished! the Messiah dies	45
To bless thy chosen race	107
To Father, Son and Holy Ghost	62
To God the Father's throne	138
To heaven I lift mine eyes	140
To Jesus, our exalted Lord	17
To thee be praise forever	175
To thee, my God, my Saviour	176
To thee, O God, when creatures	82
To the hall of the feast	206
To us a child of hope is born	95
To us a child of royal birth	43
Tremendous God with humble fear	23
Try us, O God, and search the ground	90
'Twas Jesus my Saviour	232
Unveil thy bosom, faithful tomb	21, 281
Vain, delusive world, adieu	181
Wake, O my soul, and hail	48
Watchman, tell us of the night	153
We're bound for the land of the	202
We're out on the ocean sailing	217
Weary souls that wander wide	147
We bring no glittering treasures	173
We by his Spirit prove	106
Weeping will not save me	253
We journey through a vale of tears	53
We know by faith, we know	122
Welcome delightful morn	138
Welcome sweet day of rest	125
We live as pilgrims and strangers	214
We may spread our couch with	228
We're travelling home to heaven	230
What am I, O, thou glorious God	30
What are those soul reviving strains	38
What heavenly music do I hear	196
What majesty and grace	126
What now is my object and aim	167
What poor despised company	222
What shall I do, my God to love	80
What various hindrances we meet	13
When faint and weary toiling	259
When first the Spirit left the throne	34
When God revealed his gracious	73, 77
When gracious Lord, when shall	41
When I can read my title clear	262
When Israel of the Lord beloved	39
When Israel trod the desert	27
When I survey the wondrous	35, 199
When I think of that city of light	257
When, my Saviour shall I be	141
When power divine	36
When rising from the bed of death	61, 84
When shall the voice of singing	175, 178
When shall we meet again	198
When streaming from the eastern	130
When thou my righteous Judge	134
When to the exiled seer	48
Where two or three with sweet	8
Wherewith O Lord shall I draw near	20
Which of the monarchs of the earth	79

INDEX OF FIRST LINES OF HYMNS.

	Page
While life prolongs its precious....	23
While we walk with God in light..	153
While with ceaseless course the sun	150
Whom man forsakes	7
Why do we mourn departed friends	83
Why, O my soul, O why depressed	91
Why should the children of a king..	83
Why should we start and fear......	36
With all my powers of heart	3
With joy we hail the sacred day....	92
With joy we meditate the grace....	282
With one consent let all the earth..	48
Within thy house, O Lord our God	71
Worship, and thanks and blessing..	190
Work for the night is coming	260
Ye Christian heralds, go proclaim..	40
Ye faithful souls who Jesus know..	26
Ye praying souls rejoice	284
Ye ransomed sinners hear.........	140
Ye servants of God................	182
Ye that pass by, behold the man...	21
Ye wretched starving poor........	113
Yes I will bless thee, O my God....	262
Yield to me now, for I am weak....	129

[See Page 304 for Index to Appendix.]

SELECTIONS FOR CHANTING.

	Page
As the hart panteth after the water brooks. Psa. XLII..................	269
Blessed are the dead, who die in the Lord. (Funeral)................	275
Blessed be the Lord God of Israel. Luke I. 68-71,	266
Gloria in Excelsis................	268
God be merciful unto us, and bless us. Psa. LXVII................	267
It is a good thing to give thanks unto the Lord. Psa. XCII	267
I will extol thee my God, O King. Psa. CXLV.	278
I will lift up mine eyes unto the hills. Psalm CXXI.................	273
Lord, let me know mine end. (Funeral.) Psa. XXXIX. and LXXX...........	274
O be joyful in the Lord, all ye lands Psa. C..	265
O clap your hands, all ye people. Psa. XLVII.	276
O come let us sing unto the Lord. Psa. XCV..	265
O Lord I will praise thee. Isa. XII......	276
O sing unto the Lord a new song. Psa. XCVI.	272
O sing unto the Lord a new song. Psa. XCVIII.	266
Praise the Lord, O my soul. Psa. CIII.....	268
The earth is the Lord's, and the fulness thereof. Psa. XXIV...............	270
The Lord is my light and my salvation. Psa. XXVII.................	270
The Lord is my Shepherd. Psa. XXIII. ...	278
The Lord is merciful and gracious. Psa. CIII.	271
The Lord reigneth, let the earth rejoice. PsA. XCVII.................	272
Who hath believed our report. Isa. LIII...	277

INDEX OF SUBJECTS.

Title	Page
INTRODUCTORY.	
All thanks to the Lamb	183
Another six days work is done	31
Appointed by thee we meet	183
Before Jehovah's awful throne	28
Being of beings God of love	81
Come let us join our cheerful songs	64
Come thou desire of all thy saints	95
Early my God without delay	57
Eternal power whose high abode	28
Glory to the almighty Father	164
Great God attend while Zion sings	5
Great Shepherd of thy people hear	100
Heavenly Father sov'reign Lord	144
How pleasant how divinely fair	46
Jesus we look to thee	113
Jesus where'er thy people meet	36
Lord we come before thee now	286
Lord when we bend before thy throne	62
Meet and right it is to sing	171
Not here as to the prophet's eye	25
O come loud anthems	33
Once more we come before our God	92
O thou to whom in ancient time	25
O thou whom all thy saints adore	37
Praise waits in Zion Lord for thee	49
Safely through another week	148
Thy presence gracious God afford	3
Welcome delightful morn	139
With joy we hail the sacred day	92
With one consent let all the earth	48
Within thy house O Lord our God	71
DIVINE PERFECTIONS.	
Almighty Maker God	109
Come O my soul in sacred	50
Father how wide thy glory	76
Great God to me the sight	66
Holy as thou O Lord	27
Let every tongue thy goodness speak	283
Lord of the wide extensive main	40
My Maker and my King	108
The spacious firmament on high	50
JESUS CHRIST.	
Incarnation.	
Angels from the realms of	155
Brightest and best of the sons of the morning	194
Father our hearts we lift	107
Hail to the Lord's annointed	174
Hark the glad sound the Savior	97
Hark! the herald angels sing	154
Hark what mean those holy	164
O Love divine what hast thou	130
Rejoice in Jesus' birth	110
To us a child of hope is born	95
To us a child of royal birth	43
Wake O my soul and hail	48
Death.	
Alas and did my Savior bleed	83, 225
Behold the Savior of mankind	88
Extended on a cursed tree	6
From Calvary a cry was heard	16 35
'Tis finished the Messiah dies	45
When I survey the wondrous cross	35, 199
Ye that pass by, behold the man	21
Resurrection and Ascension.	
God is gone up on high	139
Our Lord is risen from the dead	24
The Lord is risen indeed	125
The Lord of Sabbath let us praise	72
Exaltation and Intercession.	
All hail the power of Jesus' name	86
Enthroned is Jesus now	103
Glory to God on high	289
Hail thou once despised Jesus	159
Hark ten thousand harps	161
He dies the friend of sinners	42
I know that my Redeemer	87
Jesus Lord of life and glory	166
Jesus my advocate above	22
Jesus the Lord of glory died	100
Jesus thou source divine	102
The King of saints how fair	15
Thou very paschal Lamb	114
With joy we meditate the grace	232
THE HOLY GHOST.	
Come Holy Spirit, heavenly dove	65
Come Holy Ghost, inspire our songs	79
Enthroned on high, almighty Lord	65
Eternal Spirit, God of truth	67
God of all consolation	175
Gracious Spirit, love divine	143
Great Spirit by whose mighty	67
Holy Spirit fount of blessing	161
Lord we believe to us and ours	41
O Spirit of the living God	25
Sinners lift up your hearts	139
When first the Spirit left	34
INSTITUTIONS OF THE GOSPEL.	
The Ministry.	
And let our bodies part	104
Except the Lord conduct	134
Father of mercies send	99
How beauteous are their feet	118
Jesus, the name high over	87, 214
Jesus the word of mercy give	78
Jesus thy wandering sheep	51
Let Zion's watchmen all	70
Lord, if at thy command	120
O happy, happy place	125
The church.	
Daughter of Zion, from	66
Glorious things of thee are	164
God in his earthly temple lays	19
Great source of being and of	44
Hail to the brightness of	195
I love thy kingdom, Lord	124
See the gospel church secure	170
The Sabbath.	
Awake ye Saints, awake	138
Come, let us join with one	64
Day of God! thou blessed day	142
Far from my thoughts vain	31
Hail to the Sabbath day	120
Lord of the Sabbath, hear us	10
Return my soul enjoy thy rest	18
Sweet is the work, my God	5, 46
This day the Lord hath called	98
Welcome sweet day of rest	122

INDEX OF SUBJECTS.

Baptism.
	Page.
Celestial dove, come from on high	57
Come Father, Son and Holy	3
Dear Savior if these lambs	8
Great God now condescend	115
How large the promise, how divine	98
Jesus, kind inviting Lord	144
Savior who thy flock art feeding	166

Lord's Supper.
According to thy gracious	58
Called from above I rise	108
Come thou everlasting Spirit	100
Jesus all redeeming	145
Jesus at whose supreme	88
Jesus spreads his banner	160
O what delight is this	122
The King of heaven, his table	60
Thou whom my soul admires	15
To Jesus, our exalted Lord	17

SALVATION THROUGH CHRIST.
A fountain of life and of grace	168
Blow ye the trumpet, blow	137
By faith I view my Savior	237
Come ye disconsolate	223
Encompassed with clouds of	168
Grace 'tis a charming sound	102
Happy the man who finds	11
How firm a foundation	192
How great the wisdom, power	54
How sweetly flowed the gospel sound	14
I lay my sins on Jesus	176
I stood outside the gate	243
I was a wandering sheep	110
Jesus in whom but thee above	8
Jesus my all to heaven	11
Let every mortal ear attend	60
Majestic sweetness sits enthroned	282
Mercy, O thou Son of David	231
O what amazing words of	94
Rock of ages cleft for me	146
Sad and weary with my	221
Salvation, O the joyful sound	66
The gospel, O what endless	55
There is a fountain filled	58, 233
Thou very paschal Lamb	114
'Twas Jesus my Savior	232
Weeping will not save me	253
What majesty and grace	126
What shall I do my God to love	80

THE SINNER.
Character of.
Ah how shall fallen man	117
How sad our state by nature	63
Jesus, if still thou art to-day	29
Jesus thy far-extended fame	33
Lord we are vile, conceived in	6
My former hopes are fled	117

Warning and Inviting.
All yesterday is gone	115
Broad is the road that leads	20
Come, come to Jesus	231
Come hither all ye weary souls	37
Come humble sinner	89

	Page.
Come, said Jesus' sacred voice	141
Come sinners to the gospel	5
Come to Jesus	203
Come unto me when shadows	196
Come weary sinners	116
Come ye sinners poor	156, 229
Drooping souls no longer	240
From the cross uplifted high	147
Hasten sinner to be wise	144, 255
Hearts of stone, relent, relent	146
Ho, every one that thirsts	14
I've started for Canaan	230
Listen to the gentle promptings	165
Lovers of pleasure more than	62
My son know thou the Lord	114
Not to condemn the sons	33
Now the Savior stands and	238
O where shall rest be found	105
Return, O wanderer, return	50
Sinner go, will you go	224
Sinners, obey the gospel word	19
Sinners turn, while God is near	152
Sinners turn, why will ye die	145
Terrible thought shall I alone	60
The Spirit in our hearts	119
We are bound for the land of	202
We're travelling home to	230
Weary souls that wander wide	147
While life prolongs its precious	23
Ye wretched starving poor	113

DEVELOPMENT OF THE CHRISTIAN LIFE.
Repentance and Faith.
Ah, whither should I go	117
And can I yet delay	105
Author of faith to thee I cry	132
Awaked from sin's delusive	7
Because for me the Savior	61
Depth of mercy can there	145, 225
Did Christ o'er sinners weep	105
Father, if I may call thee so	20
Father, I dare believe	126
Father, I stretch my hands	57, 83
I am coming to the cross	233
Jesus, let thy pitying eye	180
Jesus, lover of my soul	152, 285
Jesus, Redeemer, Savior, Lord	74
Jesus, the sinner's friend	7, 35
Just as I am, without one plea	9
Light of the Gentile world	23
Light of those whose dreary dwelling	165
Lord at thy feet we sinners lie	61
Lord, I approach the mercy	60
Lord, I despair myself to heal	45
Mercy alone can meet my case	146
My soul before thee prostrate	22
O could I lose myself in thee	60
O disclose thy lovely face	146
O for a glance of heavenly day	32
O for that tenderness of heart	90
O Lamb of God for sinners	133
O that thou wouldst the heavens rend	77
O thou whom fain my soul would love	128
Out of the depths of woe	103
Savior, see me from above	180
Show pity, Lord, O Lord forgive	21
Stay thou insulted spirit, stay	21
Tell me the old, old story	200

	Page.
The long lost son with streaming eyes	75
Though I have grieved thy Spirit, Lord	20
When, gracious Lord, when	41
When rising from the bed of death	61, 84
Wherewith, O Lord, shall I	29
Whom man forsakes thou wilt	7

Justification and Regeneration.
And can it be that I should	128
Into thy gracious hands I fall	51
Jesus Christ who stands	147
Jesus the Lamb of God	26
Jesus to thee I now can fly	81
My God my God to thee	101
O how happy are they	185
O God most merciful and true	11
There is a spot to me more dear	256
To the hall of the feast came	206
What am I, O thou glorious	30
When God revealed his gracious	73, 77
When thou my righteous judge	134

Adoption and Assurance.
And can my heart aspire so high	71
Arise my soul arise	136, 209
Eternal source of joys divine	54
Great God indulge my humble	10
How can a sinner know	119
I listen for the voice	115
Lord how secure and blest are	18
Spirit of faith come down	111
Thou great mysterious God	133
We by his Spirit prove	106
Why should the children of a King	83

Growth in Grace.
Arise my soul on wings sublime	47
Ashamed to be a Christian	261
Author of faith eternal Word	30
Awake my soul stretch every	65
If Lord I have acceptance	16
In heavenly love abiding	178
Jesus and shall it ever be	39
Let wordly minds the world pursue	79
Lord I believe thy every word	56
My hope, my all, my Savior	22
My gracious Lord I own thy right	44
O brother be faithful	208
O for that flame of living fire	4
Still for thy loving kindness	92
This is thy will I know	115
To heaven I lift mine eyes	140
Vain delusive world	181
What now is my object and	167
Which of the monarchs of the earth	79
Ye faithful souls who Jesus	26

Consecration.
Fade fade, each earthly joy	234
Glory to thee whose powerful	49
I will follow thee my Savior	251
Jesus I my cross have taken	162
Lord I am thine entirely thine	4, 12

INDEX OF SUBJECTS.

	Page.
Lord in the strength of grace	122
Must Jesus bear the cross	74
Oh, blessed souls are they	114
O God what offering shall	127
O Lord thy heavenly grace	10
O Lord thy love's unbounded	179
O Savior, welcome to my	54
O who'll stand up for Jesus	281
Sweet the moments rich	287

Sanctification.

Come O my God the promise	71
Come O thou greater than our	19
Come Savior Jesus from	9
Come thou omniscient Son	72
Deepen the wounds thy hands	101
Forever here my rest shall be	63
God of eternal truth and grace	90
Holy Lamb who thee receive	142
I have entered the valley of	252
In hope against all human	85
Jesus hath died that I might	80
Jesus, my life thyself apply	85
Jesus, the sinner's rest thou art	58
Jesus, thine all victorious	86, 94
Jesus, thy boundless love	127
Love divine, all love excelling	159
O come and dwell in me	118
O for a heart to praise my God	89
O glorious hope of perfect love	131
O Jesus, at thy feet we wait	70
O that my load of sin were	12
Quickened with our immortal	34
Savior of the sin sick soul	149
Savior on me the grace	131
Thy loving spirit, Lord	41
Thy name to me thy nature	67
When my Savior shall I be	141

PHASES OF CHRISTIAN LIFE.

A Warfare.

Am I a soldier of the cross	87
Angels our march oppose	112
Arm me with thy whole armor	25
God is my strong salvation	173
My soul, be on thy guard	112
O, King of glory, thy rich	12
O, mny thy powerful word	128
O, when shall I see Jesus	172
Pray without ceasing, pray	112
Soldiers of Christ, arise	125
Soldiers of Christ lay hold	123
Soldiers o life's battle-field	255
When I can read my title clear	262

A Pilgrimage.

Children of the heavenly king	145
Guide me O, thou great	158
I am but a poor wayfarer	246
I'm a lonely traveller here	347
I'm a pilgrim and a stranger	237
I'm but a stranger here	234
I need thee, precious Jesus	179
In every time and place	121
My days are gliding swiftly by	213
Pilgrims, we are to Canaan	235
Rise, my soul	170
The Christian pilgrim sings	203
Through this cold world alone	229
We journey through a vale	53
We live as pilgrims and	214
We may spread our couch	228
What poor despised company	222

A Voyage.

	Page.
Land ahead its fruits are	205
Out on an ocean all boundless	214
We are out on the ocean	217

MEANS OF GRACE.

The Bible.

Bright was the guiding star	52
Jesus, the word bestow	109
Lord, I have made thy word	62
Now let my soul, eternal King	43
Thy word, Almighty Lord	113

Public and Social Prayer.

A charge to keep I have	104
Author of faith, we seek thy	45
Behold the throne of grace	106
Bid me of men beware	111
Come, my soul, thy suit	142
From every stormy wind that	13
I want a heart to pray	116
I want a principle within	100
Jesus, I fain would walk in	13
Jesus, I fain would find	121
Jesus, in whom the Godhead's	47
Jesus, my strength, my hope	111
Jesus the life, the truth	78
My faith looks up to thee	187
O, for a faith that will not	72
O Lord, thy work revive	116
O Thou who camest from	34
Our heavenly Father, hear	121
Prayer is appointed to convey	31
Savior, when in dust to thee	149
Shepherd divine, our wants	98
Sweet hour of prayer	220
Thy presence Lord, the place	54
What various hindrances we	13
Where two or three with	8

Family Devotion.

Arise my soul with rapture	38
Awake my soul and with the	43
Except the Lord our labors	14
Glory to thee, my God this	25
God of my life to thee belong	9
If death, our friends and us	135
In mercy Lord, remember me	81
Lord, in the morning thou	78
My God, how endless is thy	10
My opening eyes with rapture	44
O God, my God, my all	44
Once more my soul the rising	67
One more day's work for	259
O thou, who in the olive shade	82
Savior, breathe an	105, 246
Softly, now the light of day	283
Sun of my soul, thou Savior	7
Taught by our Lord, we will	6
There is beauty all around	242
Thou, that dost my life	141
Thus far the Lord hath led	30
When streaming from the	130

Closet.

Come, O thou traveller	129
Deathless Spirit now arise	151
Father of Jesus Christ	85
Give me the faith which can	47
I love to steal awhile away	59, 99
Sweet is the prayer, whose	93
Yield to me now for I am	129

CHRISTIAN FELLOWSHIP.

	Page.
All praise to our redeeming	86
Blest be the tie that binds	104
Brethren in Christ and	29
Centre of our hopes thou art	148
Come let us join our friends	101
How blest the sacred tie	289
Jesus, great Shepherd of	63
Jesus Lord, we look to thee	141
Jesus, united by thy grace	69, 81
Let all in whom the spirit	64
Let party names no more	120
Lift up your hearts to things	96
Mid scenes of confusion	239
Savior of all, to thee we bow	4
The glorious universe around	66
Thou God of truth and love	136
Try us, O God, and search	90
When shall we meet again	198
While we walk with God in light	153

UNFAITHFULNESS LAMENTED.

As pants the hart for cooling	80
Jesus, friend of sinners hear	181
Lord and is thy anger gone	181
O thou, who all things canst	32
Sweet was the time when first	70
Times without number have I	84

PATIENCE AND SUBMISSION.

God moves in a mysterious	75
Grant me within thy courts	77
How gentle God's commands	102
If on a quiet sea	114
If you cannot on the ocean	227
My Jesus as thou wilt	263
O deem not they are blest	17
Thou Lamb of God	45
We journey through a vale	53
When my Savior shall I be	141
When power divine	36
Why, O my soul, O why	91

DEFENCE AND DELIVERANCE.

A mighty fortress is our God	264
Consider all my sorrows, Lord	82
God is our refuge and defence	40
God is the refuge of his saints	37
God of my life whose gracious	41
God of my strength	36
He leadeth me	240
I love the Lord, he heard	75
In every trying hour	120
My Shepherd's mighty aid	188
Now to the haven of thy breast	74
O thou who driest the	93
O thou, who when we did	262
Peace troubled soul thou	34
Sad and weary with	221
The Lord is my shepherd	193
Thou very present aid	103
When Israel, of the Lord	39

PRAISE.

And are we yet alive	126
All glory and praise to Jesus our Lord	183
Awake and sing the song	118
Come away to the skies	184
Come let us tune our loftiest	3
Come sound His praise	123
Come thou fount of every	161

INDEX OF SUBJECTS.

	Page.		Page.		Page.
Come ye that love the Lord	124	As when the weary traveller	8	Jesus faithful to his word	171
From all that dwell below the	28	Away with our sorrow and	169	Lift up your heads ye friends	158
Glory to God on high	288	Brief life is here our portion	177	Lo! he comes with clouds	157
Great God let all our tuneful	51	Come all ye saints to Pisgah's	215	That awful day will surely	84
Hark the notes of angels	183	Come let us ascend	184	The day of wrath that	21
Head of the church	190	Come on my partners	132		
How sweet the name of Jesus	52	Come pilgrims	241	**MISSIONARY.**	
I hear the Savior say	208	Far from these scenes	115		
I love thee, I love thee	228	Give me the wings of faith	94	Arise great God and let	48
I love to tell the story	201	Happy the souls to Jesus joined	83	Arm of the Lord, awake	24
I will sing for Jesus	204	I long to behold him arrayed	168	From Greenland's icy	174
Jesus the very thought of thee	98	In the Christian's home	210	Jesus immortal King arise	97
Lo! God is here, let us adore	128	I will sing you a song of	220	Jesus shall reign where'er the	43
Mortals awake	97	I would not live alway	191	Jesus thy church with	42
My gracious Redeemer	169	Jerusalem my happy home	53	Jesus we bow before	29
My Savior, my Almighty	64	Jerusalem my happy home, O	69	Now be the gospel banner	175
My soul with humble fervor	32	Jerusalem the golden	177	On the mountain's top	158
Now be my heart inspired to	14	Joyfully, joyfully onward	212	Praise ye Jehovah's name	288
Now thank we all our God	263	Let me go where saints	239	Roll on thou mighty ocean	175
Of him who did salvation	18	Lo round the throne	49	See how great a flame aspires	154
O for a thousand tongues	55, 244	My heavenly home	216, 230	Shepherd of souls with	12
O God, thou art my God alone	13	My latest sun is sinking fast	211	Soon may the last glad song	24
O happy day that fixed	17, 218	No mortal eye that land	254	The morning light is breaking	172
Oh bless the Lord, my soul	108	On Jordan's stormy banks	68, 238	Though now the nations sit	10
Oh for a thousand seraph	87	O tell me no more of this	206	To bless thy chosen race	107
Praise to thee, thou great	161	O when shall we sweetly	160	Watchman tell us of the night	153
Praise ye Jehovah's name	288	There is a beautiful world	223	When shall the voice of	175, 178
Praise ye the Lord, 'tis good	38	There is a land of pure delight	68	Work for the night is	260
Praise ye the Lord	97	There is an hour of peaceful	61	Ye Christian heralds go	40
Servants of God in joyful lays	50	Though faint yet pursuing	191		
Shall we gather at the river	219	Though nature's strength	188	**SUNDAY SCHOOL.**	
Sing we the song of those who	56	We know by faith, we know	122		
Songs of praise the angels	143	When faint and weary	259	Hosanna be the children's	73
Thank and praise Jehovah's	143	When I think of that city of	257	Sweet is the time of spring	108
Thee to laud in songs divine	142			There is a glorious world of	73
The God of Abrah'm praise	189	**TIME AND ETERNITY.**		We bring no glittering	173
The world is overcome	222				
There are angels hovering	224	Come let us anew our journey	186	**MISCELLANEOUS.**	
Thou dear Redeemer, dying	53	Lo on a narrow neck of land	133		
To thee my God, my Savior	176	O God our help in ages past	91	*Erection and Dedication of Churches.*	
What are those soul reviving	53	Pass a few swiftly fleeting	35		
What heavenly music	196	Spirit, leave thy house of clay	151	And will the great eternal	42
With all my powers of heart	3	The Lord of earth and sky	139	Great is the Lord our God	109
Worship and thanks and	190	Time is winging us away	170	Lord of hosts to thee we raise	145
Ye praying souls rejoice	284	Tremendous God with humble	23	When Israel trod the desert	27
Ye ransomed sinners hear	140	While with ceaseless course	150	When to the exiled seer	48
Ye servants of God	182				
Yes I will bless thee, O my God	262	**DEATH AND RESURRECTION.**		*Public Fasts.*	
		And am I only born to die	135		
COMMUNION WITH GOD.		Hark a voice divides the sky	151	Come let our souls adore	82
Abide with me, fast falls the	197	How sweet the hour of closing	280	Dread Jehovah! God of	165
God of my life, through all my	15	O for an overcoming faith	90		
How tedious and tasteless	167	Sister thou was mild and	166	*Our Country.*	
Lord I delight in thee	284	Softly sing when I am going	236		
May I love thee and adore thee	166	The morning flowers display	46	Great God beneath whose	29
My God, my life, my love	107	The once loved form now cold	76	Great Ruler of the earth	39
My God, my portion and	55	The saints who die of Christ	21	My country 'tis of thee	187
My God, the spring of all	92	Thou art gone to the grave	248	O Lord our fathers oft save	76
My Shepherd's mighty aid	188	To thee O God when	62		
My Shepherd will supply my	93	Unveil thy bosom	21, 281	*Parting.*	
Nearer my God to thee	238	Why do we mourn departed	83		
O thou God of my salvation	155	Why should we start and fear	36	Blest be the dear uniting love	52
O 'tis delight without alloy	95			Christians, brethren ere we	144
Thou Shepherd of Israel	167	**JUDGMENT.**		Come thou soul transforming	156
				Jesus accept the praise	137
PROSPECTS AND ASSOCIATIONS OF HEAVEN.		And must I be to judgment	84	Lord dismiss us with thy	157, 160
Arise my soul to Pisgah's	245	He reigns the Lord	27, 33	DOXOLOGIES	299

GENERAL INDEX OF TUNES.

	Page
Adoration	159
Alas and did my Saviour	225
All Saints	48
America	187
Ames	19
A Mighty Fortress	264
Amsterdam	170
Angels hovering 'round	224
Antioch	96
Ariel	131
Arlington	98
Athol	126
Autumn	160
Aylesbury	117
Azmon	71

B.

Bach	61
Baden	114
Baker	115
Balerma	89
Barby	76
Bartimeus	231
Bava	4
Beethoven	171
Benevento	158
Bethany	238
Boylston	105
Brentford	14
Bridgewater	5
Broomsgrove	85
Burford	82

C.

Cambridge	66
Carmarthen	209
China	83
Choral	263
Christmas	92
Christmas Hymn	154
Cleansing Fountain	233
Clinging to the Cross	221
Communion	88
Come, let us anew	136
Come to Jesus	203
Come ye Disconsolate	223
Concord	124
Contrast	167
Corinth	90
Coronation	86
Cowper	58
Cross and Crown	74
Crucifixion	35

D.

Darwell	139
David	168
Dedham	70
Dennis	102

	Page
Depth of Mercy	225
Devizes	64
Dover	109
Dresden	230
Dunne Street	11
Duke Street	42
Dunbar	229
Dundee	62
Dunfermline	77
Durbin	161

E.

Easton	17
Effingham	44
Eisenach	3
Emmons	53
Entreaty	238
Epsilon	111
Evan	81
Evening Hymn	26
Eventide	197
Ewer	233
Ewing	177
Exhortation	68

F.

| Federal Street | 16 |
| Forest | 41 |

G.

Gabriel	234
Ganges	133
Glory to the Lamb	222
Going Home	258
Golden Hill	103
Go Work in my Vineyard	227
Grace Church	47
Grant	162
Greenville	156

H.

Hamburg	6
Hail to the Brightness	195
Hanover	194
Happy Day	218
Happy Dying	226
Harwell	163
Haydn	234
Haydn's Hymn	155
Heber	73
Hebron	30
He Leadeth Me	210
Hendon	142
Henley	196
Home Beyond the Tide	217
Home of the Soul	226
Homeward Bound	214
Hope	132
Horton	141
Howard	94

	Page
Hursley	7
Hymn	80

I.

I am trusting Lord in Thee	233
I Love Thee	228
I long to be there	257
I love to tell the story	201
I'm Going Home	230
Invocation	235
Iosco	39
Italian Hymn	288
I will follow Thee	251
I will sing for Jesus	204

J.

Jesus paid It All	208
Jesus waits for Thee	231
Joy	170
Joyfully, Joyfully	212

K.

| Kentucky | 104 |
| Kingsley | 191 |

L.

Laban	113
Lanesboro'	56
Lebanon	110
Lenox	136
Let me Go	209
Life's Battlefield	255
Lights along the Shore	207
Lisbon	125
Lischer	138
Litany Hymn	149
Lonely Traveller	247
Love at Home	242
Ludwig	236
Luton	50
Lyons	182

M.

Manoah	233
Magdalena	179
Marlow	57
Martyn	152
Magdalen	206
Mear	75
Melcombe	9
Melody	72
Meribah	134
Messiah	292
Migdol	24
Miller	10
Missionary Chant	40
Missionary Hymn	174
Monmouth	27
Mercy's Free	237
Mornington	106

GENERAL INDEX OF TUNES.

Name	Page	Name	Page	Name	Page
Mozart	235	Rothwell	38	The Sinner invited	224
Mt. Vernon	166	Rowley	184	Thompson	190
Munich	173	Royal way of the cross	228	Toplady	146
Murray	135	Russia	22	Truro	49
				Truth	237
N.		**S.**		Turner	65
Naomi	60	Sabbath Morn	148	Turn to the Lord	229
Nashville	127	Safe within the vail	205		
None but Jesus	233	Salvation	240	**U.**	
Northfield	55	Scotland	248	Union	262
Notting Hill	93	Seasons	16	Unity	198
Nuremberg	143	Seir	118	Unveil thy bosom	281
		Sessions	12	Uxbridge	25
O.		Seymour	236		
Oak	234	Shall we gather at the river	219	**V.**	
O Brother be Faithful	238	Shining shore	213	Valley of blessing	252
O how I Love Jesus	244	Shirland	107		
Old Hundred	28	Sicily	157	**W.**	
Olmutz	116	Silver street	123	Ward	34
Olney	110	Simpson	139	Walmisley	169
One more day's work for Jesus	250	Stafford	122	Ware	32
Ortonville	52	St. Ann	93	Warren	46
Osgood	230	Stephens	79	Warwick	78
Our loved ones in heaven	215	Sterling	33	Watchman	153
Outside the gate	213	St. Martin	54	Webb	172
		St. Michael	121	Weber	237
P.		St. Petersburg	130	We'll walk through the valley	215
Paddington	112	St. Stephens	128	We'll wait till Jesus comes	216
Park Street	43	St. Thomas	120	Wells	23
Parsons	63	Stonefield	29	Welton	51
Penitence	180	Sweet Hour of Prayer	220	Who'll stand up for Jesus	261
Peterboro'	67	Sweet Rest in Heaven	241	Wilmot	164
Phurah	100			Will you go	230
Pilesgrove	31	**T.**		Windham	20
Pleyel's Hymn	144	Tallis	91	Windsor	84
Portland	138	Talmar	165	Woodland	59
Portuguese	192	Tamar	101	Woodworth	8
Precious Jesus	246	Thatcher	108	Work for the night	260
Prospect	140	The Christian Pilgrim	203	World of light	223
		The Cross	199	Wrestling Jacob	129
R.		The Eden above	202		
Rapture	185	The Fountain of Mercy	232	**Y.**	
Refuge	37	The Hallowed Spot	236	Yarmouth	178
Rest for the weary	210	The Jubilee	196		
Resting by and by	239	The Land beyond the River	254	**Z.**	
Retreat	13	The Land of Beulah	211	Zephyr	36
Rockingham	18	The old, old story	200	Zerah	95
Rosedale	45	The Pilgrims	222	Zion	158
Rosefield	147	The Saint's Home	239	Zion's Pilgrim	235

[See page 304 for *Index to Appendix.*]

METRICAL INDEX.

L. M.

	Page
All Saints	48
Ames	19
Bava	4
Brentford	14
Bridgewater	5
Crucifixion	35
Dresden	280
Duane Street	11
Duke Street	42
Easton	17
Effingham	44
Eisenach	3
Evening Hymn	26
Federal Street	16
Forest	41
Grace Church	47
Hamburg	6
Hebron	30
Hursley	7
Iosco	39
Luton	50
Melcombe	9
Migdol	24
Miller	10
Missionary Chant	40
Monmouth	27
Old Hundred	28
Osgood	280
Park Street	43
Pilesgrove	31
Refuge	37
Retreat	13
Rockingham	18
Rosedale	45
Rothwell	38
Russia	22
Seasons	15
Sessions	12
Sterling	33
Stonefield	29
Sweet hour of prayer	250
Truro	49
Uxbridge	25
Unveil thy bosom	281
Ward	34
Ware	32
Warren	46
Wells	23
Welton	51
Windham	20
Woodworth	8
Zephyr	36
Zion's Pilgrim	235

C. M.

	Page
Alas and did my Savior	225
Antioch	96
Arlington	98
Azmon	71
Bach	61
Balerma	89
Barby	76
Broomsgrove	85
Burford	82
Cambridge	66
China	83
Christmas	92
Communion	88
Corinth	99
Coronation	86
Cowper	58
Cross and Crown	74
Dedham	70
Devizes	64
Dundee	62
Dunfermline	77
Emmons	53
Evan	81
Exhortation	68
Heber	73
Howard	94
Hymn	80
Lanesboro'	56
Manoah	283
Marlow	57
Mear	75
Melody	72
Messiah	282
Naomi	60
Northfield	55
Notting Hill	93
Ortonville	52
Parsons	63
Peterboro'	67
Phuvah	100
St. Ann	90
Stephens	79
St. Martin	54
Tallis	91
Tamar	101
Turner	65
Union	262
Warwick	78
Windsor	84
Woodland	59
Zerah	95

S. M.

	Page
Athol	126
Aylesbury	117
Baden	114
Baker	115
Boylston	105
Concord	124
Dennis	102
Dover	109
Epsilon	111
Ewer	283
Gabriel	284
Golden Hill	103
Haydn	214
Kentucky	104
Laban	113
Lebanon	110
Lisbon	125
Mornington	106
Olmutz	116
Olney	119
Paddington	112
Seir	118
Shirland	107
Silver Street	123
Stafford	122
St. Michael	121
St. Thomas	120
Thatcher	108

L. P. M.

	Page
Nashville	127
St. Stephens	128
St. Petersburg	130
Wrestling Jacob	129

C. P. M.

	Page
Ariel	131
Ganges	133
Hope	132
Meribah	134
Murray	135

H. M.

	Page
Darwell	139
Lenox	136
Lischer	138
Prospect	140

7s.
7s six lines.

	Page
Rosefield	147
Sabbath Morn	148
Toplady	146

7s.

	Page
Hendon	142
Horton	141
Invocation	285
Ludwig	236
Mozart	235
Nuremburg	143
Pleyel's Hymn	144
Seymour	236

7s Double.

	Page
Benevento	150
Christmas Hymn	154
Litany Hymn	149
Martyn	152
Watchman	153

METRICAL INDEX.

8s, 7s & 4s.
Adoration 159
Greenville 156
Haydn's Hymn 155
Sicily 157
Zion 158

8s & 7s Double.
Autumn 160
Durbin 161
Grant 162
Harwell 163

8s & 7s Single.
Mt. Vernon 166
Talmar 165
Truth 287
Wilmot 164
Weber 287

8s.
Contrast 167
David 168
Walmisley 169

7s & 6s (Iambic).
Ewing 177
Joy 176
Magdalena 179
Missionary Hymn 174
Munich 173
Webb 172
Yarmouth 178

7s & 6s (Trochaic.)
Amsterdam 170
Beethoven 171

7s, 6s & 8s.
Penitence 180

5s & 6s.
Lyons 182

6s & 9s.
Rowley 184
Rapture 185

10s & 11s.
Come let us anew 186

6s & 4s.
America 187

Bethany 233
Oak 234
Italian Hymn 288

6s, 8s & 4s.
Portland 189
Simpson 180

7s, 8s & 7s
Thompson 198

11s.
Kingsley 191
Portuguese 192

10s & 11s.
Hanover 194

11s & 10s.
Come ye disconsolate . . . 223
Hail to the brightness . . . 195
Henley 196

10s.
Eventide 197

6s & 5s.
Uulty 198

ADDITIONAL P. M.
A mighty fortress is our God 264
Bartimeus 231
Carmarthen 209
Cleansing Fountain 233
Clinging to the Cross . . . 221
Come to Jesus 203
Depth of Mercy 225
Dunbar 229
Entreaty 238
Glory to the Lamb 222
Going Home 258
Go work in my vineyard . 227
Happy day 218
Happy dying 236
He leadeth me 240
Home beyond the tide . . 217
Home of the soul 226
Homeward bound 214
I am trusting Lord in thee . 233
I long to be there 257
I love thee 228
I love to tell the story . . 201

I'm going home 230
I will follow thee my Saviour 251
I will sing for Jesus 204
Jesus paid it all 208
Jesus waits for thee 231
Joyfully, joyfully onward . 212
Let me go 209
Life's battle field 255
Lights along the shore . . 207
Lonely traveller 247
Love at home 242
Magdalen 206
Mercy's free 237
None but Jesus 253
Now praise we all our God 263
O brother be faithful . . . 208
O how I love Jesus 244
One more day's work for Jesus 250
Our loved ones in heaven . 215
Outside the gate 243
Precious Jesus 246
Rest for the weary 210
Resting by and by 259
Royal way of the Cross . . 228
Safe within the vail 205
Salvation 249
Scotland 248
Shall we gather at the river 219
Shining Shore 213
Sweet Rest in Heaven . . 241
The cross 199
The Christian Pilgrim . . . 203
The Eden above 202
The Fountain of Mercy . . 232
The Hallowed Spot 256
The Jubilee 196
The land beyond the river . 254
The land of Beulah 211
The old, old story 200
The Pilgrims 222
There are angels hovering
  round 224
The saint's home 239
The sinner invited 224
Turn to the Lord 229
Valley of blessing 252
We'll wait till Jesus comes 216
We'll walk through the valley 245
Who'll stand up for Jesus . 261
Will you go 230
Work for the night is coming 260
World of Light 223

APPENDIX.

All is well 6

Jesus loves even me 5

O, sing of his mighty love 3

The Great Physician 2

The Lord will provide 4

The precious blood 1

THE PRECIOUS BLOOD.

Arranged. Music and Chorus by Rev. J. H. STOCKTON.

1. The cross! the cross! the blood-stain'd cross! The hal-low'd cross I see! Re-

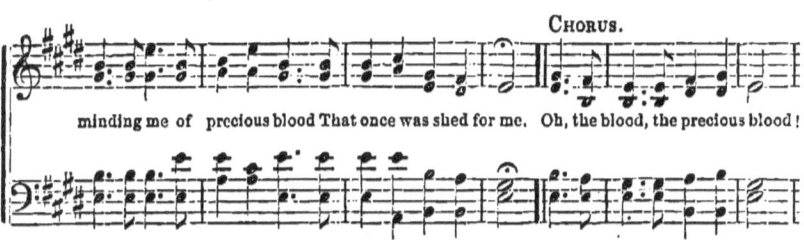

minding me of precious blood That once was shed for me. Oh, the blood, the precious blood!

That Je-sus shed for me, Up -on the cross, in crimson flood, Just now by faith I see.

2 A thousand, thousand fountains spring
    Up from the throne of God;
  But none to me such blessings bring,
    As Jesus' precious blood. CHORUS.

3 That priceless blood my ransom paid,
    While I in bondage stood;
  On Jesus all my sins were laid,
    He saved me with his blood. CHORUS.

4 By faith that blood now sweeps away
    My sins, as like a flood:
  Nor lets one guilty blemish stay:
    All praise to Jesus' blood. CHORUS.

5 This wond'rous theme will best employ
    My harp before my God,
  And make all heaven resound with joy,
    For Jesus' cleansing blood. CHORUS.

THE GREAT PHYSICIAN.

Arranged by Rev. J. H. STOCKTON. Harmonized by L. F. SNOW.

1. The great Phy-si-cian now is near, The sym-pa-thi-zing Je-sus,
He speaks the drooping heart to cheer, Oh hear the voice of..........

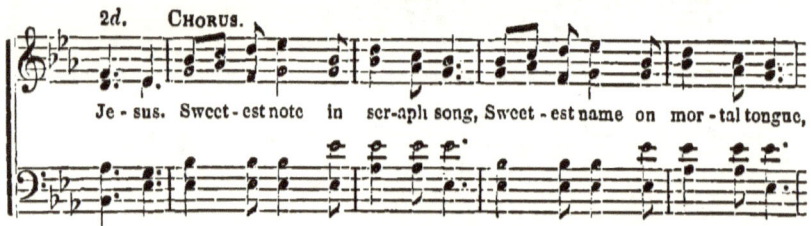

Je-sus. Sweet-est note in ser-aph song, Sweet-est name on mor-tal tongue,

Sweet-est car-ol ev-er sung, Je-sus, Je-sus, Je-sus.

2 Your many sins are all forgiven,
  Oh! hear the voice of Jesus:
Go on your way in peace to heaven,
  And wear a crown with Jesus.
      Cho.—Sweetest note, &c.

3 All glory to the dying Lamb,
  I now believe in Jesus:
I love the blessed Saviour's name,
  I love the name of Jesus.
      Cho.—Sweetest note, &c.

4 His name dispels my guilt and fear,
  No other name but Jesus:
Oh! how my soul delights to hear
  The charming name of Jesus.
      Cho.—Sweetest note, &c.

5 Come brethren, help me sing his praise,
  Oh! praise the name of Jesus:
And, sisters, all your voices raise,
  Oh! bless the name of Jesus.
      Cho.—Sweetest note, &c.

6 The children, too, both great and small,
  Who love the name of Jesus:
May now accept the gracious call,
  To work and live for Jesus.
      Cho.—Sweetest note, &c.

7 And when to that bright world above
  We rise to see our Jesus,
We'll sing around the throne of love,
  The name, the name of Jesus.
      Cho.—Sweetest note, &c.

O SING OF HIS MIGHTY LOVE.

By permission of Biglow & Main.
Words by Rev. F. BOTTOME.
Music by W. B. BRADBURY.

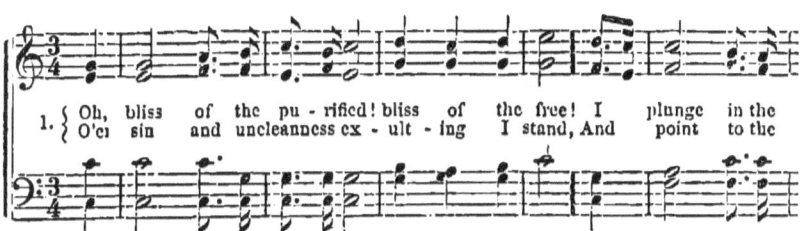

1. Oh, bliss of the pu-rified! bliss of the free! I plunge in the
   O'er sin and uncleanness ex-ult-ing I stand, And point to the

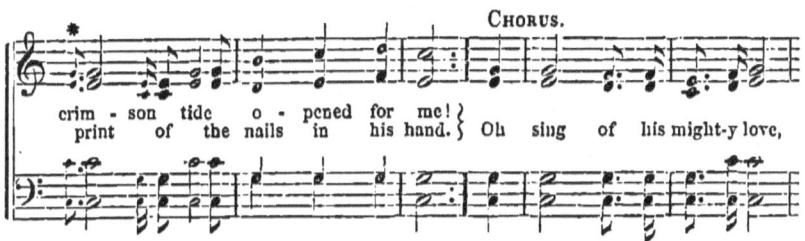

crim-son tide o-pened for me!
print of the nails in his hand.
Oh sing of his might-y love,

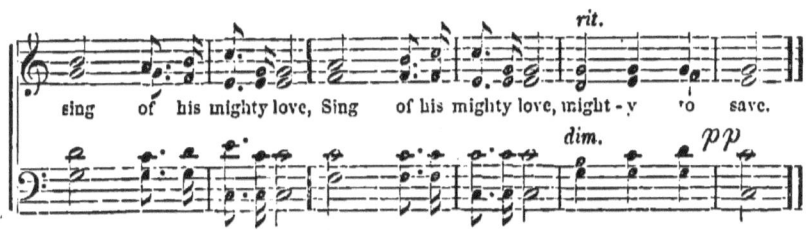

sing of his mighty love, Sing of his mighty love, might-y to save.

2 Oh, bliss of the purified! Jesus is mine,
No longer in dread condemnation I pine;
In conscious salvation I sing of his grace,
Who lifteth upon me the smiles of his face!

3 Oh, bliss of the purified! bliss of the pure!
No wound hath the soul that his blood cannot cure;
No sorrow-bowed head but may sweetly find rest,—
No tears but may dry them on Jesus' breast.

4 O Jesus the Crucified! thee will I sing!
My blessed Redeemer! my God and my King!
My soul filled with rapture shall shout o'er the grave,
And triumph in death in the Mighty to save.

* Sing the small notes to the first line only.

THE LORD WILL PROVIDE.

Prof. S. C. Harrington.

2 At some time or other the Lord will provide;
　　It may not be *my* time,
　　It may not be *thy* time,
　　And yet, in his *own* time,
　　　"The Lord will provide."

3 Despond then no longer; the Lord will provide;
　　And this be the token —
　　No word he hath spoken
　　Was ever yet broken, —
　　　"The Lord will provide."

4 March on, then, right boldly; the sea shall divide;
　　The pathway made glorious,
　　With shoutings victorious,
　　We'll join in the chorus,
　　　"The Lord will provide."

JESUS LOVES EVEN ME.

Permission of JOHN CHURCH & Co. Words and Music by P. P. BLISS.

1. I am so glad that our Father in Heav'n
Wonderful things in the Bible I see,
Tells of his love in the Book he has giv'n;
This is the dearest,— that Jesus loves me.

CHORUS.
I am so glad that Jesus loves me, Jesus loves me, Jesus loves me,

I am so glad that Jesus loves me, Jesus loves even me.

2 Though I forget him, and wander away,
Kindly he follows wherever I stray;
Back to his dear, loving arms would I flee,
When I remember that Jesus loves me.
CHORUS.

3 Oh, if there's only one song I can sing,
When in his beauty I see the great King,
This shall my song in eternity be,—
O, what a wonder that Jesus loves me.
CHORUS.

ALL IS WELL.

1. What's this that steals, that steals upon my frame, Is it death? Is it death?
That soon will quench, will quench this vital flame, Is it death? Is it........death?
If this be death, I soon shall be From ev'-ry pain and sor-row free,
I shall the King of glo-ry see, All is well, all is well.

2 Weep not, my friends, my friends, weep not for me,
 All is well, all is well.
My sins are pardoned, pardoned, I am free,
 All is well, all is well.
  There's not a cloud that doth arise,
  To hide my Saviour from my eyes,
  I soon shall mount the upper skies,
  All is well, all is well.

3 Tune, tune your harps, your harps, ye saints in glory,
 All is well, all is well.
I will rehearse, rehearse the pleasing story,
 All is well, all is well.
  Bright angels are from glory come,
  They're round my bed, they're in my room,
  They wait to waft my spirit home,
  All is well, all is well.

GOD IS LOVE.

1 What sound is this, a song thro' heaven resounding,
 God is love, God is love?
And now from earth I hear the sound rebounding,
 God is love, God is love.
  Yes, while adoring hosts proclaim—
  Love is his nature,—Love his name;
  My soul, repeat on earth the same,
  God is love, God is love.

2 This heavenly love all round is sweetly flowing,
 God is love, God is love,
And in my heart the sacred fire is glowing,
 God is love, God is love.
  This then shall be my song below,
  And when to glory I shall go,
  This strain eternally shall flow,
  God is love, God is love.

www.ingramcontent.com/pod-product-compliance
Lightning Source LLC
Chambersburg PA
CBHW030015240426
43672CB00007B/958